TAKING
SIDES

**Clashing Views
on Controversial
Social Issues**
fifth edition

---

*We are not afraid to follow truth
wherever it may lead, nor to tolerate
any error so long as reason is left free
to combat it.*

Thomas Jefferson

TÁKING
SIDES

Clashing Views
on Controversial
Social Issues

fifth edition

Edited, Selected and with Introductions by

Kurt Finsterbusch
University of Maryland

and

George McKenna
City College
City University of New York

The Dushkin Publishing Group, Inc.

To John, Alec, Ned, Laura, Maria, and Christopher who must live these issues now and in the years ahead.

Library of Congress Catalog Card Number: 87–02960
Manufactured in the United States of America
Fifth Edition, First Printing

ISBN: 0–87967–742–2

The Dushkin Publishing Group, Inc.
Sluice Dock, Guilford, CT 06437

PREFACE

The English word "fanatic" is derived from the Latin *fanum*, meaning temple. It refers to the kind of madmen often seen in the precincts of the temple in ancient times, the kind presumed to be possessed by deities or demons. The term first came into English usage during the seventeenth century to describe religious zealots, but it was soon broadened into a larger political and social context. We have come to associate the term "fanatic" with a person who acts as if his views were inspired, a person utterly incapable of appreciating opposing points of view. The nineteenth-century novelist George Eliot put it precisely: "I call a man fanatical when . . . he . . . becomes unjust and unsympathetic to men who are out of his own track." A fanatic may hear, but he is unable to listen. If he is ever confronted with those who disagree with him, he immediately vilifies them; they are not simply mistaken but evil—in fact, part of an evil conspiracy. When out of power, the fanatic is merely dangerous; in power, he is a despot, jailing and murdering those foolish enough to dissent.

Most of us would avoid the company of fanatics, but who among us is not tempted to caricature opponents instead of listening to them? Who does not put certain topics "off limits" for discussion? Who does not grasp at euphemisms to avoid facing inconvenient facts? Who has not, in George Eliot's language, sometimes been "unjust and unsympathetic" to those on a different track? Who is not, at least in certain very sensitive areas, a *little* fanatical?

The trouble with fanaticism on the individual level is that it has a way of growing suddenly larger, especially in a mass society served by communications media that pride themselves on their ability to simplify and dramatize everything. The expansion of fanaticism can lead eventually to large portions of the population calling each other names or confronting each other across barricades—or, what is worse, getting into office and silencing the opposition.

The counterweight to fanaticism is open discussion. The difficult issues that trouble us as a society have at least two sides, and we lose as a society if we hear only one side. At the individual level, the answer to fanaticism is listening.

John Stuart Mill, the nineteenth-century British philosopher, noted that the majority is not doing the minority a favor by listening to its views; it is doing *itself* a favor. By listening to contrasting points of view, we strengthen our own. In some cases we change our viewpoint completely, but in most cases we either incorporate some elements of the opposing view—thus making our own richer—or else learn how to answer the objections to our viewpoint. Either way we gain from the experience.

v

But first we must listen. That means suspending, if only temporarily, our defenses in order to appreciate what someone else is trying to say. This was our view when we first brought out *Taking Sides,* and it remains our view today. For this fifth edition, we have made some important changes in the topics and selections. We have replaced some of the earlier articles with ones that are more lively and up-to-date. We have added several new issues, including debates on whether urban life is crazy and whether women can combine careers and families.

Despite the extensive changes we have made in this edition, our underlying conviction remains the same. In our view, thoughtfulness is the best protection against fanaticism. And what is thought but self-dialogue? We have tried to stimulate internal debate by assembling the best pro and contra articles on social issues that we could find. Our hope is that readers who confront lively and thoughtful statements on *both* sides of the issues in this book will be encouraged to think about them in an atmosphere free of stereotypes and knee-jerk reflexes.

The fanatic in us all must be confronted. Our convictions, so far as they are sound, will lose nothing. They, and we, can only gain.

ACKNOWLEDGMENTS

We wish to acknowledge the encouragement and support given to this project by Rick Connelly, president of the Dushkin Publishing Group. We are grateful as well to Jeremy Brenner and to John Holland, Managing Editor, for helping us through the initial stages of this edition, and to Mimi Egan, Program Manager, for carrying us to the end. Finally, we thank our families for their patience and understanding during the period in which we prepared this book.

Kurt Finsterbusch
George McKenna

CONTENTS IN BRIEF

CONTENTS

Sociologist Irving Louis Horowitz complains that sociology has become politicized and that the work of many sociologists promotes views that make social life less humane. Alvin Gouldner counters that it is impossible and, furthermore, undesirable to eliminate all value judgments from the study of society.

Professor Edward Banfield suggests that it is the cultural outlook of the poor that tends to keep them in poverty. Psychologist Ryan responds that this view is a form of "blaming the victim."

Robert Bellah and his associates argue that Americans have become self-absorbed at the expense of transcendent values and the good of the community. Henry Fairlie suggests that such criticism fails to appreciate the extraordinary degree of freedom enjoyed by modern "mass man."

Henry Fairlie, a frequent commentator on the social scene, points out that most people flee cities whenever possible, and he enumerates the nuisances that create the exodus. C. R. Creekmore uses research findings to show that much of the criticisms of urban life is based on myths and is unfounded.

Conservative activist Phyllis Schlafly supports the traditional role of wife and mother as the source of fulfillment for women. Sociologist Barbara Deckard suggests that this role is demeaning and limiting and unvalued in our society.

Basing their remarks on a national survey, Shirley Wilkins and Thomas Miller show that most women want to combine work and family even though it may be difficult. Sociologist George Gilder argues that women are much less committed to careers than men, and he uses various data to support his conclusions.

PART 4 STRATIFICATION AND INEQUALITY 121

Harvard professor Glenn Loury contends that insistence on "ill-suited" civil rights strategies makes it impossible for blacks to achieve full equality in American society. Professor Herman Schwartz argues that we must somehow undo the cruel consequences of racism that still plague our society and its victims.

Sociologist G. William Domhoff tries to demonstrate that the American upperclass occupies a surprisingly large number of influential positions in society which enables it to rule America. Sociologist Andrew M. Greeley argues that there is no single established center of power and points to the behavior of the system as evidence to support his view.

Former Treasury Secretary William Simon argues that excessive government involvement in the economy abridges basic liberties and hurts the nation's productivity. Economist John Kenneth Galbraith says that since public services are essential to those Americans who can't afford private services, the attack on "big government" is really an attack on the poor.

Charles Murray outlines his contention that welfare programs can result in long-term dependency on the part of the poor. Social commentator Christopher Jencks argues that government aid programs are vital to meeting the needs of the poor.

Gary Imhoff looks at the recent figures on immigration and argues that excessive immigration poses serious dangers to Americans and undermines the sovereignty of the nation. Economist and social commentator Julian Simon contends that immigration invigorates and enriches America.

In arguing for an end to the nuclear arms race, Jonathan Schell, staff writer for the *New Yorker*, explores the consequences of nuclear war and its implications for the human race and the earth itself. Charles Krauthammer, senior editor of the *New Republic*, does not dispute the terror of nuclear war, but he argues that this very balance of terror is what prevents war from occurring.

PART 7 THE FUTURE: POPULATION/ENVIRONMENT/ SOCIETY

Steven Mumford, an expert in population studies, makes his case that population over-growth is the most serious threat to our lives and security. Economist Julian Simon defends his optimistic view that increased population will make greater opportunities available to future generations.

Economist Julian Simon reviews several indicators of improving environmental conditions for human life. Lester Brown and Sandra Postel, from the Worldwatch Institute, argue that many of the earth's natural systems have become seriously destabilized in environmentally destructive ways.

Former governor of Colorado Richard Lamm sees America headed into an era of economic crisis brought on by reckless spending and inadequate investment. Marshall Loeb of *Fortune* magazine predicts that America is entering a prolonged period of economic growth.

INTRODUCTION

DEBATING SOCIAL ISSUES

WHAT IS SOCIOLOGY?

"I have become a problem to myself," St. Augustine said. Put into a social and secular framework, St. Augustine's concern marks the starting point of sociology. We have become a problem to ourselves, and it is sociology that seeks to understand the problem and, perhaps, to find some solutions. The subject matter of sociology, then, is ourselves—people interacting with one another in groups.

To say that sociology involves the study of human beings in groups is immediately to turn our attention to the emotionally-charged topic of social values. Racial discrimination, poverty, democracy and despotism, civil liberties, the treatment of criminals, the relationship between the sexes—these and other "social issues" touch our most deeply-held values. These values must be established before any society can function smoothly. It is not possible to go through a day without confronting value judgments in one form or another. For example, many of us have suffered from discrimination or at least observed it. Some of us have been preyed upon by criminals and have subsequently felt frustrated with our criminal justice system. (Others at one time may have been on the other side of the law and emerged with a different set of grievances.) The list of engaging social issues goes on and on.

The purpose of sociology is to throw light on social issues and their relationship to the complex, confusing, and dynamic social world around us. It seeks to describe how society is organized and how individuals fit into it. But neither the organization of society nor the fit of individuals is perfect. Social disorganization is a fact of life—at least in modern, complex societies such as the one we live in. Here, perfect harmony continues to elude us, and "social problems" such as those mentioned above are endemic. The very institutions, laws, and policies that produce benefits also produce what sociologists call "unintended effects"—unintended and undesirable. The changes that please one sector of the society may displease another, or the changes that seem so indisputably healthy and good have a dark underside to them. The examples are endless. Modern urban life gives people privacy and freedom from snooping neighbors that the small town never afforded; yet, that very privacy seems to breed an uneasy sense of anonymity and loneliness. Or take another example: Hierarchy is necessary for organizations to function efficiently, but hierarchy leads to the creation of a ruling elite. Flatten out the hierarchy, and you may achieve social equality—but at the price of confusion, incompetence, and demoralization.

This is not to say that all efforts to effect social change are ultimately futile and that the only sound view is the tragic one that concludes "nothing works." We can be realistic without falling into despair. In many respects, the human condition has improved over the centuries and has improved as a result of conscious social policies. But improvements are purchased at a price—not only a monetary price but one involving human discomfort and discontent. The job of policymakers is to balance the anticipated benefits against the probable costs.

It can never hurt policymakers to know more about the society in which they work or the social issues they confront. That, broadly speaking, is the purpose of sociology. It is what this book is about. This volume examines social issues that are central to the study of sociology.

The Values of Sociologists
Should sociologists try to be dispassionate and scientific even when analyzing morally charged issues? Or should they cast aside their neutrality and practice a kind of advocacy sociology? In Issue 1, sociologists Irving Louis Horowitz and Alvin Gouldner develop opposing points of view on whether it is wrong to "politicize" sociology.

Perspectives on Culture
The "culture of poverty" thesis maintains that most long-term poverty in America is the result of a culture that is all too common among the poor. The implication is that those who always seek immediate material gratification will not climb out of poverty, even if they are helped by welfare and social programs. Others see most of the poor as victims of adverse conditions; they ridicule the culture of poverty thesis as a way of "blaming the victim." In Issue 2 we present a clear-cut exchange on this issue, with Edward Banfield saying "yes" to the question of whether "lower-class" culture perpetuates poverty, and William Ryan saying "no."

Cultural values are also at issue in the debate over community versus the individual in contemporary America. Has American individualism, in the sense of self-seeking, become excessive lately? Or is American individualism a vital element of American self-respect? These questions are debated by sociologists Robert Bellah et al. and journalist Henry Fairlie in Issue 3.

Cities are cultural beehives. In cities, many subgroups maintain subcultures—think of Chinatown in New York City or the haunts of the homeless. Cities are also known for a more general urban culture, which can be compared to a rural culture in terms of the pace of life, the intimacy of interactions, and the basis for social acceptance. Some, like Henry Fairlie, think urban culture is rather crazy. Others, like C. R. Creekmore, think that most urban lifestyles are satisfying for most urbanites (see Issue 4).

Sex Roles and the Family
In the flux of modernity, traditional institutions lose their sanctity. In America in recent years, the nuclear family has been depicted as a kind of prison for women that keeps them "in their place." In Issue 5, sociologist Barbara Deckard seems to agree with that view, while conservative activist Phyllis Schlafly stoutly defends the traditional family.

The women's movement has rendered problematic many of the old truths that served as cultural anchors in the past. We examine two questions relating to the debate on women's roles. Can women combine careers and families? In Issue 6, Shirley Williams and Thomas Miller present evidence that they can, while George Gilder comes to the opposite conclusion. In Issue 7, we ask: have modern women confused sex roles? Donald Singletary argues that women want many of the privileges of the traditional female sex role while at the same time they demand all the rights of modern women. Betty Winston Baye makes the same argument about men—they want to have it both ways, too.

Stratification and Inequality

Stratification theory is the backbone of sociology. Three important stratification issues are included in this volume. Does economic inequality benefit society? William Ryan and George Gilder debate this in Issue 8. Has oppression because of race significantly declined in America, or does it remain as bad as it was in the recent past? Two black sociologists, William J. Wilson and Charles V. Willie, differ in Issue 9. Then there is the controversy over affirmative action or racial quotas. Is equality promoted or undermined by such policies? Professors Glenn Loury and Herman Schwartz take opposing sides on this question in Issue 10.

The Political Economy

Sociologists study not only the poor, the workers, and the victims of discrimination but also those at the top of society—those who occupy what the late sociologist C. Wright Mills used to call "the command posts." The question is whether the "pluralist" model or the "power elite" model is the one that best fits the facts in America. Does a single power elite rule the United States or do many groups contend for power and influence so that the political process is accessible to all? In Issue 11, sociologists Andrew Greeley and William Domhoff disagree on this issue, with Greeley contending that many groups have their hands on the levers of power and Domhoff insisting that behind this seeming plurality there is a small elite which exerts the real control.

But what kind of political economy does the single or plural elites control? The United States is a capitalist welfare state. The economy is based on private enterprise and the relatively free markets of capitalism with the full support of the state. The state, however, is also committed to the welfare of those who are not provided for by the labor market.

In Issue 12, economist J. K. Galbraith and former Treasury Secretary William Simon debate the question of whether American government has gotten too big. In Issue 13, writer Charles Murray argues that the welfare programs of the "Great Society" are colossal failures and should be abandoned. On the other hand, Professor Christopher Jencks thinks the data indicate that welfare programs have been successful and that to abolish the programs would spell disaster for the poor.

Social Control and the Protection of Society

Under this heading are a variety of issues. In recent years homosexual political activists have challenged traditional assumptions concerning homosexuality in our society, and these activists have raised serious questions about our values and priorities. A core issue remains: Are homosexual relations deviant? In Issue 14, Robert Gordis argues that they are, while Jeannine Gramick develops the view that such relations are natural and normal.

Surveys indicate that concern about crime is extremely high in America. Should our society focus on deterrence by meting out sentencing on a tougher and more uniform basis? Or should our emphasis be on rehabilitating criminals and eliminating the social conditions that breed crime? These alternatives are explored in the debate between Judge David Bazelon and political scientist James Q. Wilson in Issue 15.

What is happening to our borders? The number of legal and illegal immigrants is now estimated at about a million a year. Is this new deluge of immigrants a threat to our nation's future? Or does it constitute a new and vital source of energy and productivity? These questions are explored in Issue 16, where Gary Imhoff and Julian L. Simon debate whether to limit immigration.

No nation or alliance has a monopoly of force, yet some nations possess enough force to threaten the extinction of human life. Can this force—the force of huge nuclear arsenals—be justified as an essential ingredient of a rational defense policy? Jonathan Schell thinks it cannot. Charles Krauthammer is certain that America's nuclear weapons are part of what has kept the peace and deterred aggression. Schell and Krauthammer's competing views are presented in Issue 17.

The Future

Many social commentators speculate on "the fate of the earth." The environmentalists have their own vision of Apocalypse. They foresee the human race overshooting the carrying capacity of the globe. The resulting collapse could lead to the extinction of much of the human race and the end of free societies. Population growth and increasing per capita levels of consumption, say some experts, are leading us to this catastrophe. We examine two issues that have been much debated since the ecology movement began in the late 1960s. In Issue 18, Steven Mumford and economist Julian L. Simon argue over whether the world is really threatened by "overpopulation." Issue 19 again features Julian Simon, this time arguing with ecologists Lester Brown and Sandra Postel over whether the world's physical environment is getting better or worse. Finally, we turn to projections of America's future from a different perspective. The unprecedented 508–point plunge in the stock market in October of 1987 made many observers wonder whether America may soon be headed for economic disaster. But will economic disaster occur? In Issue 20, Richard D. Lamm suggests that it is quite likely, while *Fortune* editor Marshall Loeb predicts a bright economic future for America.

OBJECTIVTY AND SUBJECTIVITY

The topics presented in this book range far and wide—from nuclear deterrence to welfare, from criminals to feminists, from the traditional family to our capitalist economy. What they all have in common is that they are at once subjective and objective issues. The point deserves some discussion.

When St. Augustine said "I have become a problem to myself," he was pondering the problem of how he could remember forgetfulness. If to forget means to obliterate from memory, how can forgetfulness be remembered? It was that riddle (which need not concern us here) that set him thinking about the vast difference between physical science and humanistic investigations. "For I am not now investigating the tracts of the heavens, or measuring the distance of the stars, or trying to discover how the earth hangs in space. I am investigating myself, my memory, my mind." The distinction is between the subjective, what is "in our heads," and the objective, that which is "out there." This is a valuable distinction, but it needs to be qualified. There is a third area, the public realm, that is partly subjective and partly objective. It consists of the actions and interactions of human beings and leads to all sorts of objective happenings; yet the subjective obviously plays a role in what happens. People act on what they believe and think and feel, and their minds, in turn, are influenced by the public environment.

At its best, sociology attempts to hold together both the objective and the subjective without allowing either to overwhelm the other.

CONCLUSION

Writing in the 1950s, a period in some ways like our own, C. Wright Mills said that Americans know a lot about their "troubles," but they cannot make the connections between seemingly personal concerns and the concerns of others in the world. If they could only learn to make those connections, he said, they could turn their concerns into *issues*. An issue transcends the realm of the personal. According to Mills, "An issue is a public matter: some value cherished by publics is felt to be threatened. Often there is a debate about what the value really is and what it is that really threatens it."

It is not only personal troubles but social issues that we have tried to present in this book. The variety of topics in it can be taken as an invitation to discover what Mills called "the sociological imagination." This imagination, said Mills, "is the capacity to shift from one perspective to another—from the political to the psychological; from examination of a single family to comparative assessment of the national budgets of the world. . . . It is the capacity to range from the most impersonal and remote transformations to the most intimate features of the human self—and to see the relations between the two." This book, with a range of issues well suited to the sociological imagination, is intended to enlarge that capacity.

UN Photo/Maggie Steber

PART 1

The Values of Sociologists

Questions of values and relevance have concerned sociologists since the discipline began. Is it the role of sociologists to passively reflect and study societies? Should they try to move society in directions that seem desirable or beneficial? These questions are fundamental to sociology.

Is It Wrong to "Politicize" Sociology?

1

ISSUE 1
Is It Wrong to "Politicize" Sociology?

YES: Irving Louis Horowitz, from "Disenthralling Sociology," *Society* (January/February 1987)

NO: Alvin Gouldner, from "Anti-Minotaur: The Myth of a Value-Free Sociology," *Social Problems* (Winter 1962)

ISSUE SUMMARY

Yes: Sociologist Irving Louis Horowitz complains that sociology has become politicized and that the work of many sociologists promotes views that make social life less humane.

No: Alvin Gouldner was the leading radical sociologist before his death and had a major role in politicizing sociology, the situation that Horowitz decries.

The issue of the politicalization of sociology is a new variation on the old debate about whether sociology should be value free or openly seek to promote values. And it is useful here to review how this debate has evolved. The patron saint of the value-free position was Max Weber (1864–1920), who differentiated between what sociologists did as sociologists and what they did as citizens. As citizens, sociologists should work hard for the causes in which they believe. As sociologists, however, they must remain objective and scientific, serving only the cause of truth, which can be a very gripping and motivating goal. Weber argued that in building a science one must not let values infect one's objectivity.

Weber's strictures against value judgements grew in part from pedagogical concerns. In the German university of his time, teachers were often tempted to turn their lecture rostrums into soap boxes by espousing one or another (or some combination) of the rich variety of "isms"—social Darwinism, socialism, communism, anarchism, syndicalism, and so on—that flourished in the late nineteenth and early twentieth centuries. Weber believed that teachers, who after all are talking to captive audiences, have no business delivering political harangues. He maintained that speeches of advocacy are perfectly appropriate in civic meetings or rallies—but not in the classroom.

Weber's insistence that values must be kept strictly apart from factual discussion grew from more fundamental considerations as well. Methodologically and epistemologically, Weber was a determined skeptic. He doubted that any philosophical or scientific system could provide truths about "ultimate" goals. Answers to such questions as the meaning of life or how it should be lived are likely to vary among individuals and cultures, and no method exists for telling us which answer is the correct one, said Weber.

2

Social science is concerned with truth, but the truth that it explores is empirical and "worldly." Social science can tell us, for example, about the effects of Calvinist theology on Western man's behavior; it cannot tell us if Calvinism is "true." It can tell us the features of charismatic leaders, but it cannot tell us whether they really possess the gift of grace. It can spell out the features of an "ideal" bureaucracy; it cannot tell us whether bureaucracy is "good" or "bad."

For at least half a century, Weber's dichotomy between facts and values was dominant in American sociology. By the early sixties, however, it had been challenged by a number of critics. Among the charges made against Weber's position, two predominated. First, critics claimed that Weber's admonishments helped to foster a trivialization of the field of sociology, particularly because sociologists had become overly cautious about making value judgments and so limited their investigations to the most remote and insignificant fragments of human concern. Secondly, critics of the early sixties maintained that "value-free" sociology could all too easily lead to opportunism. Skepticism about the possibility of affirming "ultimate" values in any objective way can subtly transform itself into the premise that sociology, and therefore sociologists, need not be concerned about ethical principles. The sociologist may end up selling his talents to the highest bidder: helping an advertising agency manipulate people or helping the CIA in some ethically questionable project.

This "revisionist" approach to sociology has now become dominant in the field. Quite recently, however, the revisionist approach itself has come under criticism. Current criticism is chiefly that value-laden sociology eventually turns into just another shrill ideology. In the following selections, Irving Louis Horowitz suggests that this has already happened in the field, while Alvin Gouldner makes the classic case for sociology as a discipline that openly embraces value judgements.

3

YES

Irving Louis Horowitz

DISENTHRALLING SOCIOLOGY

. . . Sociology has been profoundly and differentially politicized by its practitioners. Such politicization stems from an ostensibly leftward drift at the same time that American society as a whole has rediscovered such rightward verities as moral absolutes, universal standards, and inherited values. This countercyclical drift accentuates the widespread alienation of sociology as a discipline from social life and its replacement by undistilled ideology or, at times, quite distilled theology. The hectoring, badgering tone of an Old Right has now found a home in the New Left. . . .

DEVIANCE AND THE AMERICAN WAY

The key object of ideological extremism from the outset has been the total repudiation of the normative character of the social system. This is done by subjectivizing behavior and making structure nothing more than perceived idiosyncratic actions. The new moral relativists have informed their readers that without norms there be no deviance—only alternative lifestyles, contextually situated. Thus it becomes easier to declare norms null and void than to address the issues of crime and its prevention. All behavior can be interpreted in morally neutral terms, without consideration of legal or moral institutions of marriage, family, or community. If such institutions are dealt with, it is often in terms of their structural shakiness or intellectual hypocrisy. Social solidarity is old-fashioned, whereas individual swinging, whatever its larger costs, is new-fashioned. The message is clear: life has little merit or virtue apart from action. The act requires no justification beyond itself.

The one area of social science in which absolute adhesion to canons of ethical neutrality is insisted upon are studies of social deviance. The ideas of heterosexual relationships as normative in character, or marriage as a sacred or bonded state, are viewed as intolerable partisanship, lacking an evidentiary base. A transvaluation of values takes place: those formerly in the closet come out with a vengeance, and the heterosexuals come to be considered not just antiquarian, but lacking in innovative spirit or pure adventure. The revolt against cultural tradition becomes a demand for revolutionary behavior—and not unexpectedly, a new absolutism. Acquiescence to such behavior is often insisted upon at the personal level as a proof of a break with the hoary past.

By mystifying the relationship between those who commit crimes (violate norms and laws), and those who are victimized by criminals, crime is liquidated as readily as deviance. Crime simply becomes an interaction ritual, a network of evil associations. Even such a new criminology does not go far enough to suit some sociological ideologues. So a new approach has been designed which abolishes crime by fiat. Crimes are disaggregated: those with victims (murder and assault upon the person) are distinguished from those with presumably no human victim (prostitution, drugs, gambling). In this manner, crime, if not abolished, is at least greatly reduced by sociological ideologues.

Homicide alone remains as a category worthy of the label "crime." Even here we have those whose celebration of the political criminal, the intelligent criminal, comes close to excusing even homicide. In a world without good or evil, but only crime and punishment, the ultimate evildoer, the central criminal, is the state itself. The more democratic, the more criminal, since hypocrisy heads the list of crimes. This is a central theme of many talented figures of the new criminology. In their intoxication with social change, the merits of social order are simply denied, at least as long as such an order is linked to capitalism. The debates among the new criminologists refer to whether

crime itself is a meaningful category, rather than the collapse of normative structure in advanced societies.

The most avant-garde thought has now come to consider the conduct of crime as "far from being an intentional violation of a prohibition" but its opposite "the pursuit of justice . . . a mode of conflict management." Indeed, "viewed in relation to law, it [crime] is self-help." This is not a parody, but a conviction that "crime often expresses a grievance" and is thus of a piece with other forms of behavior. No effort is made to test the worthiness of the grievance, only that since "the criminality of crime is defined by law" everything is up for grabs in this sociological version of Mailerism. That author at least had the kindness to admit "that crime and its seriousness may be explained with a theory of law as a departure from common sense." Writers of sociological fiction do not bother with such demurrers.

FROM WELFARE TO TERROR

In its politicized version, the original purpose of American society is characterized as an attempt to create a collective, cooperative community. But the fall from grace engineered by the bourgeoisie substituted the base notion of personal aggrandizement, or entrepreneurialism, for the utopianism, the place of grace. Thus, the collapse of community led to the rise of repugnant individualism. This in turn led America to the cult of hero worship, primitivism, narcissistic pleasure, and private happiness at the expense of the public good. In this example of the politicization of social research, the task of social science is to restore a sense of community through collectivization and to implement planned change to achieve the good (that is, socialist) society. The failure to achieve community is seen as subversion by a new order—one far more complete than the one replaced.

Traditional liberal values are stood on their collective heads, as it turns out that every reform measure in the United States since the New Deal is doing little more than staving off the inevitable collapse of capitalism. In its purified form, welfare operates as a form of social control. In the more recent period, 1960–80, it is an integral part of governmental efforts to recommit a rebellious poor population to the existing social order. Welfare performs a social control function for the capitalist state. In this universe of tautological discourse, where the welfare system has succeeded it has done so by false consciousness, by deceiving people. Where it fails, the will of the people triumphs over capitalist antics.

The ability of American society to prosper, much less survive this welfare environment, and to be able to do so as a result of rightist rather than leftist pressure was neither anticipated nor even considered a distinct possibility. Thus the ideologists are reduced to continuously predicting the final end of capitalism. Since not even the new ideologists can overtly support terrorist attacks on the social fabric, a group of revolutionary scholars have devised methods to cleanse terror of its regnant practices by linking it with freedom struggles and/or by making opponents of such linkages the creatures of state repression or social segregation. Analyses of "powerlessness" translate into effective modes of using "insurgent power," including the "tactic" of utilizing riots and terror to create a process of "tactical integration." Under the veil of Aesoprian language the threat of gangland ("foco") styles of revolutionary behavior is approved.

In a critique of the notion of organizing the poor, some sociologists argue against helping the poor to reap the benefits of a welfare system. Instead, in manifest Leninist rhetoric, they ask, then answer: "What, then is to be done? Our position, which is implied in our criticism of separatist organizing, is that the basic task of activists who are concerned about poverty is the promotion of socialist consciousness among the rank and file in the trade unions. The response of welfare liberals to antiwelfare radicals is not reassuring: suggesting only differences in means to reach a social nirvana. There is a taken-for-granted use of sociological periodicals to vent socialist and even communist polemics and ambitions. The assumption of the legitimacy of violence in the name of sociology is a hallmark of the new ideologues.

CONSPIRATORIAL ELITES

The announcement that elites control, manipulate, and dominate corporate life in America is most fashionably argued in terms of interlocking directorates, that is, the degree to which key individuals dominate the board rooms of every industry from boots to books and liquor to lumber. The hidden predicate is that such interlockers mastermined everything from foreign policy to fiscal policy. At times, the conspiracy is even given a special geographical hideout. A belief in the existence of a unified industrial network is extended to the conclusion that there is a single unified high policy command.

We are informed, despite evidence of a decline in centralization of business authority, that "a single, unified network" of interlocking directorates exists, with "a high degree of centrality." All contrary information notwithstanding (emergence of middle-sized businesses, diversification of the labor market), the existence of conspiratorial elites remains a fixed point of faith that "power and centralization are fused in the corporate economy." How such relationships cross industrial lines, whether or not directorates actually share a common ideology, the distinction between newer and older industries in differentiating policies, all vanish before the onslaught of the interlocking directorates—an inch away from the dictatorship of the bourgeoisie (whose mythic characteristic serves to justify the real characteristic of the dictatorship of the party apparatus in the Soviet Union).

Sociological or psychological evidence to the contrary, all industries not fitting the elitist-conspiracy model, all areas not participating in the directorates, are simply dismissed. For some, American society is a cleverly rendered political conspiracy to maintain bourgeois power—now known as corporate liberalism—intact, even if and when that power is federalized. Newer developments moving to decentralize control are either dismissed as impossible without a deep restructuring of society or met with glum silence, as if every reform is a painful interlude needlessly postponing the joyful storm of industrial protest and class revolution.

The dogmas of an unadulterated Marxism burn deep only in some sociological sectors. In a tormented article on "Capitalist Resistance to the Organization of Labor Before the New Deal," we are told that "a steady structural tension, however latent it may be at any point in time, necessarily continues to exist between capital and labor because in our view, it is rooted in the very fabric of capitalism." Whatever is actually observed in labor-capital relationships, the mysterious workings of class struggles must go forth in the bowels of America. The piece concludes, predictably enough, with a statement of the New Deal "legacy" to America: "Capital's disorganization of American workers as a class in the first three decades of the twentieth century." Aside from the error of historical fact—the New Deal commenced only in the fourth decade of this century—is the metaphysical conceit that any effort to mitigate or meliorate the circumstances and lifestyles of workers is not only economically suspect but a clever political conspiracy perpetrated by President Roosevelt and his New Deal. The corruption of this form of stratification analysis has reached a point where any evolution in Western economic systems can only be described in harshly negative and disparaging terms. . . .

Increasingly, the form of scholarship, its paraphernalia, is retained, while the conclusions have a decreasing relationship to scientific methods. Conclusions that are uniformly and at times shamelessly ideological are proffered as social science. Here are the conclusions from a recent lead article in the *American Sociological Review:* "Irrespective of state interventions, there are signs that in all advanced capitalist societies hegemonic regimes are developing a despotic face.... In this period one can anticipate the working classes beginning to feel their collective impotence and the irreconcilability of their interests with the development of capitalism." And back to the *Communist Manifesto* for a little dash of inspiration: "The material interests of the working classes can be vouchsafed only beyond capitalism, beyond the anarchy of the market and beyond despotism in production." Nary a word in this article described real despotism, nor are we informed of just what great utopia is awaiting us beyond capitalism. It takes little imagination to see what this author has in store for his society.

With the notable exception of those social scientists who possess a working familiarity with European figures such as Antonio Gramsci and Leon Trotsky (Nicos Poulantzas and Ernest Mandel come most readily to mind), we have to search far and wide for any serious estimation of Soviet Communism by the new ideologists. The utter bankruptcy of the Soviet Union as a model for Western democracies has led to the displacement of utopia by myopia. The rationale for the denial of Soviet reality is varied, but almost invariably it comes down to the claim that those who live in the United States are centrally responsible to critique their own domestic scenario. Whatever goes on, or went on, in the Soviet Union, is presumably to be taken care of by the Russians. Another formulation is that it is difficult to know what is taking place in the Soviet Union, so why burden critique of America with fatuous comparisons to a foreign body. The same inhibitions do not keep such analysts from doing violence to empirical conditions or from commenting on the rest of the world.

What prevails are lengthy discourses on Marxism, socialism, radicalism; any abstraction ending in "ism" that is removed from the realities of Soviet power. In this manner the heady wine of theory is restored to its pristine primacy. In Eastern Europe discussions of Marxism and socialism are relegated to the world of black humor; but in the United States, with notable exceptions, the sacred texts of yesteryear are pored over with a sobriety and affectation that could well inspire religious zealots. The movement from a new sociology to a new ideology is, in effect, a shift from an evenhanded critical analysis of power, authority, oppression, exploitation—wherever it manifests itself and under whatever auspices—to a thinly disguised anti-Americanism that uses the rhetoric of social science to express animosities that would otherwise be quickly challenged or readily repudiated. This sad outcome of the critical tradition of power analysis must be stated frankly as unacceptable if any hope is left for a restoration of scientific principles in the present sociological environment. . . .

The metaphysical presuppositions of the politicization of sociology represent a major conversion of an "is" into an "ought." Social research is historically laden with biases, prejudices, and wrongheadedness—often caused by the elevation of a single variable into an apriority. In the past it was race, class, even nationality and geography. In our times it is more likely to be sex, gender, race (this time with reverse moral intent), and age. But the goal of social research, which is to understand and transmit the facts of social life truthfully, has been transformed into the eternality of ideology, the inevitable sociology of knowledge distortions which result from the biases of the investigator.

In part, at least, this is a consequence of a social science legacy in which theory emerged out of philosophical tradition rather than empirical observation. As a result, the social and the scientific have had a one-hundred-year history of uneasy alliance. This dualism has served to keep alive the ideological embers of nineteenth-century doctrines long after they have run out of intellectual steam and long after they have had much relevance to actual events in Europe, much less in America. In the absence of normative convictions, historical antecedents come to fill this gaping epistemic void; but such antecedents come with the baggage of every European dogma from Marx to Mosca. What was at one point brilliant observation performed with limited tools of research is turned on itself; it is transformed into derivative theory aimed at frustrating the use of scientific method, or, when that is not feasible, at least limiting such usage.

Whether by design or accident, the end product is nothing other than the subversion of sociology as both method and ideal. Ritual incantation displaces experience and experiment alike. Typical is a recent piece entitled: "It's Good Enough for Science, But Is It Good Enough For Social Action?" in which the author concludes by saying "It must be recognized generally that scientific knowledge is not objective, and hence cannot serve as the undisputed rock-hard base upon which potentially discriminatory political decisions may be erected." While we are never told on what then to base our judgments or recommendations, "analysts in the history and sociology of science" who have a unique divination into the "social nature of science" are instructed to "share this understanding with scientists, with politicians, with unionists." The queer thought that conflicts among scientists, politicians, and unionists may be what sociologists should be studying never enters the thought processes of this author (and too many like her). What we receive instead is a none-too-subtle resurfacing of the totalitarian argument concerning the "partisan" character of science, the

son of the earlier "class" and/or "race" character of science. Ideology then moves sociology from studying the social sources of distortions to a celebration of bias in the self-declared political vanguard.

Far from reacting to this sort of insurgent approach with the despairing conservative vision that "social science itself is the very disease it proposes to cure," it is more fruitful to argue that the impact of social science on the moral thinking of America is highly varied and forward-looking. The level to which ideology has come to permeate and penetrate a given discipline is the measure of disease, undermining a sense of real progress. By such a criterion, sociology is a uniquely troubled discipline precisely because it has subverted, more than any other social science discipline, the methods of science and the process of inquiry in favor of an aprioristic intellectual table-thumping. The call to disenthrall sociology is but a first step to recall the discipline to its great and good first principles.

My emphasis on the ultra-leftist effort to coopt sociology should not be interpreted as an endorsement for an ultra-conservative vision. It is no such thing. The rage for order and the faith in tradition—hallmarks of conservative ideology—remain at loggerheads with the practice of social analysis, with a sense of the present determining research agendas. Looking backwards no more than longing for utopias is what sociology examines, not what it apes. The implicit reductionism of the New Left is scarcely improved upon by the explicit moralism of the New Right. Looking for new gods to replace failed gods is neither strictly nor loosely speaking a function of social research. Sociology can survive only to the extent

sociologists from making them within the area of their expertise. If, on the contrary, technical competence provides no warrant for making value judgments then, at least sociologists are as *free* to do so as anyone else; then their value judgments are at least as good as anyone else's, say, a twelve-year-old child's. And, by the way, if technical competence provides no warrant for making value judgments, then what does? . . .

I fear that there are many sociologists today who, in conceiving social science to be value-free, mean widely different things, that many hold these beliefs dogmatically without having examined seriously the grounds upon which they are credible, and that some few affirm a value-free sociology ritualistically without having any clear idea what it might mean. Weber's own views on the relation between values and social science, and some current today are scarcely identical. While Weber saw grave hazards in the sociologist's expression of value judgments, he also held that these might be voiced if caution was exercised to distinguish them from statements of fact. If Weber insisted on the need to maintain scientific objectivity, he also warned that his was altogether different from moral indifference.

Not only was the cautious expression of value judgments deemed permissible by Weber but, he emphasized, these were positively mandatory under certain circumstances. Although Weber inveighed against the professorial 'cult of personality' we might also remember that he was not against all value-imbued cults and that he himself worshipped at the shrine of individual responsibility. A familiarity with Weber's work on these points would only be embarrassing to

many who today affirm a value-free sociology in his name. . . .

When Weber condemned the lecture hall as a forum for value-affirmation he had in mind most particularly the expression of *political* values. The point of Weber's polemic is not directed against all values with equal sharpness. It was not the expression of aesthetic or even religious values that Weber sees as most objectionable in the university, but, primarily, those of politics. His promotion of the value-free doctrine may, then, be seen not so much as an effort to amoralize as to depoliticize the university and to remove it from the political struggle. The political conflicts then echoing in the German university did not entail comparatively trivial differences, such as those now between Democrats and Republicans in the United States. Weber's proposal of the value-free doctrine was, in part, an effort to establish a *modus vivendi* among academicians whose political commitments were often intensely felt and in violent opposition. . . .

Given the historically unique conditions of nuclear warfare, where the issue would not be decided in a long-drawn-out war requiring the sustained cohesion of mass populations, national consensus is no longer, I believe, as important a condition of national survival as it once was. But if we no longer require the same degree of unanimity to *fight* a war, we do require a greater ferment of ideas and a radiating growth of political seriousness and variety within which alone we may find a way to *prevent* war. Important contributions to this have been and may further be made by members of the academic community and, perhaps, especially, by its social science sector. The question arises, however, whether this group's political intelligence can ever be adequately mobilized for these purposes so long as it remains tranquilized by the value-free doctrine. . . .

Insofar as the value-free doctrine is a mode of ensuring professional autonomy note that it does not, as such, entail an interest peculiar to the social science. In this regard, as a substantial body of research in the sociology of occupations indicates, social scientists are kin to plumbers, house painters or librarians. For most if not all occupations seek to elude control by outsiders and manifest a drive to maintain exclusive control over their practitioners.

Without doubt the value-free principle did enhance the autonomy of sociology; it was one way in which our discipline pried itself loose—in some modest measure—from the clutch of its society, in Europe freer from political party influence, in the United States freer of ministerial influence. In both places, the value-free doctrine gave sociology a larger area of autonomy in which it could steadily pursue basic problems rather than journalistically react to passing events, and allowed it more freedom to pursue questions uninteresting either to the respectable or to the rebellious. It made sociology freer—as Comte has wanted it to be—to pursue all its own theoretical implications. In other words, the value-free principle did, I think, contribute to the intellectual growth and emancipation of our enterprise.

There was another kind of freedom which the value-free doctrine also allowed; it enhanced a freedom from moral compulsiveness; it permitted a partial escape from the parochial prescriptions of the sociologist's local or native culture. Above all, effective internalization of the value-free principle has always encouraged at least a temporary suspension of the moralizing reflexes built into the sociologist by his own society. From one perspective, this of course has its dangers—a disorienting normlessness and moral indifference. From another standpoint, however, the value-free principle might also have provided a *moral* as well as an intellectual *opportunity*. For insofar as moral reactions are only suspended and not aborted, and insofar as this is done in the service of knowledge and intellectual discipline, then, in effect, the value-free principle strengthened Reason (or Ego) against the compulsive demands of a merely traditional morality. To this degree, the value-free discipline provided a foundation for the development of more reliable knowledge about men and, also, established a breathing space within which moral reactions could be less mechanical and in which morality could be reinvigorated.

The value-free doctrine thus had a paradoxical potentiality: it might enable men to make *better* value judgments rather than *none*. It could encourage a habit of mind that might help men in discriminating between their punitive drives and their ethical sentiments. Moralistic reflexes suspended, it was now more possible to sift conscience with the rod of reason and to cultivate moral judgments that expresses a man's total character as an adult person; he need not now live quite so much by his past parental programming but in terms of his more mature present.

The value-free doctrine could have meant an opportunity for a more authentic morality. It could and sometimes did aid men in transcending the morality of their 'tribe,' to open themselves to the diverse moralities of unfamiliar groups, and to see themselves and others from the standpoint of a wider range of significant cultures. But the value-free doctrine also had other, less fortunate, results as well.

Doubtless there were some who did use the opportunity thus presented; but there were, also, many who used the value-free postulate as an excuse for pursuing their private impulses to the neglect of their public responsibilities and who, far from becoming more morally sensitive, became morally jaded. Insofar as the value-free doctrine failed to realize its potentialities it did so because its deepest impulses were—as we shall note later—dualistic; it invited men to stress the separation and not the mutual connectedness of facts and values: it had the vice of its virtues. In short, the conception of a value-free sociology has had *diverse* consequences, not all of them useful or flattering to the social sciences.

On the negative side, it may be noted that the value-free doctrine is useful both to those who want to escape *from* the world and to those who want to escape *into* it. It is useful to those young, or not so young men, who live off sociology rather than for it, and who think of sociology as a way of getting ahead in the world by providing them with neutral techniques that may be sold on the open market to any buyer. The belief that it is not the business of a sociologist to make value judgments is taken, by some, to mean that the market on which they can vend their skills is unlimited. From such a standpoint, there is no reason why one cannot sell his knowledge to spread a disease just as freely as he can to fight it. Indeed, some sociologists have had no hesitation about doing market research designed to sell more cigarettes, although well aware of the implications of recent cancer research. In brief, the value-free doctrine of social science was sometimes used to justify the sale of one's talents to the highest bidder and is, far from being new, a contemporary version of the most ancient sophistry.

In still other cases, the image of a value-free sociology is the armour of the alienated sociologist's self. Although C. Wright Mills may be right in saying this is the Age of Sociology, not a few sociologists, and Mills included, feel estranged and isolated from their society. They feel impotent to contribute usefully to the solution of its deepening problems and, even when they can, they fear that the terms of such an involvement require them to submit to a commercial debasement or a narrow partisanship, rather than contributing to a truly public interest. . . .

Once committed to the premise of a value-free sociology, such sociologists are bound to a policy which can only alienate them further from the surrounding world. Social science can never be fully accepted in a society, or by a part of it, without paying its way; this means it must manifest both its relevance and concern for the contemporary human predicament. Unless the value relevances of sociological inquiry are made plainly evident, unless there are at least some bridges between it and larger human hopes and purposes, it must inevitably be scorned by laymen as pretentious word-mongering. But the manner in which some sociologists conceive the value-free doctrine disposes them to ignore current human problems and to huddle together like old men seeking mutual warmth. 'This is not our job,' they say, 'and if it were we would not know enough to do it. Go away, come back when we're grown up,' say these old men. The issue, however, is not whether we know enough; the real questions are whether we have the courage to say and use what we do know and whether anyone knows more.

There is one way in which those who desert the world and those who sell out to it have something in common. Neither group can adopt an openly critical stance toward society. Those who sell out are accomplices; they may feel no critical impulses. Those who run out, while they do feel such impulses, are either lacking in any talent for aggression, or have often turned it inward into noisy but essentially safe university politics or into professional polemics. In adopting a conception of themselves as 'value-free' scientists, their critical impulses may no longer find a target in society. Since they no longer feel free to criticize society, which always requires a measure of courage, they now turn to the cannibalistic criticism of sociology itself and begin to eat themselves up with 'methodological' criticisms.

One latent meaning, then, of the image of a value-free sociology is this: 'Thou shalt not commit a critical or negative value judgement—especially of one's own society.' Like a neurotic symptom this aspect of the value-free image is rooted in a conflict; it grows out of an effort to compromise between conflicting drives: On the one side, it reflects a conflict between the desire to criticize social institutions, which since Socrates has been the legacy of intellectuals, and the fear of reprisals if one does criticize— which is also a very old and human concern. On the other side, this aspect of the value-free image reflects a conflict between the fear of being critical and the fear of being regarded as unmanly or lacking in integrity, if uncritical.

The doctrine of a value-free sociology resolves these conflicts by making it seem that those who refrain from social criticism are acting solely on behalf of a higher professional good rather than their private interests. In refraining from social criticism, both the timorous and the venal may now claim the protection of a high professional principle and, in so doing, can continue to hold themselves in decent regard. Persuade all that no one must bell the cat, then none of the mice need feel like a rat. . . .

The problem of a value-free sociology has its most poignant implications for the social scientist in his role as educator. If sociologists ought not to express their personal values in the academic setting, how then are students to be safeguarded against the unwitting influence of these values which shape the sociologist's selection of problems, his preferences for certain hypotheses or conceptual schemes, and his neglect of others? For these are unavoidable and, in this sense, there is and can be no value-free sociology. The only choice is between an expression of one's values, as open and honest as it can be, this side of the psychoanalytical couch, and a vain ritual of moral neutrality which, because it invites men to ignore the vulnerability of reason to bias, leaves it at the mercy of irrationality.

If truth is the vital thing, as Weber is reputed to have said on his death-bed, then it must be all the truth we have to give, as best we know it, being painfully aware and making our students aware, that even as we offer it we may be engaged in unwitting concealment rather than revelation. If we would teach students how science is made, really made rather than as publicly reported, we cannot fail to expose them to the whole scientist by whom it is made, with all his gifts and blindnesses, with all his methods and his *values* as well. To do otherwise is to usher in an era of spiritless technicians who will be no less lacking in understanding than they are in passion, and who will be useful only because they can be used.

In the end, even these dull tools will through patient persistence and cumulation build a technology of social science strong enough to cripple us. Far as we are from a sociological atomic bomb, we already live in a world of systematic brainwashing of prisoners of war and of housewives with their advertising-exacerbated compulsions; and the social science technology of tomorrow can hardly fail to be more powerful than today's.

It would seem that social science's affinity for modelling itself after physical science might lead to instruction in matters other than research alone. Before Hiroshima, physicists also talked of a value-free science; they, too, vowed to make no value judgments. Today many of them are not so sure. If we today concern ourselves exclusively with the technical proficiency of our students and reject all responsibility for their moral sense, or lack of it, then we may some day be compelled to accept responsibility for having trained a generation willing to serve in a future Auschwitz. Granted that science always has inherent in it both constructive and destructive potentialities. It does not follow from this that we should encourage our students to be oblivious to the difference. Nor does this in any degree detract from the indispensable norms of scientific objectivity; it merely insists that these differ radically from moral indifference. . . .

POSTSCRIPT

Is It Wrong to "Politicize" Sociology?

Horowitz's critique of "politicized" sociology is not without irony. He worries about mixing social science with polemics, yet his essay is itself highly polemical. Of course, he could reply that sociologists are not barred from writing polemics; it is only when they are "doing" their sociology that they must be scrupulously objective and scientific. But whether even this is possible remains in question. Horowitz's own moral priorities are a case in point. He complains that his "radical" colleagues tend to decriminalize crime in America and mercilessly criticize our government while remaining silent on the evils of the Soviet system. Would he be so concerned about the insertion of "values" into sociological analysis if the values were more in accord with his own?

Gouldner's difficulties are the reverse of Horowitz's. He wants a free-wheeling sociology that is unafraid of value judgments. He urges his colleagues in sociology to "take the lid off." The question is whether this kind of uninhibited politicalization might undermine the credibility of the profession. If sociology has been more respected than soapbox oratory, has it not been because people have considered it more rigorous and objective? What happens to scientific rigor when everyone in the field decides to "take the lid off"?

Countless sociological works, including textbooks, have been written with a conscious attempt to avoid value judgments. Among the representative works are those of the late Talcott Parsons, who remains perhaps the single most influential figure in American sociology. See in particular his *The Social System* (The Free Press, 1964) and *Structure and Process in Modern Societies* (The Free Press, 1960). Another major sociologist who adopted the value-free approach is George Lundberg. See his *Foundations of Sociology* (Longman, 1964). For a critique of these and other efforts to construct a value-free sociology, see Alvin Gouldner's *The Coming Crisis in Western Sociology* (Basic Books, 1970). For an extremely thoughtful critique of Weber's fact/value dichotomy, see Leo Strauss' *Natural Right and History* (University of Chicago, 1953), pages 36–78.

EPA/Documerica

PART 2

Perspectives on Culture

How does our culture influence our lives? Many of our attitudes and values are culture-related, but there may be detrimental aspects of our culture that, if recognized, could be changed to improve the lives of all the members of the society. Are changes necessary?

Does "Lower Class" Culture Perpetuate Poverty?

Has Individualism Become Excessive?

Is Urban Life Crazy?

ISSUE 2

Does "Lower-Class" Culture Perpetuate Poverty?

YES: Edward Banfield, from *The Unheavenly City Revisited* (Little, Brown, 1970)

NO: William Ryan, from *Blaming the Victim* (Pantheon, 1971)

ISSUE SUMMARY

YES: Sociologist Edward Banfield suggests that it is the cultural outlook of the poor that tends to keep them in poverty.
NO: Psychologist William Ryan responds that this is a form of "blaming the victim" for the conditions that surround him.

The Declaration of Independence proclaims the right of every human being to "life, liberty, and the pursuit of happiness." It never defines "happiness," but Americans have put their own gloss on the term. Whatever else happiness means, Americans tend to agree, it includes doing well, getting ahead in life, and a comfortable standard of living.

The fact, of course, is that millions of Americans do not do well and do not get ahead. They are mired in poverty and seem unable to get out of it. On the face of it, this fact poses no contradiction to America's commitment to the pursuit of happiness. To pursue is not necessarily to catch; it certainly does not mean that everyone should feel entitled to a life of material prosperity. "Equality of opportunity," the prototypical American slogan, is vastly different from the socialist dream of "equality of condition," which perhaps is one reason socialism has so few adherents in America.

The real difficulty in reconciling the American ideal with American reality is not the problem of income differentials but of the *persistence* of poverty from generation to generation. Often, parent, child, and grandchild seem to be locked into a hopeless cycle of destitution and dependence. One explanation is that a large segment of the poor do not really try to get out of poverty. In its more vicious form this view portrays these poor as lazy, stupid, or base. Their poverty is not to be blamed on defects of American society but on their own defects. After all, this account of poverty continues, many successful Americans have worked their way up from humble beginnings, and many immigrant groups have made progress in one generation. Therefore, the United States provides opportunities for all who will work hard and make something of themselves. Another explanation, however, could be that the poor have few opportunities and many obstacles to overcome to climb out of poverty. If so, then America is not the land of opportunity for the poor and the American dream is reserved for the more fortunate.

That first explanation above of the persistence of poverty holds that among some groups there is a *culture* that breeds poverty because it is antithetical to the self-discipline and hard work that enable others to climb out of their poverty. In other words, the poor have a culture all their own that is at variance with middle-class culture and hinders their success. While it may keep people locked into what seems to be an intolerable life, this culture nevertheless has its own compensations and pleasures: It is full of "action" and it does not demand that people postpone pleasure, save money, or work hard. It is, for the most part, tolerable to those who live in it. Furthermore, according to this argument, not all poor people embrace the culture of poverty, and those who embrace middle-class values should be given every workable form of encouragement—material and spiritual—for escaping poverty. But for those poor who embrace lower-class culture, very little can be done. These poor will always be with us.

According to the second explanation of poverty, most of the poor will become self supporting if they are given a decent chance. Their most important need is for decent jobs that can go somewhere. But often they cannot find jobs, and when they do, the jobs are dead-end or degrading. Some need job training or counseling to give them more self confidence before navigating the job market. Others need temporary help through programs such as rent supplements, inexpensive housing, income supplements, protection from crime, medical services, or better education to help them help themselves.

The culture of poverty thesis shields the economic system from blame for poverty and honors better-off Americans. But it is a lie. Most of the poor are as committed to taking care of themselves and their families through hard work as the middle class, and a sense of dignity is common to all classes. Critics judge the culture of poverty thesis to be a smug, self-righteous justification by spokesmen for the middle and upper classes for the economic system that rewards them so handsomely while subjecting the poor to an intolerable existence. The culture of the poor is similar to the culture of the middle class. Where they do differ, however, the difference is because the culture of the poor is materially different. Change their material conditions and their culture will change rather quickly.

Proponents of the culture of poverty thesis maintain that it is not the material that controls the culture but the other way around; only the abandonment of lower-class culture will get the poor out of poverty. This is Harvard sociologist Edward C. Banfield's argument. On the other side is the late William Ryan, a psychologist and social activist, who says that the Banfield approach is a typical case of "blaming the victim."

YES

Edward Banfield

THE FUTURE OF THE LOWER CLASS

So long as the city contains a sizable lower class, nothing basic can be done about its most serious problems. Good jobs may be offered to all, but some will remain chronically unemployed. Slums may be demolished, but if the housing that replaces them is occupied by the lower class it will shortly be turned into new slums. Welfare payments may be doubled or tripled and a negative income tax instituted, but some persons will continue to live in squalor and misery. New schools may be built, new curricula devised, and the teacher-pupil ratio cut in half, but if the children who attend these schools come from lower-class homes, they will be turned into blackboard jungles, and those who graduate or drop out from them will, in most cases, be functionally illiterate. The streets may be filled with armies of policemen, but violent crime and civil disorder will decrease very little. If, however, the lower class were to disappear—if, say, its members were overnight to acquire the attitudes, motivations, and habits of the working class—the most serious and intractable problems of the city would all disappear with it.

[The] serious problems of the city all exist in two forms—a normal-class and a lower-class form—which are fundamentally different from each other. In its normal-class form, the employment problem, for example, consists mainly of young people who are just entering the labor market and who must make a certain number of trials and errors before finding suitable jobs; in its lower-class form, it consists of people who prefer the "action" of the street to any steady job. The poverty problem in its normal-class form consists of people (especially the aged, the physically handicapped, and mothers with dependent children) whose only need in order to live decently is money; in its lower-class form it consists of people who live in squalor and misery even if their incomes were doubled or tripled. The same is true with the other problems—slum housing, schools, crime, rioting; each is really two quite different problems.

The lower-class forms of all problems are at bottom a single problem: the existence of an outlook and style of life which is radically present-oriented and which therefore attaches no value to work, sacrifice, self-improvement, or service to family, friends, or community. Social workers, teachers, and law-

Excerpts from *The Unheavenly City Revisited,* by Edward Banfield (Boston: Little, Brown and Company), pp. 125–131, 210–211. Copyright © 1970, 1974 by Edward C. Banfield. Reprinted by permission of Little, Brown and Company.

enforcement officials—all those whom Gans calls "caretakers"—cannot achieve their goals because they can neither change nor circumvent this cultural obstacle. . . .

Robert Hunter described it in 1904:

> They lived in God only knows what misery. They ate when there were things to eat; they starved when there was lack of food. But, on the whole, although they swore and beat each other and got drunk, they were more contented than any other class I have happened to know. It took a long time to understand them. Our Committees were busy from morning until night in giving them opportunities to take up the fight again, and to become independent of relief. They always took what we gave them; they always promised to try; but as soon as we expected them to fulfill any promises, they gave up in despair, and either wept or looked ashamed, and took to misery and drink again,—almost, so it seemed to me at times, with a sense of relief.

In Hunter's day these were the "undeserving," "unworthy," "depraved," "debased," or "disreputable" poor; today, they are the "troubled," "culturally deprived," "hard to reach," or "multiproblem." In the opinion of anthropologist Oscar Lewis, their kind of poverty "is a way of life, remarkably stable and persistent, passed down from generation to generation among family lines." This "culture of poverty," as he calls it, exists in city slums in many parts of the world, and is, he says, an adaptation made by the poor in order to defend themselves against the harsh realities of slum life.

The view that is to be taken here [is that] there is indeed such a culture, but that poverty is its effect rather than its cause. (There are societies even poorer than the ones Lewis has described—primitive ones, for example—in which nothing remotely resembling the pattern of behavior here under discussion exists.) Extreme present-orientedness, not lack of income or wealth, is the principal cause of poverty in the sense of "the culture of poverty." Most of those caught up in this culture are unable or unwilling to plan for the future, to sacrifice immediate gratifications in favor of future ones, or to accept the disciplines that are required in order to get and to spend. Their inabilities are probably culturally given in most cases—"multi-problem" families being normal representatives of a class culture that is itself abnormal. No doubt there are also people whose present-orientedness is rationally adaptive rather than cultural, but these probably comprise only a small part of the "hard core" poor.

Outside the lower class, poverty (in the sense of hardship, want, or destitution) is today almost always the result of external circumstances—involuntary unemployment, prolonged illness, the death of a breadwinner, or some other misfortune. Even when severe, such poverty is not squalid or degrading. Moreover, it ends quickly once the (external) cause of it no longer exists. Public or private assistance can sometimes remove or alleviate the cause—for example, by job retraining or remedial surgery. Even when the cause cannot be removed, simply providing the nonlower-class poor with sufficient income is enough to enable them to live "decently."

Lower-class poverty, by contrast, is "inwardly" caused (by psychological inability to provide for the future, and all that this inability implies). Improvements in external circumstances can affect this poverty only superficially: One problem of a "multiproblem" family is no sooner solved than another arises. In principle, it is possible to eliminate the poverty (material lack) of such a family, but only at great expense, since the capacity of the radically improvident to waste money is almost unlimited. Raising such a family's income would not necessarily improve its way of life, moreover, and could conceivably even make things worse. Consider, for example, the H. family:

Mrs. H. seemed overwhelmed with the simple mechanics of dressing her six children and washing their clothes. The younger ones were running around in their underwear; the older ones were unaccounted for, but presumably were around the neighborhood. Mrs. H. had not been out of the house for several months; evidently her husband did the shopping. The apartment was filthy and it smelled. Mrs. H. was dressed in a bathrobe, although it was mid-afternoon. She seemed to have no plan or expectations with regard to her children; she did not know the names of their teachers and she did not seem to worry about their school work, although one child had been retained one year and another two years. Mrs. H. did seem to be somewhat concerned about her husband's lack of activity over the weekend—his continuous drinking and watching baseball on television. Apparently he and she never went out socially together nor did the family ever go anywhere as a unit.

If this family had a very high income—say, $50,000 a year—it would not be considered a "culture of poverty" case. Mrs. H. would hire maids to look after the small children, send the others to boarding schools, and spend her time at fashion shows while her husband drank and watched TV at his club. But with an income of only moderate size—say 100 percent above the poverty line—they would probably be about as badly off as they are now. They might be even worse off, for Mrs. H. would be able to go to the dog races, leaving the children alone, and Mr. H. could devote more time to his bottle and TV set. . . .

Welfare agencies, recognizing the difference between "internally" and "externally" caused poverty, have long been trying first by one means and then another to improve the characters or, as it is now put, to "bring about personal adjustment" of the poor. In the nineteenth century, the view was widely held that what the lower class individual needed was to be brought into a right relation with God or (the secular version of the same thing) with the respectable (that is, middle- and upper-class) elements of the community. The missionary who distributed tracts door to door in the slums was the first caseworker; his—more often, her—task was to minister to what today would be called "feelings of alienation."

The stranger, coming on a stranger's errand, becomes a friend, discharging the offices and exerting the influence of a friend. . . .

Secularized, this approach became the "friendly visitor" system under which "certain persons, under the direction of a central board, pledge themselves to take one or more families who need counsel, if not material help, on their visiting list, and maintain personal friendly relations with them." The system did not work; middle- and upper-class people might be "friendly," but they could not sympathize, let alone communicate, with the lower class. By the beginning of the twentieth century the friendly visitor had been replaced by the "expert." The idea now was that the authority of "the facts" would bring about desired changes of attitude, motive, and habit. As it happened, however, the lower class did not recognize the authority of the facts. The expert then became a supervisor, using his (or her) power to confer or withhold material benefits in order to force the poor to do the things that were supposed to lead to "rehabilitation" (that is, to a middle-class style of life). This method did not work either; the lower class could always find ways to defeat and exploit the system. They seldom changed their ways very much and they never changed them for long. Besides, there was really no body of expertise to tell caseworkers how to produce the changes desired. As one caseworker remarked recently in a book addressed to fellow social service professionals:

> Despite years of experience in providing public aid to poor families precious little is yet known about how to help truly inadequate parents make long term improvements in child care, personal maturity, social relations, or work stability.

Some people understood that if the individual's style of life was to be changed at all, it would be necessary to change that of the group that produced, motivated, and constrained him. Thus, the settlement house. As Robert A. Woods explained:

> The settlements are able to take neighborhoods in cities, and by patience bring back to them much of the healthy village life, so that the people shall again know and care for one another. . . .

When it became clear that settlement houses would not change the culture of slum neighborhoods, the group approach was broadened into what is called "community action." In one type of community action ("community development"), a community organizer tries to persuade a neighborhood's informal leaders to support measures (for instance, measures for delinquency control) that he advances. In another form of it ("community organization"), the organizer tries to promote self-confidence, self-respect, and attachment to the group (and, hopefully, to normal society) among lower-class people. He attempts to do this by encouraging them in efforts at joint action, or by showing them how to conduct meetings, carry on discussions, pass resolutions, present requests to politicians, and the like. In still another form ("community mobilization"), the organizer endeavors to arouse the anger of lower-class persons against the local "power structure," to teach them the techniques of mass action—strikes, sit-ins, picketing, and so on—and to show them how they may capture power. The theory of community organization attributes the malaise of the poor to their lack of self-confidence (which is held to derive largely from their "inexperience"); community mobilization theory, by contrast, attributes it to their feelings of "powerlessness." According to this doctrine, the best cure for poverty is to give the poor power. But since power is not "given," it must be seized.

The success of the group approach has been no greater than that of the caseworker approach. Reviewing five years of effort on the part of various community action programs, Marris and Rein conclude:

> . . . the reforms had not evolved any reliable solutions to the intractable problems with which they struggled. They had not discovered how in general to override the intransigent autonomy of public and private agencies, at

any level of government; nor how to use the social sciences practically to formulate and evaluate policy; nor how, under the sponsorship of government, to raise the power of the poor. Given the talent and money they had brought to bear, they had not even reopened very many opportunities.

If the war on poverty is judged by its ability "to generate major, meaningful and lasting social and economic reforms in conformity with the expressed wishes of poor people," writes Thomas Gladwin, " . . . it is extremely difficult to find even scattered evidence of success." . . . Although city agencies have sent community organizers by the score into slum neighborhoods, the lower-class poor cannot be organized. In East Harlem in 1948, five social workers were assigned to organize a five-block area and to initiate a program of social action based on housing, recreation, and other neighborhood needs. After three years of effort, the organizers had failed to attract a significant number of participants, and those they did attract were upwardly mobile persons who were unrepresentative of the neighborhood. In Boston a "total community" delinquency control project was found to have had "negligible impact," an outcome strikingly like that of the Cambridge-Somerville experiment— a "total caseworker" project—a decade earlier. Even community mobilization, despite the advantages of a rhetoric of

hate and an emphasis on "action," failed to involve lower-class persons to a significant extent. Gangsters and leaders of youth gangs were co-opted on occasion, but they did not suffer from feelings of powerlessness and were not representative of the class for which mobilization was to provide therapy. No matter how hard they have tried to appeal to people at the very bottom of the scale, community organizers have rarely succeeded. Where they have appeared to succeed, as, for example, in the National Welfare Rights Organization, it has been by recruiting people who had some of the *outward* attributes of the lower class— poverty, for example—but whose outlook and values were not lower class; the lower-class person (as defined here) is incapable of being organized. Although it tried strenuously to avoid it, what the Mobilization for Youth described as the general experience proved to be its own experience as well:

> Most efforts to organize lower-class people attract individuals on their way up the social-class ladder. Persons who are relatively responsible about participation, articulate and successful at managing organizational "forms" are identified as lower-class leaders, rather than individuals who actually reflect the values of the lower-class groups. Ordinarily the slum's network of informal group associations is not reached.

NO   William Ryan

BLAMING THE VICTIM

Twenty years ago, Zero Mostel used to do a sketch in which he impersonated a Dixiecrat Senator conducting an investigation of the origins of World War II. At the climax of the sketch, the Senator boomed out, in an excruciating mixture of triumph and suspicion, "What was Pearl Harbor *doing* in the Pacific?" This is an extreme example of Blaming the Victim.

Twenty years ago, we could laugh at Zero Mostel's caricature. In recent years, however, the same process has been going on every day in the arena of social problems, public health, anti-poverty programs, and social welfare. A philosopher might analyze this process and prove that, technically, it is comic. But it is hardly every funny.

Consider some victims. One is the miseducated child in the slum school. He is blamed for his own miseducation. He is said to contain within himself the causes of his inability to read and write well. The shorthand phrase is "cultural deprivation," which, to those in the know, conveys what they allege to be inside information: that the poor child carries a scanty pack of cultural baggage as he enters school. He doesn't know about books and magazines and newspapers, they say. (No books in the home: the mother fails to subscribe to *Reader's Digest*.) They say that if he talks at all—an unlikely event since slum parents don't talk to their children—he certainly doesn't talk correctly. Lower-class dialect spoken here, or even—God forbid!—Southern Negro. *(Ici on parle nigra.)* If you can manage to get him to sit in a chair, they say, he squirms and looks out the window. (Impulse-ridden, these kids, motoric rather than verbal.) In a word he is "disadvantaged" and "socially deprived," they say, and this, of course, accounts for his failure (*his* failure, they say) to learn much in school.

Note the similarity to the logic of Zero Mostel's Dixiecrat Senator. What is the culturally deprived child *doing* in the school? What is wrong with the victim? In pursuing this logic, no one remembers to ask questions about the collapsing buildings and torn textbooks, the frightened, insensitive teachers, the six additional desks in the room, the blustering, frightened principals, the relentless segregation, the callous administrator, the irrelevant curriculum, the bigoted or cowardly members of the school board, the insulting

Excerpts from *Blaming the Victim*, by William Ryan (New York: Pantheon Books), pp. 3–9, 121–125, 236–237. Copyright © 1971 by William Ryan. Reprinted by permission of Pantheon Books, a division of Random House, Inc.

history book, the stingy taxpayers, the fairy-tale readers, or the self-serving faculty of the local teachers' college. We are encouraged to confine our attention to the child and to dwell on all his alleged defects. Cultural deprivation becomes an omnibus explanation for the educational disaster area known as the inner-city school. This is Blaming the Victim.

Pointing to the supposedly deviant Negro family as the "fundamental weakness of the Negro community" is another way to blame the victim. Like "cultural deprivation," "Negro family" has become a shorthand phrase with stereotyped connotations of matriarchy, fatherlessness, and pervasive illegitimacy. Growing up in the "crumbling" Negro family is supposed to account for most of the racial evils in America. Insiders have the word, of course, and know that this phrase is supposed to evoke images of growing up with a long-absent or never-present father (replaced from time to time perhaps by a series of transient lovers) and with bossy women ruling the roost, so that the children are irreparably damaged. This refers particularly to the poor, bewildered male children, whose psyches are fatally wounded and who are never, alas, to learn the trick of becoming upright, downright, forthright all-American boys. Is it any wonder the Negroes cannot achieve equality? From such families! And, again, by focusing our attention on the Negro family as the apparent *cause* of racial inequality, our eye is diverted. Racism, discrimination, segregation, and the powerlessness of the ghetto are subtly, but thoroughly, downgraded in importance.

The generic process of Blaming the Victim is applied to almost every American problem. The miserable health care of the poor is explained away on the

grounds that the victim has poor motivation and lacks health information. The problems of slum housing are traced to the characteristics of tenants who are labeled as "Southern rural migrants" not yet "acculturated" to life in the big city. The "multiproblem" poor, it is claimed, suffer the psychological effects of impoverishment, the "culture of poverty," and the deviant value system of the lower classes; consequently, though unwittingly, they cause their own troubles. From such a viewpoint, the obvious fact that poverty is primarily an absence of money is easily overlooked or set aside.

The growing number of families receiving welfare are fallaciously linked together with the increased number of illegitimate children as twin results of promiscuity and sexual abandon among members of the lower orders. Every important social problem—crime, mental illness, civil disorder, unemployment—has been analyzed within the framework of the victim-blaming ideology. In the following pages, I shall present in detail nine examples that relate to social problems and human services in urban areas.

It would be possible for me to venture into other areas—one finds a perfect example in literature about the underdeveloped countries of the Third World, in which the lack of prosperity and technological progress is attributed to some aspect of the national character of the people, such as lack of "achievement motivation"—but I plan to stay within the confines of my own personal and professional experience, which is, generally, with racial injustice, social welfare, and human services in the city.

I have been listening to the victim-blamers and pondering their thought processes for a number of years. That process is often very subtle. Victim-blaming is cloaked in kindness and concern, and bears all the trappings and statistical furbelows of scientism; it is obscured by a perfumed haze of humanitarianism. In observing the process of Blaming the Victim, one tends to be confused and disoriented because those who practice this art display a deep concern for the victims that is quite genuine. In this way, the new ideology is very different from the open prejudice and reactionary tactics of the old days. Its adherents include sympathetic social scientists with social consciences in good working order, and liberal politicians with a genuine commitment to reform. They are very careful to dissociate themselves from vulgar Calvinism or crude racism; they indignantly condemn any notions of innate wickedness or genetic defect. "The Negro is *not born* inferior," they shout apoplectically. "Force of circumstance," they explain in reasonable tones, "has *made* him inferior." And they dismiss with self-righteous contempt any claims that the poor man in America is plainly unworthy or shiftless or enamored of idleness. No, they say, he is "caught in the cycle of poverty." He is trained to be poor by his culture and his family life, endowed by his environment (perhaps by his ignorant mother's outdated style of toilet training) with those unfortunately unpleasant characteristics that make him ineligible for a passport into the affluent society.

Blaming the Victim is, of course, quite different from old-fashioned conservative ideologies. The latter simply dismissed victims as inferior, genetically defective, or morally unfit; the emphasis is on the intrinsic, even hereditary, defect. The former shifts its emphasis to the environmental causation. The old-fashioned conservative could hold firmly to the belief that the oppressed and the victimized were born that way—that way being defective or inadequate in character or ability. The new ideology attributes defect and inadequacy to the malignant nature of poverty, injustice, slum life, and racial difficulties. The stigma that marks the victim and accounts for his victimization is an acquired stigma, a stigma of social, rather than genetic, origin. But the stigma, the defect, the fatal difference—though derived in the past from environmental forces—is still located *within* the victim, inside his skin. With such an elegant formulation, the humanitarian can have it both ways. He can, all at the same time, concentrate his charitable interest on the defects of the victim, condemn the vague social and environmental stresses that produced the defect (some time ago), and ignore the continuing effect of victimizing social forces (right now). It is a brilliant ideology for justifying a perverse form of social action designed to change, not society, as one might expect, but rather society's victim.

As a result, there is a terrifying sameness in the programs that arise from this kind of analysis. In education, we have programs of "compensatory education" to build up the skills and attitudes of the ghetto child, rather than structural changes in the schools. In race relations, we have social engineers who think up ways of "strengthening" the Negro family, rather than methods of eradicating racism. In health care, we develop new programs to provide health information (to correct the supposed ignorance of the poor) and to reach out and discover cases of untreated illness and disability (to compensate for their supposed unwillingness to seek treatment). Meanwhile, the gross inequities of our medical care delivery systems are left completely unchanged. As we might expect, the logical outcome of analyzing social problems in terms of the deficiencies of the victim is the development of programs aimed at correcting those deficiencies. The formula for action becomes extraordinarily simple: change the victim.

All of this happens so smoothly that it seems downright rational. First, identify a social problem. Second, study those affected by the problem and discover in what ways they are different from the rest of us as a consequence of deprivation and injustice. Third, define the differences as the cause of the social problem itself. Finally, of course, assign a government bureaucrat to invent a humanitarian action program to correct the differences.

Now no one in his right mind would quarrel with the assertion that social problems are present in abundance and are readily identifiable. God knows it is true that when hundreds of thousands of poor children drop out of school—or even graduate from school—they are barely literate. After spending some ten thousand hours in the company of professional educators, these children appear to have learned very little. The fact of failure in their education is undisputed. And the racial situation in America is usually acknowledged to be a number one item on the nation's agenda. Despite years of marches, commissions, judicial decisions, and endless legislative remedies, we are confronted with unchanging or even widening racial differences in achievement. In addition, despite our assertions that Americans get the best health care in the world, the poor stubbornly remain unhealthy. They lose more work because of illness, have more carious teeth, lose more babies as a result of both miscarriage and infant death, and die considerably younger than the well-to-do.

The problems are there, and there in great quantities. They make us uneasy. Added together, these disturbing signs reflect inequality and a puzzlingly high level of unalleviated distress in America totally inconsistent with our proclaimed ideals and our enormous wealth. This thread—this rope—of inconsistency stands out so visibly in the fabric of American life, that it is jarring to the eye. And this must be explained, to the satisfaction of our conscience as well as our patriotism. Blaming the Victim is an ideal, almost painless, evasion.

The second step in applying this explanation is to look sympathetically at those who "have" the problem in question, to separate them out and define them in some way as a special group, a group that is *different* from the population in general. This is a crucial and essential step in the process, for that difference is in itself hampering and maladaptive. The Different Ones are seen as less competent, less skilled, less knowing—in short, less human. . . .

The ultimate effect is always to distract attention from the basic causes and to leave the primary social injustice untouched. And, most telling, the proposed remedy for the problem is, of course, to work on the victim himself. Prescriptions for cure, [are] invariably conceived to revamp and revise the victim, never to change the surrounding circumstances. They want to change his attitudes, alter his values, fill up his cultural deficits, energize his apathetic soul, cure his character defects, train him and polish him and woo him from his savage ways.

. . . The old, reactionary exceptionalistic formulations are replaced by new progressive, humanitarian exceptionalistic formulations. In education, the outmoded and unacceptable concept of racial or class differences in basic inherited intellectual ability simply gives way to the new notion of cultural deprivation: there is very little functional difference between these two ideas. In taking a look at the phenomenon of poverty, the old concept of unfitness or idleness or laziness is replaced by the newfangled theory of the culture of poverty. In race relations, plain Negro inferiority—which was good enough for old-fashioned conservatives—is pushed aside by fancy conceits about the crumbling Negro family. With regard to illegitimacy, we are not so crass as to concern ourselves with immorality and vice, as in the old days; we settle benignly on the explanation of the "lower-class pattern of sexual behavior," which no one condemns as evil, but which is, in fact, simply a variation of the old explanatory idea. Mental illness is no longer defined as the result of hereditary taint or congenital character flaw; now we have new causal hypotheses regarding the ego-damaging emotional experiences that are supposed to be the inevitable consequence of the deplorable child-rearing practices of the poor.

In each case, of course, we are persuaded to ignore the obvious: the continued blatant discrimination against the Negro, the gross deprivation of contraceptive and adoption services to the poor, the heavy stresses endemic in the life of the poor. And almost all our make-believe liberal programs aimed at correcting our urban problems are off target; they are designed either to change the poor man or to cool him out. . . .

But, in any case, are the poor really all that different from the middle class? Take a common type of study, showing that ninety-one percent of the upper class, compared to only sixty-eight percent of the poor, prefer college education for their children. What does that tell us about the difference in values between classes?

First, if almost seventy percent of the poor want their children to go to college, it doesn't make much sense to say that the poor, as a group, do not value education. Only a minority of them—somewhat less than one-third—fail to express a *wish* that their children attend college. A smaller minority—one in ten—of the middle class give similar responses. One might well wonder why this small group of the better-off citizens of our achieving society reject higher education. They have the money; many of them have the direct experience of education; and most of them are aware of the monetary value of a college degree. I would suggest that the thirty percent of the poor who are unwilling to express a wish that their children go to college are easier to understand. They know the barriers—financial, social, and for black parents, racial—that make it very difficult for the children of the poor to get a college education. That seven out of ten of them nevertheless persist in a desire to see their children in a cap and gown is, in a very real sense, remarkable. Most important, if we are concerned with cultural or subcultural differences, it seems highly illogical to emphasize the values of a small minority of one group and then to attribute these values to the whole group. I simply cannot accept the evidence. If seventy percent of a group values education, then it is completely illogical to say that the group as a whole does *not* value education.

A useful formulation is to be found in Hyman Rodman's conception of the "lower class value stretch" which, to give a highly oversimplified version, proposes that members of the lower class *share* the dominant value system but *stretch* it to include as much as possible of the variations that circumstances force upon them. Rodman says:

> Lower class persons in close interaction with each other and faced with similar problems do not long remain in a state of mutual ignorance. They do not maintain a strong commitment to middle class values that they cannot attain, and they do not continue to respond to others in a rewarding or punishing way simply on the basis of whether these others are living up to the middle class values. A change takes place. They come to tolerate and eventually to evaluate favorably certain deviations from the middle class values. In this way they need not be continually frustrated by their failure to live up to unattainable values. The resultant is a stretched value system with a low degree of commitment to all the values within the range, including the dominant, middle class values.

In Rodman's terms, then, differences in range of values and commitments to specific elements within that range occur primarily as an *adaptive* rather than as a *cultural* response. . . .

The most recent, and in many ways the best information on [the related issue of child rearing] comes to us from the Hylan Lewis child-rearing studies, which I have mentioned before. Lewis has demonstrated (finally, one hopes) that there really *is* no "lower class child-rearing pattern." There are a number of such patterns—ranging from strict and over-controlled parenting, to permissiveness, to down-right neglect—just as in Lewis' sample there are a variety of different kinds of families—ranging from those

with rigid, old-fashioned standards of hard work, thrift, morality and obsessive cleanliness, to the disorganized and disturbed families that he calls the "clinical poor." Lewis says:

> . . . it appears as a broad spectrum of pragmatic adjustments to external and internal stresses and deprivation. . . . Many low income families appear here as, in fact, the frustrated victims of what are thought of as middle class values, behavior and aspirations.

We return, finally, to where we began: the concept of Deferred Need Gratification. The simple idea that lower class folk have, as a character trait, a built-in deficiency in ability to delay need gratification has been explored, analyzed and more or less blown apart by Miller, Riessman, and Seagull. They point out that the supposed commitment of the middle classes to the virtues of thrift and hard work, to the practices of planning and saving for every painfully-chosen expenditure is, at this point in time, at best a surviving myth reflecting past conditions of dubious prevalence. The middle classes of today are clearly consumption-minded and debt-addicted. So the comparison group against which the poor are judged exists largely as a theoretical category with a theoretical behavior pattern. They go on to raise critical questions, similar to those I have raised earlier in this chapter. For example, on the question of what one would do with a two thousand dollar windfall, there was a difference between class groups of only five percent—about seventy percent of the middle class said they would save most of it, compared with about sixty-five percent of the lower class. On the basis of this small difference (which was statistically, but not practically, significant) the researchers, you will remember, had concluded that working-class people had less ability to defer need gratification. This conclusion may reflect elegant research methodology, but it fails the test of common sense. . . .

As for the idea that the poor share a culture in the sense that they subscribe to and follow a particular, deviant prescription for living—a poor man's blueprint for choosing and decision-making which accounts for the way he lives—this does not deserve much comment. Every study—with the exception of the egregious productions of Walter Miller—shows that, at the very least, overwhelming numbers of the poor give allegiance to the values and principles of the dominant American culture.

A related point—often the most overlooked point in any discussion of the culture of poverty—is that there is not, to my knowledge, *any evidence whatever* that the poor perceive their way of life as good and preferable to that of other ways of life. To make such an assertion is to talk pure nonsense. . . .

Perhaps the most fundamental question to ask of those who are enamored of the idea that the poor have one culture and the rich another is to ask, simply, "So what?" Suppose the mythical oil millionaire behaves in an unrefined "lower class" manner, for example. What difference does that make as long as he owns the oilwells? Is the power of the Chairman of the Ways and Means Committee in the state legislature diminished or enhanced in any way by his taste in clothing or music? And suppose every single poor family in America set as its long-range goal that its sons and daughters would get a Ph.D.—who would pay the tuition?

The effect of tastes, child-rearing practices, speech patterns, reading habits, and other cultural factors is relatively small in comparison to the effect of wealth and influence. What I am trying to suggest is that the inclusion in the analytic process of the elements of social stratification that are usually omitted—particularly economic class and power—would produce more significant insights into the circumstances of the poor and the pressures and deprivations with which they live. The simplest—and at the same time, the most significant—proposition in understanding poverty is that it is caused by lack of money. The overwhelming majority of the poor are poor because they have, first: insufficient income; and second: no access to methods of increasing that income—that is, no power. They are too young, too old, too sick; they are bound to the task of caring for small children, or they are simply discriminated against. The facts are clear, and the solution seems rather obvious—raise their income and let their "culture," whatever it might be, take care of itself.

The need to avoid facing this obvious solution—which is very uncomfortable since it requires some substantial changes and redistribution of income—provides the motivation for developing the stabilizing ideology of the culture of poverty which acts to sustain the *status quo* and delay change. The function of the ideology of lower class culture, then, is plainly to maintain inequality in American life.

The millionaire, freshly risen from the lower class, whose crude tongue and appalling table manners betray the newness of his affluence, is a staple of American literature and folklore. He comes on stage over and over, and we have been taught exactly what to expect with each entrance. He will walk into the parlor in his undershirt, gulp tea from a saucer, spit into the Limoges flower pot, and, when finally invited to the society garden party, disgrace his wife by saying "bullshit" to the president of the bank. When I was growing up, we had daily lessons in this legend from Jiggs and Maggie in the comic strip.

This discrepancy between *class* and *status*, between possession of economic resources and life style, has been a source of ready humour and guaranteed fascination for generations. The centrality of this mythical strain in American thought is reflected again in the strange and perverse ideas emerging from the mouths of many professional Pauper Watchers and Victim Blamers.

In real life, of course, Jiggs' character and behavior would never remain so constant and unchanging over the decades. The strain between wealth and style is one that usually tends to be quickly resolved. Within a fairly short time, Jiggs would be coming into the parlor first with a shirt, then with a tie on, and, finally, in one of his many custom-made suits. He would soon be drinking tea from a Limoges cup, and for a time he would spit in an antique cuspidor, until he learned not to spit at all.

At the garden party, he would confine his mention of animal feces to a discussion of the best fertilizer for the rhododendron. In real life, style tends to follow close on money, and money tends to be magnetized and attracted to power. Those who try to persuade us that the process can be reversed, that a change in style of life can lead backward to increased wealth and greater power, are preaching nonsense. To promise that improved table manners can produce a salary increase; that more elegant taste in clothes will lead to the acquisition of stock in IBM; that an expanded vocabulary will automatically generate an enlargement of community influence—these are pernicious as well as foolish. There is no record in history of any *group* having accomplished this wondrous task. (There may be a few clever individuals who have followed such artful routes to money and power, but they are relatively rare.) The whole idea is an illusion of fatuous social scientists and welfare bureaucrats blinded by the ideology I have painstakingly tried to dissect in the previous chapters. . . .

POSTSCRIPT

Does "Lower-Class" Culture Perpetuate Poverty?

The debate over the culture of poverty thesis is as strong today as it was fifteen years ago when Banfield and Ryan were debating. In 1981 George Gilder incorporated the culture of poverty thesis in his book, *Wealth and Poverty* (Basic Books) and argued that hard work is the tried and true path from poverty to wealth (see issue 8). He also agrees that many welfare programs perpetuate poverty by breeding dependence and supporting the culture of poverty. This criticism of welfare has been forcefully argued with ample statistics by Charles Murray in *Losing Ground* (Basic Books, 1984) (see issue 13). Both Gilder and Murray view the welfare system as an important contributor to the culture of poverty, whereas Banfield sees the culture of poverty as virulent long before welfare became a major fact in the lives of poor people.

On the other side of the debate are the countless works that describe the crushing and numbing conditions of the poor. Charles Dickens is the patron saint of these crusaders and Michael Harrington is their leading living prophet. He described the widespread poverty that has existed in affluent America in his book, *The Other America* (Macmillan, 1963) and helped launch the "War on Poverty" of the Kennedy-Johnson administrations. Thomas Gladwin in *Poverty USA* (Little, Brown, 1967) and Nick Katz in *Let Them Eat Promises* (Prentice-Hall, 1969) sought to maintain the national concern about poverty in the late 1960s by documenting its prevalence even though the poverty rate dropped from 30 percent in 1950 to 13 percent in 1970. In 1968, however, the administration changed and the crusade against poverty died down. Nevertheless, public welfare expenditures rose mainly because Social Security, Medicare and Medicaid kept expanding.

The anti-poverty warriors soon had new worries as unemployment rose to record levels since the Depression because of the economic difficulties of the 1970s. Two new developments were that female-headed families became the largest group below the poverty line and in the 1980s the homeless became a major public concern. These developments compelled Michael Harrington to again take up his pen and write for the cause of the poor in *The New American Poverty* (Holt, Rinehart and Winston, 1984). More recently William Wilson has described the horrid conditions of the poor and the macroeconomic forces that cause these conditions in *The Truly Disadvantaged* (University of Chicago Press, 1987).

ISSUE 3
Has Individualism Become Excessive?

YES: Robert Bellah et al., from *Habits of the Heart: Individualism and Commitment in American Life* (Harper & Row, 1986)

NO: Henry Fairlie, from *Spoiled Child of the Western World* (Doubleday, 1975)

ISSUE SUMMARY

YES: Robert Bellah and his associates argue that the tendency of Americans has been to become absorbed in the self at the expense of transcendent values and the good of the community.

NO: Henry Fairlie suggests that the critics of "consumerism" fail to appreciate the extraordinary degree of freedom enjoyed by modern "mass man."

Many observers have called attention to the "Lockean" qualities of the American people. The reference is to John Locke, the English philosopher of the seventeenth century, whose writings were much quoted by Americans of the eighteenth century. Parts of our Declaration of Independence sound like they came almost word for word from Locke. The Declaration reaffirms Locke's belief in "unalienable rights," which are identified as "life, liberty, and the pursuit of happiness" (for Locke there were "life, liberty, and property").

Locke championed individualism. He postulated a "state of nature," in which humans lived before they established governments. In that natural state, human beings were all "free, equal, and independent." While the raw products of nature (the trees, the fruit, the deer, and so on) belonged to all, the moment a human being "worked on" one of these products—by killing and skinning a deer, by picking a fruit, or otherwise mixing one's labor with the product of nature—the product then became one's own, to do with as one pleased. Not incidentally, the product then became more valuable. The moral: work produces both wealth and private property.

Locke was popular in America because his theory seemed to fit the American experience. Lacking Europe's class distinctions and restrictions on economic activity, America offered unprecedented opportunities to the ambitious and the industrious. Writers like Benjamin Franklin won great renown by showing Americans the "uses of virtue." Franklin demonstrated that thrift, self-denial, temperance, patience, hard work, and other Puritan virtues could bring rewards not only in Heaven but in this world too. The compelling American value became the "pursuit of happiness."

The pursuit was in full swing by the time Alexis de Tocqueville arrived in America in the 1830s. The famous French observer was struck by the driving ambition of Americans. "The passions that stir the Americans most deeply are commercial and not political ones," he noted, adding that "private interest" seems to be the dominant force in America. Yet de Tocqueville also noted the tendency of Americans to form associations and work together for common goals. Americans, he said, are farsighted enough to appreciate the individual advantage in common action. "It thus happens that ambition can make a man care for his fellows, and, in a sense, he often finds his self-interest in forgetting about himself."

Perhaps there was a bit of wishful thinking in this analysis. Or, even assuming that de Tocqueville was correct about Americans in the 1830s, is it as obvious today that Americans combine self-seeking and community spirit? If we insist on defining the "pursuit of happiness" as the chase after wealth or whatever else it is that pleases us, won't this individual self-seeking at some point destroy the community? These are not meant to be rhetorical questions. It may well be that individualism and community spirit do fit together, or can be made to fit. But they certainly point different ways. Individualism emphasizes freedom and choice; it prizes incentive, competitiveness, and material reward. Community stresses the need for cooperation, the joy of companionship, and the warmth of familiarity. By the same token, community and individualism both have darker potentialities. Community cooperation can turn into regimentation, and too much familiarity may breed contempt. Yet excessive individualism may lead to the "atomization" of society, in which persons are reduced to faceless and soulless integers. This is the "mass society" that European philosophers have been writing about since the 1930s. Such thinkers as José Ortega y Gasset, Hannah Arendt, and Erich Fromm have warned us that too much individualism lays the groundwork for ugly anti-democratic movements that exploit mass loneliness.

In the following selections, sociologist Robert Bellah and his colleagues seem to share some of the concerns of the European critics and conclude that individualism has gone too far, causing painful psychic and moral wounds. Journalist Henry Fairlie, however, suggests that there is nothing intrinsically wrong, and much that is exciting and liberating, in the way sovereign individuals pursue happiness in America.

37

YES

Robert N. Bellah et al.

INDIVIDUALISM AND COMMITMENT
IN AMERICAN LIFE

How ought we to live? How do we think about how to live? Who are we, as Americans? What is our character? These are questions we have asked our fellow citizens in many parts of the country. We engaged them in conversations about their lives and about what matters most to them, talked about their families and communities, their doubts and uncertainties, and their hopes and fears with respect to the larger society. We found them eager to discuss the right way to live, what to teach our children, and what our public and private responsibilities should be, but also a little dismayed by these subjects. These are important matters to those to whom we talked, and yet concern about moral questions is often relegated to the realm of private anxiety, as if it would be awkward or embarrassing to make it public. We hope this book will help transform this inner moral debate, often shared only with intimates, into public discourse. In these pages, Americans speak with us, and indirectly, with one another, about issues that deeply concern us all. As we will see, many doubt that we have enough in common to be able mutually to discuss our central aspirations and fears. It is one of our purposes to persuade them that we do.

The fundamental question we posed, and that was repeatedly posed to us, was how to preserve or create a morally coherent life. But the kind of life we want depends on the kind of people we are—on our character. Our inquiry can thus be located in a longstanding discussion of the relationship between character and society. In the eighth book of the *Republic*, Plato sketched a theory of the relationship between the moral character of a people and the nature of its political community, the way it organizes and governs itself. The founders of the American republic at the time of the Revolution adopted a much later version of the same theory. Since for them, as for Americans with whom we talked, freedom was perhaps the most important value, they were particularly concerned with the qualities of character necessary for the creation of a free republic.

In the 1830s, the French social philosopher Alexis de Tocqueville offered the most comprehensive and penetrating analysis of the relationship between

Excerpts from *Habits of the Heart: Individualism and Commitment in American Life*, by Robert N. Bellah et al. (New York: Harper & Row Publishers, Inc.). Copyright © 1985 by Robert N. Bellah. Reprinted by permission of Harper & Row Publishers, Inc.

character and society in America that has ever been written. In his book *Democracy in America*, based on acute observation and wide conversation with Americans, Tocqueville described the mores—which he on occasion called "habits of the heart"—of the American people and showed how they helped to form American character. He singled out family life, our religious traditions, and our participation in local politics as helping to create the kind of person who could sustain a connection to a wide political community and thus ultimately support the maintenance of free institutions. He also warned that some aspects of our character—what he was one of the first to call "individualism"—might eventually isolate Americans one from another and thereby undermine the conditions of freedom.

The central problem of our book concerns the American individualism that Tocqueville described with a mixture of admiration and anxiety. It seems to us that it is individualism, and not equality, as Tocqueville thought, that has marched inexorably through our history. We are concerned that this individualism may have grown cancerous—that it may be destroying those social integuments that Tocqueville saw as moderating its more destructive potentialities, that it may be threatening the survival of freedom itself. We want to know what individualism in America looks and feels like, and how the world appears in its light. . . .

Living well is a challenge. Brian Palmer, a successful businessman, lives in a comfortable San Jose suburb and works as a top-level manager in a large corporation. He is justifiably proud of his rapid rise in the corporation, but he is even prouder of the profound change he has made recently in his idea of success. "My value system," he says, "has changed a little bit as the result of a divorce and reexamining life values. Two years ago, confronted with the work load I have right now, I would stay in the office and work until midnight, come home, go to bed, get up at six, and go back in and work until midnight, until such time as it got done. Now I just kind of flip the bird and walk out. My family life is more important to me than that, and the work will wait, I have learned." A new marriage and a houseful of children have become the center of Brian's life. But such new values were won only after painful difficulties.

Now forty-one, his tall, lean body bursting with restless energy, Brian recalls a youth that included a fair amount of hell-raising, a lot of sex, and a considerable devotion to making money. At twenty-four, he married. Shouldering the adult responsibilities of marriage and children became the guiding purpose of his life for the next few years.

Whether or not Brian felt his life was satisfying, he was deeply committed to succeeding at his career and family responsibilities. He held two full-time jobs to support his family, accepting apparently without complaint the loss of a youth in which, he himself reports, "the vast majority of my time from, say, the age of fifteen to twenty-two or twenty-three was devoted toward giving myself pleasure of one sort or another." Brian describes his reasons for working so hard after he married quite simply. "It seemed like the thing to do at the time," he says. "I couldn't stand not having enough money to get by on, and with my wife unable to contribute to the family income, it seemed like the thing to do. I guess self-reliance is one of the characteristics I have pretty high up in my value system. It was second nature. I didn't even question the thing. I just went out and did it." Brian and his wife came to share very little in their marriage, except, as he thought, good sex, children, and devotion to his career. With his wife's support, he decided to "test" himself "in the Big League," and he made it, although at a great cost to his marriage and family life. "What was my concept of what constituted a reasonable relationship? I guess I felt an obligation to care for materially, provide for, a wife and my children, in a style to which I'd like to see them become accustomed. Providing for my family materially was important. Sharing wasn't important. Sharing of my time wasn't important. I put in extremely long hours, probably averaging sixty to sixty-five hours a week. I'd work almost every Saturday. Always in the office by 7:30. Rarely out of the office before 6:30 at night. Sometimes I'd work until 10:30 or 11. That was numero uno. But I compensated for that by saying, I have this nice car, this nice house, joined the Country Club. Now you have a place you can go, sit on your butt, drink, go into the pool. I'll pay the bills and I'll do my thing at work."

For Brian's wife, the compensations apparently weren't enough. After almost fifteen years of marriage, "One day I came home. In fact, our house was for sale, and we had an offer on the house. My wife said, 'Before you accept this offer, you should probably know that once we sell this house, we will live in different houses.' That was my official notification that she was planning to divorce me."

The divorce, "one of the two or three biggest surprises of my life," led Brian to reassess his life in fundamental ways and to explore the limits of the kind of success he had been pursuing. "I live by

establishing plans. I had no plan for being single, and it gave me a lot of opportunity to think, and in the course of thinking, I read for the first time in many, many years. Got back into classical music for the first time since my college years. I went out and bought my first Bach album and a stereo to play it on. Mostly the thinking process of being alone and relating to my children." . . .

The revolution in Brian's thinking came from a reexamination of the true sources of joy and satisfaction in his life. And it is particularly in a marriage to a women very different from his first wife that Brian has discovered a new sense of himself and a different understanding of what he wants out of life. He has a new sense of what love can be. "To be able to receive affection freely and give affection and to give of myself and know it is a totally reciprocal type of thing. There's just almost a psychologically buoyant feeling of being able to be so much more involved and sharing. Sharing experiences of goals, sharing of feelings, working together to solve problems, etc. My viewpoint of a true love, husband-and-wife type of relationship is one that is founded on mutual respect, admiration, affection, the ability to give and receive freely." His new wife, a divorcee his own age, brings four children to their marriage, added to Brian's own three. They have five children still living at home, and a sense of energy, mutual devotion, and commitment sufficient to make their family life a joy.

In many ways, Brian's is an individual success story. He has succeeded materially, and he has also taken hold of the opportunity to reach out beyond material success to a fuller sense of what he wants from life. Yet despite the personal triumph Brian's life represents, despite the fulfillment he seems to experience, there is still something uncertain, something poignantly unresolved about his story.

The difficulty becomes most evident when Brian tries to explain why it is that his current life is, in fact, better than his earlier life built around single-minded devotion to his career. His description of his reasons for changing his life and of his current happiness seems to come down mainly to a shift in his notions of what would make him happy. His new goal—devotion to marriage and children—seems as arbitrary and unexamined as his earlier pursuit of material success. Both are justified as idiosyncratic preference rather than as representing a larger sense of the purpose of life. Brian sees himself as consistently pursuing a utilitarian calculus—devotion to his own self-interest—except that there has been an almost inexplicable change in his personal preferences. In describing the reasons for this change, he begins, "Well, I think I just reestablished my priorities." He sometimes seems to reject his past life as wrong; but at other times, he seems to say he simply got bored with it. "That exclusive pursuit of success now seems to me not a good way to live. That's not the most important thing to me. I have demonstrated to myself, to my own satisfaction, that I can achieve about what I want to achieve. So the challenge of goal realization does not contain that mystique that it held for me at one time. I just have found that I get a lot of personal reward from being involved in the lives of my children."

American cultural traditions define personality, achievement, and the purpose of human life in ways that leave the individual suspended in glorious, but terrifying, isolation. These are limita-tions of our culture, of the categories and ways of thinking we have inherited, not limitations of individuals such as Brian who inhabit the culture. People frequently live out a fuller sense of purpose in life than they can justify in rational terms, as we see in Brian's case and many others.

Brian's restless energy, love of challenges, and appreciation of the good life are characteristics of much that is most vital in American culture. They are all qualities particularly well-suited to the hard-driving corporate world in which he works. When Brian describes how he has chosen to live, however, he keeps referring to "values" and "priorities" not justified by any wider framework of purpose or belief. What is good is what one finds rewarding. If one's preferences change, so does the nature of the good. Even the deepest ethical virtues are justified as matters of personal preference. Indeed, the ultimate ethical rule is simply that individuals should be able to pursue whatever they find rewarding, constrained only by the requirement that they not interfere with the "value systems" of others. "I guess I feel like everybody on this planet is entitled to have a little bit of space, and things that detract from other people's space are kind of bad," Brian observes. "One of the things that I use to characterize life in California, one of the things that makes California such a pleasant place to live, is people by and large aren't bothered by other people's value systems as long as they don't infringe upon your own. By and large, the rule of thumb out here is that if you've got the money, honey, you can do your thing as long as your thing doesn't destroy someone else's property, or interrupt their sleep, or bother their privacy, then that's fine. If you want to go in your house and smoke marijuana and shoot dope and get all screwed up, that's your business, but don't bring that out on the street, don't expose my children to it, just do your thing. That works out kind of neat." . . .

Each of the individuals that we have described in this chapter is drawn from one of the four research projects on which the book is based.* We are less concerned with whether they are average than with the fact that they represent the ways in which Americans use private and public life to make sense of their lives. This is the central issue with which our book is concerned. Brian Palmer finds the chief meaning of his life in marriage and family; Margaret Oldham in therapy. Thus both of them are primarily concerned with private life. Joe Gorman gives his life coherence through his active concern for the life of his town; Wayne Bauer finds a similar coherence in his involvement in political activism. Both of them have integrated the public world deeply into their lives. Whether chiefly concerned with private or public life, all four are involved in caring for others. They are responsible and, in many ways, admirable adults. Yet when each of them uses the moral discourse they share, what we call the first language of individualism, they have difficulty articulating the richness of their commitments. In the language they use, their lives sound more isolated and arbitrary than, as we have observed them, they actually are.

Thus all four of the persons whose voices we have heard assume that there is something arbitrary about the goals of

*Only Brian Palmer's story is reprinted here. Margaret Oldham, Joe Gorman and Wayne Bauer are the other individuals whose lives are examined in *Habits of the Heart.*—Eds.

a good life. For Brian Palmer, the goal of a good life is to achieve the priorities you have set for yourself. But how do you know that your present priorities are better than those of your past, or better than those of other people? Because you intuitively appreciate that they are right for you at the present time. For Joe Gorman, the goal of a good life is intimate involvement with the community and family into which he happens to have been born. But how do you know that in this complicated world, the inherited conventions of your community and your family are better and more important, and, therefore, more worthy of your allegiance, than those of other communities and families? In the end, you simply prefer to believe that they are better, at least for you. For Margaret Oldham, the goal of a good life is liberation from precisely the kinds of conventions that Joe Gorman holds dear. But what do you aim for once you have been liberated? Simply what you yourself decide is best for you. For Wayne Bauer, the goal of a good life is participation in the political struggle to create a more just society. But where should political struggle lead us? To a society in which all individuals, not just the wealthy, will have power over their own lives. But what are they going to *do* with that power? Whatever they individually choose to do, as long as they don't hurt anybody.

The common difficulties these four very different people face in justifying the goals of a morally good life point to a characteristic problem of people in our culture. For most of us, it is easier to think about how to get what we want than to know what exactly we should want. Thus Brian, Joe, Margaret, and Wayne are each in his or her own way confused about how to define for themselves such things as the nature of success, the meaning of freedom, and the requirements of justice. Those difficulties are in an important way created by the limitations in the common tradition of moral discourse they—and we—share. . . .

PRIVATE AND PUBLIC

Sometimes Americans make a rather sharp dichotomy between private and public life. Viewing one's primary task as "finding oneself" in autonomous self-reliance, separating oneself not only from one's parents but also from those larger communities and traditions that constitute one's past, leads to the notion that it is in oneself, perhaps in relation to a few intimate others, that fulfillment is to be found. Individualism of this sort often implies a negative view of public life. The impersonal forces of the economic and political worlds are what the individual needs protection against. In this perspective, even occupation, which has been so central to the identity of Americans in the past, becomes instrumental—not a good in itself, but only a means to the attainment of a rich and satisfying private life. But on the basis of what we have seen in our observation of middle-class American life, it would seem that this quest for purely private fulfillment is illusory: it often ends in emptiness instead. On the other hand, we found many people, some of whom we introduced earlier in this chapter, for whom private fulfillment and public involvement are not antithetical. These people evince an individualism that is not empty but is full of content drawn from an active identification with communities and traditions. Perhaps the no-

tion that private life and public life are at odds is incorrect. Perhaps they are so deeply involved with each other that the impoverishment of one entails the impoverishment of the other. Parker Palmer is probably right when he says that "in a healthy society the private and the public are not mutually exclusive, not in competition with each other. They are, instead, two halves of a whole, two poles of a paradox. They work together dialectically, helping to create and nurture one another."

Certainly this dialectical relationship is clear where public life degenerates into violence and fear. One cannot live a rich private life in a state of siege, mistrusting all strangers and turning one's home into an armed camp. A minimum of public decency and civility is a precondition for a fulfilling private life. On the other hand, public involvement is often difficult and demanding. To engage successfully in the public world, one needs personal strength and the support of family and friends. A rewarding private life is one of the preconditions for a healthy public life.

For all their doubts about the public sphere, Americans are more engaged in voluntary associations and civic organizations than the citizens of most other industrial nations. In spite of all the difficulties, many Americans feel they must "get involved." In public life as in private, we can discern the habits of the heart that sustain individualism and commitment, as well as what makes them problematic. . . .

For several centuries, we have been embarked on a great effort to increase our freedom, wealth, and power. For over a hundred years, a large part of the American people, the middle class, has imagined that the virtual meaning of life lies in the acquisition of ever-increasing status, income, and authority, from which genuine freedom is supposed to come. Our achievements have been enormous. They permit us the aspiration to become a genuinely humane society in a genuinely decent world, and provide many of the means to attain that aspiration. Yet we seem to be hovering on the very brink of disaster, not only from international conflict but from the internal incoherence of our own society. What has gone wrong? How can we reverse the slide toward the abyss?

In thinking about what has gone wrong, we need to see what we can learn from our traditions, as well as from the best currently available knowledge. What has failed at every level—from the society of nations to the national society to the local community to the family—is integration: we have failed to remember "our community as members of the same body," as John Winthrop put it. We have committed what to the republican founders of our nation was the cardinal sin: we have put our own good, as individuals, as groups, as a nation, ahead of the common good. . . .

What we fear above all, and what keeps the new world powerless to be born, is that if we give up our dream of private success for a more genuinely integrated societal community, we will be abandoning our separation and individuation, collapsing into dependence and tyranny. What we find hard to see is that it is the extreme fragmentation of the modern world that really threatens our individuation: that what is best in our separation and individuation, our sense of dignity and autonomy as persons, requires a new integration if it is to be sustained.

The notion of a transition to a new level of social integration, a newly vital social ecology, may also be resisted as absurdly utopian, as a project to create a perfect society. But the transformation of which we speak is both necessary and modest. Without it, indeed, there may be very little future to think about at all. . . .

If we are right in our stress on a revitalized social ecology, then one critically important action that government could take in a new political atmosphere would be, in Christopher Jenck's words, to reduce the "punishments of failure and the rewards of success." Reducing the inordinate rewards of ambition and our inordinate fears of ending up as losers would offer the possibility of a great change in the meaning of work in our society and all that would go with such a change. To make a real difference, such a shift in rewards would have to be part of a reappropriation of the idea of vocation or calling, a return in a new way to the idea of work as a contribution to the good of all and not merely as a means to one's own advancement.

If the extrinsic rewards and punishments associated with work were reduced, it would be possible to make vocational choices more in terms of intrinsic satisfactions. Work that is intrinsically interesting and valuable is one of the central requirements for a revitalized social ecology. For professionals, this would mean a clearer sense that the large institutions most of them work for really contribute to the public good. A bright young lawyer (or a bright old lawyer, for that matter) whose work consists in helping one corporation outwit another is intelligent enough to doubt the social utility of what he or she is doing. The work may be interesting—even challenging and exciting—yet its intrinsic meaninglessness in any larger moral or social context necessarily produces an alienation that is only partly assuaged by the relatively large income of corporate lawyers. Those whose work is not only poorly rewarded but boring, repetitive, and unchallenging are in an even worse situation. Automation that turns millions of our citizens into mere servants of robots is already a form of despotism, for which the pleasures of private life—modest enough for those of minimum skill and minimum wage—cannot compensate. The social wealth that automation brings, if it is not siphoned into the hands of a few, can be used to pay for work that is intrinsically valuable, in the form of a revival of crafts (that already flourish in supplying goods for the wealthy) and in the improvement of human services. Where routine work is essential, its monotony can be mitigated by including workers in fuller participation in their enterprises so that they understand how their work contributes to the ultimate product and have an effective voice in how those enterprises are run.

Undoubtedly, the satisfaction of work well done, indeed "the pursuit of excellence," is a permanent and positive human motive. Where its reward is the approbation of one's fellows more than the accumulation of great private wealth, it can contribute to what the founders of our republic called virtue. Indeed, in a revived social ecology, it would be a primary form of civic virtue. And from it would flow a number of positive consequences. For one thing, the split between private and public, work and family, that has grown for over a century, might begin to be mended. If the ethos of work were less brutally competitive and more ecologically harmonious, it would be

more consonant with the ethos of private life and, particularly, of family life. A less frantic concern for advancement and a reduction of working hours for both men and women would make it easier for women to be full participants in the workplace without abandoning family life. By the same token, men would be freed to take an equal role at home and in child care. In this way, what seemed at first to be a change only in the nature of work would turn out to have major consequences for family life as well.

Another consequence of the change in the meaning of work from private aggrandizement to public contribution would be to weaken the motive to keep the complexity of our society invisible. It would become part of the ethos of work to be aware of our intricate connectedness and interdependence. There would be no fear of social catastrophe or hope of inordinate reward motivating us to exaggerate our own independence. And with such a change, we might begin to be better able to understand why, though we are all, as human beings, morally deserving of equal respect, some of us begin with familial or cultural advantages or disadvantages that others do not have. Or perhaps, since we would not conceive of life so much in terms of a race in which all the prizes go to the swiftest, we might begin to make moral sense of the fact that there are real cultural differences among us, that we do not all want the same thing, and that it is not a moral defect to find other things in life of interest besides consuming ambition. In short, a restored social ecology might allow us to mitigate the harm that has been done to disadvantaged groups without blaming the victims or trying to turn them into carbon copies of middle-class high achievers. . . .

SIGNS OF THE TIMES

Few of those with whom we talked would have described the problems facing our society in exactly the terms we have just used. But few have found a life devoted to "personal ambition and consumerism" satisfactory, and most are seeking in one way or another to transcend the limitations of a self-centered life. If there are vast numbers of a selfish, narcissistic "me generation" in America, we did not find them, but we certainly did find that the language of individualism, the primary American language of self-understanding, limits the ways in which people think.

Many Americans are devoted to serious, even ascetic, cultivation of the self in the form of a number of disciplines, practices, and "trainings," often of great rigor. There is a question as to whether these practices lead to the self-realization or self-fulfillment at which they aim or only to an obsessive self-manipulation that defeats the proclaimed purpose. But it is not uncommon for those who are attempting to find themselves to find in that very process something that transcends them. For example, a Zen student reported: "I started Zen to get something for myself, to stop suffering, to get enlightened. Whatever it was, I was doing it for myself. I had hold of myself and I was reaching for something. Then to do it, I found out I had to give up that hold on myself. Now it has hold of me, whatever 'it' is." What this student found is that the meaning of life is not to be discovered in manipulative control in the service of the self. Rather, through the disciplined practices of a religious way of life, the student found his self more grasped than grasping. It is not surprising that "self-realization" in this case has

occurred in the context of a second language, the allusive language of Zen Buddhism, and a community that attempts to put that language into practice.

Many Americans are concerned to find meaning in life not primarily through self-cultivation but through intense relations with others. Romantic love is still idealized in our society. It can, of course, be remarkably self-indulgent, even an excuse to use another for one's own gratification. But it can also be a revelation of the poverty of the self and lead to a genuine humility in the presence of the beloved. We have noted in the early chapters of this book that the therapeutically inclined, jealous though they are of their personal autonomy, nonetheless seek enduring attachments and a community within which those attachments can be nurtured. As in the case of self-cultivation, there is in the desire for intense relationships with others an attempt to move beyond the isolated self, even though the language of individualism makes that sometimes hard to articulate.

Much of what is called "consumerism," and often condemned as such, must be understood in this same ambiguous, ambivalent context. Attempts to create a beautiful place in which to live, to eat well and in a convivial atmosphere, to visit beautiful places where one may enjoy works of art, or simply lie in the sun and swim in the sea, often involve an element of giving to another and find their meaning in a committed relationship. Where the creation of a consumption-oriented lifestyle, which may resemble that of "the beautiful people" or may simply involve a comfortable home and a camper, becomes a form of defense against a dangerous and meaningless world, it probably takes on a greater burden than it can bear. In that case, the effort to move beyond the self has ended too quickly in the "little circle of family and friends" of which Tocqueville spoke, but even so the initial impulse was not simply selfish.

With the weakening of the traditional forms of life that gave aesthetic and moral meaning to everyday living, Americans have been improvising alternatives more or less successfully. They engage, sometimes with intense involvement, in a wide variety of arts, sports, and nature appreciation, sometimes as spectators but often as active participants. Some of these activities involve conscious traditions and demanding practices, such as ballet. Others, such as walking in the country or jogging, may be purely improvisational, though not devoid of some structure of shared meaning. Not infrequently, moments of intense awareness, what are sometimes called "peak experiences," occur in the midst of such activities. At such moments, a profound sense of well-being eclipses the usual utilitarian preoccupations of everyday life. But the capacity of such experiences to provide more than a momentary counterweight to pressures of everyday life is minimal. Where these activities find social expression at all, it is apt to be in the form of what we have called the lifestyle enclave. The groups that form around them are too evanescent, too inherently restricted in membership, and too slight in their hold on their members' loyalty to carry much public weight. Only at rare moments do such largely expressive solidarities create anything like a civic consciousness, as when a local professional sports team wins a national championship and briefly gives rise to a euphoric sense of metropolitan belongingness. . . .

THE POVERTY OF AFFLUENCE

At the very beginning of the modern era, Thomas Hobbes painted a picture of human existence that was to be all too prophetic of the society coming into being. He compared "the life of man" to a race and said, "But this *race* we must suppose to have no other *goal*, nor other *garland*, but being foremost, and in it [to give only a few of his many specifications]:

> To consider them behind, is *glory*,
> To consider them before, is *humility*,
> To fall on the sudden, is disposition to *weep*,
> To see another fall, is disposition to *laugh*,
> Continually to be out-gone, is *misery*,
> Continually to out-go the next before, is *felicity*,
> And to forsake the course, is to *die*.

In *Leviathan*, Hobbes summed up his teaching about human life by arguing that the first "general inclination of mankind" is "a perpetual and restless desire of power after power, that ceaseth only in death." But we are beginning to see now that the race of which he speaks has no winner, and if power is our only end, the death in question may not be merely personal, but civilizational.

Yet we still have the capacity to reconsider the course upon which we are embarked. The morally concerned social movement, informed by republican and biblical sentiments, has stood us in good stead in the past and may still do so again. But we have never before faced a situation that called our deepest assumptions so radically into question. Our problems today are not just political. They are moral and have to do with the meaning of life. We have assumed that as long as economic growth continued, we could leave all else to the private sphere. Now that economic growth is faltering and the moral ecology on which we have tacitly depended is in disarray, we are beginning to understand that our common life requires more than an exclusive concern for material accumulation.

Perhaps life is not a race whose only goal is being foremost. Perhaps true felicity does not lie in continually outgoing the next before. Perhaps the truth lies in what most of the world outside the modern West has always believed, namely that there are practices of life, good in themselves, that are inherently fulfilling. Perhaps work that is intrinsically rewarding is better for human beings than work that is only extrinsically rewarded. Perhaps enduring commitment to those we love and civic friendship toward our fellow citizens are preferable to restless competition and anxious self-defense. Perhaps common worship, in which we express our gratitude and wonder in the face of the mystery of being itself, is the most important thing of all. If so, we will have to change our lives and begin to remember what we have been happier to forget.

We will need to remember that we did not create ourselves, that we owe what we are to communities that formed us, and to what Paul Tillich called "the structure of grace in history" that made such communities possible. We will need to see the story of our life on this earth not as an unbroken success but as a history of suffering as well as joy. We will need to remember the millions of suffering people in the world today and the millions whose suffering in the past made our present affluence possible.

Above all, we will need to remember our poverty. We have been called a people of plenty, and though our per capita GNP has been surpassed by several other nations, we are still enormously affluent. Yet the truth of our condition is poverty. We are finally defenseless on this earth. Our material belongings have not brought us happiness. Our military defenses will not avert nuclear destruction. Nor is there any increase in productivity or any new weapons systems that will change the truth of our condition.

We have imagined ourselves a special creation, set apart from other humans. In the late twentieth century, we see that our poverty is as absolute as that of the poorest of nations. We have attempted to deny the human condition in our quest for power after power. It would be well for us to rejoin the human race, to accept our essential poverty as a gift, and to share our material wealth with those in need.

Such a vision is neither conservative nor liberal in terms of the truncated spectrum of present American political discourse. It does not seek to return to the harmony of a "traditional" society, though it is open to learning from the wisdom of such societies. It does not reject the modern criticism of all traditions, but it insists in turn on the criticism of criticism, that human life is lived in the balance between faith and doubt. Such a vision arises not only from the theories of intellectuals, but from the practices of life that Americans are already engaged in. Such a vision seeks to combine social concern with ultimate concern in a way that slights the claims of neither. Above all, such a vision seeks the confirmation or correction of discussion and experiment with our friends, our fellow citizens.

NO   Henry Fairlie

THE FICTION OF THE MASSES

The masses do not exist. But the idea of "the masses," although it is a fiction, the invention of a few minds, dominates the way in which we both think of our societies and even of ourselves. It helps to nourish both the rebellion of the self and the revolt of the privileged, since everyone would like to distinguish himself from "the masses." None of us believes that he is a mass man, and we do not think of those whom we meet as mass men. We live by anecdote, and anecdotes are about what is particular, an individual or an occasion. We do not say in the evening, "I met a mass man today, called Petermass, and he was exactly like Philipmass, the mass man whom I was telling you about yesterday." If that was all that we had to say, we would have nothing to tell; we would have no anecdote.

We can test this from our own experiences. We all have a story to tell about the conversation of an Italian taxi driver who has just driven us from La Guardia Airport to the centre of Manhattan. No story is every quite the same; the words of the Italian taxi driver which we report this evening are not the same as the words of the Italian taxi driver who drove us on that evening a week ago. Others interrupt with their own stories of Italian taxi drivers; and, although there is something common to them all, which is a part of their point, they are also all different, which is why we tell them. Again, we notice when one mailman is replaced by another. He performs for us the same service, at about the same time each day, in approximately the same way, as did his predecessor; and we are grateful that he does, it is not eccentricity that we expect of him. But we also notice that there is something different about him, and it is this we mention to our neighbours: "I wish we had the old mailman back, he always had time for a chat." . . . "Thank goodness the old mailman's gone, he always wanted to talk when I was busy."

This is how people talk. They have been touched by individuals during the day, whom they have observed as individuals, and on whose individuality they report in the evening with a story. We call our buses "mass transit"; but we get on a bus in the rush hour, and the driver is either welcoming or he does not have the time of day for us. "He's a sourpuss," we say as we take our seats, and stick out our tongues behind his back. We do not lament, "Alas and alack! Mass man is driving us today." We know that the next morning the driver may be Irish, with a "top of the morning" for us. In the common situations that we share from day to day, we notice individuals who behave in their own ways, not as a mass.

Unless we are from day to day aware of this—how each retains his individuality, not in the isolation of his-self, but in his dealings with others in our state—we will again be persuaded that as a social being he is inauthentic. We will learn to think of our companions in the estate only as "the masses," and the estate itself only as "mass society." The rebellion of the self will be justified by what we have been taught is the condition of our society. We must be ready to go out each morning and return each evening, and ask ourselves in our ordinary encounters whom we met during the day who was a mass man, who was less of an individual than ourselves; against the ways in which we are taught to imagine our situation, we must bring the evidence of our own senses. . . .

IN DEFENCE OF THE SUPERMARKET

. . . The homogenization of "the masses," as it has been foretold and feared for so long, has not occurred; least of all has it occurred in America, which was described by Ortega as "the paradise of the masses." Instead, there has been the most astonishing individualization of whole classes of people who throughout all previous history have been undifferentiated. Let us consider,

for example, "the consumer" in our "consumer societies," which is another of the symbols by which we represent "the masses" in our "mass societies." "The consumer" is commonly taken to be marked by the uniformity of his tastes; but, if we look closely, we will find that his true mark is an increasing individualization of his tastes.

One of the most common symbols of the "consumer society" is, in turn, the replacement of the village (or neighbourhood or corner) shop by the supermarket. One did not know, until one read their writings, that so many of our intellectuals, including some of the most prominent of them, spend so much of their time buying the groceries; or that they suffer such a delicate feeling of estrangement from their fellow men, from society, from nature, from god, or from whatever they feel alienated, when they enter a supermarket. To someone who in fact enjoys trundling his cart round a supermarket, this expression of their feelings is worrying, since it suggests that his own sensibility may be peculiarly dull; and it is even more worrying if he in fact grew up where there were only village (or neighbourhood or corner) shops, and his memory of them, far from being pleasant, is quite the opposite: that they were not pleasant places to go.

Again and again, in the kind of literature we are discussing, we are given a picture of the village woman who used to shop at the village store, where she was served by the village shopkeeper, with whom she discussed the latest gossip, and who is now "at a loss in the metropolitan supermarket where her demands are no longer dictated by her needs, but on the contrary dictated by an abundant supply." At the checkout counter, there is no time for gossip, and she receives only a small slip of paper with the words "Thank you" printed on it, "more for the sake of public than personal relationships. The shopkeeper, focal point in rural face-to-face relationships, has been replaced by machines and anonymous functionaries." The writers seem almost to repeat each other. C. Wright Mills, for example, said that "the small shop serving the neighbourhood is replaced by the anonymity of the national corporation: mass advertisement replaces the personal influence of opinion between merchant and customer."

But the village shop, as one knew it personally, and as one can read about it in fiction, was usually an unattractive place, and frequently a malignant one. The gossip which was exchanged was, as often as not, inaccurate and cruel. Although there were exceptions, one's main memory of the village shopkeeper, man and wife, is of faces which were hard and sharp and mean, leaning forward to whisper into ears that were cocked and turned to hear all that they could of the misfortunes or the disgrace of a neighbour. Whisper! Whisper! Whisper! This has always been the chief commodity of the village shop. And not only whispers, because the village shopkeeper, informed or misinformed, could always apply sanctions against those to whom disgrace or misfortune was imputed.

The anonymity of the supermarket is in fact a gain in privacy, even in the equalization of dignity. Anyone can shop at a supermarket without the whole of his life being known and examined; if he is living in sin, or his daughter is mad, or he has dodged the draft, it is of no consequence to the manager or the checkout girl, as long as he can pay the bill.

But let us suppose that the customer is respectable by the standards that prevail: what of the choice, in making a purchase, which is available? There is an impenetrable obscurity in the suggestion that, whereas in the village shop, the customer's demands were dictated by his or her needs, in the supermarket they are dictated by an abundant supply. One really has to do better than that. The demands of most customers at a village shop were dictated, not by their needs, but by their purses; and their purses were very rarely in equation with their needs. The majority of villagers were always poor, and were known to be poor.

It is true that too often at too many supermarkets one may still observe the really poor as they desperately try to balance their purses against their needs, as they rummage for a last penny at the checkout counter. But there is a saving grace in the supermarket even for them. They no longer go into the village shop to be told by the shopkeeper, "Ah! Mrs. Smith, I have saved a few neckbones for you," as if she had no choice, and he was the author of a benefaction. They now enter the supermarket anonymously; no one says to them, "We know what you can afford." They diddle around at the meat counter, as we all do, and even if they in the end have to settle for the neckbones or the chicken feet, they have known, not merely the illusion of choice, as some would say, but something of the experience of choice. The possibility of choice was there, present to them; it was reduced, as they calculated, by the fact of their poverty, but it was not a denial from the beginning, made by others on their behalf, an ordering of the fates, in the person of the village shopkeeper.

What is more, the poor in the supermarket can refuse, with the dignity that anonymity confers, the reduction of their choice. One does not need to imagine, one can remember all too well, Mrs. Smith announcing in a village store that she was tired of cabbage and would try some peas for a change. At once she was reproved by the village shopkeeper—the entertaining fellow—"Ah! Mrs. Smith, you know that the cabbage will go much farther than the peas, with all of those mouths to feed," and before she can remonstrate, the cabbage has been popped into her bag. But in a supermarket one can watch the poor decide for themselves that this week they will waste a little money on a frill, and nobody will challenge or reprove them. . . .

THE RELEASE FROM CUSTOM

But let us leave aside the really poor, and consider the choice that is available at the supermarket to the large majority of Americans, and increasingly to a large number of men and women in comparable societies. Let us watch them also as they shop. Their demands are not dictated by an abundant supply; their demands on the abundant supply are restricted by their purses. The choice of the poor is reduced to the point at which the nature of the choice is changed; the choice of the majority is restricted, but its nature is not affected, it is a limitation only of degree.

Restriction by the purse becomes more serious if the variety of goods that are available is itself restricted. This has always been one of the faults of the village shop. Not only are its goods more expensive than in a supermarket, because its turnover is not so great, but the variety of goods which it carries is limited. This means that the customer is doubly sub-

ject to the necessity, week after week, to purchase the same foods, in order to make the same meals. The choice in the supermarket, if the customer wishes to take advantage of it, is much wider. He can determine to spend more on a foreign cheese—which would probably not be available in the village store in any case—knowing that he can save the extra money that he has spent on the cheese by buying a cheaper vegetable.

These may not seem to be important increases in human freedom, until one considers how astonishingly more varied are the personal tastes of ordinary people than they were even a quarter of a century ago. From this point of view, the recent proliferation of small shops—delicatessens, health-food stores, boutiques—ought to be seen, not as an alternative to the supermarket and the department store, but as an extension of them; they are certainly an extension of the "consumer society," and the true significance of the "consumer society" is this increasing differentiation of tastes. The vegetable counter of almost any supermarket is an invitation to the individual customer to experiment and discriminate with his own taste and, although the significance of this may seem to be slight, it is an expression of individualization, as it is an education in it, far removed from the notion of "the masses."

Not to have to eat the same food that one was brought up to eat, not to have to eat the same food that one ate last week, not to have to eat the same food for all one's life: this is a release from custom, and from its bondage; and there again one can observe how the critics of "the masses" have a point and then misconstrue it. Even in this simple matter of food, the release from custom does indeed mean the destruction of an old culture variety. Germans no longer eat only German food, and German food is no longer eaten only by Germans. When the critics of "mass society" talk of the homogenization of tastes, it is usually to the destruction of this cultural variety that they are referring. But this destruction has been accompanied by an individualization of personal tastes that is elaborately various. German food is not lost to the human memory, the arts of German cooking are not forgotten; they have merely become the property, not of a culture, but of individuals, if that is their taste. What is more, the sharing of individual tastes can then become an opportunity for human companionship and interchange, of associations that are voluntary and not just customary. . . .

"The masses" whom one remembers even from one's own childhood and youth, the working classes and the lower middle classes, ate the same food from day to day, wore the same clothes from year to year, and were uniform in taste and appearance. In contrast, their children or grandchildren are today astonishingly various and colourful in these everyday expressions of their individuality. These gains may seem to be small; but they have their reflections at a more serious level. One does not wish to exaggerate their importance; but it is time that we challenged some of the images in which our society is represented to us, so that we grow to disdain it. The privileged man who was a dandy in the past ought not to be contemptuous or resentful of the construction worker who today is making something of a dandy of himself under his hard hat, which is perched improbably on his mannered tresses, tolerated even by his employer, and now scarcely noticed by passers-by. . . .

THE INDIVIDUAL BECOMES SELF-CONSCIOUS

. . . The distinction between the individual and his society, and between his society and the state, has been the work of the modern age, and not only is this double distinction most precious to us, there is no way in which we can properly understand either ourselves or our societies if we do not strenuously hold to it. When we talk of "the masses" in our "mass societies," we ought to be talking, first, of the individuals who compose them, each equal in his rights and in his claims on his society and, secondly, of the fact that their relations with their society are personal, not mediated by hierarchy or status, by guild or community, by church or even now by family. The relationships of the individual have ceased to be more important than himself. This is the positive gain of the modern age, of which we are the beneficiaries. If we have lost a sense of community, it is because we have gained a sense of the individual; and this is why the placing of the individual citizen in a direct relationship with his society is today so urgent a task.

The individuality that has seemed to the European to be so threatened by "the masses" was, in fact, a kind of cultural variety; in particular, it was the individuality of a superior class, as Dewey remarked when he said that the "prized and vaunted individuality of European culture was a very limited affair," in which the peasant and the proletariat did not participate. At no time when the European idea was in the ascendant was there any possibility that this individuality would be conceived and realized as the self-evident and equal possession of all; neither in the French Revolution nor in the Russian Revolution was the individual as such a genuine concern, he was not brought to the fore.

Only in the American idea has there lain this double affirmation of the individuality of each, and of the equality of each with all: the idea of the I released in the En-Masse. . . .

Amazingly, because it has never before been true in history, the individual who is self-conscious as an individual is the unit round which our societies must organize themselves. He is the man who finds his dignity, as it was put by George Herbert Mead, in the fact that, when he calls upon himself, he finds himself at home. If we are bound to imagine the individual in this manner, we are no less bound to reimagine our societies in such a way that he will be enabled to participate fully as an individual in the common life, so that each may know and feel that he is a citizen. . . .

THE MODEL IN AMERICA

One is not denying that immensity of the challenge—to imagine and then to create a society in which the individual day by day negotiates with it as himself, and it day by day addresses him as an individual—but at least we have a model before us. Whatever its faults, the vast commonalty of the middle class of the United States is a society of individuals, in the sense that we are trying to imagine; it is here that most obviously the I has been released in the En-Masse, with no mediator between the two. The result is not yet rewarding to the individual, or satisfactory to society; but there can be no doubt that here is where the challenge may be met, that it is in "the paradise of the masses" that the I must be established,

not only as an individual in his own right, but as fully a citizen.

It ought to be a boast, not a lament, that the example of the En-Masse is being spread by America to the rest of the world, with its power and its commerce. "We do indeed share a common culture," says Edgar Z. Friedenberg of the United States. "And the commonness goes further. American mass gratifications, from soft drinks to comic books and movies, have turned out to be the common coin of the mass culture the world over. This is not conquest, but genuine culture diffusion. All over the world, man in the mass has turned out to be exactly our type of fellow." His point is correct, but the voice is familiar in its disaffection. As always, the emphasis is put only on the material manifestations—and these the grossest—of the culture that is being spread.

But it was again Dewey, whose voice is so sorely needed at this time, who invited us to look deeper and farther ahead:

> . . . a peasantry and proletariat which have been released from intellectual bondage will for a time have its revenge. Because there is no magic in democracy to confer immediately the power of critical discrimination upon the masses . . . it does not follow that the ineptitude of the many is the creation of democracy.

It is not only the wholesomeness of this voice, the lack of pettiness in its vision, to which we need to listen, but its truth. The idea of the revenge of "the masses" has been prominent in the literature, not least in the work of Ortega; but more than fifty years after Dewey wrote his careful words, the evidence is that the desire for revenge has been neither deep nor long-lasting.

The questioning of traditional standards has not proved to be the negation of all standards; the desire to replace has not proved to be an ambition to destroy, the claim of equality has not proved to be a denial of liberty. We have only to look around us in the public estate of America to see that the I released in the En-Masse is neither impatient nor placid, that even in so short a time, year by year, generation after generation, the search is being made for new forms to replace the dead forms of the past. Perhaps it requires an outsider to affirm that the commonalty of the middle class in America is experimental and invigorating and rich in promise, and that it needs only a further exercise of our imaginations to recover for it a sense of direction and a common understanding of its purpose.

There are "situations in social life—exceptional situations, to be sure—when it might be said that history is 'free,'" Francis D. Wormuth has said: "the resolution of a small group of leaders who can capture the revolutionary movement can turn it into a channel which it could not follow without their action." This is a prescription for the kind of revolutionary action of a Lenin or a Mao or a Castro; and the answer of the United States must be, as it can be, that history is "free" in its society, not exceptionally, but habitually. It is free in this sense because it is the I who has been released as the main actor, never for long to be subdued even in the En-Masse. . . .

POSTSCRIPT

Has Individualism Become Excessive?

Bellah and his associates are critical of Brian Palmer for changing his life-style without being able to justify the change in terms of "a larger sense of the purpose of life." But is that necessary? Do we have to employ widely shared value systems to guide the changes in our lives? Fairlie, on the other hand, likes supermarkets, where we can choose without having to explain our choices. But living our lives is different than picking products from a shelf. "How ought we to live? How do we think about how to live?" Perhaps Bellah and his associates are right to force these questions on us.

America's perennial "Lockeanism" is the theme of Louis Hartz's classic *The Liberal Tradition in America* (Harvest Books, 1955). For the limitations of this approach, see Dorothy Ross, "The Liberal Tradition Revisited and the Republican Tradition Addressed," in John Higham and Paul K. Conking, eds., *New Directions in American Intellectual History* (Johns Hopkins, 1979). Some studies suggest that Americans are quite adept at forming community networks, even in our "impersonal" cities. See for example, Claude S. Fischer et al., *Networks and Places* (Free Press, 1977), and Peggy Wireman, *Urban Neighborhoods, Networks, and Families* (Lexington Books, 1984). Others, however, take a more pessimistic view of our capacities for joint action, See, for example, Christopher Lasch, *The Culture of Narcissism* (Norton, 1979), and Richard Sennett, *The Fall of Public Man* (Knopf, 1976).

ISSUE 4
Is Urban Life Crazy?

YES: Henry Fairlie, from "The Idiocy of Urban Life," *New Republic* (January 5 and 12, 1987)

NO: C. R. Creekmore, from "Cities Won't Drive You Crazy," *Psychology Today* (January 1985)

ISSUE SUMMARY

YES: Journalist Henry Fairlie points out that most people flee the city for the suburbs, mountains, or countryside whenever possible and notes the nuisances that create the exodus.
NO: C. R. Creekmore, a free-lance writer, uses research findings to show that many of the criticisms of urban life are unsubstantiated; they are myths.

The city has been seen as the worst and the best expression of human society. The city of Babel and its magnificent tower greatly offended God, according to the account in Genesis, as did the famous cities of Sodom, Nineveh, and Babylon. On the other hand, Jerusalem was often called the city of God in the Bible. And the future perfect Kingdom of God among men is to be headquartered in a new Jerusalem according to the book of Revelation. The Greek city-state of Athens is commonly viewed as the pinnacle of social achievement in the ancient world of the Occident, and ancient writers saw cities as centers of civilization surrounded by barbarism. But, too, cities in the ancient world have also been seen as centers of decay.

The debate on the virtues and vices of cities has been continuous. Contemporary critics point to the high rates of crime and violence in cities and the desperate conditions of inner city ghettoes. Drugs, gangs, corruption, inefficient bureaucracies, and "bossism" are added by the critics to the list of vices. These, critics say, cannot be balanced by professional orchestras, baseball teams, and theaters. Next come the complaints about the nuisance factors: noise, dirt, bad air, trash, traffic jams, crowding, cramped apartments, and high prices. Finally, the critics expand the vice list of cities to include the porno section, the bums and street people, the open homosexuality, and the "deviant" life-styles. The defenders of cities often point to the fact that people choose voluntarily to live in cities. They leave, in droves, those areas without vices and move to cities. Every day millions of people indicate by their actions that they judge the virtues of cities to outweigh the vices.

The vices of cities identified so far are obvious and visible, but deeper criticism concerns the character of a city dweller's social life. Near the end of the nineteenth century, a German sociologist named Ferdinand Toennies differentiated between rural and urban types of relationships. Rural relationships he identified as *Gemeinschaft* (translated as community). They are intimate, all-embracing, and involve shared commitments. Close friends and relatives relate to one another in this way. Urban relationships he identified as *Gesellschaft* (translated as society). They are impersonal, superficial, and merely matters of convenience and practical needs. If we go to a supermarket or a bank we are likely to relate to the cashier or the teller in such a manner. Chances are we know nothing about their personal life and have no concern about it. Our relationship with them has to do with cash or commerce, and it is these things that are on our minds rather than the people with whom we happen to deal.

Toennies' observations on the superficiality of urban relationships have been deepened by modern research. Because city dwellers are flooded with stimuli and pass close to hundreds of people a day, they naturally learn to screen out most of what happens around them. Their selective inattention to stimuli helps them cope, but, at the extreme, it means that they pay no attention to screams in the night for help. On the other hand, modern research also finds that urbanites are involved in networks of intimate friendships and associations of common interests. The research even finds neighborhoods with many of the *Gemeinschaft* features of rural villages. In other words, urban life can be socially and psychologically very satisfying.

In the following selections Henry Fairlie and C. R. Creekmore debate whether cities make good sense socially and psychologically. Henry Fairlie uses wit, satire, and an observant eye to point out the craziness of urban life. C. R. Creekmore sees Fairlie's viewpoint as a myth, and he uses research on rural-urban comparisons to build his case that cities are great places to live.

YES   Henry Fairlie

THE IDIOCY OF URBAN LIFE

Between about 3 a.m. and 6 a.m. the life of the city is civil. Occasionally the lone footsteps of someone walking to or from work echo along the sidewalk. All work that has to be done at those hours is useful—in bakeries, for example. Even the newspaper presses stop turning forests into lies. Now and then a car comes out of the silence and cruises easily through the blinking traffic lights. The natural inhabitants of the city come out from damp basements and cellars. With their pink ears and paws, sleek, well-groomed, their whiskers combed, rats are true city dwellers. Urban life, during the hours when they reign, is urbane.

These rats are social creatures, as you can tell if you look out on the city street during an insomniac night. But after 6 a.m., the two-legged, daytime creatures of the city begin to stir; and it is they, not the rats, who bring the rat race. You might think that human beings congregate in large cities because they are gregarious. The opposite is true. Urban life today is aggressively individualistic and atomized. Cities are not social places.

The lunacy of modern city life lies first in the fact that most city dwellers who can do so try to live outside the city boundaries. So the two-legged creatures have created suburbs, exurbs, and finally rururbs (rubs to some). Disdaining rural life, they try to create simulations of it. No effort is spared to let city dwellers imagine they are living anywhere but in a city: patches of grass in the more modest suburbs, broader spreads in the richer ones further out; prim new trees planted along the streets; at the foot of the larger backyards, a pretense to bosky woodlands. Black & Decker thrives partly on this basic do-it-yourself rural impulse in urban life; and with the declining demand for the great brutes of farm tractors, John Deere has turned to the undignified business of making dinky toy tractors for the suburbanites to ride like Roman charioteers as they mow their lawns.

In the city itself gentrification means two tubs of geraniums outside the front door of a town house that has been prettified to look like a country cottage. The homes, restaurants, and even offices of city dwellers are planted thick with vegetation. Some executives have window boxes inside their high-rise offices; secretaries, among their other chores, must now be horticulturists. Commercials on television, aimed primarily at city dwellers, have more themes of the countryside than of urban life. Cars are never seen in a traffic jam, but whiz through bucolic scenery. Lovers are never in tenements, but drift through sylvan glades. Cigarettes come from Marlboro Country. Merrill Lynch is a bull. Coors is not manufactured in a computerized brewery, but taken from mountain streams.

The professional people buy second homes in the country as soon as they can afford them, and as early as possible on Friday head out of the city they have created. The New York intellectuals and artists quaintly say they are "going to the country" for the weekend or the summer, but in fact they have created a little Manhattan-by-the-Sea around the Hamptons, spreading over the Long Island potato fields whose earlier solitude was presumably the reason why they first went there. City dwellers take the city with them to the country, for they will not live without its pamperings. The main streets of America's small towns, which used to have hardware and dry goods stores, are now strips of boutiques. Old-fashioned barbers become unisex hairdressing salons. The brown rats stay in the cities because of the filth the humans leave during the day. The rats clean it up at night. Soon the countryside will be just as nourishing to them, as the city dwellers take their filth with them.

The recent dispersal of the urban middle-class population is only the latest development in this now established lunatic pattern. People who work in Cleveland live as far out as lovely Geauga and Ashtabula counties in northeast Ohio, perhaps 30 or 50 miles away. A bank manager in Chardon, which used to be a gracious market town in Geauga, once explained to me how the city people who come to live there want about five acres of land. "But they want the five acres for themselves alone, and not for others who come to follow their example, though no one is going to supply the services—electricity, gas, sewerage, water—for a few people living on their five acres. So the place fills up, and soon they've rebuilt the urban life they said they were escaping. What is more, they don't like paying for those services, since the rich come out to escape the high city taxes." They also force up the price of land and old houses, so that real estate is put beyond the reach of farmers and others who must work there.

In the old industrial cities, people lived near their places of work. The mill hands lived around the cotton mill, and the mill owner lived close at hand, in the big house on the hill, looking down on the chimney stacks belching out the smoke that was the evidence they were producing and giving employment. The steelworkers and the steel magnate lived close to the steel mill. The German brewer Miller lived next to his brewery in Milwaukee. The city churches had congregations that were representative of both the resident population and the local working population. It wasn't so much that work gave meaning to life as that it created a community that extended into and enriched the residential community, and sustained solidarity among the workers. It was the automakers, especially the ever revolutionary Henry Ford, who realized that their own product enabled them to build factories far from the dispersed homes of the workers, and not unconsciously they appreciated that dispersed work force would be docile.

Work still gives meaning to rural life, the family, and churches. But in the city today work and home, family and church, are separated. What the office workers do for a living is not part of their home life. At the same time they maintain the pointless frenzy of their work hours in their hours off. They rush from the office to jog, to the gym or the YMCA pool, to work at their play with the same joylessness. In the suburbs there is only an artificial community life—look at the notice board of community activities in a new satellite town like Reston, outside Washington. They breathlessly exhort the resident to a variety of boring activities—amateur theatricals, earnest lectures by officers of the United Nations Association sing-songs—a Tupperware community culture as artificial as the "lake" in the supposed center of the town. These upright citizens of Reston were amazed one day when they found that their bored children were as hooked on drugs as those in any ghetto.

Even though the offices of today's businesses in the city are themselves moving out to the suburbs, this does not necessarily bring the workers back closer to their workplace. It merely means that to the rush-hour traffic into the city there is now added a rush-hour traffic out to the suburbs in the morning, and back around and across the city in the evening. As the farmer walks down to his farm in the morning, the city dweller is dressing for the first idiocy of his day, which he not only accepts but even seeks—the journey to work.

This takes two forms: solitary confinement in one's own car, or the discomfort of extreme overcrowding on public transport. Both produce angst. There are no more grim faces than those of the single drivers we pedestrians can glimpse at the stoplights during the rush hour. It is hard to know why they are so impatient in the morning to get to their useless and wearisome employments; but then in the evening, when one would have thought they would be relaxed, they are even more frenetic. Prisoners in boxes on wheels, they do not dare wonder why they do it. If they take to public transit, there may still be the ritual of the wife driving the breadwinner to the subway station, and meeting him in the evening. Life in the suburbs and exurbs has become a bondage to the hours of journeying.

The car, of course, is not a vehicle suitable to the city. The problems of traffic in the city, over which urban planners have wracked their brains for years, could be simply eliminated if private cars were banned, or if a swinging tax were levied on those who drive into the city alone. The dollar toll in New York should be raised to five dollars—each way. There should be a toll on all the bridges crossing the Potomac from Virginia, and at every point where the rush hour drivers cross the District line from Maryland. The urban dwellers in Virginia and Maryland make sure that their jurisdictions obstruct any legitimate way the District might force the suburban daytime users of the city to pay for its manifold services. But ten dollars a day to cross into Washington, in addition to parking fees, would soon cut down the urban idiocy of bringing a small room to work and parking it in precious space for eight hours.

On the bus or subway each morning and evening other urban dwellers endure the indignity of being crushed into unwelcome proximity with strangers whom they have no wish to communicate with except in terms of abuse, rancor, and sometimes violent hostility. The wonder is not that there is an occasional shooting on public transit, but that shootings are not daily occurrences. The crushing of people together on the subway can have unintended results. One of my memories is of being on a London tube at rush hour in my younger days, pressed against a young woman who was with her boyfriend. To my surprise, though not unwelcome, her hand slipped into mine. It squeezed. Mine squeezed back. Her expression when they got out at Leicester Square, and she found she'd been holding my hand, and even had begun pulling me off the train, has not been easy to forget in 35 years. But generally even eye contact on public transport is treated as an act of aggression or at least harassment.

This primary urban activity of getting to and from work has other curious features. As every Englishman visiting America for the first time remarks, the smell of deodorants on a crowded bus or subway in the morning is overpowering. Even the stale smell of the human body would be preferable. It must account for the glazed looks—perhaps all deodorants contain a gas introduced by the employers to numb the urban office workers to the fatuity of their labors.

But whether they have come by car or public transit, the urban office workers must continue their journey even after they have gotten to the city. They then must travel in one of the banks of elevators that often run the height of three city blocks or more. Once again they are herded into confined spaces. City people are so used to moving in herds that they even fight to cram themselves into the elevators, as they do into buses or subway cars, as if it mattered that they might get to their pointless occupations a minute later. The odd thing about the elevators themselves is that there are no fares for distances often longer than those between two bus stops. Office elevators are public transit, free to anyone who needs to use them—but there's no such thing as a free elevator ride, as the president will tell you. Banks of elevators occupy large areas of valuable city land on every floor. This and the costs of running and maintaining them is written into the rents paid by the employers. If the urban workers had not been reduced to a docile herd, they would demand that the employers who expect them to get to work subsidize all the public transport into the city, while leaving those who bring their rooms on wheels to pay for them themselves.

In the modern office building in the city there are windows that don't open. This is perhaps the most symbolic lunacy of all. Outdoors is something you can look at through glass but not to touch or hear. These windows are a scandal because they endanger the lives of office workers in case of fire. But no less grievous, even on the fairest spring or fall day the workers cannot put their heads outside. The employers do not mind this, may have even conspired with the developers to dream up such an infliction, because the call of spring or fall would distract their employers. Thus it's not surprising that the urban worker has no knowledge of the seasons. He is aware simply that in some months there is air conditioning, and in others through the same vents come fetid central heating. Even outside at home in their suburbs the city dwellers may know that sometimes it's hot, and sometimes cold, but no true sense of the rhythms of the seasons is to be had from a lawn in the

back yard and a few spindly trees struggling to survive.

City dwellers can now eat the vegetables of their choice at almost any time of
the year—always with the proviso that
they will never taste a fresh vegetable,
even though the best supermarkets have
various ways to touch them up. Anyone
who has not eaten peas picked that
morning has never tasted a pea. The
simple fact is that some frozen vegetables
(frozen within hours of being picked) are
fresher than the alleged fresh vegetables
on the produce counter of the supermarkets. The suburbanite again struggles
to simulate the blessings of rural life by
maintaining a vegetable patch in the back
yard. The main consequence of this melancholy pursuit comes in high summer,
when office workers bring in their home-
grown tomatoes to share with their colleagues, ill-colored, lump-faced objects
with scars all over them, since they have
not been staked correctly.

The city dweller reels from unreality to
unreality through each day, always trying to recover the rural life that has been
surrendered for the city lights. (City life,
it is worth noticing, has produced almost
no proverbs. How could it when proverbs
—a rolling stone gathers no moss, and so
on—are a distillation from a sane existence?) No city dweller, even in the suburbs, knows the wonder of a pitch-dark
country lane at night. Nor does he naturally get any exercise from his work.
When jogging and other childish pursuits began to exercise the unused bodies
of city dwellers, two sensible doctors (a
breed that has almost died with the general practitioner) said that city workers
could get their exercise better in more
natural ways. They could begin by walking upstairs to their office floors instead
of using the elevators.

Every European points out that Americans are the most round-shouldered
people in the world. Few of them carry
themselves with an upright stance, although a correct stance and gait is the
first precondition of letting your lungs
breathe naturally and deeply. Electric
typewriters cut down the amount of
physical exertion needed to hit the keys;
the buttons of a word processor need
even less effort, as you can tell from the
posture of those who use them. They
might as well be in armchairs. They rush
out to jog or otherwise Fonda-ize their
leisure to try to repair the damage done
during the day.

Dieting is an urban obsession. Country dwellers eat what they please, and
work it off in useful physical employments, and in the open air, cold or hot,
rainy or sunny. Mailmen are the health-
iest city workers. When was your mailman last ill for a day? If one reads the
huge menus that formed a normal diet in
the 19th century, you realize that even
the city dwellers could dispatch these
gargantuan repasts because they still
shared many of the benefits of rural life.
(Disraeli records a meal at the house of
one lordly figure that was composed of
nine meat or game entrees. The butler
asked after the eighth, "Snipe or pheas-
ant, my lord?") They rode horseback to
work or to Parliament even in the coldest
weather, and nothing jolts and enlivens
the liver more than riding. Homes were
cold in the winter, except in the immediate vicinity of the hearth or stove. Cold
has a way of eating up excess fat. No
wonder dieting is necessary in a cosset-
ted life in which the body is forced to do
no natural heavy work.

Everything in urban life is an effort
either to simulate rural life or to compensate for its loss by artificial means. The

greatest robbery from the country in recent years has of course been Levi's, which any self-respecting farmer or farm worker is almost ashamed to wear nowadays. It was when Saks Fifth Avenue began advocating designer jeans years ago that the ultimate urban parody of rural life was reached. The chic foods of the city have to be called health foods, which would seem a tautology in the country. And insofar as there used to be entertainment in the city that enticed, these can now be enjoyed more than sufficiently on VCRs and stereos.

It is from this day-to-day existence of unreality, pretense, and idiocy that the city people, slumping along their streets even when scurrying, never looking up at their buildings, far less the sky, have the insolence to disdain and mock the useful and rewarding life of the country people who support them. Now go out and carry home a Douglas fir, call it a Christmas tree, and enjoy 12 days of contact with nature. Of course city dwellers don't know it once had roots.

_____

NO

C. R. Creekmore

CITIES WON'T DRIVE YOU CRAZY

Trapped in one of those Olympian traffic jams on the Garden State Parkway in New Jersey, I waited to pay my toll for the Newark exit. Horns, insults and exhaust fumes had settled in a noisy, dark-tempered cloud. As I finally reached the end of the exact-change line, I faced a sudden dilemma. There was the automatic toll collector, side-by-side with a human toll taker standing in his little both. I stared into the impersonal mouth of the collecting machine, then at the person, and chose him. The man looked shocked. He regarded the quarter I thrust him as if it were a bug. "Grow up!" he screamed at me with a sense of indignation that I assumed was generated by a life dedicated to the parkway system. "Grow up and use the machine!"

To me, the incident has always summed up the essence of what cities are: hotbeds of small embarrassments, dehumanizing confrontations, monetary setbacks, angry people and festering acts of God.

Many Americans agree with this stereotype and believe firmly that the dirty, crowded, dangerous city must gradually destroy an urbanite's psyche. This belief has a corollary: Rural life, haven of natural purity, wholesome values and the spirit of self-reliance, is the wellspring of physical and mental health.

A large body of research, conducted in the past 15 years by a diverse group of social scientists, challenges these heartfelt prejudices. These studies conclude that metropolitan living is more than OK. In many ways, researchers have found, city pavements outshine the sticks as healthy places to live and work.

Jonathan Freedman, chairperson of the psychology department at the University of Toronto, is an authority on how cities affect those who live in them. On the physical side, he believes that life expectancy is higher for people in urban areas and infant mortality rates are lower. The potentially unhealthy aspects of city life, such as pollution, stress and crime, are more than offset by better medical care, better water supplies and sewage systems and better systems for handling emergencies of all kinds.

What about mental illness? Surely the fabled rat race must eventually sap mental endurance and lead to breakdowns. Not according to mental health statistics. In a now classic study of the subject, *Mental Health in the Metropolis: The Midtown Manhattan Study*, sociologist Leo Srole and five colleagues compared mental-health statistics in Manhattan with those in small towns. They concluded that small towns have a slightly higher rate of mental illness.

This doesn't mean that cities are easy to live in. Manhattan psychiatrist Herbert E. Walker and C. Ray Smith, a writer on urban planning, point out in an article that certain environmental stress comes with the urban territory: automobile traffic, air pollution, high noise levels, lack of privacy and such architectural faults as poor lighting, tight spaces and inadequate seating.

With all this to contend with, why don't cities drive more people around the bend? One answer is that we learn to cope with the multiple problems. "It's not a bad environment, just a very complex one," says Gerda McCahan, chairperson of the department of psychology at Furman University in Atlanta, who once worked as a clinical psychologist in New York City. "An effect of living in the big city is that with time people learn to insulate themselves in a psychological sense. They learn not to allow a lot of stimuli to impinge on their consciousness. They sift out things that do not concern them."

Another answer is that mental illness goes deeper than environmental stress. "Severe mental illness is not caused by the kinds of environmental stimuli characteristic of a city—loud noises, noxious odors, density of population and high levels of activity, for instance," Freedman explains. "Rather, it is caused by complex human and social problems such as genetic defects, interpersonal relationships and the stresses of dealing with one's needs. And these problems are carried wherever you go. City stimuli might affect your mood temporarily, but they are unlikely to cause real mental illness."

Crowding is perhaps the most studied problem of city living. As urbanites do battle with blitzing cabdrivers, crammed subway cars, the frustrations of traffic and deadly competition for parking spaces, they have one big thing going for them. As McCahan suggests, their saving grace is superior adaptability.

Take some of the ways city folk deal with common crowding situations. They live on many levels, so the entire population is not constantly milling together on the ground. They have complex social rules (walk on the right; stop at red lights; wait in line for services) for pedestrian traffic. Cities now install bicycle, horse and foot paths that connect parks and open space and make movement safer and more pleasant. Freeways are built to travel to and from downtown faster. And planners use a variety of methods (rotaries, coordinated traffic lights, one-way roads) to improve traffic flow in the most crowded areas.

Other improvements are on the way. "One feature now becoming standard on urban expressways is noise barriers," says Dorn McGrath Jr., a professor of urban and regional planning at George Washington University. "That's because research carried on over the last 15 years has determined that highway noise is not only annoying to nearby residents, but can be psychologically and physiologically harmful."

This type of human adaptability is one reason Freedman is skeptical about the relevance of experiments that test the effect of crowding on rats and other animals—research that typically shows heightened levels of aggression, competitiveness, infant neglect and early death. Freedman feels that these findings can't be usefully applied to human crowding conditions. "Humans are much more adaptable creatures than other animals," he explains. Additionally, "the level of density you are talking about with laboratory animals is extraordinary, a level that would never appear in the real world."

Other researchers are less certain about the harmlessness of crowding to humans. For example, psychologists Janice Zeedyk-Ryan and Gene F. Smith report that crowding took its toll when 16 undergraduates volunteered to stay in a 12-foot-by-18-foot civil-defense shelter for 18 hours. Compared to a group of six students who occupied the same shelter in a second test, the densely packed students became markedly more hostile and anxious as the hours passed.

In another experiment, psychologists Yakov M. Epstein, Robert L. Woolfolk and Paul M. Lehrer created an environment that approximated the close conditions found in rush-hour mass-transit systems. They then compared the students' reactions under these conditions to what happened when they were put with the same number of strangers in a normal-sized room. The researchers found that the crowded students had higher blood pressure, reported that they felt unfriendlier and less in control and were rated by the strangers (who were actually working with the experimenters as observers) as tenser and more uncomfortable and annoyed than the uncrowded students.

Studies such as these suggest that crowding cramps the style of city dwellers and produces stress. Freedman has another interpretation. "Density intensifies people's reactions to events around them," he explains. "If you get people who are feeling aggressive for other reasons—who have been angered at home or work, for instance—and you put them under high-density conditions, they are likely to be more aggressive. On the other hand, if the same people are feeling good and cooperative, density will also intensify that."

Freedman uses loud music as an analogy. If people like the music being played, turning it up usually enhances the experience. If they don't, increased volume makes the experience even more unpleasant.

Thus, when crowding occurs in situations normally considered negative, such as commuting to work or waiting in line for service in a bank or store, it intensifies those negative feelings. But place the same crowds in an amusement park, at a cocktail party or in a basketball arena, and crowding enhances the fun.

One recent study indicates that under the right conditions, population density can actually improve relations in a neighborhood. Sociologists Lois M. Verbrugge and Ralph B. Taylor explained how this worked in a study they did in Baltimore. As population density increases, some environmental resources diminish and people start to compete for limited space, ease of movement, services and other resources.

The ultimate result of this competition, however, is that people adapt. They add services, make adjustments in how they live and increase social interaction to make up for scarce resources. Think of the Guardian Angels, patrolling neighborhoods to augment police services. Or consider those neighborhood characters who direct people to vacant parking spaces and act as traffic cops for alternate-side-of-the-street parking changes. In adaptive ways of this kind, neighbors get together.

"Local social resources actually increase," Verbrugge and Taylor point out. "High density provides opportunities for informal contact and assistance because people are more accessible . . . It is very possible that increasing density enhances social ties."

Crowding aside, it seems obvious that other stimuli peculiar to cities can be harmful to many people. In their article on urban stress, Walker and Smith list anxiety, depression, back pain, ulcers and heart attacks as diseases that can be traced to the high level of environmental stress in the city. "But for those people equipped to handle it," McCahan argues, "the city is the absolute optimum habitat." And, she adds, people can find their share of stress in the country as well. The boredom, lack of variety and low level of stimulation can be just as stressful as city living for those not accustomed to it.

Cities can also provide ties that help inhabitants handle stress better than their country cousins do. Home economist David Imig of the University of Missouri investigated the impact of life stress on 37 rural and 64 urban families with similar economic and educational backgrounds. He discovered that when the families suffered unemployment, money problems, relocation, illness and divorce, the city people suffered considerably less disruption in family relationships than did the rural families.

The difference seems to lie in the support systems that influence people's perception of stress. Urban families, Imig says, usually have closer connections to their social environment. They operate within a wide-ranging network of secondary relationships that may not involve close kinship or friendship, but which do offer informal support and exchange of services. You take my kid to dance class; I take yours to the ball game.

By contrast, rural families usually limit their support networks to a few close primary ties. This means that urban families have more outlets to diffuse stress. "Rural families don't have the large support system that urban families do," Imig believes. "They don't have anyone to turn to, to fall back on, when stress concentrates on their few close ties."

Another popular urban myth was depicted humorously in the movie *Terms of Endearment*. In one scene, an Iowa banker chastises a rude and insensitive cashier by noting, "You must be from New York."

Many studies contradict this stereotype of the cold, impersonal city. We have already seen that dense population can improve social ties, and that the city support network often works better than that in the country. In a study reported in *Psychology Today* (April 1981), environmental psychologist Karen Franck and two colleagues at the City University of New York found that although good friends come slowly in the city, friendships there eventually seem to become more intimate and more highly valued than those in nonurban settings. City friendships also tend to be more varied, broadening people's perspectives and opportunities.

"You have access to people at your own level in intellectual pursuits, sports, artistic interests—any area that you select," McCahan explains. "And you can seek out people at or above your own level who stimulate your growth."

Another measure of an area's elusive sense of warmth and personality is whether its inhabitants help one another in times of need. Do people help less in cities than in the country? The jury is still out on that one.

"A majority of studies find more help in rural areas," says Erwin Staub, a professor of psychology at the University of Massachusetts who has studied helping behavior extensively. "But some find no difference. And a minority even find more help in urban areas.

"The more confusing a situation, the more complex the stimuli, the more people's attention tends to be distracted," Staub says. "So the complexity of a city situation might distract people from helping." But, he points out, some areas also feature helping networks that can spur onlookers to come to the aid of victims.

People living in an urban neighborhood with a strong sense of identity—a Little Italy, a Chinatown or a rehabilitated neighborhood, for example—see emergency situations as their responsibility. After all, it's their turf. Cities also have concentrations of people with special helping skills such as CPR expertise, civil-defense training or medical backgrounds, and these people help in emergencies because they are conditioned to do so.

One of the most important mechanisms for triggering a person's helping response, Staub proposes, is a "prosocial orientation," previous experience being helpful. Since cities are the regional centers for charitable causes, social campaigns and reform efforts, many people learn to be helpers.

Thus, the whole process of solving city problems is part of a healthy cycle of activity. "If you want to look for problems that need addressing," says urban planner McGrath, "cities are the places where they tend to accumulate." Among the problems that he lists are "the awesome fabric of despair and difficulty" that covers our ghettos; bad traffic flow with its accompanying pollution and psychological frustration; noise; pollution of the environment; and frightening rises in already frightening urban crime rates.

"As one consequence, there are people drawn to deal with these problems. The whole process acts to revitalize a city," McGrath continues. "And the very problems that accumulate also serve to get meaning and satisfaction into the lives of the people who live there by giving them causes."

McGrath's viewpoint is another indication that the key to living in a city is adaptability. Stress is in the eye and mind of the beholder. An urbanite must be able to take apparently unpleasant stimuli and use them to his or her advantage.

Can people learn this psychological backflip? Yes, according to Walker and Smith, who tell in their article how to manipulate city stress. "Urban stress should be seen as a stimulus," they say. And to relieve pressure, they advise exercising regularly in enjoyable, varied places, attending a wide range of entertainments, living in a pleasant, well-lighted space, being assertive when a situation demands it and adopting a positive attitude about the city and its complexity.

"To flourish in the city, you must have a good sense of self-esteem and be able to tolerate competition," McCahan adds. "You must be able to pit yourself against the best and, win or lose, learn something positive about yourself. And you must be relatively assertive. If you are a shy person, the city can eat you up."

The city can also do you in if you are saddled with competitive handicaps; if you are financially, socially, physically or mentally restricted from competing. But for those geared to compete, city life can be a horn of plenty. "I always think of living in the city as a potential growth center for human beings," McCahan says. "One reason is that cities attract the best of everything."

There are good jobs. The city offers the opportunity, according to McCahan, of "seeking your own milieu" and level of competence, whatever your calling. You can see good plays and artsy movies. Professional and collegiate sports abound. You can go to street fairs and ethnic festivals in the park. Take your pick of music, art galleries and cultural exhibits. Or you can spend your days wandering among various periods of architecture,

testing Lewis Mumford's observation that "in the city, time becomes visible."

And, of course, you can always take advantage of a city's most notable amenity—going out for Chinese food at 3 a.m.

All of this activity is what makes a city go: a great, roiling, collective energy. "It is as if, far down in the rocky bowels . . . some vast, secret turbine were generating an extra source of power, capable of being shared by all the inhabitants of the city," wrote author Brendan Gill about New York's psychic energy. "It is a power that gives them the means of meeting the city on its own fierce terms of constant stress. And it is profoundly the case that your true (urbanite) rejoices in stress; the crowds, the dirt, the stench, the noise. Instead of depressing him, they urge him onto an unexpected 'high,' a state of euphoria in which the loftiest of ambitions seems readily attainable."

POSTSCRIPT

Is Urban Life Crazy?

C. R. Creekmore points out that increased stimuli can either annoy or delight depending upon one's attitude toward the stimuli. A crowded rock concert is exciting, a crowded subway is irritating. From this it is easy to conclude that both the critics and defenders of urban life are right. Urban life is both good and bad, depending on how one reacts to it. Those who thrive in cities know how to plug into a variety of networks and to master the complexities of urban life. It helps to be tolerant, open to new experiences, and capable of finding meaning and purpose without pat answers. The relevant issue for the urban community itself should be how can urban life be made better. For the politicians and businessmen the answer is economic development. The answer of some young urban professionals is gentrification. The answer of urban sociologists is building community.

The issue of quality urban life is a growing problem because the world is rapidly urbanizing. In 1950 the world was only 29 percent urban, but in 1975 it was 39 percent urban, and the world is expected to become 50 percent urban by 2000 and 90 percent by 2100. In the last quarter of this century over two billion people are expected to migrate from countryside to city. Several commentators, including Rashmi Mayers (*The Futurist*, August 1985), predict that dislocating changes on this scale could lead to the ". . . breakdown of the local and even global social fabric." This urban-ward migration involves more people than lived in the world in 1930, and many of the migrants will end up in slums, shantytowns, or on the street. Homelessness has become a problem in American cities, but the American problem is infinitesimal compared to the problem in many Third World cities. Bombay has 500,000 people (more than the entire population of Atlanta, Georgia) living on sidewalks.

The world's homeless make us aware that millions of people do not have the basic means to live—they migrate to cities in desperation. The human family is hurting and many of the worse-off members of the human family are huddling in the shadows of the urban skyscrapers. In cities, the contrasts in power and wealth between rich and poor are dramatic and dangerous. Some cities could literally erupt in the next decade. Even cities that remain stable, however, must deal with the quality-of-life issues of love and meaning. Cities must be places where people can become connected to others and coparticipants in rewarding activities.

Recent research on social relations in urban settings have demonstrated that urban and suburban residents have friendship networks and social interaction rates that are equal to or greater than rural residents, so individuals are not as isolated in metropolitan areas as is often supposed. See, for example, Claude S. Fischer et al., *Networks and Places* (Free Press, 1977), Claude S. Fischer, *To Dwell Among Friends: Personal Networks in Town and City* (University of Chicago Press, 1982), and Peggy Wireman, *Urban Neighborhoods, Networks and Families: New Forms of Old Values* (Lexington Books, 1984). Bert E. Swanson et al. provides a thorough empirical description of what small communities are like in *Small Towns and Small Towners* (Sage, 1979). A very informative recent community study is *Middletown Families: Fifty Years of Change and Continuity* by Theodore Caplow et al. (University of Minnesota Press, 1983).

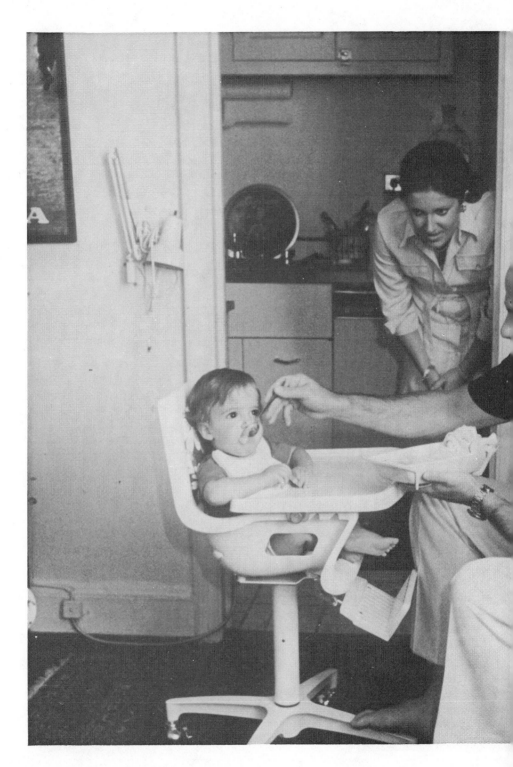

UN Photo

PART 3

Sex Roles and the Family

The family is a primary social institution, but is the nuclear family still the core of a stable social structure in our society? Every society assigns different roles to men and women according to their sex. What is happening to sex roles in our society, and what are the effects of changing sex roles?

Are Traditional Families More
Successful?

Can Women Combine Careers and
Families?

The "New Woman": Has She
Confused Sex Roles?

ISSUE 5

Are Traditional Families More Successful?

YES: Phyllis Schlafly, from *The Power of the Positive Woman* (Arlington House, 1977)

NO: Barbara Deckard, from *The Women's Movement* (Harper & Row, 1979)

ISSUE SUMMARY

YES: Conservative activist Phyllis Schlafly supports the traditional role of wife and mother as a source of fulfillment for women.

No: Sociologist Barbara Deckard suggests that this role is demeaning and limiting.

The family has become the subject of intense controversy in recent years. Even defining the term is difficult without getting into ideological disputes. A scheduled White House Conference on the Family in 1980 had its name changed to a White House Conference on *Families* after some participants objected that the use of the singular would imply that there exists only one form of the family—the traditional nuclear family of husband, wife, and children—and that any other form of living together is somehow aberrant or abnormal. The conference, despite bitter protest from its more traditional participants, ended up including in its definition of "family" divorced single-parent homes (which used to be called "broken homes"), single people living together with or without children, communal arrangements, and homosexual unions.

Twenty years earlier, such a tolerant approach to "family" would have been almost unthinkable. During the 1950s and early 1960s, there was a broad consensus that the nuclear family was the normal and universal means of fulfilling what were considered the four basic needs of any society: the regulation of sex and the creation, socialization, and support of children. Each of these presumed societal "needs" became problematic in the 1970s. During that decade, there was a significant increase in (and at least a partial legitimization of) premarital and extramarital sex, suggesting that the regulation of sex in America had lost some of its urgency. Procreation, the second function of the nuclear family, also declined in significance. Demographers and ecologists expressed concern about population overgrowth, and feminists claimed that childbearing was often another link in the chain of women's oppression. The last two functions of the nuclear family, the socialization and support of children, seemed increasingly to be taken over by what historian Christopher Lasch has termed "The helping professions"—social workers, teachers, psychiatrists, and family therapists—and by the welfare state in general.

Whether because of institutional obsolescence or a larger breakdown in society, the middle-class nuclear family which had occupied an almost sacred place (in theory, if not always in practice) since the early nineteenth century, has come under increasingly critical scrutiny. Is the family critical to child development? Aren't there many cases where it has stifled development through overprotectiveness and "momism"? Have those "moms" and wives been able to explore their full creative potential within the bounds of the traditional family? Aren't there a number of successful alternatives to it, from extended family arrangements, to communal families, to two-career families? Finally, can the nuclear family even be called "the norm" anymore in a society where divorce is as common as it is in America today?

Such questions touch the deepest roots of American values. To some people, the traditional family is the rock of social morality and even to ask these questions suggests decay. To others, the traditional family has been a retrogressive force holding back the development of people's full potential and the new critical attitude toward it has to be taken as a sign of progress.

In the following selections, Phyllis Schlafly defends the traditional family and Barbara Deckard states her opposition to it. Schlafly, the well-known opponent of almost the entire feminist agenda, develops the "pro-family" position that the nuclear family is a socializing institution that has protected and fulfilled women. Thus, she argues, "the positive woman" is one who not only accepts but rejoices in her biologically-influenced role of housewife and mother. Deckard, a feminist sociologist, regards the Schlafly position as one derived less from empirical study than from "popular stereotypes." In her view, the available evidence indicates that the happy housewife is relatively rare and that the frustrated, repressed housewife is more common.

YES
Phyllis Schlafly

THE POWER OF THE POSITIVE WOMAN

The first requirement for the acquisition of power by the Positive Woman is to understand the differences between men and women. Your outlook on life, your faith, your behavior, your potential for fulfillment, all are determined by the parameters of your original premise. The Positive Woman starts with the assumption that the world is her oyster. She rejoices in the creative capability within her body and the power potential of her mind and spirit. She understands that men and women are different, and that those very differences provide the key to her success as a person and fulfillment as a woman. . . .

Another feature of the woman's natural role is the obvious fact that women can breast-feed babies and men cannot. This functional role was not imposed by conspiratorial males seeking to burden women with confining chores, but must be recognized as part of the plan of the Divine Architect for the survival of the human race through the centuries and in the countries that know no pasteurization of milk or sterilization of bottles.

The Positive Woman looks upon her femaleness and her fertility as part of her purpose, her potential, and her power. She rejoices that she has a capability for creativity that men can never have. . . .

The Positive Woman knows that, while there are some physical competitions in which women are better (and can command more money) than men, including those that put a premium on grace and beauty, such as figure skating, the superior physical strength of males over females in competitions of strength, speed, and short-term endurance is beyond rational dispute. . . .

The Positive Woman recognizes the fact that, when it comes to sex, woman are simply not the equal of men. The sexual drive of men is much stronger than that of women. That is how the human race was designed in order that it might perpetuate itself. The other side of the coin is that it is easier for women to control their sexual appetites. A Positive Woman cannot defeat a man in a wrestling or boxing match, but she can motivate him, inspire him, encourage him, teach him, restrain him, reward him, and have power over him that he can never achieve over her with all his muscle. How or whether a Positive Woman uses her power is determined solely by the way she alone defines her goals and develops her skills.

The differences between men and women are also emotional and psychological. Without woman's innate maternal instinct, the human race would have died out centuries ago. . . .

The overriding psychological need of a woman is to love something alive. A baby fulfills this need in the lives of most women. If a baby is not available to fill that need, women search for a baby-substitute. This is the reason why women have traditionally gone into teaching and nursing careers. They are doing what comes naturally to the female psyche. The schoolchild or the patient of any age provides an outlet for a woman to express her natural maternal need. . . .

Finally, women are different from men in dealing with the fundamentals of life itself. Men are philosophers, women are practical, and 'twas ever thus. Men may philosophize about how life began and where we are heading; women are concerned about feeding the kids today. No woman would ever, as Karl Marx did, spend years reading political philosophy in the British Museum while her child starved to death. Women don't take naturally to a search for the intangible and the abstract. The Positive Woman knows who she is and where she is going, and she will reach her goal because the longest journey starts with a very practical first step. . . .

One of the endemic defects of the women's liberation movement is that it is mostly made up of women who think they should be television station managers or vice presidents of General Motors, or hold positions of similar authority over other lesser mortals. They are living in a make-believe world in which they postulate that the ultimate fulfillment for all women is to spend their adult life in the paid-employment market. The big percentage of jobs in the world—both male and female—fulfill a need for money, but little else. Whether a woman's ambition, training, and skill lead her into a "job" or into a "career" will usually determine how eager she is to enter the paid-employment labor force and then stay in it all her life. It is an impudent presumption of the women's liberationists to assume that *all* women seek or find self-fulfillment in a lifetime in the paid-employment market.

This is because women have another career option available—one that is seldom recommended in "women's studies" courses or seminars—namely, marriage and motherhood. The desire for this career binds those who seek "jobs" and those who see "careers" with a psychological bond that truly unites women of all disparate groups: educated and unskilled, rich and poor, black and white. The human problems involved in marriages and motherhood are common to women of all groups, but the problems of the job market can never be.

Virginia Slims, a source that must be considered at least friendly to the women's liberation movement, commissioned the Roper Organization to conduct an in-depth survey during 1974 of women's attitudes. The survey showed that a majority of women would like to include both marriage and a career in their life plan, but that, when confronted with having to make a choice of marriage *or* a paid-employment career, only a tiny 2 percent would choose "career." Two-thirds of women feel strongly that "having a loving husband who is able to take care of me is much more important than making it on my own." That is probably an accurate assessment of women's attitudes. . . .

The women's liberation movement makes much of the fact that, despite laws requiring equal pay for equal work, statistics show that women hold only a small minority of the high-paying executive and professional positions. The statistics are accurate, but the reason is not discrimination. No person, man or woman, rises to those high-income ranks on a forty-hour week. Ask any successful doctor, lawyer, or business executive. They have invariably spent years working nights and weekends, bringing home briefcases bulging with work, and serving clients or customers in a steady stream outside of office hours.

Top business and professional men and women have all paid a big price for their success in terms of long hours every week, missed vacations, canceled social engagements, and a constant sacrifice of time with their families—in addition to the physical and mental strain demanded by the highly competitive rat race that sometimes causes heart attacks, high blood pressure, and early death or physical collapse.

For any man or women who chooses that life, there is plenty of room at the top. The stakes are high, and it is a personal decision as to whether the rewards of money, power, and prestige are worth the sacrifices and the risks. Many men think they are. The plain fact is that most women don't. Why? It certainly is not because they lack a willingness to do hard and sustained work, and it probably is not even because they lack a capacity for competition. It is because, for most women, something else comes first in their lives—namely, marriage and motherhood—and business or professional success does not rate high enough in their scale of values to permit it to steal so much time from the home. Many talented women may want to have some of both careers, but home remains primary in their scale of values, while a business or professional career is secondary. . . .

What does a woman want out of life? If you want to love and be loved, marriage offers the best opportunity to achieve your goal. Men may want, or think they want, a cafeteria selection of lunch counter sex. But most women continue to want what the popular song calls "a Sunday kind of love." A happy marriage is the perfect vehicle for the Positive Woman. Marriage and motherhood give a woman new identity and the opportunity for all-round fulfillment as a woman.

Are you looking for security—emotional, social, financial? Nothing in this world is sure except death and taxes, but marriage and motherhood are the most reliable security the world can offer. . . .

Do you want the satisfaction of achievement in your career? No career in the world offers this reward at such an early age as motherhood. In the business or professional world, a man or a woman may labor for years, or even decades, to acquire the satisfaction of accomplishment. A mother reaps that reward within months of her labor when she proudly shows off her healthy and happy baby. She can have the satisfaction of doing her job well—and being recognized for it.

It is generally conceded that former Israeli Premier Golda Meir is the outstanding career woman of our time. She achieved more in a man's world than any woman in any country—and she did it on sheer ability, not on her looks or her legs. The Gallup Poll repeatedly identified her as "the most-admired woman" in the world. Yet Golda Meir said without hesitation that having a baby is the most fulfilling thing a woman can ever do, and she put down the women's liberationists as a bunch of "bra-burning nuts." . . .

Consider another highly successful career woman: Oriana Fallaci, the Italian journalist whose interviews with heads of state are the envy of most reporters and whose financial success in her chosen profession has brought her two homes in Italy and an apartment in Manhattan. When she gave a personal interview to *The New York Times*, she conceded that the crushing disappointment of her life is that she never had a baby. Even though she reached the pinnacle of her profession, career success was not enough for her self-fulfillment as a woman. She still yearns to satisfy her natural maternal urge.

Amelia Earhart has been a long-time heroine of feminists because she lived such an independent and exciting life. Yet when her true story was dramatized on national television in October, 1976, she was shown cuddling another woman's baby—and wishing it were her own.

One of the most successful writers of the twentieth century was Taylor Caldwell. *Family Weekly* asked her if it didn't give her solid satisfaction to know that her novel *Captains and the Kings* was to be seen as a nine-hour television production. She replied:

There is no solid satisfaction in any career for a woman like myself. There is no home, no true freedom, no hope, no joy, no expectation for tomorrow, no contentment. I would rather cook a meal for a man and bring him his slip-

pers and feel myself in the protection of his arms than have all the citations and awards and honors I have received worldwide, including the Ribbon of the Legion of Honor and my property and my bank accounts.

In unguarded moments, women's liberationists often reveal the womanly desires lurking behind their negative attitude toward men and marriage. One who heard me extol the rewards of marriage and motherhood could not restrain the tears in her eyes even in front of live television cameras. Another, with a glamorous network television job, whispered off camera: "I'd rather be scrubbing floors in my own home than working on this program." A third said, "If you find one of those nice guys who would like to support a wife, please bring him around; I'd like to meet him." A fourth conceded in a public debate, "I envy the happily married woman."

Mrs. Ronald Reagan summed it up in a November 1975, interview: "I believe a woman's real happiness and fulfillment come from within her home with a husband and children."

Anne Morrow Lindbergh spoke for the big majority of women when she described her own priorities in *Hour of Gold, Hour of Lead*:

To be deeply in love is, of course, a great liberating force and the most common experience that frees—or seems to free—young people. The loved one is the liberator. Ideally, both members of a couple in love free each other to new and different worlds. I was no exception to the general rule. The sheer fact of finding myself loved was unbelievable and changed my world, my feelings about life and myself. I was given confidence, strength, and almost a new character. The man I was to marry believed in me and what I could do, and consequently, I found I could do more than I realized, even in that mysterious outer world that fascinated me but seemed unattainable. He opened the door to "real life" and although it frightened me, it also beckoned. I had to go. . . .

The first months of motherhood were totally normal, joyful, and satisfying and I would have been content to stay home and do nothing else but care for my baby. This was "real life" at its most basic level.

Marriage and motherhood, of course, have their trials and tribulations. But what lifestyle doesn't? If you look upon your home as a cage, you will find yourself just as imprisoned in an office or a factory. The flight from the home is a flight from yourself, from responsibility, from the nature of woman, in pursuit of false hopes and fading illusions.

If you complain about servitude to a husband, servitude to a boss will be more intolerable. Everyone in the world has a boss of some kind. It is easier for most women to achieve a harmonious working relationship with a husband than with a foreman, supervisor, or office manager.

The women's liberationists point to the Bible as proof that marriage forces women into a subservient role from which they must be liberated. The feminists get livid at any reading of Ephesians 5, wherein Saint Paul says; "Wives, submit yourselves unto your own husbands, as unto the Lord. For the husband is the head of the church." The fringe group called Saint Joan's Alliance often pickets in front of churches when Saint Paul is scheduled to be read at the Sunday service.

The first answer to these anti-Scripture agitators is that Ephesians also states:

Husbands, love your wives, even as Christ also loved the church, and gave Himself for it. . . . Let everyone of you in particular so love his wife even as himself; and the wife see that she reverence her husband.

The Positive Woman recognizes that there is a valid and enduring purpose behind this recognition of different roles for men and women which is just as relevant in the twentieth century as it was in the time of Saint Paul.

Any successful vehicle must have one person at the wheel with ultimate responsibility. When I fly on a plane or sail on a ship, I'm glad there is one captain who has the final responsibility and can act decisively in a crisis situation. A family cannot be run by committee. The committee system neutralizes a family with continuing controversy and encumbers it with psychological impedimenta. It makes a family as clumsy and slow as a hippopotamus (which might be defined as a race horse designed by a committee).

Every successful country and company has one "chief executive officer." None successfully functions with responsibility equally divided between cochairmen or copresidents. The United States has a president and a vice president. They are not equal. The vice president supports and carries out the policies enunciated by the president. Likewise with the presidents and vice presidents of all business concerns. Vice presidents can and do have areas of jurisdiction delegated to them but there is always one final decision maker. The experience of the ages has taught us that this system is sound, practical, and essential for success. The republic of ancient Rome tried a system of two consuls of equal authority, and it failed.

If marriage is to be a successful institution, it must likewise have an ultimate decision maker, and that is the husband. Seen in this light, the laws that give the husband the right to establish the domicile of the marriage and to give his surname to his children are good laws designed to keep the family together. They are not anachronisms from a bygone era from which wives should be liberated in the name of equality. If a woman does not want to live in her husband's home, she is not entitled to the legal rights of a wife. Those women who preach that a wife should have the right to establish her own separate domicile do not stay married very long. That "equal right" is simply incompatible with a happy lifetime marriage.

The women's liberationists look upon marriage as an institution of dirty dishes and dirty diapers. They spend a lot of energy writing marriage contracts that divide up what they consider the menial, degrading chores. The much quoted "Shulmans' marriage agreement," for example, includes such provisions as "Husband does dishes on Tuesday, Thursday; and Sunday. Wife does Monday, Wednesday and Saturday, Friday is split...," and "wife strips beds, husband remakes them." If the baby cries in the night, the chore of "handling" the baby is assigned as follows: "Husband does Tuesdays, Thursday and Sunday. Wife does Monday, Wednesday and Saturday, Friday is split...." Presumably, if the baby cries for his mother on Tuesday night, he would be informed that the marriage contract prohibits her from responding.

It is possible, in such a loveless home, that the baby would never call for his mother at all. Most wives remember those years of diapers and tiny babies as the happiest of their lives.

Are dirty dishes all that bad? It's all in whether you wake up in the morning with a chip on your shoulder or whether you have a positive mental attitude. One happy wife I know has this poem hanging on her kitchen wall:

Thank God for dirty dishes,
They have a tale to tell.
While others may go hungry
We're eating very well.
With home, health and happiness,
I wouldn't want to fuss;
By the stack of the evidence,
God's been very good to us.

If you think diapers and dishes are a never-ending, repetitive routine, just remember that most of the jobs outside the home are just as repetitious, tiresome, and boring. Consider the assembly-line worker who pulls the same lever, pushes the same button, or inspects thousands of identical bits of metal or glass or paper, hour after weary hour; the stenographer who turns out page after page of typing; the telephone operator; the retail clerk who must repeatedly bite her lip because "the customer is always right."

Many people take such jobs because they need or want the money. But it is ludicrous to suggest that they are more self-fulfilling than the daily duties of a wife and mother in the home. The plain fact is that most women would rather cuddle a baby than a typewriter or factory machine. Not only does the baby provide a warm and loving relationship that satisfies the woman's maternal instinct and returns love for service, but it is a creative and growing job that builds for the future. After twenty years of diapers and dishes, a mother can see the results of her own handiwork in the good citizen she has produced and trained. After twenty years of faithful work in the business world, you are lucky if you have a good watch to show for your efforts.

Those who want to be hermits and live in isolation are welcome to make that choice. Most people want and need human companionship in facing life's trials. Family living requires many social compromises, but it is worth the price, especially for women. . . .

The Positive Woman knows that there are two main pillars of a happy marriage and that she has the capability to build both. The first is that a wife must appreciate and admire her husband. Whereas a woman's chief emotional need is active (i.e., to love), a man's prime emotional need is passive (i.e., to be appreciated or admired).

The Positive Woman recognizes this fundamental difference and builds her male/female relationship accordingly. She knows that this does not in any sense make her inferior, but that it is one key to personal fulfillment for both herself and her husband. Knowledge of this factor gives the Positive Woman the power to build and retain that most fragile but most rewarding of all human relationships, the happy marriage.

It is really just as easy as it sounds. Those who fight it, or try to bypass it or suppress it, face endless frustration and battles that lead to bitter dead ends. How often have you thought, as you noticed a contented couple, "What on earth does he see in her?" The answer is always very simple: She knows how to make him feel like a man—and to remember always that she is a woman.

Is this degrading to the wife? Humiliating? Subservient? Or any of the other extravagant liberationist adjectives? How ridiculous! It is just the application of the Golden Rule with a simple male/female variation. Most women think that the prize is worth the price.

A satisfying and rewarding relationship between a man and a woman can last through the years only if she is willing to give him the appreciation and the admiration his manhood craves. There are a thousand ways a woman can devise—public and private, obvious and subtle, physical and intellectual. It makes little difference how—so long as it is personal, pervasive, perennial, and genuine.

Take, for example, two such totally different women as Queen Victoria and Katharine Hepburn. Although poles apart in morals and milieu, they were alike in being extremely strong-minded in temperament and independent in action. Both spoke with the voice of authority and were forceful to the point of being domineering in their dealings with their fellow human beings, male and female. Except for one person, that is. Victoria's relationship with her husband, Prince Albert, was that of the dutiful wife, deferring always to her husband's wishes in their domestic partnership.

Recent revelations of Katharine Hepburn's twenty-seven-year love affair with Spencer Tracy (who had a wife) show that, to him alone in all the world, this assertive, headstrong, free-thinking spitfire of a woman was submissive and more abnegating than any wife this side of the Orient. She often sat at his feet when they were together, and metaphorically, she was always there. The bond that pulled them together was the abundance of admiration she lavished on him. A really Positive Woman, she had enough self-confidence that she could afford to accord to her man a preeminence in their personal relationship. . . .

NO

Barbara Deckard

THE MYTH OF THE AMERICAN FAMILY

They stare at you from the television screen, the pages of magazines, the billboards—the pretty, smiling woman; the tall, competent-looking man; the cute, clean children. No labeling is necessary for us to recognize them as the typical American family. Ask any man or woman on the street and they will tell you that the family consisting of husband, wife, and children is not just typical but natural and universal—decreed by God or determined by biology. An occasional fun-loving bachelor may have escaped marriage; a few women are simply too ugly to catch any man; some couples are unable to have children, poor things. These cases are exceptions and are abnormal. The proper, accepted, normal state for an adult is marriage and parenthood. Furthermore, the closer one comes to the typical family of advertising fame, the happier and certainly the more normal one will be. The pretty wife stays home taking care of her gadget-full house and cute children; the husband goes out to work to make the gadgets and a college education for the children possible. this division of labor is not just typical; it is natural, universal, and good.

Popular stereotypes can hardly be considered scientific knowledge. What do social scientists have to tell us about the family? Sociologists of the structural-functional school agree to a remarkable extent with the popular stereotypes, although of course their language is much more impressive. These sociologists say that the nuclear family, consisting of a man, a woman, and their children, is universal. It is universal because it performs certain functions that are necessary if the society is to survive. Some functions that used to be performed within the family (economic production, for example) are now performed elsewhere. The family still acts as the "primary agent of socialization of the child" and is the "primary basis of security for the normal adult." For the family to function effectively, a division of labor is required: the husband's function is instrumental (i.e., task oriented); the wife's, expressive (i.e., she provides emotional support). In concrete terms, the husband works outside the home so as to support the family financially; the wife is housekeeper, mother, and binder of psychic wounds for both husband and children.

The structural-functional theorists essentially agree with the popular view that the nuclear family and the present division of labor within it is both natural and good. They do not provide evidence that the functions the family performs cannot be performed by other institutions. They do not explain why the woman should invariably perform the expressive function and the man the instrumental. More basically, they do not ask whether the maintenance of society as it now is should be the overriding goal. Certainly the abolition of the nuclear family would result in major societal changes, but would these changes be for the better or for the worse? The answer depends to a large extent on how one evaluates the present situation. Instead of asking whether the nuclear family is functional for society, we should ask if it is functional for its component units—for the woman, the man, and the children. . . .

THE MYTH

What does a young woman expect of marriage, and what does she actually get? She has been taught that the choice of a marriage partner is the most important decision she will ever make. In marriage she expects to fulfill her true nature as loving wife and mother. This, she has been taught, is the most creative career possible for a woman. She is, in effect, promised instant and complete happiness.

Especially if she is quite young, the bride's image of marriage is likely to come straight from the pages of popular magazines and the TV screen. She sees herself as the glamorous, creative homemaker decorating her house a la *House Beautiful* and cooking gourmet meals.

Beautifully dressed, she greets her smiling husband when he comes home from work. They spend a peaceful, intimate hour discussing the events of the day. She, of course, is an interested and sympathetic listener; he, of course, wants to share all aspects of his life with her and values her advice. Some evenings they entertain couples as beautiful and smiling as themselves; other evenings they go out.

Did the young woman have dreams or plans for doing something more with her life? She will, she is sure, manage to keep up in some way. If she has artistic talent, she can write or paint at home. Otherwise, she can at least read good books. This will provide intellectual stimulation for her and keep her interesting to her husband.

Not long after marriage she will become pregnant. Having a baby—an act that she has been told is more creative than painting the *Last Supper*—will complete her happiness. She sees a cute, smiling baby that she can play with, take for walks, and show off to her friends. She may look a few years further into the future and see herself, still vivacious and pretty, as the mother of several clean, attractive grammar school children. Throughout, she is happy and fulfilled as wife, mother, and homemaker. She has lived the American dream.

REALITY:
THE MIDDLE-CLASS VERSION

The middle-class, like the working-class, woman is increasingly likely to work until she is pregnant with her first child. During the time she is working outside the home, she finds she has two jobs. She is expected to do most of the housework. It is, after all, woman's work. Her husband may help out, but it is clearly understood that the inside housework is her responsibility.

Whether she is working or not, the first part of the myth crumbles quickly. Housework is neither interesting nor creative; in the expressive phrase of the women's movement, it is "shit work." For those with the talent and interest, decorating and gourmet cooking are creative and fun. But most housework consists of mopping floors, washing dishes, and cleaning toilet bowls. Not only is it boring, it is repetitive and never-ending. Housework does not stay done; a chore done today must be done again tomorrow or, at best, next week. Thus it provides no real feeling of accomplishment. Studies have found that doing housework is a perfect job for the feeble-minded. . . .

A man generally expects his wife to center her life around him. She should not need anything but a husband who is a good provider and healthy children to make her happy. After all, both he and she have been taught that a normal woman finds total fulfillment in this way. He is surprised and upset if the pretty, admiring girl he married turns into a nagging shrew. Being barred from achieving on her own, the wife may put all her excess energy into her husband's career. He may be satisfied with his present position; she demands greater and greater success. Aware of his weak spots, she may question his masculinity if he does not live up to her expectations. He will be hurt and angry; he may seek out other female companionship to provide the stroking his wife withholds. He probably considers his wife overly money hungry and status conscious. He is unlikely to realize that she is trying to live his life because she does not have one of her own.

The traditional American family structure does not seem to be good for the wife and can also be pretty hard on the husband. What about the children? Surely the children must benefit from having a loving mother always around. Child psychologists have found that the answer is often no. Children can be over-mothered. Such children are overly dependent on their mothers; they tend to be passive and remain infantile. Over-mothering stunts a child's emotional and intellectual development. Small children who are not given independence to explore and solve problems on their own are unlikely to develop the ability to think analytically. Such children often do not develop an independent sense of self-worth.

The woman may be overmothering her children because she believes this is the proper mother's role. Child care books and popular Freudian psychology convey the impression that, by sins of omission or commission, she can easily scar her child for life. Her full-time loving presence is said to be essential for the child's healthy development. She is never told that she can scar her children as well as herself by paying too much attention to them.

Excessive mothering is often a result of the woman's lack of a life of her own. She may attempt to live vicariously through her children. Through them she will experience all the things she has missed. Her daughter must be the prettiest and most popular girl in her class; her son, the smartest and most athletically proficient. She may push her daughter into absurdly early dating so that she can relive the most exciting part of her life. She will give up anything and everything for her children. Nothing is too good for them. They need not help around the house or get part-time jobs. The only thing she will not give them is their independence.

When their children leave home, such supermothers find adjustment especially difficult. Depression severe enough to require hospitalization is a not-infrequent problem. For most full-time housewives, the children's leaving home means a loss of function and, often, of identity. The woman frequently feels that no one needs her anymore, and because she has based her life on satisfying others' needs, she now sees herself as superfluous. She has nothing to live for, nothing to do. All the extra time is seen as a curse, not a benefit. Because over the years her interests have been so narrowly centered on her family, wider interests have atrophied. Now she has no idea what to do with the 20 or 30 years of life left to her.

Even if her husband understands her problem, there is often little he can do to help. If he is successful, his career may well require increasing amounts of time. Even if he does have time to spend with his wife, they may find they have so little in common that neither finds much satisfaction in their being together.

The middle-class American ideal is the companionate marriage in which husband and wife are friends. The typical division of labor in the family along sex lines makes the ideal almost impossible to achieve. Friendship requires common interests. The very different lives that husband and wife lead tend to erode any common interests they may have had and does not encourage the development of new ones. Friendship also requires equality. Even if the couple consciously try to attain an egalitarian marriage, so long as the traditional division of labor is maintained, the husband will be "more equal." He is the provider not only of money but of status. Especially if he is successful, society values what he does; she is just a housewife. Their friends are likely to be his friends and coworkers; in their company, she is just his wife. Because his provider function is essential for the family's survival, major family decisions are made in terms of how they affect his career. He need not and usually does not act like the authoritarian paterfamilius of the Victorian age. His power and status are derived from his function in the family and are secure so long as the traditional division of labor is maintained.

REALITY: THE WORKING-CLASS VERSION

Companionate marriage, while seldom attained, is the middle-class ideal. In the working class, older, traditional values are more prevalent. Mirra Komarovsky, in her study of blue-collar marriage, found that many of the couples interviewed, especially those with less than a high school education, did not expect friendship in marriage. Men and women are seen as having sufficiently different interests that cross-sex friendship is not really possible. According to one young woman, "Regular guys don't mess around with women except when they want what a woman's got to give them. Men and women are different. The fellows got their interests and the girls got theirs, they go their separate ways."

This view is not universal. The high school graduates in the sample, in particular, tend to feel that husband and wife should be friends. Yet companionship was rarely attained. Many of the women complained that their husbands did not talk to them enough and that the husbands did not listen. Husbands, particularly the less educated ones, simply do not understand their wives' complaints: "What is it about women that they want to talk about things when there is really nothing to talk about? Why do they have to hash it over? They talk about screwy things. Keep quacking, like beating a dead horse."

On this inability to communicate, Komarovsky comments, "Husbands and wives need not share identical mental worlds to understand one another, but their two separate worlds must be in contact at some points. This overlapping of interest is so narrow for a number of Glenton couples that neither partner can serve as a satisfactory audience for the other."

The lack of overlap seems to be due in part to the socialization process. Sex role stereotypes are emphasized in working-class families to a greater extent than in middle-class ones. The male role is defined in such a way that it produces in the man a "trained incapacity to share." According to Komarovsky, "the ideal of masculinity into which they were socialized inhibits expressiveness both directly, with its emphasis on reserve, and indirectly by identifying personal exchange with the feminine role."

Highly traditional views on the division of labor within the family further reduce the range of common interests. In 80 percent of the families, women do all of the cooking, cleaning, and laundry. In only one-third of the families do the men help with the dishes. Only one-third of the fathers frequently or regularly help with the care of babies; most are more involved in the care of older children.

Any help the husband gives is seen by both sexes as a favor, not as his responsibility. According to one young husband, "I'd be glad to help but when she insisted it was my job to do it—well, I didn't like it." A mother of four says: "If a man likes to take care of children, it's all right; if he doesn't, he shouldn't be expected to do it unless his wife is sick."

MARRIAGE AND THE FAMILY— IS IT GOOD FOR HUMAN BEINGS?

If the description of the family presented earlier is correct, the traditional family structure is not good for human beings. The woman in particular is trapped in a situation that provides little opportunity for intellectual growth or the satisfactions of achievement. The man at least gets a maid.

But surely the picture is overdrawn. Betty Friedan says that when she was interviewing for her book she never found a happy housewife who was only that. Hers was not a scientific survey; certainly there must be women content with the traditional female role of housewife and mother.

Available evidence indicates that the happy housewife may indeed be relatively rare. A number of studies have found that women of all social classes express more dissatisfaction with marriage than do men. "More wives than husbands report marital frustration and dissatisfaction; more report negative feelings; more wives than husbands report marital problems; more wives than husbands consider their marriages unhappy, have considered separation or divorce, have regretted their marriages; and fewer report positive companionship."

Many widows do not want to remarry. A study by the Department of Health, Education and Welfare of 390 Chicago widows found that only one-fifth said they would like to marry again. The other 80 percent said no and gave as their reason, "I'm free and independent now." A study of people over 65 found that the wives envied the widows for their freedom, independence, and fun in life. The wives felt "they were unfortunate, in contrast with the widows, in being stuck in the house at the beck and call of a usually temperamental and demanding retired husband."

More disturbing are the figures on mental health. According to Jessie Bernard, "being a housewife makes women sick." When married men and married women are compared, the men show up much better on various indexes of mental health. "More married women than married men show phobic reactions, depression and passivity; greater than expected frequency of symptoms of psychological distress; and mental-health impairment."

Perhaps women are simply psychologically less stable than men. No; the poorer mental health of married women is not due to a general sex difference. On the same measures, unmarried women show up as mentally healthier than both married women and unmarried men. "Many symptoms of psychological distress show up more frequently than expected among married women: nervous breakdowns, nervousness, inertia, insomnia, trembling hands, nightmares, perspiring hands, fainting, headaches, dizziness and heart palpitations. They show up less frequently than expected among unmarried women." Unmarried women's mental health also compares very favorably with that of unmarried men. "Single women show far less than expected frequency of symptoms of psychological distress as compared with single men. . . . Single women suffer far less than single men from neurotic and antisocial tendencies. More single men than single women are depressed and passive." When unmarried women and married men are compared, little overall mental health difference is found, although the women show a markedly smaller incidence of psychological distress symptoms such as nervousness and insomnia.

The data would seem to show that marriage is good for men and bad for women. Perhaps, however, some of these differences are due to selective factors. That is, maybe mentally healthy men and mentally sick women tend to marry more frequently than mentally sick men and mentally healthy women. Bernard believes that such selection may account for some but far from all of the difference. "In our society, the husband is assigned superior status. It helps if he actually *is* somewhat superior in ways—in height, for example, or age or education or occupation—for such superiority, however slight, makes it easier for both partners to conform to the structural imperatives."

Men may tend to marry women to whom they can feel superior; women to marry men they can look up to. If women tend to marry up and men to marry down, then "bottom-of-the-barrel" men and "cream-of-the-crop" women are least likely to marry.

The selective process cannot, however, completely explain the poor mental health of wives because almost everyone does eventually get married. Something about the woman's marriage must account for the problem. A comparison between working women, many of whom are married, and housewives is illuminating. Working women, whatever their marital status, are on the average far healthier mentally than housewives. "Far fewer than expected of the working women and more than expected of the housewives, for example, had actually had a nervous breakdown. Fewer than expected of the working women and more than expected of the housewives suffered from nervousness, inertia, insomnia, trembling hands, nightmares, perspiring hands, fainting, headaches, dizziness, and heart palpitations." Clearly being only a housewife is the problem: It literally makes many women sick. . . .

THE AMERICAN FAMILY AND MYTH AS SOCIAL SCIENCE

A critique of the nuclear family is useful only if better alternatives can be found. Many people, social scientists as well as laymen, contend that this is not possible. The nuclear family is universal and is based on our biological nature, they contend. Women must have babies for their own good, not just for the continuation of the species. Motherhood is a biological imperative; no woman can find true fulfillment without having children. The division of labor within the family is decreed by nature; since women have the babies, they must stay home and take care of them. Any absence of the mother will have disastrous psychological and intellectual effects on the child. The father performs the instrumental function; he is the provider, a role for which (the biological determinists contend) he is well fitted by virtue of his natural aggressiveness, innovativeness, and independence. According to the sociologists, however, the male cannot effectively perform his function unless the female performs her expressive function. That is, the husband is dependent on his wife for

emotional support or, in Bernard's term, stroking. The female's effective performance of the stroking function is dependent on her being in a position that the male sees as not competitive with his own. If a woman has a career in the cruel, competitive world outside the home, she is unlikely to be effective at stroking, since her husband will see her as a competitor and not as a quiet port in a stormy world. According to Talcott Parsons, if both husband and wife have careers, the resulting competition between them is likely to have a disruptive effect on the solidarity of the marriage.

If we are to determine whether alternatives to the nuclear family are possible and desirable, each of these tenets must be examined.

George Murdock, a well-known anthropologist, contends that the nuclear family is universal. When one examines his much-reprinted article on the topic, one finds that his definition of the term is very broad. So long as a man, a woman, and their children live together, no matter who else lives with them, this is, according to Murdock, a nuclear family. Under this definition Murdock includes both polygamous and extended families, since in these forms of the family a man, a woman, and their children also live together. In common usage the term *nuclear family* refers to the isolated nuclear family, composed solely of a man, a woman, and their children. Of the 192 societies on which Murdock had data, 42 had isolated nuclear families, 53 had polygamous families and 92, some form of extended family. Obviously the isolated nuclear family is atypical. Furthermore, a few cases of "visit" marriages, in which a man does not live with his wife and children, have since been discovered.... Data so far presented show clearly that the nuclear family consisting solely of a man, a woman, and their children is far from universal and thus cannot be biologically determined.

Is motherhood natural? This question really consists of two parts. Do women need to be mothers in order to find fulfillment? Does mothering, that is, taking care of children, come naturally to women?

There is no evidence that women have a biological need for children. "Women don't need to be mothers anymore than they need spaghetti," says Dr. Richard Rabkin, a New York psychiatrist. "But if you're in a world where everyone is eating spaghetti, thinking they need it, and want it, you will think so too."

If there were such a biological need, the motherhood-is-bliss myth and all the social pressures on women to become mothers would be unnecessary. As sociologist William Goode says, "There is no innate drive for children. Otherwise, the enormous cultural pressures that there are to reproduce wouldn't exist. There are no cultural pressures to sell you on getting your hand out of the fire."

A woman's desire to have children is due to her psychological, not her biological, state. Do women, then, have a psychological need for children? To the extent that they do, the need is a socially developed one. Nevertheless, despite the motherhood-is-bliss myth, many women find it more frustrating than blissful. As one young mother said, "In the abstract sense, I'd have several (children). . . . In the non-abstract, I would not have any. . . ." A number of studies have found that childless marriages are happier.

None of the arguments for maintaining the status quo are persuasive. As so often happens, social scientists have attempted "to justify a particular, local and almost certainly, temporary, economic and cultural pattern as an eternal biological law."

What is needed now is more serious consideration of alternatives. Restructuring the professions to allow both men and women to work part-time and thus share child care would be a first step. High-quality child care centers staffed by both men and women are needed. Experiments in communal living should be encouraged. Perhaps most important is recognition that no one life style will meet the needs of everyone. We do not expect everyone to do the same work or have the same interests and hobbies. Why should we expect everyone to have the same kind of family life? . . .

POSTSCRIPT

Are Traditional Families More Successful?

The discerning reader may have noticed that both Deckard and Schlafly sustain their arguments by using stereotypes. For Deckard, housework is "mopping floors" and "cleaning toilet bowls," while a career is "stimulating" and "creative." For Schlafly the imagery is reversed: the housewife "is a home executive: planning, organizing, leading, coordinating, and controlling," in contrast to the wretch who works on an assembly-line "hour after weary hour," or who labors behind a cash register, "knuckling under" to the infallible customer, or who toils behind an office typewriter, grinding out "page after page" for the boss. For the sake of realism, it would probably be better for Schlafly to concede that changing diapers is not an experience that makes those years of women's marriage "the happiest of their lives" and for Deckard to concede that drudgery is not confined to homemaking.

The debate featured in this section concerns what families should be like. A related issue is what modern families are like and how they differ from families in the past. Theodore Caplow and others replicated a study done fifty years earlier in Muncie, Indiana and find many continuities and relatively few changes in family patterns. See *Middletown Families: Fifty Years of Change and Continuity* (University of Minnesota Press, 1983). They find little evidence of the disintegration of the family as an institution, a theme also developed by Mary Jo Bane in *Here to Stay: American Families in the Twentieth Century* (Basic Books, 1976). Continuity is also the theme in the collection of essays on women's familial roles, *Women and the Family: Two Decades of Change*, edited by Beth B. Hess and Marvin B. Sussman (Haworth Press, 1984), while change is emphasized in Andrew Cherlin, *Marriage, Divorce, Remarriage* (Harvard University Press, 1981).

Most of the literature on the family tends to be alarmist. For example, in 1970 David Cooper wrote *The Death of the Family* (Vintage). Maxine L. Margolis relates changes in the American economy to transformations in the way the lives of women (especially her familial roles) are viewed in *Mothers and Such: Views of American Women and Why They Have Changed* (University of California Press, 1984). Barbara Ehrenreich argues a radical view that the male revolt against his traditional role of family breadwinner has spawned the women's movement for greater independence in *The Hearts of Men: American Dreams and the Flight from Commitment* (Anchor, 1983).

ISSUE 6
Can Women Combine Careers and Families?

YES: Shirley Wilkins and Thomas A. W. Miller, from "Working Women: How It's Working Out," *Public Opinion* (October/November 1985)

NO: George Gilder, from "Women in the Workforce" *Atlantic Monthly* (September 1986)

ISSUE SUMMARY

YES: Shirley Wilkins and Thomas Miller use a national survey to show that most women want to combine work and family even though it may be difficult.
NO: Sociologist George Gilder points out that only slightly more than one-third of working-age women held full-time year-round jobs, and he argues that women are much less committed to careers than men.

Women have come a long way, but there seems to be much confusion about where they are now. It is well known that most working-age women are in the paid labor force, but it is not clear what women have gained and lost thereby, particularly women with families. Are women happy to be leaving the home? Surveys show that most women want both family and career. If they had to choose between the two, 51 per cent said they would choose their career. On the other hand, Betty Friedan, who launched the modern women's movement with her book *The Feminine Mystique* (Norton, 1963), has more recently acknowledged the strong natural desire of some women for children and motherhood. Can a woman handle both career and family even when she wants to? The numbers suggest that they are doing both, but the literature currently highlights the many problems of doing so.

What problems are women with families having? According to Barbara Berg, who interviewed nearly 1,000 working women, "guilt was their greatest emotional problem." In "The Guilt That Drives Working Mothers Crazy" (*Ms.*, May 1987), she writes about her own experience: "But as soon as I reached for my briefcase, they [her two toddlers] would burst into inconsolable tears. 'Please don't go. Please don't leave us,' they would chorus pitifully, sometimes wrapping their little bodies around my legs in an effort to keep me home." These women also felt guilty for working late and missing dinner, for having little interest in sex, for being short-tempered with their children, for not disciplining more, and for not earning more. They also felt guilty for taking time off from work to attend school plays or to meet other family needs.

Guilt heads a long and painful list of problems for working mothers. It obviously includes overwork, exhaustion, and inattention to personal needs. Sylvia Ann Hewlett describes many of these problems in her controversial book, *A Lesser Life: The Myth of Women's Liberation in America* (Morrow, 1986). She argues that working mothers are forced to carry an impossible double burden of a job plus the bulk of the housework and child caring. "It is now possible to become a successful career woman, provided one has the right educational credentials, has stayed on track, and has been sensible enough not to have children. But putting these roles together is an invitation for failure." Her message is that society does not support working mothers, and maternity leaves, child care, and early childhood education programs are necessary. The controversial aspect of her message is her criticism of the women's movement for failing to advocate and obtain these supports.

So where are women today? In the selections that follow, Shirley Wilkins and Thomas Miller argue that not only are the majority of women working, but the majority are committed to their work. George Gilder, on the other hand, argues that women work less and are less committed to work.

YES

**Shirley Wilkins and
Thomas A. W. Miller**

WORKING WOMEN:
HOW IT'S WORKING OUT

Lynn and John are in their early thirties, married, and both lawyers. They are about to have their first child—and their first big marital problem.

How are they to raise their child? Which of these talented individuals will be called upon to make the greater professional sacrifice? Whose career will be at least temporarily, if not permanently, derailed in order to have a family?

The couple does have some options. Lynn is eligible for several months of maternity leave, but she worries that she will be taken off the interesting and important cases. John can take a more limited amount of paternity leave, but, frankly, it would be frowned upon. They certainly have the combined income to be able to afford a full-time nanny, but they are not anxious to entrust their child's early education to a professional—no matter how sensitive and intelligent that person may be. Day-care centers are available, but there the problem of paying an outsider to do their child-rearing is compounded by an environment that, however well managed, is in no sense a home.

In brief, Lynn and John do not want to be absentee parents—and yet both of them derive enormous personal satisfaction from their work.

This couple's problem is by no means an isolated one. Writ large, it exemplifies a growing challenge for a rapidly increasing number of American women and men: how to combine careers and families when both spouses work. Time is of the essence—and for working couples, their time is particularly pressed. How can all of the things that people want for themselves—children, a happy marriage, a job—be fit into a twenty-four-hour day?

The 1985 Virginia Slims American Women's Opinion Poll, conducted by the Roper Organization, has monitored and tracked Americans' opinions on social, familial, and personal issues since 1970. The fifth in a series of polls sponsored by Virginia Slims, this one is based on a representative nationwide sample of 3,000 adult women and 1,000 adult men. The results of this

From "Working Women: How It's Working Out," by Shirley Wilkins and Thomas A. W. Miller, *Public Opinion*, October/November 1985, pp. 44–48. Reprinted by permission of American Enterprise Institute for Public Policy Research.

year's survey suggest that changing attitudes toward women's role in society, toward marriage, and toward the essential components of a full and satisfying personal life portend major social changes in the future. The traditional organization of family life, and the very nature of work itself, may never be the same.

ONCE A BREAD BAKER, NOW A BREAD WINNER

If one word could sum up the vast progress made by women in the past fifteen years, it would be "choice." The freedom to choose a fulfilling individual lifestyle—and, simultaneously, tolerance of others' choices—has been the essential force underlying the social transformations of this period.

And a key element in this ongoing social evolution has been, and undoubtedly will continue to be, women's move into the workplace. Over the past fifteen years, the percentage of women employed full time has doubled; combined with part-time workers, this brings the total percentage of working women to more than half (52 percent) of the adult female population.

It is not simply out of economic necessity, moreover, that this fast-rising number of women choose to work. When asked whether they would continue to work even if financially secure, an identical proportion of employed women and employed men (66 percent) reply that they would. Perhaps more to the point, for the first time ever a majority of women (51 percent) would prefer to have a job rather than stay at home and take care of a family, if that were their only choice. In 1970, six out of ten women chose home over the workplace.

In the opinion of a growing majority of women, the most personally satisfying and interesting life is one that combines marriage, a career, and children (see Table 1). Particularly among younger women and better-educated ones, this preference for a full professional *and* family life is pronounced (see Table 2). This result leads to two conclusions. First, as younger women mature, they may be more likely to stay in the workforce even as they attempt to raise a family. Second, as more women enroll in colleges and universities, so too will they tend to seek the best of both these worlds. It appears that the desire for a "working marriage"—in which career, marriage, and a family all contribute to a woman's personal satisfaction—is bound to spread in the future.

Table 1

Question: Now let me ask you a somewhat different question. Considering the possibilities for combining or not combining marriage, children, and a career, and assuming you had a choice, which *one* of these possibilities do you think would offer *you* the most satisfying and interesting life? (card shown respondent)

	Women 1974	1985
Combining marriage, career, and children	52%	63%
Marrying, having children, but not having career	38	26
Having career and marrying, but not having children	4	4
Having career, but not marrying or having children	2	3
Marrying, but not having children or career	1	1
Don't know	3	2

Source: Surveys by the Roper Organization for Virginia Slims, latest that of March 1985.

Table 2

Preferences for Marriage, Children, and Career by Demographic Groups, 1985

	Combining marriage, career, and children	Marrying, having children, but not having career	Having career and marrying, but not having children	Having career, but not marrying or having children	Marrying, but not having children or career
All women	63%	26%	4%	3%	1%
White	63	26	5	3	1
Black	63	26	3	7	1
18–29 years	70	19	6	3	1
30–39 years	66	21	6	5	1
40–49 years	66	22	4	5	1
50 years and over	54	37	3	2	*
Non-high school graduate	53	37	3	4	1
High school graduate	63	28	3	3	*
College graduate	70	17	7	4	1

Note: * = less than .5%.

Source: Survey by the Roper Organization for Virginia Slims, March 1985.

Table 3

Efforts to Strengthen Women's Status

Question: Do you favor or oppose most of the efforts to strengthen and change women's status in society today?

	Women		Men	
	Favor	Oppose	Favor	Oppose
1970	40%	42%	44%	39%
1972	48	36	49	36
1974	57	25	63	19
1980	64	24	64	23
1985	73	17	69	17

Source: Surveys by the Roper Organization for Virginia Slims, latest that of March 1985.

This move of women into a traditionally male domain—the workplace—has enormous social consequences. In the first place, it is clearly linked to women's improving status in our society—and to women's increasing self-confidence as their own, ardent advocates. According to three-quarters of women and men, women's role in society will continue to change, and larger majorities today (69 percent of women, 67 percent of men) than in 1980 think those roles *should* continue to change.

What is more, overwhelming majorities favor efforts to improve the status of women, and for the first time ever, more women than men support such efforts (see Table 3). This is indeed a dramatic shift in opinion from fifteen years ago, when a slight plurality of women *opposed* efforts to improve their status. They were fearful of the unknown and were much more comfortable with the status quo. Men, not being the object of such efforts, either could afford to be more objective or were reluctant to appear too self-interested. Now, however, women have observed what has happened to many other women as a result of these efforts and have, apparently, decided that the result is good.

In step with women's changing roles, furthermore, has come greater respect for women as individuals, which helps to explain why growing majorities favor efforts to improve women's status. Today, 60 percent of women and 61 percent of men believe that women are more respected now than they were ten years ago. This, too, represents quite a change from the attitudes of 1970, when only 38 percent of women and 40 percent of men thought that women were more respected compared to ten years previously. And, once again, the young and college-educated are among the most optimistic women.

Despite such growing respect for women, however, working women have encountered difficulties in the professional world. Sexual discrimination does persist, and the consensus of both women and men is that, all things considered, there are more advantages in being a man in today's world. Yet it is heartening that majorities of working women say they stand an equal chance with men in three vital areas concerning their jobs: salary, responsibility, and promotion possibilities. The major barrier that remains, according to a plurality of these women (45 percent), is being promoted to a top management position (see Table 4).

Nevertheless, women with actual work experience think that things are generally better now than they were five years ago. But men do not agree. Men are *less* inclined today than they were in 1980 to think that women have equal chances in the workplace. Thus, those who are allegedly discriminated against believe that the situation is improving; those who are supposed to be doing the discriminating think it is getting worse. What explains this fascinating contradiction?

It would seem that men's attitudes toward this problem have been influenced, at least to some extent, by the increasing amount of information on sexual discrimination in general. That is, men have become more aware that there is a problem, and this is influencing their opinions about possible unfairness in the workplace. Men are now more sensitive, and perhaps even more defensive, about equal professional opportunities, even though the attitudes of working women suggest that real progress is being made.

Of course, it would be premature to declare that battle for equal economic

Table 4

Equal Opportunity on the Job, 1985

Question: Do you feel you stand an equal chance with the men you work with in the following areas?

	Working women say they have:			Men say working women have:		
	Equal chance	Not equal	Don't know	Equal chance	Not equal	Don't know
Salary	57%	33%	10%	48%	46%	6%
Responsibility	73	18	9	61	33	6
Promotion	53	35	12	45	49	7
Becoming an executive	38	45	17	37	54	9

Source: Survey by the Roper Organization for Virginia Slims, March 1985.

opportunity, for completely nondiscriminatory treatment at work, over. Certain issues, such as the complex and emotional one of comparable worth, are still on the public agenda. Yet, women *have* come far in seeking and obtaining meaningful jobs for themselves. They *are* moving into occupations once considered the sole preserves of men, as Sally Ride's space flight in 1983 and Geraldine Ferraro's vice presidential nomination in 1984 symbolize. There *is* a widespread feeling today that a talented and capable woman can succeed in whatever profession she chooses.

More and more, women's professional potential is obstructed not by discrimination *in* the workplace but rather by obligations *outside* it. Women may increasingly enjoy equal opportunities at work, but, compared to men, they have relatively little time to capitalize on those opportunities. The major challenges for the future—challenges created by women's very success in moving into the workplace over the past fifteen years—concern the organization of *domestic* life. The problem is to find a new balance between work and home for both women and men—and, further down the road, perhaps to alter the structure of work in order to have a fuller and more satisfying family life.

MARRIAGES OF MUTUAL RESPONSIBILITY

Marriage these days is enjoying something of a comeback, despite all the attention typically paid to the divorce rate in this country. Although fewer men and women today are married and living with their spouses than in 1980—in part, it must be said, because the baby boom generation is still in its marrying years and tends to marry later—other signs indicate that attitudes about marriages may be changing.

Nine out of ten women and men say, for instance, that marriage is their preferred lifestyle. Substantially fewer people today than in 1970 believe that marriage as an institution is weaker now than ten years ago.

The fact is that marriage and the nuclear family have always been, and will long continue to be, the core of American society. True, large majorities say that people can be happy without being married. And they also think that a happy marriage does not require children. Yet, there has been virtually no increase since 1972 in the number of Americans who have or plan to have no children, and the extremely high proportion (90 percent) saying that marriage is their preferred lifestyle has remained remarkably constant. Instead, these attitudes toward the role of marriage and children in personal happiness demonstrates Americans' growing tolerance of alternative lifestyles—of those minorities who choose to remain single or childless.

Yet by far the most significant change in Americans' views of marriage concerns the *kind* of marriage that people want. Today, majorities of men and women desire a marriage of shared responsibility—one in which both spouses work and divide housekeeping and childrearing equally. Merely a decade ago, a majority of women and a plurality of men opted for a traditional marriage, in which he was the financial provider and she ran the house and took care of the children (see Table 5).

Once again, enthusiasm for this new type of marriage is most pronounced among younger women and men, which suggests that it will increasingly become the norm. But more indicative of the challenges ahead, and the problems obstructing such shared-responsibility marriages, is that women have more eagerly embraced this concept than men.

The main reasons for this divergence in attitudes of women and men is that, while women have moved quickly into the "male" domain of the workplace, men have been much slower to help out with "female" tasks in the home. For instance, 30 percent of married women who are employed full time assert they do nearly all of the household chores, and another 44 percent claim they do a lot but their husbands help out some. Merely 24 percent say these tasks are evenly divided between the spouses. Men with working wives tend to be more charitable toward themselves—28 percent claim that the chores are evenly divided—but even so, the imbalance is evident.

Another factor that helps to explain men's relative reluctance about the shared-responsibility marriage is that they, much more than women, derive a greater sense of their personal identity from their work. For many men, their careers are the key element defining their place in society and even their concept of self-worth. Women, however, have long relied on other sources—particularly, perhaps their children—to establish their sense of identity, precisely because customarily they have spent so much time with kids in the home. One indication of this major difference between the sexes can be found in attitudes toward work. A majority of employed men (56 percent) consider their work to be a career, while a majority of employed women (58 percent) say their work is "just a job."

Yet what exactly do these figures mean? Is work just a stopgap measure or a kind of pastime for many women? This is hardly the appropriate conclusion, given that a majority of women consider work to be an essential ingredient of a full and satisfying life, that two-thirds of employed women would continue to work even if financially secure, that more employed women than employed men derive a great deal of personal satisfaction from their work, and that a majority of *all* women would choose a job instead of staying home. Instead, the proper conclusion would appear to be that women place a different *degree* of importance on their work—that, in the grand scheme of life, work may be somewhat less important than it is to many men.

Table 5

Question: In today's society, there are different lifestyles, and some that are acceptable today that weren't in the past. Regardless of what you may have done or plan to do with your life, and thinking just of what would give *you personally* the most satisfying and interesting life, which one of these different ways of life do you think would be the best as a way of life? (Card shown respondent)

	1974		1985					
	Total women	Total men	Total women	18–29 years	30–39 years	40–49 years	50 years and over	Total men
Marriage where husband and wife share responsibilities more—both work, share housekeeping and child responsibilites	46%	44%	57%	69%	65%	58%	42%	50%
Traditional marriage with husband assuming responsibility for family and wife running house and taking care of children	50	48	37	24	30	34	52	43
Living with someone of opposite sex, but not marrying	3	3	2	3	1	2	1	3
Remaining single and living alone	1	1	2	1	1	4	2	3
Remaining single and living with others of the same sex	—	—	—	—	—	—	—	1
Living in large family of people with similar interests in which some are married and some are not	1	1	1	1	1	—	1	1

Source: Surveys by the Roper Organization for Virginia Slims, latest that of March 1985.

WORKING TOWARD
A MORE BALANCED FUTURE

It may sound rather radical to suggest that the very nature of the work may change as a result of these evolving attitudes, but that may be the case—someday. If so, what will be the most obviously affected?

First, a larger number of employed women will probably consider their work to be a career rather than "just a job." Already the opinions of college-educated women on this issue are identical to the beliefs of college-educated men: more than six in ten say they are pursuing a career, not working a job. The very meaning of a career, however, could well be transformed. Career paths in most professions were established when men overwhelmingly dominated them. That is no longer the case. Some better mechanism will have to be found to accommodate these career-minded women—and their aspirations for a happy family life as well.

Second, working couples will face more difficult decisions about whose career should take priority. Right now, large majorities of women and men think a woman should quit her job if her husband is offered a very good one elsewhere; at the same time, majorities also believe that a wife should turn down a very good job offer in another city so that her husband can continue his present career. In part this can be explained by the probability that the man has a higher salary and hence is the main source of income for the family. It may simply reflect the public's acceptance of economic reality. But as the earnings of both spouses draw closer together, issues concerning career advancement will become more complex—and Americans' attitudes toward them more ambivalent.

There may also be greater pressure from such two-income families for employers to allow more flexibility in work schedules. Staggering the hours that the parents are at work or shortening the work week could help alleviate some of the problems associated with day care. Or shared jobs, half-time jobs, and other forms of part-time work may take on even greater significance in the future, allowing at least one parent to spend more time with the family.

In the same vein, the provision of day-care services by employers—and perhaps better policies on maternity and paternity leave—may eventually come to be seen as more valuable employee benefits. Employers who provide these kinds of options will be better placed to attract talented individuals from two-income households.

These general attitudes also indicate that the trend toward smaller families is firmly established and will, in all likelihood, continue. It is one thing to hold down a job while attempting to care for two children, quite another if the parents have to look after five.

And even the nature of relationships between women and men undergo some fundamental changes. Hackneyed as the cliché may be, there is power in the purse—psychological as well as economic. Among other things, men's habit of paying for things may fade, in part out of deference to the more independent status of women and in part, perhaps, out of necessity. Plus, they will undoubtedly have to help out a lot more around the home, or the couple will have to learn to tolerate a less clean, orderly environment. But offsetting this, men may get to know their children a little bit better, because they spend more time with them. In fact, children who are raised more equally by both parents may well turn out to be different in many respects from previous generations.

These are just some of the adjustments, it seems, that Americans will be making in coming years. In many respects, this will be a period of consolidation, of sorting out how best to cope with the changing responsibilities of women and men. As Walt Whitman once wrote to Ralph Waldo Emerson: "Women in these States approach the day of that organic equality with men, without which, I see, men cannot have organic equality among themselves." The poet was simply a century and a half before his time.

NO

George Gilder

WOMEN IN THE WORK FORCE

Drastic shifts in sex roles seem to be sweeping through America. From 1890 to 1985 the participation in the work force of women between the ages of twenty-five and forty-four soared from 15 to 71 percent, with the pace of change tripling after 1950. At the end of the Second World War only 10 percent of married women with children under the age of six held jobs or were seeking them. Since then mothers of preschool children have thronged the job market: by 1985 the census had classified more than half of these young mothers as participants in the work force.

Women seem to be crowding into sectors of the work force traditionally occupied by men. From 1972 to 1985 women's share of professional jobs increased from 44 to 49 percent and their share of "management" jobs nearly doubled—growing from 20 to 36 percent. The sociologist Andrew Hacker reported in *The New York Times Magazine* in 1984 that from 1960 to 1983 the percentage of lawyers who are women had risen from 2 to 15 and the percentage of jobs in banking and financial management held by women had risen from 9 to 39.

According to Hacker, a similar shift had occurred in blue-collar work. He cited as examples the fact that from 1970 to 1984 the number of female butchers in packinghouses had risen by more than a third and that by 1984 nearly 80 percent of new bartending jobs were going to women. Moreover, Hacker pointed out, the number of male flight attendants rose by 10,000 during the 1970s. In a poll conducted in 1983 by *The New York Times*, 21 percent of married men declared that they would prefer to stay home and care for the children if they could.

The future apparently promises yet more blurring of traditional sex roles in the work force. Half of all 1985 college graduates were women, and women are earning a steadily rising share of all advanced degrees, including close to one third of all degrees in law, business, accounting, and computer and information sciences.

Every year seems to bring new evidence of radical change in the masculine and feminine roles around which most Americans have oriented their lives and expectations. Yet this "revolution"—for all its numerical weight and anecdotal pervasiveness —is largely a statistical illusion.

Many of the statistics that have been cited in the stories of sexual revolution are reflections instead of the Industrial Revolution. The entrance of women into the work force has accompanied, at a slower pace, their departure from farms. As recently as eighty years ago 36 percent of American families were engaged in agriculture; today fewer than three percent are. This shift is truly a revolution, and it has transformed the official labor statistics for women. Although these statistics show women entering the work force in record numbers, the fact is that women have always worked. Their labor on farms, however—in an array of arduous jobs beyond the hearth and cribside—was never monitored by statisticians.

Some 80 percent of single (that is, never married) women between the ages of twenty-five and forty-four now work for pay, and this percentage has not changed significantly since 1950. (The rest presumably include welfare recipients and women of independent means.) Although work-force participation by married women in this age group has increased dramatically—from 26 percent in 1950 to some 67 percent in the mid-1980s—the vast majority of married women, like their grandmothers on the farm, seek part-time or seasonal work convenient to their homes.

As of 1984—the most recent year for which detailed figures are available—only 37 percent of all women between the ages of twenty and sixty-four and 41 percent of all women between the ages of twenty-five and forty-four held full-time year-round jobs (including teaching jobs). Also as of 1984 only 29 percent of married women held full-time year-round jobs. That same year married women contributed an average of only 18.6 percent of the total incomes of their families. From 1960 to 1980 the incomes of working wives actually fell in relation to the incomes of working husbands: from 40 percent to 38 percent.

Statistics such as these are generally interpreted as evidence of tenacious discrimination against women. Such discrimination unquestionably exists, but one can argue that it is only a small part of what the statistics reflect.

It is possible that the data also reflect choices that women themselves are making. A study conducted in the mid-1970s by the Institute for Research on Poverty at the University of Wisconsin, with the assistance of the U.S. Department of Health, Education, and Welfare, lends support to the hypothesis that the job priorities of married women are not the same as those of married men. The study uncovered a sharp difference between wives and husbands in the extent to which they exploit what the researchers termed their "earnings capacity," or potential, as defined by a complex formula that includes such variables as age, location, education, experience, training, and physical health. For women the researchers considered one other variable: discrimination. Because the researchers allowed for discrimination in their calculation of the extent to which women exploit their earnings capacity, discrimination alone cannot explain the differences they found.

The study showed that single men and single women are about equally successful in the extent to which they exploit their earnings capacity (68 percent for single men, 64 percent for single women). However, whereas married men of working age exploit 87 percent of their earnings capacity, married women exploit only 33 percent. Thus, according to the study, married men are more than twice as successful in realizing their financial potential as married women are.

More significant still is the difference that the institute found between the most highly educated married women and men. The women with the best credentials and qualifications—the top 10 percent in earnings capacity—exploited on quarter as much of their financial potential as did similarly qualified men. In direct contrast with the pattern exhibited by married men, the more earnings capacity commanded by married women the less they used it—that is, the less likely they were to work full-time all year at a demanding and highly remunerative job. The inadequacies of day care cannot account for this discrepancy; these women presumably have a potential income high enough to cover an array of options in child care.

The institute based its study on data from the early 1970s, but more recent data are compatible with its findings. The gap in earnings between married men and women still widens dramatically as age and schooling increase. As of 1983 married women with a graduate education earned 11 percent less than married men with a high school education. However, single women who work full-time year-round have long earned about as much as their single male peers. Therefore, the pattern of low earnings by highly qualified wives seems a reflection more of personal choice than of discrimination against women.

A Louis Harris poll conducted in 1980 revealed basic differences between the sexes in attitudes toward work. Unlike the working men surveyed, who overwhelmingly preferred full-time jobs, working women expressed a preference for part-time over full-time work by a 41 to 17 percent margin. The women with the highest earnings capacity—managerial, professional, and executive women—preferred part-time work by a 51 to 19 percent margin.

Large numbers of women are using entrepreneurial activity to satisfy their apparent preference for work in the home. From knitting mittens to selling real estate and writing software packages for personal computers, more and more women are working for themselves, launching small businesses in their homes. From 1972 to 1982 the percentage of self-employed workers in nonagricultural industries who are women rose from 26 to 32. For the past two years women have actually formed sole proprietorships at a faster rate than men.

The more education and the better credentials women have, the more freedom they have to choose the extent to which they will work outside their homes. Female physicians, for example, see 38 percent fewer patients per hour and work fewer hours than male physicians; female professors write fewer books and research papers than male professors.

A study in 1979 by the Brookings Institution showed that women in the prime earning years were eleven times more likely to leave the work force voluntarily—if often temporarily—than men were. Current data from the Bureau of Labor Statistics indicate that women work only 70 percent as long for a given employer as men do. According to a study of census data done for the Civil Rights Commission by Solomon Polachek in 1984, the differences in the number of years of continuous service in the work force—and resulting differences in training and experience—explain "close to 100 percent of the wage gap" between men and women in the job market.

Although polls show an increasing desire for jobs on the part of women, in a 1985 Roper survey only 10 percent of women declared that a husband should turn down a very good job in another city "so the wife can continue her job." This percentage has not increased since 1980 and offers a reason, beyond maternity, why women leave their jobs so often: they still rate their own employment as less important than their husband's.

The most recent data on occupational trends, released by the Bureau of Labor Statistics for 1985, show little sign that sex roles in the work force are disappearing. The percentage of women in such blue-collar jobs as plumbing, electrical work, and carpentry has scarcely changed. Federal contractors and private firms, including Sears, Roebuck and Co., that have attempted to hire women for jobs traditionally held by men have consistently failed to meet their own goals, for lack of applicants.

Regardless of the evidence of polls and of labor-force-participation rates that include part-time workers, women do not seem to be behaving like men in the labor market. While the government is pressuring private firms to employ and promote more women, the government itself fails to show employment patterns much different from those in the private sector. Even in November of 1980—the final year of a Democratic Administration that made equal rights for women a prime goal—only seven percent of the employees in the top five GS ratings were women, while more than three quarters in the bottom grades were.

In fact, the pattern of employment in the federal government would suffice to justify an anti-discrimination suit if the government were a private institution. Yet the government may not be discriminating against women, and private companies may not be either. Let us at least consider the possibility that many women, deliberately rejecting the values of male careerists, are discriminating against the job "rat race" and in favor of their families.

POSTSCRIPT

Can Women Combine Careers and Families?

Gilder is not at all impressed by the types of statistics that are presented by Wilkins and Miller. "Every year seems to bring new evidence of radical change in the masculine and feminine roles around which most Americans have oriented their lives and expectations. Yet this 'revolution'—for all its numerical weight and anecdotal pervasiveness—is largely a statistical illusion." Single women have always worked and "the vast majority of married women, like their grandmothers on the farms, seek part-time or seasonal work convenient to their homes." So where is the revolution? Furthermore, according to his reading of the evidence most mothers are not trying to combine career with family but rather are trying to find part-time work to fit around their family life.

Gilder's analysis suggests that women's lives could be significantly improved if much more part-time work were available in all lines of work. Wilkins and Miller's analysis suggests that working mothers are more interested in institutional supports (i.e., job protection, leave policies, quality child care centers, preschools, flexible work schedules, and flexible career ladders than) in shorter hours at work.

Much of the literature on career and family are articles in magazines, but two key books are Sylvia Ann Hewlett's *A Lesser Life: The Myth of Women's Liberation in America* (Morrow, 1986) and Barbara Berg's *The Crisis of the Working Mother* (Summit, 1986). See also Berg's article, "The Guilt that Drives Working Mothers Crazy" (*Ms.*, May 1987; Kathleen Gerson's "Briefcase, Baby or Both?" (*Psychology Today*, November 1986); Karl Zinsmeister's "Family's Tie to the American Dream" (*Public Opinion*, September/October 1986); and Cheryl Russell's "The New Homemakers" (*American Demographics*, October 1985). For germane time-use studies see F. Thomas Juster et al.,

Time, Goods, and Well-Being (University of Michigan Press, 1985) and William Michelson, *From Sun to Sun—Daily Obligations and Community Structure in the Lives of Employed Women and Their Families* (Rowman and Allanheld, 1985). Two books in addition to Hewlett's that are trying to redirect the women's movement to focus more on family-related issues are Betty Friedan's *The Second Stage* (Summit, 1981) and Ruth Sidel's *Women and Children Last* (Viking, 1986). Three articles address these issues in response to Hewlett's book: "What Now?" by Dorothy Wickenden (*The New Republic,* May 5, 1986); "Family Ties: Feminism's Next Frontier" by Joan Walsh (*The Progressive,* September 1986); and "Feminism, Stage Three" by Michael Levin (*Commentary,* August 1986). For an important study of the problems of women in the corporate world see Liz Roman Gallese's *Women Like Us* (Morrow, 1985).

ISSUE 7
The "New Woman":
Has She Confused Sex Roles?

YES: Donald Singletary, from "You New Women Want It Both Ways!" *Essence* (July 1985)

NO: Betty Winston Baye, from "You Men Want it All!" *Essence* (July 1985)

ISSUE SUMMARY

YES: Donald Singletary accuses modern young women of wanting all the advantages of being liberated women but also wanting many of the advantages of being traditional women.
NO: Betty Winston Baye makes the same argument about men. They want educated, independent, money-earning women, but their egos cannot handle a true equal. And they really want to continue the traditional unequal division of labor in the household.

In 1970 Alvin Toffler wrote *Future Shock* (Random House) "to describe what happens to people when they are overwhelmed by change." He argued that the increased pace of life, the break from past traditions, the throw-away habit, the frequent change of residence, the pursuit of novelty, and the accelerated technical changes disturbed people, so much so that most suffered from "future shock." He emphasized technological changes and their impacts on psychological security and mental health.

Toffler's emphasis on the disrupting impacts of technological change may have been overstated. When we compare our lives with our parents we find that we drive in cars that behave very much like our parents' cars; we live in houses similar to theirs; we have furniture that in some cases may be even older than theirs, we eat foods that are not much different from theirs; do work that may not be essentially different from theirs! The landing on the moon, CDs, and other technological breakthroughs may change our lives, but it is hard to see how they "shock" us.

Yet the spirit of Toffler's book—or at least its title—is not irrelevant to our times, for we do live in an age of sociological shock. Traditional ways of living, traditional expectations and mores, and traditional roles are being challenged. The biggest differences between our lives and our parents' lives are in the roles that men and women play in our society.

Major changes in social roles do not occur smoothly. They are confusing; they raise lots of questions. How should the sexes behave toward one another? Is "chivalry" possible without condescension? Are there indeed certain "men's jobs"? Should women be "feminine"? What does "feminine" mean? Is there some legitimate meaning of "separate but equal" for the sexes? Modern industrial society has never been quite certain about the answers to these questions, though there have been short-term answers provided from time to time. The brief span of time between the end of World War II and the early 1960s was one such period. Caricaturists may picture it as a time of Doris Day movies and crinolines, but during those years there was an attempt to reassert a more traditional relationship between the sexes after the disruption caused by the war years. This was the "baby boom" era, and a woman's role as mother and homemaker was emphasized. Men were seen as breadwinners and protectors. It was fine for certain women to be "sexy," but their sexiness contained elements of passivity and submissiveness. Women were assumed to be incompetent at typically "male" roles, such as driving motor vehicles or firing guns. Politically, women could vote and were expected to do so, though it was assumed (correctly, according to the polls later conducted) that their political views were strongly influenced by the men in their lives. Memories of earlier feminist movements had largely faded, or else the movements were seen as having been wholly successful in their objectives and thus of no particular relevance to the present.

By the end of the 1960s, this consensus had been shattered. The publication of Betty Friedan's *The Feminine Mystique* in 1963 helped start a movement that certainly questioned and to some extent changed traditional sex roles. By the end of the 1970s, women were upper classmen at West Point and were working as telephone linemen and corporate presidents. Women reporters were interviewing athletes in men's locker rooms, and girls were playing Little League baseball. Affirmative action guidelines set minimum hiring quotas for women in many occupations, and three successive presidents and their wives endorsed a proposed Equal Rights Amendment to the Constitution that would make gender an irrelevant distinction under the law.

By the end of the 1970s, however, the march toward equality changed course. First, an anti-feminist backlash erupted and helped defeat the ERA. Second, Betty Friedan wrote another book in 1981 that acknowledged the desire of many women for children and nurturing. She admitted that some differences between sex roles should perhaps be retained. Third, many career women were remaining single or becoming divorced. They claimed that few men could handle intimate relationships with self-actualizing women and that most men still felt more comfortable with dependent women.

The sex role revolution has succeeded in tearing down traditional sex role norms but has not yet succeeded in establishing a new set of sex role norms. The unresolved conflict between the old and the new is as yet unresolved, as is illustrated by the following debate between Betty Winston Baye and Donald Singletary.

YES

Donald Singletary

YOU NEW WOMEN WANT IT ALL!

1A: Why is it always sex, sex, sex? Can't a man talk to me as a professional?

1B: All men want to do is talk business; there's no romance.

2A: These guys are together all day at work; now they come in the club and they're still over there in a group talking to each other.

2B: Damn, I can't even come in here to have a quiet drink with my girlfriend without men coming around to hit on us.

3A: I feel that as a woman today I can have just as much freedom as a man. That means a casual affair is okay.

3B: I don't understand men. They want to jump into bed as fast as they can. They don't want any commitment.

In each of the above, statements A and B were made by the same woman at different times. In the second example they were made in the same evening.

Imagine eating in an expensive restaurant. You pick up the shaker and it reads: "salt or sugar." Or picture the announcer's voice at the beginning of a boxing match: "In this corner we have the liberated woman. And in the same corner we have the woman who wants to be 'kept.' " Let's place the man in the role of referee: How does he judge this fight? Yes, it is confusing, isn't it? Not to mention annoying. It is very annoying. What we have there are examples of mixed messages, conflicting signals. And to put it bluntly, it is the women who are sending the confusing signals and the men who are getting confused. Not to mention angry.

In the last few years—since women began their quest for greater personal independence, better jobs and pay comparable to men's and the right to make decisions about what they do with their bodies—men have struggled to understand this "new woman." The signals that we are getting are that women want to take charge of their own destinies. They want to compete alongside men for the fruits of success in society. They no longer wish to rely on men for the things that they want out of life. Instead they have opted to get it themselves. Although these changes do in fact create some anxiety among men, many feel that they will ultimately free men from some of the traditional male responsibilities society has imposed upon them. Ideally, this should mean men no longer have to carry the full burden of financial support, decision making and being the aggressor in romantic pursuits. Right?

Wrong! That's one message women send. But there is another message that says, "I'll have my cake and eat yours too."

A perplexed former coworker of mine once said, "You would hope that a woman making, say, $35,000 a year could go out with whoever she wants—even the guy in the mail room. But no, she wants somebody who makes $45,000 a year! Why? Because she's still looking to be taken care of."

For this man and for many others, the assumption is that once a woman has the necessary financial security, the need to form relationships on the basis of what a man earns is gone.

Not so.

It's what some of us call the "my money, our money" syndrome. Here's a typical example: A man and woman meet through a mutual friend. Both single, they begin chatting about themselves. They are both professionals, make approximately the same money, and each has attended a good college.

SHE: You're very nice to talk to. It's so refreshing. A lot of men these days can't deal with an independent woman. They seem to always want the upper hand, and if you are making the same bread, they become insecure. I think they still expect women to be impressed with what they do.

HE: That's true. I even see it in some of my own friends. But I like a professional woman, not one who's dependent on a man.

SHE: That's me. Hey, why don't we have dinner sometime? I know a great little place.

They go out to dinner at an expensive restaurant that she choses. At last, he thinks, a woman who doesn't wait for the man to take the initiative, an independent woman! Wow, I never thought I'd be taken any place like this by a woman.

The check comes, and she waits patiently for him to pick it up. Thank goodness our hero has his American Express card up to date. I know guys who've had to excuse themselves from the table and dash out into the streets in search of a bank cash machine. In fact, I've been one of those guys. It's tough. You have to run out in the bitter cold (it's *always* cold) without your coat because you don't want the waiter to think you've left without paying. As one of my cronies put it, "Women want it all today, from soup to nuts—and the man has to pay for the meal."

No one is suggesting, least of all me, that women *have* to pay or date "dutch." But when one professes her liberation, as did this woman, the man has the right to expect her to follow through. The emerging new woman has not only created confusion for men; she has created some problems for women as well. At least one of them, as you might expect, is a paradoxical one. Now that women have more money and more mobility, there don't seem to be any men around. Not *any* men, mind you, but those with the "right stuff." In conversations between women and men, women and women, coast to coast, the question "Where are all the men?" always rears its head.

I defy you to find one man, one *real* man, who actually believes there is a shortage of men. Yes, I know what the statistics say. But what I and other men see is quite different. We see women who walk around as if they couldn't care less about a man. Women don't have time.

One of my own former girlfriends once told me that she was having a difficult time deciding on what to do with her new status. She had recently passed the New York bar and had gotten a new job. "I don't know what I should be: a socialite, a hard-boiled attorney, or sort of work out a blend of my professional and social life," she mused. Curiously, none of the choices included me, so I asked, "Where do I fit in?" She stared blankly for a moment, as if she'd come home and discovered she'd forgotten to buy catsup. Then she said, "You know, Donald, sometimes I think you really have a place in my life, and sometimes I think if you walked out the door and never came back, it wouldn't faze me at all."

I had to ask.

Had it not been about nine below zero (it's *always* cold) that February night, I would have left right then. (I have since garnered lots more pride.)

Women sit at tables in fours and fives wondering where all the men are, while the men sit a few feet away at the bar. The women almost never initiate anything. Believe me, if there were only ten eligible women in New York, I'd have two of them. If I didn't, it wouldn't be because I didn't try.

It is baffling to men why women are not more aggressive. One has to assume that they are simply not interested. Here are some examples of what "eligible" men are saying.

Women don't have time for you these days. I swear, making a date is like making a business appointment. Everybody's got calendars and datebooks.

While women are in their twenties, they party like crazy and tell you not to pressure them into relationships. Then all of a sudden they hit 30 and uh-oh! Everybody races the clock to get married and make that baby.

What are we, sperm factories? I'm supposed to get married so you can have cut crystal?

It's quality I'm looking for, not quantity. I don't care how many women there are out there, it's quality I want. By the time you weed out the workaholics, the ones so bitter about their past lovers that they hate every man, the ones that want you only for your money/prestige, the druggies (yes, women do that too) and star seekers (noncelebrities need not apply) and ones who want fathers for their children, the margin really narrows.

I'll believe women are liberated when one walks up to me, says, 'Hey, good-lookin', ' buys me dinner, pats me on the cakes and suggests we go to her place for a nightcap.

It's ironic. Women are always telling me that men are intimidated by independent, assertive women. Where are they? On a recent *Donahue* show dedicated to single men, one man posed this question: "How many women out there would drive two hours to pick me up, take me out and spend $100, bring me back home and leave?" Yes, I'm certain some have done it. Just as I know there are some readers who have figured out the number of angels on the head of a pin. However, although the number of miles and dollar amount might seem exaggerated, the routine is one that is typical and expected of men.

I remember once being headed out the door at about 9:30 on a Saturday night when the phone rang. It was a woman I dated once in a while, and she invited me out that night. Already headed elsewhere, I respectfully declined. "Well, excuse me," she said, obviously miffed. "I guess I have to book ahead."

I remember that I really had something to do that night, I think it was open-heart surgery or something, so I explained that to her. She wouldn't have cared if it really had been open-heart surgery; she felt rejected, humiliated.

I hate to tell you this, but whenever you ask someone out, there is a possibility they will say no. Men know it, they live with it. I'll never like it, but I have gotten used to it.

Oh, you thought we had it easy, huh? Women, I honestly think, believe it is easy for men to approach them. If that were true, I would be dating Jayne Kennedy *and* Diahann Carroll. Talking to a woman for the first time, especially without an introduction, is always a crap shoot. For me, it is worse. It is tantamount to walking down a dark alley knowing a psychopath with a big baseball bat and little mercy is in there. Approaching someone means you have to bare yourself and lay some of your cards on the table. That's not easy—particularly with the "new woman" who waltzes into a room like it's the set of *Dynasty*. Thumbs up if she likes you; to the lions if not.

I'm certain that it's easier for many men. And I'm equally certain that I've fooled lots of women with my cool, sophisticated facade. It comes with years of practice and experience.

What men are seeing and hearing from women, either directly or indirectly, is that there is a very bad problem with self-image. I'm not quite sure why. It seems contradictory. There are more women than ever before who are well educated, have lucrative careers and are well dressed and good-looking.

Therein may lie the problem. Women are insecure not only about the shortage of men but also about the increasing number of what they see as competition—other women.

I've said it myself. A woman walks into the room and I'm introduced to her and I think, *Okay, you went to a good school, you've got a good job and you look good. So what? So do most of the women in this room. In fact, so do most of the ones I meet.*

Increasingly, there is nothing exceptional about being young, gifted and cute. It has, in many circles, become a given. Male friends of mine often say, "Why do women place so much emphasis on what they do professionally?" That automatically sets up a false criterion that men fall prey to. It creates a value system that emphasizes material things. Women, of course, are not solely responsible for that. Throughout history men have shown off their uniforms, three-piece suits and jobs since shepherding paid top dollar. However, at the same time, our criteria for women were based largely on hair, ankles, calves—you get the picture.

Nowadays we find ourselves asking more questions about education, career goals and so on. These are valid questions for anyone to ask, mind you, but they are not by any means the sole criterion for what makes a good human being, let alone a good relationship. It does, on the other hand, keep the mind beyond the ankles, which is a step in the right direction.

Years ago men chose women who could cook, take care of a house and raise children. Women chose men who would make good providers. Today more and more men do their own cooking and cleaning, are becoming closer to their children. Women, on the other hand, are becoming more self-supporting. This sounds to me like a marvelous opportunity for people to find some other reasons for relationships and shed some old ones. However, that does not seem to be happening.

It becomes extremely difficult to decipher the signals. One says, "I want a man who's sensitive, caring, spiritual and warm." The other says, "I have this list of things that I feel I should have. I want a man who can help me achieve them and move up in society."

There is a curious other side to the pursuit of Mr. Right Stuff. When women settle for less, it is *far* less. I'm talkin' triflin' here. But for some reason, Brother Rat seems to capture their attention. The story has become a tired soap opera.

I knew a woman, a professional, good school, good job, condo, the whole ball of wax. She could never find a guy good enough. She always broke off the relationships, saying that the men would feel bad because she made more money; their fragile egos would be crushed. She went out with a good guy. A professional, a nice person. They were to be married. At the last minute she shifted gears and decided she wanted more time as a career woman. She left him. She spent her days bemoaning the fact that she had nobody. Then she met a rogue. Not the charming, sophisticated, Billy Dee Williams type, but a sleazy, coke-dealing, never-had-an-honest-job type. She let him move into her apartment; he spent her money and left her in debt and with a great loss of self-esteem. Yet at a given opportunity, whenever he came through town, she would take him in for a few days and, yes, lend him money.

Figure it out.

I have spent nearly all my adult life in the communications business as a writer, journalist and media specialist, and ten years in corporate public relations. None of these things, however, prepared me for the biggest communications gap of all—that between men and women.

It happened so suddenly. Things hadn't changed very much for decades. Then came the middle sixties, while the Black movement was in full fury, and eventually people began questioning, challenging, their sexual roles. Age-old ideas about love, marriage, sex, family and children began to change for women—and for men as well.

When women were fragile little princesses (they never really were, but they played the part), it was a lot more palatable for men to play the role of Prince Charming. There is, at least among college-educated, professional women, little impetus for a man to feel he has to sweep you off your feet as you stand together, pinstripe to pinstripe, Gucci to Gucci, M.B.A. to M.B.A. But there you stand, waiting for him to open the door and take you to dinner. During the day he holds the door at work and she's furious. At night she stands in place until he opens it.

What's a guy to do?

How does one approach the new woman? Should he be forward? More aggressive and to the point? Or should he be more subtle? Should he try to appeal to her intellect through conversation? Or should he be more romantic? Can he assume she is more sexually liberated or that she is seeking only a "meaningful relationship?" How do you separate platonic friendships from romantic inclinations? Who pays the bill? Does the fact that she's "career oriented" mean that she doesn't want or have time for a relationship?

Women are facing a backlash from men that will rival the white backlash of the seventies and eighties. And, like the white liberals in the sixties, the disenchanted men are the "nice guys"—the guys who feel they have been gentlemanly, supportive, considerate. All of a sudden the message they are getting is one of distrust, as they're portrayed as abusers, ne'er-do-wells, drug abusers and cheats. And after struggling to survive the street, college and/or military service and the day-to-day strife of the work world, they are being sent messages that say women's struggles make theirs pale by comparison. Not only that—they are the ones responsible for it!

Liberation. Independence. They're words that imply hard-won, newfound freedom. Freedom from the shackles of the past. That should include the freedom to look at relationships in a new light. Taking one or two bad experiences into each relationship thereafter is not being liberated. It is being shackled, weighed down, by your past. Understanding that the changes that took place for women also changed the perspective of many men is important. It means that realignments in relationships are necessary.

I once had the experience of working with a group of five women. All of them had previously worked together and had been friends for some time. Their businesslike demeanor made me want to straighten my tie, let alone my files and desk. We would have group meetings prior to every division meeting. They would stress how we would go in as a group, pose a common front. But once inside the meeting, something interesting happened. They broke ranks, and each tried to impress the boss. How? By fluttering eyelashes, flashing toothy smiles and laughing at all his dumb jokes.

It caused one of my male coworkers to remark, "You know who the new woman is? She's the old woman, only she can't cook"—a sexist response evoked by a group of women who lapsed into a stereotypical role.

As bleak as some of this may seem, things are actually getting better. Change did move in very swiftly, and we are all, men and women alike, getting used to it. Certainly most of us over 30 grew up in an America where girls played nurse and boys played soldier. So it will take a while. But regardless of the changes, and the time it takes, there will always be a misread signal somewhere.

And it will *always* be on a cold night.

NO

Betty Winston Baye

MEN WANT IT BOTH WAYS!

I thought the 1980's would be different, especially after the revolutionary sixties, when it was common to hear some Black men hollering about how Black women should walk ten paces behind their "kings" and have babies for the revolution. I thought that in the eighties, Black men and women had declared a truce in the war between the sexes and we had reached, or were striving to reach, a level where we could enjoy each other's company as equals.

I know now, however, that I hoped for much too much. Though I don't presume to paint all Black men with one broad brush stroke, it seems to me that there are men—too many—who, for reasons that only they and God understand, find it necessary to lie and pretend that they just love independent women. That's what they say at first, but as their relationships develop, it becomes painfully obvious that what they really want are women who work to help bring home the bacon but also cook, clean and take care of them and their babies on demand. These new men want women who are articulate and forceful when they're taking care of business but who, behind closed doors, become simpering sycophants who heed their every wish.

I am an independent woman, and I'll tell anybody that what my mother and many of the women of her generation did to keep home and family together I won't do, not for love or money! Whenever I meet a man who says he's interested in me, I tell him up front that I don't do no windows. I don't love housework. I don't love to cook, and I certainly don't reach climax thinking about having to clean up behind a bunch of kids and some mother's son. If a man wants somebody to make him home bread and fresh collard greens every night, then I'm definitely not the girl of his dreams.

Now, I realize that I'm not every man's cup of tea. But take it or leave it, that's where I'm coming from. I'll gladly work every day to help bring home the money so that my man and I can pool our resources to go out to dinner every once in a while, take a few trips during the year and to pay somebody willing (or needing) to cook, clean and do laundry.

Surprisingly, my attitudes don't turn too many men off—in fact, brothers seem turned on by my honesty and independence. My ex-husband is one case in point. At the dawn of our relationship, he swore to me I was just what the doctor had ordered. Said he'd never met a woman like me—intelligent, witty, educated, self-sufficient and not all that hard on the eyes. He went on about how he was just so thrilled that I had "chosen" him.

At first, everything was wonderful. But soon after I acquired a sweet contract to write my first book, the shit was on. It occurred to me that my beloved husband was just a bit jealous of my success. Before I knew it, I realized that he got some kind of perverse pleasure out of trying to insult me and make me look small in the eyes of my friends and professional colleagues. I remember how one time, for no special reason, he got up and announced in front of my childhood friend, her husband and their children that I was "a stupid bitch." Now, he had already published a novel, and to me he was a fine writer who could handle the English language as smoothly as butter sliding down a hot roll. But my book, and the money I got, just seemed to set him off. Not surprisingly, the marriage was finished before the book hit the shelves.

Had what happened in my marriage been an isolated case, I might have concluded that it was just "my problem"— something we women tend to do a lot. But it wasn't isolated. All around me, women friends of mine were and still are bailing out of relationships with men who say one thing, then do another.

A friend of mine got married a few years ago to a man she'd been dating for more than a year. This was a marriage made in heaven, or so she thought. Both she and her husband were talented go-getters who seemed to want the same things out of life. When they first met, she says, he told her he didn't dig her just for her body but also for her sharp mind. Before long, however, it became clear that the only thing he wanted to do with her mind was to cause her to lose it. She says he wanted her to be dynamic by day and servile by night. Finally, after much verbal and physical abuse, she split. Thankfully, her memorable excur-sion into his insanity didn't last for long. Now she's recovering quite nicely.

Strong, dynamic, intelligent, independent women are what men of the eighties say they want. They claim they want their women to go that extra mile, but what they really mean is that we should work twice as hard but not forget our responsibilities at home. When a woman spends time with *their* children, cleans the house or cooks for *their* family, it often goes unnoticed. No matter how tired she is after a demanding day at work, the expectation is that these are *her* responsibilities. But when a man spends time with *their* children, cooks food for *their* family or cleans *their* house once a month, he acts like he deserves an Academy Award.

Money is another area that has the brothers confused. For example, there are the men who say that if we women want to be truly liberated we should be willing, on occasion, to pick up the tab for dinner or for a night on the town. The fact that many of these same men often get their jaws wired when women, in the presence of a waiter or others at the table, reach for their wallet and pull out the cash or credit card says they're not ready for liberation. They don't mind women paying but would much prefer that they slip them the money under the table, the way women used to do.

And there are also the double-talking men who claim they can handle a wo-man who makes more money than they do. At first, everything is all right, but in order to assuage their egos, some men start thinking that "just because" they are men, they must exert control over their women's money and become personal financial managers of sorts. She's smart enough to make the money, he knows, but he believes she doesn't have enough sense to know how to spend it, invest it or manage it. "Are you sure you can afford this?" is a common question, but one rarely asked out of concern for a woman's finances. He knows she can afford it; he'd prefer to think she can't.

Many of the same men rattle on about how if we women want equality, we should buy gifts for them, as they allegedly have always done for us. Gift giving is nice, but for women, it can be a double-edged sword. One well-known singer tells the story of how she bought gifts for her man, which he gratefully accepted. But she says that after a time, the man got nasty and told her that he couldn't be bought—he wasn't for sale.

And, of course, there are the men who seem to think that success drops out of the sky—that it doesn't require hard work and long hours. I've seen men hotly pursue women whom they know are busy and then get bent out of shape if the sister pulls out her datebook to see when she's free. These women say they are tired of feeling guilty and trying to explain to some yo-yo that they can't just saunter off to dinner on the spur of the moment when they've got a report to finish or a meeting to attend.

Brothers are all for liberation when it works to their advantage. Yet, what we have found out is that when men don't want a serious commitment, they encourage us to be independent—to be open-minded enough to accept the terms of an "open relationship." But try that same rap on them, and we're in for trouble. Try saying, "Okay, baby, I don't want a commitment either"; or better yet, beat them to the punch. All of a sudden they've decided that they're in love and want to settle down. They get jealous and accuse us of "using" them.

And what about men who claim they want total honesty with their women? For many men, total honesty means that they want the freedom to talk openly about their prior involvements, including relating to their women intimate details about how many other women they've slept with or how many have aborted their babies. In return, a man like this often demands that his woman tell all her business to keep things in balance. Unfortunately, what many sisters have found—often after they are laid out on a stretcher or when they've had their past sexual exploits thrown in their faces in the heat of an argument—is that many men can't handle total honesty, especially if it's sexual honesty. Many men still seem to buy into the Madonna/whore syndrome. They still believe that their peccadillos are understandable because everyone knows that "boys will be boys." Women, however, especially *their* women, are supposed to be innocents who somehow, perhaps through osmosis, instinctively know how to turn them on in bed.

There are dozens of other ways that men send out mixed signals to the women in their lives and show, through their words and deeds, that they really want it both ways. They want us to drive the car—but from the backseat. Mostly what they want is for things to be the way they used to be. That, however, is a pipe dream. Black women, like their counterparts of other races, are liberating their minds and their bodies from the shackles of the past. Increasingly, women are refusing to waste their lives trying to decode men's mixed messages and buying into some man's macho fantasies. Instead, many women who are or want to be high achievers are accepting the fact that the price of success may be temporary loneliness. And even that loneliness is relative, since many of us have learned that having a man isn't all there is to life.

POSTSCRIPT

The "New Woman": Has She Confused Sex Roles?

If both Singletary and Baye have valid complaints, the sex roles are very confused, and confused sex roles mean a lot of pain. Anger and resentment build up on both sides, as illustrated in both essays. Male-female relationships get conducted on a minefield. Misunderstanding, broken relationships, and loneliness are the lot of many men and women as they date and consider marriage. Amanda Spake writes about these issues when she describes herself and many of her friends: "Our lives reflect what has, in my view, become the hallmark of relations between the sexes these days—a crushing ambivalence. It is an ambivalence about sex and intimacy with one another, ambivalence about whether or not the trade-offs now required of *both* men and women in relationships are, after all, worth the price and pain they extract" ("The Choices that Brought Me Here," *Ms.*, November 1984).

The other side of the issue is the question of what men expect of women. The literature is much quieter on this question. Pete Hamill freely offers his opinion based on journalistic interviews and personal observation in "Great Expectations" (*Ms.*, September 1986). The perfect wife for many men, according to Hamill, is well-educated, beautiful, great in bed, faithful, and "heroically juggling career, husband, children, and self-respect in the forging of the happy fulfilling life." She can be liberated and successful in her career as long as she also fulfills her husband's emotional needs. If Hamill is right, men do not want women to change sex roles too drastically. How far has the sex role revolution brought men?

For a broad discussion of sex roles see Marie Richmond-Abbot's *Masculine and Feminine: Sex Roles Over the Life Cycle* (Addison-Wesley, 1983); Laurel Waburn Richardson's *The Dynamics of Sex and Gender* (Houghton Mifflin, 1981); and Carol Tavris and Carol Wade's *The Longest War: Sex Differences in Perspective*, Second Edition (HBJ, 1984). For a focus on women's perspectives and sex roles see Margaret L. Anderson, *Thinking About Women* (Macmillan, 1983). For a focus on men's sex roles see Clyde W. Franklin, *The Changing Definition of Masculinity* (Plenum, 1984); James N. Doyle, *The Male Experience* (William M. Brown, 1983); Deborah David and Robert Brannon, eds., *The Forty-Nine Percent Majority: The Male Sex Role* (Addison-Wesley, 1976); and Warren Farrell, *Why Men Are the Way They Are* (McGraw Hill, 1986).

UAW/Bob Gummpert

PART 4

Stratification and Inequality

Our society has long maintained that there is equal opportunity for success for anyone willing to work hard to achieve it. That contention has been challenged by those who are out of the mainstream of society and see no room for themselves at "the top." Is our society knowingly divided into layers? Is there room at the upper levels to accommodate those who are willing and ready to work? Is every member of the society considered equal? These are among the most significant questions examined by sociologists.

Is Economic Inequality Beneficial to Society?

Is Racial Oppression Declining in America?

Is Affirmative Action Reverse Discrimination?

ISSUE 8

Is Economic Inequality Beneficial To Society?

YES: George Gilder, from *Wealth and Poverty* (Basic Books, 1981)

NO: William Ryan, from *Equality* (Pantheon Books, 1981)

ISSUE SUMMARY

YES: Sociologist George Gilder praises the American political economy that provides so many incentives for people to get ahead and make money. He maintains that the economy is dynamic and all classes benefit.

NO: Psychologist William Ryan contends that income inequalities in America are excessive and immoral because they vastly exceed differences of merit and result in tremendous hardships for the poor.

No one thinks that the President of the United States should be paid the same salary as a professor of sociology or a teaching assistant. Everyone benefits when the financial rewards for being president are large enough to motivate the most capable members of society to compete for the job. A society is better off with income inequality than with income equality as long as everyone has an equal opportunity to compete for the high paying jobs. Pay differentials are needed to get the best possible fit between people and jobs. But how much income inequality is desirable? On this issue, people strongly disagree, and they carry their disagreement into the political arena.

Income inequality, however, should be viewed as only one type of inequality. Four other essential dimensions of equality/inequality are the degree of equality of opportunity, legal rights, political power, and social status. The American creed is fully committed to equality of opportunity and equality of legal and political rights. We believe everyone should have an equal opportunity to compete for jobs and awards. Laws forbidding discrimination and free public school education are the major means for providing equal opportunities to U.S. citizens. Whether society should also compensate for handicaps such as disadvantaged family backgrounds or the ravages of past discrimination, however, is a knotty issue, which has divided the country. Policies such as Head Start, income-based scholarships, quotas, and Affirmative Action are hotly debated. Equality of legal rights has been promoted by the civil rights and women's movements. The major debate in this area, of course, is the Equal Rights Amendment (ERA). However, the disagreement is not over the principle of equality but over whether ERA is good or bad for women. America's commitment to political equality is strong in principle, though less strong in practice. Everyone over eighteen gets one vote, and all votes are counted equally, but the political system tilts in the direction of special interest groups; those who belong to no such groups are seldom heard. Furthermore, money plays an increasingly important role in political campaigns. Clearly, there is room for improvement here. The final dimension of equality/inequality is status. Inequality of status involves differences in prestige and it is arguable whether it can or should be eliminated. Ideally, the people who contribute the most to society are the most highly esteemed. The reader can judge the extent to which this principle holds true in the United States.

In the Declaration of Independence, our forefathers claimed that "all men are created equal," and they went on to base the law of the land on the principle of equality. The equality they were referring to was equality of opportunity and legal and political rights for white, property-owning males. They did not mean equality of income or status, though they recognized that too much inequality of income would jeopardize democratic institutions. In the following two centuries non-whites and women struggled for and won considerable equality of opportunity and rights. Meanwhile, income gaps have been widening (except from 1929 to 1945 when the crash harmed the wealthy and wartime full employment favored the poor).

Should America now move toward greater income equality? Must this dimension of inequality be rectified in order for society to be just? George Gilder strongly believes that people must try hard, work hard, innovate, compete, aspire and accept risks and that they must be rewarded for their efforts. He maintains that welfare, public enterprise, highly progressive taxes and many other egalitarian measures are sapping American initiative, crippling American enterprise, slowing the American economy, and perpetuating the poverty of the poor. According to Gilder, the free enterprise system, with all of its inequalities, stimulates individual effort and enterprise, and this is what makes America great and prosperous. On the other hand, William Ryan makes the case that the existing income inequalities are obscene and offensive to moral sensibilities. He believes some reduction of inequalities is essential to social justice. Ryan contends that the rich and their propagandists justify existing inequalities by claiming that the system is fair and the inequalities result largely from differential effort, skill and achievement. He tries to show that this justification is weak.

YES

George Gilder

THE DIRGE OF TRIUMPH

The most important event in the recent history of ideas is the demise of the socialist dream. Dreams always die when they come true, and fifty years of socialist reality, in every partial and plenary form, leave little room for idealistic reverie. In the United States socialism chiefly rules in auditoria and parish parlors, among encounter groups of leftist intellectuals retreating from the real world outside, where socialist ideals have withered in the shadows of Stalin and Mao, Sweden and Tanzania, gulag and bureaucracy.

The second most important event of the recent era is the failure of capitalism to win a corresponding triumph. For within the colleges and councils, governments and churches where issue the nebulous but nonetheless identifiable airs and movements of new opinion, the manifest achievements of free enterprise still seem less comely than the promise of socialism betrayed. . . .

A prominent source of trouble is the profession of economics. Smith entitled Book One of *The Wealth of Nations*, "Of the Causes of Improvement in the productive Powers of Labour and the Order according to which its Produce is naturally distributed among the different Ranks of the people." He himself stressed the productive powers, but his followers, beginning with David Ricardo, quickly became bogged down in a static and mechanical concern with distribution. They all were forever counting the ranks of rich and poor and assaying the defects of capitalism that keep the poor always with us in such great numbers. The focus on distribution continues in economics today, as economists pore balefully over the perennial inequalities and speculate on brisk "redistributions" to rectify them.

This mode of thinking, prominent in foundation-funded reports, best-selling economics texts, newspaper columns, and political platforms, is harmless enough on the surface. But its deeper effect is to challenge the golden rule of capitalism, to pervert the relation between rich and poor, and to depict the system as "a zero-sum game" in which every gain for someone implies a loss for someone else, and wealth is seen once again to create poverty. As Kristol has said, a free society in which the distributions are widely seen as unfair cannot long survive. The distributionist mentality thus strikes at the living heart of democratic capitalism.

Whether of wealth, income, property, or government benefits, distributions always, unfortunately, turn out bad: highly skewed, hugely unequal, presumptively unfair, and changing little, or getting worse. Typical conclusions are that "the top 2 percent of all families own 44 percent of all family wealth, and the bottom 25 percent own none at all"; or the "the top 5 percent get 15.3 percent of the pretax income and the bottom 20 percent get 5.4 percent." . . .

Statistical distributions, though, can misrepresent the economy in serious ways. They are implicitly static, like a picture of a corporate headquarters, towering high above a city, that leaves out all the staircases, escalators, and elevators, and the Librium® on the executive's desk as he contemplates the annual report. The distribution appears permanent, and indeed, like the building, it will remain much the same year after year. But new companies will move in and out, executives will come and go, people at the bottom will move up, and some at the top will leave their Librium® and jump. For example, the share of the tobacco industry commanded by the leading four firms has held steady for nearly thirty years, but the leader of the 1950s is now nearly bankrupt. The static distributions also miss the simple matter of age; many of the people at the bottom of the charts are either old, and thus beyond their major earning years, or young, and yet to enter them. Although the young and the old will always be with us, their low earnings signify little about the pattern of opportunity in a capitalist system.

Because blacks have been at the bottom for centuries now, economists often miss the dynamism within the American system. The Japanese, for example, were interned in concentration camps during World War II, but thirty years later they had higher per capita earnings than any other ethnic group in America except the Jews. Three and one-half million Jewish immigrants arrived on our shores around the turn of the century with an average of nine dollars per person in their pockets, less than almost any other immigrant group. Six decades later the mean family income of Jews was almost double the national average. Meanwhile the once supreme British Protestants (WASPs) were passed in per capita earnings after World War II not only by Jews and Orientals but also by Irish, Italians, Germans, and Poles (which must have been the final Polish joke), and the latest generation of black West Indians.

It is a real miracle that learned social scientists can live in the midst of these continuing eruptions and convulsions, these cascades and cataracts of change, and declare in a tone of grim indignation that "Over the last fifty years there has been no shift in the distribution of wealth and income in this country." . . .

The income distribution tables also propagate a statistical illusion with regard to the American rich. While the patterns of annual income changed rather little in the 1970s, there was a radical shift in the distribution of wealth. In order to understand this development, it is crucial to have a clear-eyed view of the facts and effects of inflation, free of the pieties of the Left and the Right: the familiar rhetoric of the "cruelest tax," in which all the victims seem to be widows and orphans. In fact, widows and orphans—at least the ones who qualified for full social security and welfare benefits—did rather well under inflation. Between 1972 and 1977, for example, the median household income of the elderly rose from 80 to 85 percent of the entire population's. As Christopher Jencks of Harvard University and Joseph Minarek of the Brookings Institution, both men of the Left, discovered in the late 1970s, inflation hit hardest at savers and investors, largely the rich. . . .

Wealth consists of assets that promise a future stream of income. The flows of oil money do not become an enduring asset of the nation until they can be converted into a stock of remunerative capital—industries, ports, roads, schools, and working skills—that offer a future flow of support when the oil runs out. Four hundred years ago, Spain was rich like Saudi Arabia, swamped by a similar flood of money in the form of silver from the mines of Potosi in its Latin American colonies. But Spain failed to achieve wealth and soon fell back into its previous doldrums, while industry triumphed in apparently poorer parts of Europe.

A wealthy country must be able to save as well as to consume. Saving is often defined as deferred consumption. But it depends on investment: the ability to produce consumable goods at that future date to which consumption has been deferred. Saving depends on having something to buy when the deposit is withdrawn. For an individual it sounds easy; there must always be *something* to buy after all. But for a nation, with many savers, real wealth is hard work, requiring prolonged and profitable production of goods. . . .

Work, indeed, is the root of wealth, even of the genius that mostly resides in sweat. But without a conception of goals and purposes, well-paid workers consume or waste all that they earn. Pop singers rocking and rolling in money, rich basketball stars who symbolize wealth to millions, often end up deep in debt with nothing solid to show for their efforts, while the poorest families can often succeed in saving enough to launch profitable businesses. The old adages on the importance of thrift are true not only because they signify a quantitative rise in investible funds, but because they betoken imagination and purpose, which make wealth. Few businesses begin with bank loans, and small businesses almost never do. Instead they capitalize labor.

For example, ten years ago a Lebanese family arrived in Lee, Massachusetts, with a few dollars and fewer words of English. The family invested the dollars in buying a woebegone and abandoned shop beside the road at the edge of town, and they started marketing vegetables. The man rose at five every morning to drive slowly a ramshackle truck a hundred miles to farms in the Connecticut Valley, where he purchased the best goods he could find as cheaply as possible to sell that morning in Lee. It was a classic entrepreneurial performance, arbitrage, identifying price differentials in different markets, and exploiting them by labor. But because both the labor and the insight was little compensated, it was in a sense invisibly saved and invested in the store. All six children were sources of accumulating capital as they busily bustled about the place. The store remained open long hours, cashed checks of locals, and began to build a clientele. A few years later one had to fight through the crowds around it in summer, when the choice asparagus or new potted plants went on sale. Through the year it sold flowers and Christmas trees, gas and dry goods, maple syrup and blackberry jam, cider and candies, and wines and liquors, in the teeth of several supermarkets, innumerable gas stations, and other shops of every description, all better situated, all struggling in an overtaxed and declining Massachusetts economy.

The secret was partly in the six children (who placed the family deep in the statistics of per capita poverty for long after its arrival) and in the entrepreneurial vision of the owner, which eluded all the charts. Mr. Michael Zabian is the man's name, and he recently bought the biggest office building in the town, a three-story structure made of the same Lee marble as the national capitol building. He owns a large men's clothing store at street level and what amounts to a small shopping center at his original site; and he preens in three-piece suits in the publicity photos at the Chamber of Commerce.

As extraordinary as may seem his decade of achievement, though, two other Lebanese have performed similar marvels in the Berkshires and have opened competing shops in the area. Other immigrants in every American city—Cubans in Miami, Portuguese in Providence and Newark, Filipinos in Seattle, Koreans in Washington, D.C., and New York, Vietnamese in Los Angeles, to mention the more recent crop—have performed comparable feats of commerce, with little help from banks or government or the profession of economics.

Small firms, begun by enterprising men, can rise quickly to play important roles in the national economy. Berkshire Paper Company, for example, was started by Whitmore (Nick) Kelley of Glendale, Massachusetts, as a maker of scratch pads in the rural town of Great Barrington. One of the array of paper manufacturers along the Housatonic River, the firm endured repeated setbacks, which turned into benefits, and, by 1980, it was providing important capital and consumer goods to some of the nation's largest and fastest growing corporations, though Kelley himself had no inherited wealth or outside support.

From the onset, the company's capital consisted mostly of refuse. Like the copper and steel companies thriving on the contents of slag heaps, Berkshire Paper Company employed paper, machinery, and factory space rejected as useless by other companies. Berkshire Paper, in fact, was launched and grew with almost no recourse to resources or capital that was accorded by any value at all in any national economic accounts. Yet the company has now entered the semiconductor industry and holds virtual monopolies in three sophisticated products. The story of its rise from scratch pads to semiconductor products shows the irrelevance of nearly all the indices of economic value and national wealth employed by the statisticians of our economy.

As a sophomore in college, Nick Kelley used to visit his stepfather at Clark-Aiken, a manufacturer of papermaking machine tools in Lee, Massachusetts. Within and around the factory, he noticed random piles of paper and asked his stepfather what was done with them. He was told they were leftovers from machinery tests and would be loaded into a truck and taken to the Lee dump. Kelley asked whether he could have them instead.

He took a handful of paper to an office-supply store, Gowdy's in Pittsfield, and asked the proprietor what such paper was good for. Scratch pads, he was told. After long trial and error, and several visits to a scratch pad factory in the guise of a student, he figured out how to make the pads. With the help of his stepfather he purchased and repaired a broken paper-cutting machine, and he even found a new method of applying glue, replacing the usual paintbrush with a paint roller. He then scoured much of the Northeast for markets and created a thriving scratch pad business that, again with his stepfather's help, even survived Kelley's stint in Southeast Asia during the Vietnam War.

In every case, setbacks led to innovation and renewed achievement. Deprived of paper from Clark-Aiken, he learned how to purchase it from jobbers in New York. Discovering that it cost two cents a pound more in sheets than in rolls (nine cents rather than seven cents), he computed that the two pennies represented a nearly 30 percent hike in cost and determined to contrive a sheeter out of old equipment. Finally, his worst setback drove him out of the scratch pad business altogether and allowed him to greatly expand his company.

Attempting to extend his marketing effort to Boston, Kelley approached the buyer for a large office-supply firm. The buyer said he doubted that Kelley could meet the competition. Kelley demanded to know how anyone could sell them for less, when the raw materials alone cost some fourteen cents a pound, and he sold the pads for eighteen cents. He went off to investigate his rival, a family firm run by Italians in Somerville. Kelley found a factory in an old warehouse, also filled with old equipment, but organized even more ingeniously than Kelley's own. He had to acknowledge that the owner was "the best." "He had me beat." Kelley said, "I decided then and there to go out of scratch pad manufacturing." Instead he resolved to buy pads from the Somerville factory and use his

own marketing skills to sell them. He also purchased printing equipment and began adding value to the pads by printing specified lines and emblems on them.

This effort led to a request from Schweitzer, a large paper firm in the Berkshires, that Kelley print up legal pads, and then later, in a major breakthrough, that he cut up some tea bag paper that the Schweitzer machines could not handle. Although Kelley had only the most crude cutting machinery, he said sure, he could process tea bags. He took a pile of thin paper and spent several days and nights at work on it, destroying a fourth of the sheets before his machine completely jammed and pressed several of the layers together so tightly that he found he could easily cut them. This accident gave Kelley a reputation as a worker of small miracles with difficult and specialized papermaking tasks, and the large companies in the area began channeling their most difficult production problems to him.

These new assignments eventually led to three significant monopolies for the small Berkshire firm. One was in making women's fingernail mending tissue (paper with long fibers that adhere to the nail when it is polished) for cosmetic firms from Avon to Revlon. Another was in manufacturing facial blotting tissue (paper that cleans up dirt and makeup without rubbing) for such companies as Mary Kaye and Bonne Belle. His third and perhaps most important project, though—a task that impelled Kelley to pour endlessly through the literature of semiconductor electronics, trafficking in such concepts as microns (one-thousandth of a centimeter) and angstroms (one thousandth of a micron)—was production of papers for use in the manufacture of microprocessors and other semiconductor devices. This required not only the creation of papers sufficiently lint free to wrap a silicon wafer in (without dislodging an electron), but also a research effort to define for the companies precisely what impurities and "glitches" might remain. Kelley now provides this paper, along with the needed information, to all leading semiconductor companies, from National Semiconductor to Intel and Motorola, and he continues research to perfect his product.

Throughout his career, Kelley had demonstrated that faith and imagination are the most important capital goods in the American economy, that wealth is a product less of money than of mind.

The official measures miss all such sources of wealth. When Heilbroner and Thurow claim that 25 percent of American households owned zero net wealth in 1969, they are speaking of families that held above 5 billion dollars' worth of automobiles, 16 billion dollars of other consumer durables, such as washers and television sets, 11 billion dollars' worth of housing (about one-third had cars and 90 percent TVs), as well as rights in Medicaid, social security, housing, education, and other governmental benefits. They commanded many billions of dollars' worth of human capital, some of it rather depreciated by age and some by youthful irresponsibilities (most of these poor households consisted either of single people or abandoned mothers and their offspring). Their net worth was zero, because their debts exceeded their calculable worth. Yet some 80 percent of these people who were poor in 1969 escaped poverty within two years, only to be replaced in the distributions by others too young, too old, too improvident, or too beset with children to manage a positive balance in their asset accounts.

Now it may be appropriate to exclude from the accounting such items as rights in government welfare and transfer programs, which often destroy as much human worth as they create. But the distribution tables also miss the assets of the greatest ultimate value. For example, they treated as an increment of poverty, bereft of net worth, the explosive infusion of human capital that arrived on our shores from Lebanon in the guise of an unlettered family.

Families of zero wealth built America. Many of the unincorporated businesses that have gained some 500 billion dollars in net value since World II (six times more than all the biggest corporations combined) were started in households of zero assets according to the usual accounts. The conception of a huge and unnegotiable gap between poverty and wealth is a myth. In the Berkshires, Zabian moving up passed many scions of wealth on their way down. . . .

In the second tier of wealth-holders, in which each member would average nearly 2 million dollars net worth in 1970 dollars, 71 percent reported no inherited assets at all, and only 14 percent reported substantial inheritance. Even in the top group of multimillionaires, 31 percent received no inherited assets, and 9 percent only small legacies. Other studies indicate that among the far larger and collectively more important group of wealth-holders of more than $60,000 in 1969, 85 percent of the families had emerged since 1953. With a few notable exceptions, which are always in the news, fast movement up or down in two generations has been the fate of the American rich. . . .

In attacking the rich, tax authorities make great use of the concept of "unearned income," which means the returns from money earned earlier, heavily taxed, then saved or invested. Inheritances receive special attention, since they represent undemocratic transfers and concentrations of power. But they also extend the time horizons of the economy (that is, business), and retard the destruction of capital. That inheritance taxes are too high is obvious from the low level of revenue they collect and the huge industry of tax avoidance they sustain. But politically these levies have long been regarded as too attractive to forgo at a time of hostility toward the rich.

Nonetheless, some of the most catalytic wealth in America is "unearned." A few years before Michael Zabian arrived on our shores, Peter Sprague, now his Berkshire neighbor, inherited 400,000 dollars, largely from the sale of Sprague Electric Company stock. Many heirs of similar legacies have managed to lose most of it in a decade or so. But Sprague set out on a course that could lose it much faster. He decided on a career in venture capital. To raise the odds against him still further, he eventually chose to specialize in companies that faced bankruptcy and lacked other sources of funds.

His first venture was a chicken hatchery in Iran, which taught him the key principles of entrepreneurship—chiefly that nothing happens as one envisions it in theory. The project had been based on the use of advanced Ralston-Purina technology, widely tested in Latin America, to tap the rapidly growing poultry markets of the Middle East. The first unexpected discovery was two or three feet of snow; no one had told him that it *snowed* in Iran. Snow ruined most of the Ralston-Purina equipment. A second surprise was chicanery (and sand) in the chicken

feed business. "You end up buying two hundred pounds of stone for every hundred pounds of grain." But after some seven years of similar setbacks, and a growing capital of knowledge, Sprague began to make money in Iran; growing a million trees fertilized with chicken manure, cultivating mushrooms in abandoned ice houses, and winding up with the largest cold storage facilities in the country. The company has made a profit through most of the seventies.

In 1964, three years after starting his Iranian operations, Sprague moved in on a failing electronics company called National Semiconductor. Sprague considered the situation for a week, bought a substantial stake, and became its chairman. The firm is now in the vanguard of the world-wide revolution in semiconductor technology and has been one of America's fastest growing firms, rising from 300 employees when Sprague joined it to 34,000 in 1980.

Also in the mid-sixties Sprague bought several other companies, including the now fashionable Energy Resources, and rescued Design Research from near bankruptcy (the firm finally folded in 1976). In 1969, he helped found Auton Computing Company, a firm still thriving in the business of detecting and analyzing stress in piping systems in nuclear and other power plants, and in 1970 he conducted a memorably resourceful and inventive but finally unsuccessful Republican campaign for the New York City congressional seat then held by Edward Koch (who is now mayor).

He then entered the latest phase of his career rescuing collapsing companies. A sports car buff, he indicated to some friends an interest in reviving Aston-Martin, which had gone out of business six months earlier, in mid-1974. Arriving in England early in 1975 with a tentative plan to investigate the possibilities, he was besieged by reporters and TV cameras. Headlines blared: MYSTERY YANK FINANCIER TO SAVE ASTON MARTIN. Eventually he did, and the company is now securely profitable. . . .

A government counterpart of Sprague's investment activity was Wedgewood Benn's National Enterprise Board in England, which spent some 8 billion dollars attempting to save various British companies by drowning them in money. Before Sprague arrived in England Benn had adamantly refused to invest in Aston-Martin—dismissing the venerable firm as a hopeless case—and instead subsidized a large number of other companies, most of which, unlike Aston, still lose money, and some of which ended up bankrupt. The British, however, did find 104 million dollars—fifty times more than Sprague had to invest in Aston-Martin—to use in luring John DeLorean's American luxury car project to Northern Ireland and poured 47.8 million dollars into the effort to create Ininos, a British nationalized semiconductor firm that has yet to earn any money and technologically remains well in the wake of Sprague's concern. With 400,000 dollars inheritance and his charismatic skills, Sprague has revived many times more companies than Wedgewood Benn with the British Treasury. One entrepreneur with energy, resolution, and charisma could turn 400,000 dollars into a small fortune for himself and a bonanza for the economy, accomplishing more than any number of committee-bound foundations, while a government agency usually requires at least 400,000 dollars to so much as open an office.

Nonetheless, considering the sometimes unedifying spectacle of the humpty-dumpty heirs of wealth—and often focusing on the most flamboyant and newsworthy consumers of cocaine and spouses—it is all too easy to forget that the crucial role of the rich in a capitalist economy is not to entertain and titillate the classes below, but to invest: to provide unencumbered and unbureaucratized cash. The broad class of rich does, in fact, perform this role. Only a small portion of their money is consumed. Most of it goes to productive facilities that employ labor and supply goods to consumers. The rich remain the chief source of discretionary capital in the economy.

These are the funds available for investment outside the largely sterile channels of institutional spending. This is the money that escapes the Keynesian trap of compounded risk, created by the fact that a bank, like an entrepreneur, may lose most of its investment if an enterprise fails, but only the entrepreneur can win the large possible payoff that renders the risk worthwhile. Individuals with cash comprise the wild card—the mutagenic germ—in capitalism, and it is relatively risky investments that ultimately both reseed the economy and unseat the rich. . . .

The risk-bearing role of the rich cannot be performed so well by anyone else. The benefits of capitalism still depend on capitalists. The other groups on the pyramid of wealth should occasionally turn from the spectacles of consumption long enough to see the adventure on the frontiers of the economy above them—an adventure not without its note of nobility, since its protagonist families will almost all eventually fail and fall in the redeeming struggle of the free economy.

In America the rich should not be compared to the Saudi Arabians or be seen in the image of Midas in his barred cage of gold. . . . Under capitalism, when it is working, the rich have the anti-Midas touch, transforming timorous liquidity and unused savings into factories and office towers, farms and laboratories, orchestras and museums—turning gold into goods and jobs and art. That is the function of the rich: fostering opportunities for the classes below them in the continuing drama of the creation of wealth and progress. . . .

THE NATURE OF POVERTY

To get a grip in the problems of poverty, one should also forget the idea of overcoming inequality by redistribution. Inequality may even grow at first as poverty declines. To lift the incomes of the poor, it will be necessary to increase the rates of investment, which in turn will tend to enlarge the wealth, if not the consumption, of the rich. The poor, as they move into the work force and acquire promotions, will raise their incomes by a greater percentage than the rich; but the upper classes will gain by greater absolute amounts, and the gap between the rich and the poor may grow. All such analyses are deceptive in the long run, however, because they imply a static economy in which the *numbers* of the rich and the middle class are not growing.

In addition, inequality may be favored by the structure of a modern economy as it interacts with demographic changes. When the division of labor becomes more complex and refined, jobs grow more specialized; and the increasingly specialized workers may win greater rents for their rare expertise, causing their incomes to rise relative to common labor. This tendency could be height-ened by a decline in new educated entrants to the work force, predictable through the 1990s, and by an enlarged flow of immigration, legal and illegal. Whatever the outcome of these developments, an effort to take income from the rich, thus diminishing their investment, and to give it to the poor, thus reducing their work incentives, is sure to cut American productivity, limit job opportunities, and perpetuate poverty.

Among the beneficiaries of inequality will be the formerly poor. Most students of the problems of poverty consider the statistics of success of previous immigrant groups and see a steady incremental rise over the years, accompanied by the progressive acquisition of educational credentials and skills. Therefore, programs are proposed that foster a similar slow and incremental ascent by the currently poor. But the incremental vision of the escape from poverty is mostly false, based on a simple illusion of statistical aggregates that conceals everything important about upward mobility. Previous immigrants earned money first by working hard; their children got the education.

The rising average incomes of previous groups signify not the smooth progress of hundreds of thousands of civil-service or bureaucratic careers, but the rapid business and professional successes of a relative few, who brought their families along and inspired others to follow. Poor people tend to rise up rapidly and will be damaged by a policy of redistribution that will always hit new and unsheltered income and wealth much harder than the elaborately concealed and fortified winnings of the established rich. The poor benefit from a dynamic economy full of unpredictable capital gains (they have few capital losses!) more than from a stratified system governed by educational and other credentials that the rich can buy.

The only dependable route from poverty is always work, family, and faith. The first principle is that in order to move up, the poor must not only work, they must work harder than the classes above them. Every previous generation of the lower class has made such efforts. But the current poor, white even more than black, are refusing to work hard. Irwin Garfinkel and Robert Haveman, authors of an ingenious and sophisticated study of what they call *Earning Capacity Utilization Rates*, have calculated the degree to which various income groups use their opportunities—how hard they work outside the home. This study shows that, for several understandable reasons, the current poor work substantially less, for fewer hours and weeks a year, and earn less in proportion to their age, education, and other credentials (even *after* correcting the figures for unemployment, disability, and presumed discrimination) than either their predecessors in American cities or those now above them on the income scale (the study was made at the federally funded institute for Research on Poverty at the University of Wisconsin and used data from the census and the Michigan longitudinal survey). The findings lend important confirmation to the growing body of evidence that work effort is the crucial unmeasured variable in American productivity and income distribution, and that current welfare and other subsidy programs substantially reduce work. The poor choose leisure not because of moral weakness, but because they are paid to do so.

A program to lift by transfers and preferences the incomes of less diligent groups is politically divisive—and very unlikely—because it incurs the bitter resistance of the real working class. In addition, such an effort breaks the psychological link between effort and reward, which is crucial to long-run upward mobility. Because effective work consists not in merely fulfilling the requirements of labor contracts but "in putting out" with alertness and emotional commitment, workers have to understand and feel deeply that what they are given depends on what they give—that they must supply work in order to demand goods. Parents and schools must inculcate this idea in their children both by instruction and example. Nothing is more deadly to achievement than the belief that effort will not be rewarded, that the world is a bleak and discriminatory place in which only the predatory and the specially preferred can get ahead. Such a view in the home discourages the work effort in school that shapes earnings capacity afterward. As with so many aspects of human performance, work effort begins in family experiences, and its sources can be best explored through an examination of family structure.

Indeed, after work the second principle of upward mobility is the maintenance of monogamous marriage and family. Adjusting for discrimination against women and for child-care responsibilities, the Wisconsin study indicates that married men work between two and one-third and four times harder than married women, and more than twice as hard as female family heads. The work effort of married men increases with their age, credentials, education, job experience, and birth of children, while the work effort of married women steadily declines. Most important in judging the impact of marriage, husbands work

50 percent harder than bachelors of comparable age, education, and skills.

The effect of marriage, thus, is to increase the work effort of men by about half. Since men have higher earnings capacity to begin with, and since the female capacity-utilization figures would be even lower without an adjustment for discrimination, it is manifest that the maintenance of families is the key factor in reducing poverty.

Once a family is headed by a woman, it is almost impossible for it to greatly raise its income even if the woman is highly educated and trained and she hires day-care or domestic help. Her family responsibilities and distractions tend to prevent her from the kind of all-out commitment that is necessary for the full use of earning power. Fewer women with children make earning money the top priority in their lives.

A married man, on the other hand, is spurred by the claims of family to channel his otherwise disruptive male aggressions into his performance as a provider for a wife and children. These sexual differences alone, which manifest themselves in all societies known to anthropology, dictate that the first priority of any serious program against poverty is to strengthen the male role in poor families.

These narrow measures of work effort touch on just part of the manifold interplay between family and poverty. Edward Banfield's *The Unheavenly City* defines the lower class largely by its lack of an orientation to the future. Living from day to day and from hand to mouth, lower class individuals are unable to plan or save or keep a job. Banfield gives the impression that short-time horizons are a deepseated psychological defect afflicting hundreds of thousands of the poor.

There is no question that Banfield puts his finger on a crucial problem of the poor and that he develops and documents his theme in an unrivaled classic of disciplined social science. But he fails to show how millions of men, equally present oriented, equally buffeted by impulse and blind to the future, have managed to become farseeing members of the middle classes. He also fails to explain how millions of apparently future-oriented men can become dissolute followers of the sensuous moment, neglecting their jobs, dissipating their income and wealth, pursuing a horizon no longer than the most time-bound of the poor.

What Banfield is in fact describing in his lower-class category is largely the temperament of single, divorced, and separated men. The key to lower-class life in contemporary America is that unrelated individuals, as the census calls them, are so numerous and conspicuous that they set the tone for the entire community. Their congregation in ghettos, moreover, magnifies greatly their impact on the black poor, male and female (though, as Banfield rightly observes, this style of instant gratification is chiefly a male trait).

The short-sighted outlook of poverty stems largely from the breakdown of family responsibilities among fathers. The lives of the poor, all too often, are governed by the rhythms of tension and release that characterize the sexual experience of young single men. Because female sexuality, as it evolved over the millennia, is psychologically rooted in the bearing and nurturing of children, women have long horizons within their very bodies, glimpses of eternity within their wombs. Civilized society is dependent upon the submission of the short-term sexuality of young men to the extended maternal horizons of women. This is what happens in monogamous marriage; the man disciplines his sexuality and extends it into the future through the womb of a woman. The woman gives him access to his children, otherwise forever denied him; and he gives her the product of his labor, otherwise dissipated on temporary pleasures. The woman gives him a unique link to the future and a vision of it; he gives her faithfulness and a commitment to a lifetime of hard work. If work effort is the first principle of overcoming poverty, marriage is the prime source of upwardly mobile work.

It is love that changes the short horizons of youth and poverty into the long horizons of marriage and career. When marriages fail, the man often returns to the more primitive rhythms of singleness. On the average, his income drops by one-third and he shows a far higher propensity for drink, drugs, and crime. But when marriages in general hold firm and men in general love and support their children, Banfield's lower-class style changes into middle-class futurity. . . .

Adolph A. Berle, contemplating the contrast between prosperous and dominantly Mormon Utah and indigent, chiefly secular Nevada next door, concluded his study of the American economy with the rather uneconomic notion of a "transcendental margin," possibly kin to Leibenstein's less glamorous X-efficiency and Christopher Jencks's timid "luck."

Lionel Tiger identifies this source of unexplained motion as "evolutionary optimism—the biology of hope," and finds it in the human genes. Ivan Light, in his fascinating exploration of the sources of difference between entrepreneurial Orientals and less venturesome blacks, resolved on "the spirit of moral community." Irving Kristol, ruminating on the problems of capitalism, sees the need for a "transcendental justification." They are all addressing, in one way or another, the third principle of upward mobility, and that is faith.

Faith in man, faith in the future, faith in the rising returns of giving, faith in the mutual benefits of trade, faith in the providence of God are all essential to successful capitalism. All are necessary to sustain the spirit of work and enterprise against the setbacks and frustrations it inevitably meets in a fallen world; to inspire trust and cooperation in an economy where they will often be betrayed; to encourage the forgoing of present pleasures in the name of a future that may well go up in smoke; to promote risk and initiative in a world where the rewards all vanish unless others join the game. In order to give without the assurance of return, in order to save without the certainty of future value, in order to work beyond the requirements of the job, one has to have confidence in a higher morality: a law of compensations beyond the immediate and distracting struggles of existence. . . .

NO   William Ryan

EQUALITY

. . . It should not surprise us [that] the clause "all men are created equal" can be interpreted in quite different ways. Today, I would like to suggest, there are two major lines of interpretation: one, which I will call the "Fair Play" perspective, stresses the individual's right to pursue happiness and obtain resources; the other, which I will call the "Fair Shares" viewpoint, emphasizes the right of access to resources as a necessary condition for equal rights to life, liberty and happiness.

Almost from the beginning, and most apparently during the past century or so, the Fair Play viewpoint has been dominant in America. This way of looking at the problem of equality stresses that each person should be equally free from all but the most minimal necessary interferences with his right to "pursue happiness." . . . Given significant differences of interest, of talents, and of personalities, it is assumed that individuals will be variably successful in their pursuits and that society will consequently propel to its surface what Jefferson called a "natural aristocracy of talent," men who because of their skills, intellect, judgment, character, will assume the leading positions in society that had formerly been occupied by the hereditary aristocracy—that is, by men who had simply been born into positions of wealth and power. In contemporary discussions, the emphasis on the individual's unencumbered pursuit of his own goals is summed up in the phrase "equality of opportunity." Given at least an approximation of this particular version of equality, Jefferson's principle of a natural aristocracy—spoken of most commonly today as the idea of "meritocracy"—will insure that the ablest, most meritorious, ambitious, hardworking, and talented individuals will acquire the most, achieve the most, and become the leaders of society. The relative inequality that this implies is seen not only as tolerable, but as fair and just. Any effort to achieve what proponents of Fair Play refer to as "equality of results" is seen as unjust, artificial, and incompatible with the more basic principle of equal opportunity.

The Fair Shares perspective, as compared with the Fair Play idea, concerns itself much more with equality of rights and of access, particularly the implicit rights to a reasonable share of society's resources, sufficient to sustain life at a decent standard of humanity and to preserve liberty and freedom from compulsion. Rather than focusing on the individual's pursuit of his own happiness, the advocate of Fair Shares is more committed to the principle that all members of the society obtain a reasonable portion of the goods that society produces. From his vantage point, the overzealous pursuits of private goals on the part of some individuals might even have to be bridled. From this it follows, too, that the proponent of Fair Shares has a different view of what constitutes fairness and justice, namely, an appropriate distribution throughout society of sufficient means for sustaining life and preserving liberty.

So the equality dilemma is built into everyday life and thought in America; it comes with the territory. Rights, equality of rights—or at least interpretations of them—clash. The conflict between Fair Play and Fair Shares is real, deep, and serious, and it cannot be easily resolved. Some calculus of priorities must be established. Rules must be agreed upon. It is possible to imagine an almost endless number of such rules:

• Fair Shares until everyone has enough; Fair Play for the surplus

• Fair Play until the end of a specified "round," then "divvy up" Fair Shares, and start Fair Play all over again (like a series of Monopoly games)

• Fair Play all the way, except that no one may actually be allowed to starve to death.

The last rule is, I would argue, a perhaps bitter parody of the prevailing one in the United States. Equality of opportunity and the principle of meritocracy are the clearly dominant interpretation of "all men are created equal," mitigated by the principle (usually defined as charity rather than equality) that the weak, the helpless, the deficient will be more or less guaranteed a sufficient share to meet their minimal requirements for sustaining life.

FAIR PLAY AND UNEQUAL SHARES

The Fair Play concept is dominant in America partly because it puts forth two most compelling ideas: the time-honored principle of distributive justice and the cherished image of America as the land of opportunity. At least since Aristotle, the principle that rewards should accrue to each person in proportion of his worth or merit has seemed to many persons one that warrants intuitive acceptance. The more meritorious person—merit being some combination of ability and constructive effort—*deserves* a greater reward. From this perspective it is perfectly consistent to suppose that *unequal* shares could well be *fair* shares; moreover, within such a framework, it is very unlikely indeed that equal shares could be fair shares, since individuals are not equally meritorious.

The picture of America as the land of opportunity is also very appealing. The idea of a completely open society, where each person is entirely free to advance in his or her particular fashion, to become whatever he or she is inherently capable of becoming, with the sky the limit, is a universally inspiring one. This is a picture that makes most Americans proud.

But is it an accurate picture? Are these two connected ideas—unlimited opportunity and differential rewards fairly distributed according to differences in individual merit—congruent with the facts of life? The answer, of course, is yes and no. Yes, we see some vague congruence here and there—some evidence of upward mobility, some kinds of inequalities that can appear to be justifiable. But looking at the larger picture, we must answer with an unequivocal "No!: The fairness of unequal shares and the reality of equal opportunity are wishes and dreams, resting on a mushy, floating, purely imaginary foundation. Let us look first at the question of unequal shares.

Fair Players and Fair Sharers disagree about the meaning, but not about the fact, of unequal shares and of the significant degree of inequality of wealth and income and of everything that goes along with wealth and income—general life conditions, health, education, power, access to services and to cultural and recreational amenities, and so forth. Fair Sharers say that this fact is the very *essence* of inequality, while Fair Players define the inequalities of condition that Fair Sharers decry as obvious and necessary *consequences* of equality of opportunity. Fair Players argue, furthermore, that such inequalities are for the most part roughly proportional to inequalities of merit. . . .

There [are] some patterns of ownership that are reasonably consistent with the Fair Play paradigm. In the distribution of such items as automobiles, televisions, appliances, even homes, there are significant inequalities, but they are not extreme. And if the Fair Player is willing to concede that many inequities remain to be rectified—and most Fair Players are quite willing, even eager, to do so—these inequalities can, perhaps, be swallowed.

It is only when we begin to look at larger aspects of wealth and income— aspects that lie beyond our personal vision—that the extreme and, I believe, gross inequalities of condition that prevail in America become evident. Let us begin with income. How do we divide up the shares of what we produce annually? In 1977 about one American family in ten had an income of less than $5,000 and about one in ten had an income of $35,000 a year and up ("up" going all the way to some unknown number of millions). It is difficult to see how anyone could view such a dramatic disparity as fair and justified. One struggles to imagine any measure of merit, any sign of membership in a "natural aristocracy," that would manifest itself in nature in such a way that one sizable group of persons would "have" eight or ten or twenty times more of it—whatever "it" might be—than another sizeable group has.

Income in the United States is concentrated in the hands of a few: one-fifth of the population gets close to half of all the income, and the top 5 percent of this segment get almost one-fifth of it. The bottom three-fifths of the population— that is, the majority of us—receive not much more than one-third of all income. . . .

As we move [to] the reality of living standards, the pertinent questions are: How much do people spend and on what? How do the groups at the different tables, that is, different income groups in America, live? Each year the Bureau of Labor Statistics publishes detailed information on the costs of maintaining three different living standards, which it labels "lower," "intermediate," and "higher"; in less discreet days it used to call the budgets "minimum," "adequate," and "comfortable." The adequate, intermediate budget is generally considered to be an index of a reasonably decent standard of living. It is on this budget, for example, that newspapers focus when they write their annual stories on the BLS budgets.

To give some sense of what is considered an "intermediate" standard of living, let me provide some details about this budget as it is calculated for a family of four—mother, father, eight-year-old boy, and thirteen-year-old girl. As of the autumn of 1978, for such a family the budget allows $335 a month for housing, which includes rent or mortgage, heat and utilities, household furnishings, and all household operations. It allows $79 a week for groceries, which extends to cleaning supplies, toothpaste, and the like. It allows $123 a month for transportation, including car payments. It allows $130 a month for clothing, clothing care or cleaning, and all personal-care items.

In his book *The Working Class Majority*, Andrew Levinson cites further details about this budget from a study made by the UAW:

A United Auto Workers study shows just how "modest" that budget is: The budget assumes, for example, that a family will own a toaster that will last for thirty-three years, a refrigerator and a range that will each last for seventeen years, a vacuum cleaner that will last for fourteen years, and a television set that will last for ten years. The budget assumes that a family will buy a two-year-old car and keep it for four years, and will pay for a tune-up once a year, a brake realignment every three years, and front-end alignment every four years. . . . The budget assumes that the husband will buy one year-round suit every four years . . . and one topcoat every eight and a half years. . . . It assumes that the husband will take his wife to the movies once every three months and that one of them will go to the movies alone once a year. The average family's two children are each al-lowed one movie every four weeks. A total of two dollars and fifty-four cents per person per year is allowed for admission to all other events, from football and baseball games to plays or concerts. . . . The budget allows nothing whatever for savings.

This budget, whether labeled intermediate, modest, or adequate, is perhaps more accurately described by those who call it "shabby but respectable." . . .

In 1978 the income needs by an urban family of four in order to meet even this modest standard of living was $18,622. This is a national average; for some cities the figure was much higher: in Boston, it was $22,117, in metropolitan New York, $21,587, in San Francisco, $19,427. More than *half* of all Americans lived *below* this standard. As for the "minimum" budget (which, by contrast with the "intermediate" budget, allows only $62 rather than $79 for groceries, $174 rather than $335 for housing, $67 rather than $123 for transportation, and $93 rather than $130 for clothing and personal care), the national average cost for an urban family in 1978 was $11,546. Three families out of ten could not afford even *that* standard, and one family in ten had an income below $5,000 which is *less than half enough* to meet minimum standards.

These dramatically *unequal* shares are —it seems to me—clearly *unfair* shares. Twenty million people are desperately poor, an additional forty million don't get enough income to meet the minimal requirements for a decent life, the great majority are just scraping by, a small minority are at least temporarily comfortable, and a tiny handful of persons live at levels of affluence and luxury that most persons cannot even imagine.

The myth that America's income is symmetrically distributed—an outstanding few at the top getting a lot, an inadequate few at the bottom living in poverty, and the rest clustered around the middle—could hardly be more false. The grotesquely lopsided distribution of our yearly production of goods and services is well illustrated by Paul Samuelson's famous image:

> A glance at the income distribution in the United States shows how pointed is the income pyramid and how broad its base. "There's always room at the top" is certainly true; this is so because it is hard to get there, not easy. If we make an income pyramid out of a child's blocks, with each layer portraying $1000 of income, the peak would be far higher than the Eiffel Tower, but almost all of us would be within a yard of the ground.

When we move from income to wealth —from what you *get* to what you *own*— the *degree* of concentration makes the income distribution look almost fair by comparison. About one out of every four Americans owns *nothing*. Nothing! In fact, many of them *owe* more than they have. Their "wealth" is actually negative. The persons in the next quarter own about 5 percent of all personal assets. In other words, half of us own 5 percent, the other half own 95 percent. But it gets worse as you go up the scale. Those in the top 6 percent own half of all the wealth. Those in the top 1 percent own one-fourth of all the wealth. Those in the top ½ percent own one-fifth of all the wealth. That's one-half of 1 percent— about one million persons, or roughly 300,000 families.

And even this fantastic picture doesn't tell the whole story, because "assets" include homes, cars, savings accounts, cash value of life insurance policies—the kinds of assets that the very rich don't bother with very much. The very rich put their wealth into the ownership of things that produce more wealth—corporate stocks and bonds, mortgages, notes, and the like. Two-thirds of their wealth is in this form and the top 1 percent owns 60 percent of all that valuable paper. The rest of it is owned by only an additional 10 percent, which means that nine people out of ten own none of it—and, if they're like me, they probably have never seen a real stock certificate in their lives.

America, we are sometimes told, is a nation of capitalists, and it is true that an appreciable minority of its citizens have a bank account here, a piece of land there, along with a few shares of stock. But quantitative differences become indisputably qualitative as one moves from the ownership of ten shares of General Motors to the ownership of ten thousand. There are capitalists, and then there are capitalists. . . .

Another way of grasping the extreme concentration of wealth in our society is to try to imagine what the ordinary person would have if that wealth were evenly distributed rather than clumped and clotted together in huge piles. Assuming that all the personal wealth was divided equally among all the people in the nation, we would find that every one of us, man, woman, and child, would *own* free and clear almost $22,000 worth of goods: $7,500 worth of real estate, $3,500 in cash, and about $5,000 worth of stocks and bonds. For a family of four that would add up to almost $90,000 in assets, including $30,000 equity in a house, about $14,000 in the bank, and about $20,000 worth of stocks and bonds. That much wealth would also bring in an extra $3,000 or $4,000 a year in income.

If you have any doubts about the reality of grossly unequal shares, compare the utopian situation of that imaginary "average" family with your own actual situation. For most of us, the former goes beyond our most optimistic fantasies of competing and achieving and getting ahead. Actually only about ten million persons in the country own as much as that, and, as I suggested before, the majority of us have an *average* of less than $5,000 per family including whatever equity we have in a home, our car and other tangible assets, and perhaps $500 in the bank.

Still another way of thinking about this is to remark that the fortunate few at the top, and their children, are more or less guaranteed an opulent standard of living because of what they own, while the majority of American families are no more than four months' pay away from complete destitution.

All of this, of course, takes place in the wealthiest society the world has ever known. If we extended our horizons further and began to compare the handful of developed, industrial nations with the scores of underdeveloped, not to say "over-exploited," nations, we would find inequalities that are even more glaring and appalling. . . .

THE VULNERABLE MAJORITY

Stripped down to its essentials, the rule of equal opportunity and Fair Play requires only that the best man win. It doesn't necessarily specify the margin of victory, merely the absence of unfair barriers. The practical test of equal opportunity is *social mobility*—do talented and hardworking persons, whatever their backgrounds, actually succeed in rising to higher social and economic positions?

The answer to that of course, is that they do. Remaining barriers of discrimination notwithstanding, it is plain that many persons climb up the social and economic ladder and reach much higher rungs than those their parents attained and than those from which they started. Fair Players prize these fortunate levitations as the ultimate justification of their own perspective and as phenomena that must be protected against any erosion caused by excessive emphasis upon Fair Shares.

It is necessary, then, to look seriously at the question of mobility. Among the questions to be asked are the following:

• How much mobility can we observe? No matter how rigidly hierarchical it might be, every society permits some mobility. How much movement up and down the scale is there in ours?

• How far do the mobile persons move?

• Is mobility evident across the whole social and economic range? Do the very poor stay poor, or do they, too, have an equal chance to rise? Are the very rich likely to slide *down* the ladder very often?

Given our great trove of rags-to-riches mythology, our creed that any child (well, any man-child) can grow up to be president—if not of General Motors, at least of the United States—we clearly assume that our society is an extraordinarily open one. And everyone knows, or has a friend who knows, a millionaire or someone on the way to that envied position: the patient, plodding peddler who transformed his enterprise into a great department store; the eccentric tinkerer in his garage whose sudden insight produced the great invention that everyone had been saving his pennies to buy.

At lesser levels of grandeur, we all know about the son of the illiterate cobbler who is now a wealthy neurosurgeon, the daughter of impoverished immigrants who sits in a professional chair at Vassar or Smith—or even Princeton. In America social mobility is an unquestioned fact.

But how many sons of illiterate cobblers become physicians, on the other hand, and how many become, at best, literate cobblers? And how many settle for a job on the assembly line or in the sanitation department? And all of those daughters of impoverished immigrants—how many went on to get Ph.D.'s and become professors? Very few. A somewhat larger number may have gone to college and gotten a job teaching sixth grade. But many just finished high school and went to work for an insurance company for a while, until they married the sons of other impoverished immigrants, most of them also tugging at their bootstraps without much result.

About all of these facts there can be little dispute. For most people, there is essentially no social mobility—for them, life consists of rags to rags and riches to riches. Moreover, for the relatively small minority who do rise significantly in the social hierarchy, the *distance* of ascent is relatively short. Such a person may start life operating a drill press and eventually become a foreman or even move into the white-collar world by becoming a payroll clerk or perhaps an accountant. Or he may learn from his father to be a cobbler, save his money, and open a little cobbler shop of his own. He hardly ever starts up a shoe factory. It is the son of the owner of the shoe factory who gets to do that. So there is mobility—it is rather common, but also rather modest, with only an occasional dramatic rise from rags to riches.

To provide some specific numbers, it has been calculated that for a young man

born into a family in which the father does unskilled, low-wage manual work, the odds against his rising merely to the point of his becoming a nonmanual white-collar worker are at least three or four to one; the odds against his rising to the highest level and joining the wealthy upper class are almost incalculable. For the son of a middle-level white-collar worker, the odds against his rising to a higher-level professional or managerial occupation are two or three to one. On the other hand, the odds are better than fifty to one that the son of a father with such a high-level occupation will not descend the ladder to a position as an unskilled or semiskilled manual worker. Upward mobility is very limited and usually involves moving only one or two levels up the hierachy. . . .

Finally, we have to look carefully to see that, for all our social mobility, the very rich almost all stay at the top and welcome only a select handful to their ranks. The rich of one generation are almost all children of the rich of the previous generation, partly because more than half of significant wealth is inherited, partly because all the other prerogatives of the wealthy are sufficient to assure a comfortable future for Rockefeller and Du Pont toddlers. It may well take more energy, ingenuity, persistence, and single-mindedness for a rich youngster to achieve poverty than for a poor one to gain wealth.

The dark side of the social-mobility machine is that it is, so to speak, a reciprocating engine—when some parts go up, others must come *down*. Downward mobility is an experience set aside almost exclusively for the nonrich, and it is grossly destructive of the quality of life.

The majority of American families are constantly vulnerable to economic disaster—to downward mobility to the point where they lack sufficient income to meet their most basic needs—food, shelter, clothing, heat, and medical care. Included in this vulnerable majority, who have at least an even chance of spending some portion of their lives in economic distress, are perhaps three out of four Americans.

This does to accord with the common view of poverty. We have been given to understand that "the poor" form a fairly permanent group in our society and that those who are above the poverty line are safe and perhaps even on their way up. This thought is comforting but false. A number of small studies have raised serious questions about this static picture; recently we have received massive evidence from one of the most comprehensive social and economic investigations ever mounted. This study, under the direction of James Morgan, has traced the life trajectories of five thousand American families over a period, to date, of eight years, concentrating on the nature of and possible explanations for economic progress or the lack of it.

Five Thousand American Families indicates that over a period of eight years, although only one in ten families is poor during *every one* of the eight years, over one-third of American families are poor for *at least one* of those eight years.

From the Michigan study, the census data, and other sources, we can readily estimate that a few are permanently protected against poverty because they *own things*—property, stocks, bonds—that provide them with income sufficient to meet their needs whether or not they work or have any other source of income. Another small minority of Americans own only *rights*—virtual job tenure, a guaranteed pension—but these rights

also give effective protection against poverty. At the bottom of the pyramid, there are a few who might be called permanently poor. Between these extremes come persons whose income is primarily or wholly dependent on salaries or wages. This is the core of the vulnerable majority—not poor now, but in jeopardy. In any given year one family out of six in that vulnerable majority will suffer income deficit, will go through a year of poverty. Over a five-year period nearly half of them will be poor for at least one year. If we project this over ten or fifteen years, we find that well over half will be poor for at least one year. On adding this group to the permanently poor, we arrive at the startling fact that a *substantial majority* of American families will experience poverty at some point during a relatively short span of time.

Several elements in our socioeconomic structure help account for income deficiency. Let us consider, for example, those who are more or less permanently poor. Why do they stay mired in poverty? The answer in most cases is simple: they remain poor because it has been deliberately *decided* that they should remain poor. They are, for the most part, dependent on what we impersonally call transfer payments—mostly Social Security, some private pensions, some welfare. To put it as simply as possible, these transfer payments are not enough to live on, not enough to meet basic needs. Countrywide, public assistance payments provide income that is only 75 percent of what is required to pay for sufficient food, adequate shelter, clothing, and fuel; the percentage decreases as the size of the family increases. For very large families, welfare provides only half of what is needed to live on. The poverty of the permanently poor is thus easily explained by the fact that the income assistance that we provide them is simply too small.

For the vulnerables, however, economic hills and valleys are created by the job situation. Economic status, progress, and deficit are determined by what social scientists call "family composition and participation in the labor force." In plain English that means they depend on the number of mouths to be fed and on the number of people working—that is, on how many children there are, on whether both wife and husband are working, and so forth. But this, of course, is only synonymous with the natural ebb and flow in the life of almost any family. It should not be an economic catastrophe, after all, when people get married and have children. . . . So, children are born and they grow up, sometimes work awhile, and then leave home. One parent, usually the mother, is tied to the home during some periods, free to work during others. A family member finds a job, loses a job, gets sick or injured, sometimes dies tragically young. All of these events are the landmarks in the life of a family, most of them are common enough, and some are inevitable sources of joy or sorrow. Yet these ordinary occurrences have a drastic impact on families, because they lead to greater changes in one or both sides of the ratio of income and needs. In most cases they are direct causes of most of the economic progress or distress that a family experiences. . . .

WHY NOT FAIR SHARES?

I have been trying to show, in a preliminary way, that the beliefs and assumptions associated with the Fair Play rendering of equality are quite inconsistent with the facts of life as we know them, although its principles are paraded as a version—in fact, the correct version—of equality and are widely accepted as quite plausible, indeed obvious. To the extent that there is any competition between Fair Players and Fair Sharers for the mind of the public, the former usually win hands down. Yet, as we have seen, the Fair Play idea appears to condone and often to endorse conditions of inequality that are blatant and, I would say, quite indefensible. Such equal opportunities for advancing in life as do exist are darkly overshadowed by the many head starts and advantages provided to the families of wealth and privilege. As for the workings out of the solemnly revered principles of meritocracy, they are—like many objects of reverence—invisible to most persons and rarely discernible in the lives of the vulnerable majority of us. Barely two centuries after its most persuasive formulation, the Fair Play concept of equality has shriveled to little more than the assertion that a few thousand individuals are fully licensed to gather and retain wealth at the cost of the wasteful, shameful, and fraudulent impoverishment of many millions. . . .

A Fair Shares egalitarian would hold that all persons have a *right* to a reasonable share of material necessities, a right to do constructive work, and a right of unhindered access to education, to gratifying social memberships, to participation in the life and decisions of the community, and to all the major amenities of society. This principle doesn't lend itself to the calculation of "equal results," and it certainly doesn't imply a demand for uniformity of resources. No one in his right mind would entertain some cockeyed scheme in which everyone went to school for precisely thirteen years; consumed each year 19,800 grams of protein and 820,000 calories; read four works of fiction and six of non-fiction; attended two concerts, one opera, and four basketball games, and voted in 54 percent of the elections. . . . Unfortunately, many persons who are upset about the present state of inequality tend to talk vaguely about the need "to redistribute income" or even "to redistribute wealth." When such ideas are tossed out without consideration of the fact that they will then be discussed within the framework of Fair Play, we have a surefire prescription for disaster. From that viewpoint, which is, after all, the dominant one in America, such ideas appear both extremely inpracticable and not particularly desirable. For example, are we to take redistribution of income to mean that every individual will somehow receive the same compensation, no matter what work he or she does or whether he works at all? And would we try to redistribute wealth by giving every person, say, a share of stock in GM, Exxon, IBM, and the local paperbag factory? Hardly. Fair Players can make mincemeat of such silly ideas, and they love to pretend that that's Fair Share egalitarians are proposing. I don't think many of us have strong objections to inequality of monetary income as such. A modest range, even as much as three or four to one, could, I suspect, be tolerable to almost everybody. (And one would suppose that, given some time for adjustment and perhaps some counseling and training in homemaking and budgeting skills, those who now get a lot more could learn to scrape by on something like eight or nine hundred dollars a week.) The current range in annual incomes—from perhaps $3,000 to some unknown number of *millions*—is, however, excessive and intolerable, impossible to justify rationally, and plain inhuman.

The problem of wealth is more fundamental. Most of the evils of inequality derive from the reality that a few thousand families control almost all the necessities and amenities of life, indeed the very conditions of life. The rest of us, some 200 million, have to pay tribute to them if we want even a slight illusion of life, liberty, and the pursuit of happiness. But the solution to this problem is certainly not simply the fragmentation of ownership into tiny units of individual property. This naive solution has been well criticized by serious proponents of equality, perhaps most gracefully by R.H. Tawney:

> It is not the division of the nation's income into eleven million fragments, to be distributed, without further ado, like cake as a school treat, among its eleven million families. It is, on the contrary, the pooling of its surplus resources by means of taxation, and use of the funds thus obtained to make accessible to all, irrespective of their income, occupation, or social position, the conditions of civilization which, in the absence of such measures, can only be enjoyed by the rich. . . .
>
> It can generalize, by collective action, advantages associated in the past with ownership of property. . . . It can secure that, in addition to the payments made to them for their labour, its citizens enjoy a social income, which is provided from the surplus remaining after the necessary cost of production and expansion have been met, and is available on equal terms for all its members. . . .

The central problem of inequality in America—the concentration of wealth and power in the hands of a tiny minority—cannot, then, be solved, as Tawney makes clear, by any schemes that rest on the process of long division. We need, rather, to accustom ourselves to a different method of holding resources, namely, holding them in common, to be *shared* amongst us all—not divided up and parceled out, but shared. That is the basic principle of Fair Shares, and it is not at all foreign to our daily experience. To cite a banal example, we share the air we breathe, although some breathe in penthouses or sparsely settled suburbs and others in crowded slums. In a similar fashion, we share such resources as public parks and beaches, although, again, we cannot overlook the gross contrast between the size of vast private waterfront holdings and the tiny outlets to the oceans that are available to the public. No one in command of his senses would go to a public beach, count the number of people there, and suggest subdividing the beach into thirty-two-by-twenty-six-foot lots, one for each person. Such division would not only be unnecessary, it would ruin our enjoyment. If I were assigned to Lot No. 123, instead of enjoying the sun and going for a swim, I might sit and watch that sneaky little kid with the tin shovel to make sure he did not extend the sand castle onto my beach. We own it in common; it's *public*; and we just plain *share* it.

We use this mode of owning and sharing all the time and never give it a second thought. We share public schools, streets, libraries, sewers, and other public property and services, and we even think of them as being "free" (many libraries even have the word in their names). Nor do we need the "There's no such thing as a free lunch" folks reminding us that they're not really free; everyone is quite aware that taxes support them. We don't feel any need to divide up all the books in the library among all the citizens. And there's no sensible way of looking at the use of libraries in terms of "equal opportunity" as opposed to "equal results." Looking at the public library as a tiny example of what Fair Shares equality is all about, we note that it satisfies the principle of equal access if no one is *excluded* from the library on the irrelevant grounds of not owning enough or of having spent twelve years in school learning how not to read. And "equal results" is clearly quite meaningless. Some will withdraw many books; some, only a few; some will be so unwise as to never even use the facility.

The *idea* of sharing, then, which is the basic idea of equality, and the *practice* of sharing, which is the basic methodology of Fair Shares equality, are obviously quite familiar and acceptable to the American people in many areas of life. There are many institutions, activities, and services that the great majority believe should be located in the public sector, collectively owned and paid for, and equally accessible to everyone. We run into trouble when we start proposing the same system of ownership for the resources that the wealthy have corralled for themselves. . . .

Most of the good things of life have either been provided free by God (nature, if you prefer) or have been produced by the combined efforts of many persons, sometimes many generations. As all share in the making, so all should share in the use and the enjoyment. This may help convey a bit of what the Fair Shares idea of equality is all about.

POSTSCRIPT

Is Economic Inequality Beneficial to Society?

The spirit of personal initiative seems to be alive in the hearts of Michael Zabian, the vegetable stand owner, Nick Kelley, the scratch paper dealer, and Peter Sprague, the venture capitalist, whose success stories are related by George Gilder. But how typical are their experiences? What about the government's bail-outs of Lockheed and Chrysler and the trials of U.S. Steel, General Motors, and many other corporations? What about the limitation of individual initiative in countless corporations guided by decisions made by committees and teams of experts? And what about the issues of fairness raised by William Ryan? Perhaps the basic question is: "Can the system be made more just, fair and humane without squelching enterprise and drive?"

Stratification and social mobility are two of the central concerns of sociology, and much literature has been produced discussing these issues. Two major publications of research on census statistics are Peter M. Blau and Otis Dudley Duncan's *The American Occupational Structure* (John Wiley & Sons, 1967), and Robert M. Hauser and David L. Featherman's *The Process of Social Stratification* (Academic Press, 1972). For general works, see Gerhard Lenski's *Power and Privilege* (McGraw-Hill, 1966) and Leonard Beeghley's *Social Stratification in the United States* (Goodyear, 1978). Many have written about the rich and their power, including Ferdinand Lundberg in *The Rich and the Super Rich* (Lyle Stuart, 1968); E. Digby Baltzell, *The Protestant Establishment* (Random House, 1964); and G. William Dornhoff in *Who Rules America?* (Prentice-Hall, 1967) and *The Higher Circles* (Random House, 1970). For a journalistic account of the process of climbing up the ladder of success, see Vance Packard's *The Pyramid Climbers* (McGraw Hill, 1962). A number of important works look at the poor and their disadvantages, including Joe Feagin's *Subordinating the Poor* (Prentice-Hall, 1975); Richard Sennett and Jonathan Cobbs, *The Hidden Injuries of Class* (Alfred A. Knopf, 1973); Michael Harrington's *The Other America* (Macmillan, 1962) and *The New American Poverty* (Holt, Rinehart and Winston, 1984); William Wilson's *The Truly Disadvantaged* (University of Chicago Press, 1987); and Elliot Liebow's *Tally's Corner* (Little, Brown, 1967).

Some studies of the social origins of elites include Suzanne Keller's *Beyond the Ruling Class* (Random House, 1963), and Floyd Warner and James Abegglen's *Big Business Leaders in America* (Harper, 1955). An interesting study of how the rich view themselves and the poor and income inequalities is *Equality in America: The View from the Top*, by Sidney Verber and Gary Orren (Harvard University Press, 1985).

ISSUE 9

Is Racial Oppression Declining in America?

YES: William Julius Wilson, from *The Declining Significance of Race* (University of Chicago Press, 1978)

NO: Charles V. Willie, from "The Inclining Significance of Race," *Society* (July/August 1978)

ISSUE SUMMARY

YES: University of Chicago sociologist William J. Wilson argues that class, rather than race, is now the dominant factor in determining a person's life chances.
NO: Educator Charles V. Willie counters that race remains the primary consideration.

"We didn't land on Plymouth Rock, my brothers and sisters—Plymouth Rock landed on *us*." Malcolm X's observation is borne out by the facts of American history. Snatched from their native land, transported thousands of miles, and sold into slavery, blacks were reduced to the legal status of cattle. The *Dred Scott* decision of the Supreme Court in 1857 declared them to be "private property." The Civil War and the subsequent Reconstruction period gave many the hope that slavery and its vestiges would be abolished forever. But even before the last federal troops were withdrawn from the South in 1877, the Southern "bourbons" had begun to regain control of the legislatures of the South. Before long, the gains made by blacks at the close of the war were wiped out. There was little public outcry and only one dissent on the bench when the Supreme Court in 1883 declared unconstitutional a Reconstruction statute that had prohibited segregation in public accommodations. In 1896, in the case of *Plessy v. Ferguson*, the Supreme Court sealed the fate of civil rights by upholding state-imposed segregation.

Not for another half-century was there any relief from the deliberate and systematic oppression of blacks. In 1954, in *Brown v. Board of Education*, the Supreme Court in effect reversed the *Plessy* decision of 1896 by outlawing state-imposed racial segregation. As a result of the civil rights movement in the 1960s, more improvements were won: Congress passed a series of statutes protecting voting rights and prohibited discrimination in employment, housing, and public accommodations. It also created offices within the executive branch to enforce and administer its new laws. By any fair estimation, these are remarkable gains, but there still remains a legacy of three hundred years of oppression. Blacks had been confined to the most menial jobs. In addition, they had first been forbidden, then denied, education. Later they were given only the most rudimentary schooling and found the doors to advancement were closed everywhere. As a result, by practically every index—employment, income, education, and even health and longevity—blacks have trailed whites by large margins.

In economic terms, the past twenty years have been years of both progress and retrogression for blacks. During the 1960s, black family income increased steadily. By 1969, it was 61% of white income (compared to 53% in 1961). By 1979, however, the ratio had fallen to 57% and 56% in 1983. Why? According to some observers, it was related to the erosion of liberal policies in the 1970s combined with an economic downturn. Yet, that explanation seems to be belied by the fact that for some black families the gap between black and white incomes *continued* to narrow during the 1970s. In that category were black married couples with both spouses working and younger educated blacks. (In the latter case, black income was essentially equal to that of whites.) The more likely explanation for the overall slippage is the fact that the number of female-headed single-parent families among blacks increased dramatically—from 21% in 1960 to 42% in 1983. Only 12% of white families fell into that category in 1983.

Though the picture is complex, one fact is starkly clear: Overall, a wide disparity in income and in general well-being still exists between blacks and whites in America. The question is whether this social inequality is still related, in any meaningful sense, to American racism. To put it simply: Are blacks still being oppressed in America simply because they are black?

The question has been hotly debated. In the following selections William Julius Wilson, a black sociologist, argues that race is much less significant than class in explaining the gap between black and white income, while another black social scientist, Charles V. Willie, considers it premature to conclude that oppression has become color-blind in America.

YES

William Julius Wilson

THE DECLINING SIGNIFICANCE OF RACE

Race relations in the United States have undergone fundamental changes in recent years, so much so that now the life chances of individual blacks have more to do with their economic class position than with their day-to-day encounters with whites. In earlier years the systematic efforts of whites to suppress blacks were obvious to even the most insensitive observer. Blacks were denied access to valued and scarce resources through various ingenious schemes of racial exploitation, discrimination, and segregation, schemes that were reinforced by elaborate ideologies of racism.

But the situation has changed. However determinative such practices were in the previous efforts of the black population to achieve racial equality, and however significant they were in the creation of poverty-stricken ghettoes and a vast underclass of black proletarians—that massive population at the bottom of the social class ladder plagued by poor education and low-paying unstable jobs—they do not provide a meaningful explanation of the life chances of black Americans today. The traditional patterns of interaction between blacks and whites, particularly in the labor market, have been fundamentally altered.

NEW AND TRADITIONAL BARRIERS

In the pre-Civil War period, and in the latter half of the nineteenth through the first half of the twentieth century, the continuous and explicit efforts of whites to construct racial barriers profoundly affected the lives of black Americans. Racial oppression was designed, overt, and easily documented. As the nation has entered the latter half of the twentieth century, however, many of the traditional barriers have crumbled under the weight of the political, social, and economic changes of the civil rights era. A new set of obstacles has emerged from basic structural shifts in the economy.

These obstacles are therefore impersonal, but may prove to be even more formidable for certain segments of the black population. Specifically, whereas the previous barriers were usually designed to control and restrict

Excerpt from *The Declining Significance of Race,* by William Julius Wilson (Illinois: The University of Chicago Press), pp. 1, 2, 146–154. Copyright © 1978 by William Julius Wilson. Reprinted by permission of The University of Chicago Press.

the entire black population, the new barriers create hardships essentially for the black underclass; whereas the old barriers were based explicitly on racial motivations derived from intergroup contact, the new barriers have racial significance only in their consequences, not in their origins. In short, whereas the old barriers portrayed the pervasive features of racial oppression, the new barriers indicate an important and emerging form of class subordination.

It would be shortsighted to view the traditional forms of racial segregation and discrimination as having essentially disappeared in contemporary America; the presence of blacks is still firmly resisted in various institutions and social clubs. However, in the economic sphere class has become more important than race in determining black access to privilege and power. It is clearly evident in this connection that many talented and educated blacks are now entering positions of prestige and influence at a rate comparable to or, in some situations, exceeding that of whites with equivalent qualifications. It is equally clear that the black underclass is in a hopeless state of economic stagnation, falling further and further behind the rest of society. . . .

CLASS AND RACE RELATIONS

Except for the brief period of fluid race relations in the North between 1870 and 1890 and in the South during the Reconstruction era, racial oppression is the single best term to characterize the black experience prior to the twentieth century. In the antebellum South both slaves and free blacks occupied what could best be described as a caste position, in the sense that realistic changes for occupational mobility simply did not exist. In the antebellum North a few free blacks were able to acquire some property and improve their socioeconomic position, and a few were even able to make use of educational opportunities. However, the overwhelming majority of free northern Negroes were trapped in menial positions and were victimized by lower-class white antagonism, including the racial hostilities of European immigrant ethnics (who successfully curbed the black economic competition). In the postbellum South the system of Jim Crow segregation wiped out the small gains blacks had achieved during Reconstruction, and blacks were rapidly pushed out of the more skilled jobs they had held since slavery. Accordingly, there was very little black occupational differentiation in the South at the turn of the century.

Just as the shift from a plantation economy to an industrializing economy transformed the class and race relations in the postbellum South, so too did industrialization in the North change the context for race-class interaction and confrontation there. On the one hand, the conflicts associated with the increased black-white contacts in the early twentieth century North resembled the forms of antagonism that soured the relations between the races in the postbellum South. Racial conflicts between blacks and whites in both situations were closely tied to class conflicts among whites. On the other hand, there were some fundamental differences. The collapse of the paternalistic bond between the blacks and the southern business elite cleared the path for the almost total subjugation of blacks in the South and resulted in what amounted to a white racial movement that solidified in the system of Jim Crow segregation.

However, a united white movement against blacks never really developed in the North. In the first quarter of the twentieth century, management attempted to undercut white labor by using blacks as strikebreakers and, in some situations, as permanent replacements for white workers who periodically demanded higher wages and more fringe benefits. Indeed, the determination of industrialists to ignore racial norms of exclusion and to hire black workers was one of the main reasons why the industry-wide unions reversed their racial policies and actively recruited black workers during the New Deal era. Prior to this period the overwhelming majority of unskilled and semiskilled blacks were nonunionized and were available as lower-paid labor or as strikebreakers. The more management used blacks to undercut white labor, the greater were the racial antagonisms between white and black labor.

Moreover, racial tension in the industrial sector often reinforced and sometimes produced racial tension in the social order. The growth of the black urban population created a housing shortage during the early twentieth century which frequently produced black "invasions" or ghetto "spillovers" into adjacent poor white neighborhoods. The racial tensions emanating from labor strife seemed to heighten the added pressures of racial competition for housing, neighborhoods, and recreational areas. Indeed, it was this combination of racial friction in both the economic sector and the social order that produced the bloody riots in East Saint Louis in 1917 and in Chicago and several other cities in 1919.

In addition to the fact that a united white movement against blacks never really developed in the North during the industrial period, it was also the case that the state's role in shaping race relations was much more autonomous, much less directly related to developments in the economic sector. Thus, in the brief period of fluid race relations in the North from 1870 to 1890, civil rights laws were passed barring discrimination in public places and in public institutions. This legislation did not have any real significance to the white masses at that time because, unlike in the pre-Civil War North and the post-Civil War South, white workers did not perceive blacks as major economic competitors. Blacks constituted only a small percentage of the total population in northern cities; they had not yet been used in any significant numbers as cheap labor in industry or as strikebreakers; and their earlier antebellum competitors in low-status jobs (the Irish and German immigrants) had improved their economic status in the trades and municipal employment.

POLITY AND RACIAL OPPRESSION

For all these reasons liberal whites and black professionals, urged on by the spirit of racial reform that had developed during the Civil War and Reconstruction, could pursue civil rights programs without firm resistance; for all these reasons racial developments on the political front were not directly related to the economic motivations and interests of workers and management. In the early twentieth century the independent effect of the political system was displayed in an entirely different way. The process of industrialization had significantly altered the pattern of racial interaction, giving rise to various manifestations of racial antagonism.

Although discrimination and lack of training prevented blacks from seeking higher-paying jobs, they did compete with lower-class whites for unskilled and semiskilled factory jobs, and they were used by management to undercut the white workers' union movement. Despite the growing importance of race in the dynamics of the labor market, the political system did not intervene either or mediate the racial conflicts or to reinforce the pattern of labor-market racial interaction generated by the system of production. This was the case despite the salience of a racial ideology system that justified and prescribed unequal treatment for Afro-Americans. (Industrialists will more likely challenge societal racial norms in situations where adherence to them results in economic losses.)

If nothing else, the absence of political influence on the labor market probably reflected the power struggles between management and workers. Thus legislation to protect the rights of black workers to compete openly for jobs would have conflicted with the interests of management. To repeat, unlike the South, a united white movement resulting in the almost total segregation of the work force never really developed in the North.

But the state's lack of influence in the industrial sector of private industries did not mean that it had no significant impact on racial stratification in the early twentieth century North. The urban political machines, controlled in large measure by working-class ethnics who were often in direct competition with blacks in the private industrial sector, systematically gerrymandered black neighborhoods and excluded the urban black masses from meaningful political participation throughout the early twentieth century. Control by the white ethnics of the various urban political machines was so complete that blacks were never really in a position to compete for the more important municipal political rewards, such as patronage jobs or government contracts and services. Thus the lack of racial competition for municipal political rewards did not provide the basis for racial tension and conflict in the urban political system. This political racial oppression had no direct connection with or influence on race relations in the private industrial sector.

In sum, whether one focuses on the way race relations were structured by the system of production or the polity or both, racial oppression (ranging from the exploitation of black labor by the business class to the elimination of black competition for economic, social, and political resources by the white masses) was a characteristic and important phenomenon in both the preindustrial and industrial periods of American race relations. Nonetheless, and despite the prevalence of various forms of racial oppression, the change from a preindustrial to an industrial system of production did enable blacks to increase their political and economic resources. The proliferation of jobs created by industrial expansion helped generate and sustain the continuous mass migration of blacks from the rural South to the cities of the North and West. As the black urban population grew and became more segregated, institutions and organizations in the black community also developed, together with a business and a professional class affiliated with these institutions. Still, it was not until after World War II (the modern industrial period) that the black class structure started to take on some of the characteristics of the white class structure.

CLASS AND BLACK LIFE CHANCES

Class has also become more important than race in determining black life chances in the modern industrial period. Moreover, the center of racial conflict has shifted from the industrial sector to the sociopolitical order. Although these changes can be related to the more fundamental changes in the system of production and in the laws and policies of the state, the relations between the economy and the polity in the modern industrial period have differed from those in previous periods. In the preindustrial and industrial periods the basis of structured racial inequality was primarily economic, and in most situations the state was merely an instrument to reinforce patterns of race relations that grew directly out of the social relations of production.

Except for the brief period of fluid race relations in the North from 1870 to 1890 the state was a major instrument of racial oppression. State intervention in the modern industrial period has been designed to promote racial equality, and the relationship between the polity and the economy has been much more reciprocal, so much so that it is difficult to determine which one has been more important in shaping race relations since World War II. It was the expansion of the economy that facilitated black movement from the rural areas to the industrial centers and that created job opportunities leading to greater occupational differentiation in the black community (in the sense that an increasing percentage of blacks moved into white-collar positions); and it was the intervention of the state (responding to the pressures of increased black political resources and to the racial protest movement that re-

moved many artificial discrimination barriers by municipal, state, and federal civil rights legislation, and that contributed to the more liberal racial policies of the nation's labor unions by protective union legislation. And these combined political and economic changes created a pattern of black occupational upgrading that resulted, for example, in a substantial drop in the percentage of black males in the low-paying service, unskilled labor, and farm jobs.

However, despite the greater occupational differentiation within the black community, there are now signs that the effect of some aspects of structural economic change has been the closer association between black occupational mobility and class affiliation. Access to the means of production is increasingly based on educational criteria (a situation which distinguishes the modern industrial from the earlier industrial system of production) and thus threatens to solidify the position of the black underclass. In other words, a consequence of the rapid growth of the corporate and government sectors has been the gradual creation of a segmented labor market that currently provides vastly different mobility opportunities for segments of the black population.

On the one hand, poorly trained and educationally limited blacks of the inner city, including that growing number of black teenagers and young adults, see their job prospects increasingly restricted to the low-wage sector, their unemployment rates soaring to record levels (which remain high despite swings in the business cycle), their labor force participation rates declining, their movement out of poverty slowing, and their welfare roles increasing. On the other hand, talented and educated blacks are experiencing unprecedented job opportunities in the growing government and corporate sectors, opportunities that are at least comparable to those of whites with equivalent qualifications. The improved job situation for the more privileged blacks in the corporate and government sectors is related both to the expansion of salaried white-collar positions and to the pressures of state affirmative action programs.

In view of these developments, it would be difficult to argue that the plight of the black underclass is solely a consequence of racial oppression, that is, the explicit and overt efforts of whites to keep blacks subjugated, in the same way that it would be difficult to explain the rapid economic improvement of the more privileged blacks by arguing that the traditional forms of racial segregation and discrimination still characterize the labor market in American industries. The recent mobility patterns of blacks lend strong support to the view that economic class is clearly more important than race in predetermining job placement and occupational mobility. In the economic realm, then, the black experience has moved historically from economic racial oppression experienced by virtually all blacks to economic subordination for the back underclass. And as we begin the last quarter of the twentieth century, a deepening economic schism seems to be developing in the black community, with the black poor falling further and further behind middle and upper-income blacks.

SHIFT OF RACIAL CONFLICT

If race is declining in significance in the economic sector, explanations of racial antagonism based on labor-market con-flicts, such as those advanced by economic class theories of race, also have less significance in the period of modern industrial race relations. Neither the low-wage sector nor the corporate and government sectors provide the basis for the kind of interracial job competition and conflict that plagued the economic order in previous periods. With the absorption of blacks into industrywide labor unions, protective union legislation, and equal employment legislation, it is no longer feasible for management to undercut white labor by using black workers. The traditional racial struggles for power and privilege have shifted away from the economic sector and are now concentrated in the sociopolitical order. Although poor blacks and poor whites are still the main actors in the present manifestations of racial strife, the immediate source of the tension has more to do with racial competition for public schools, municipal political systems, and residential areas than with the competition for jobs.

To say that race is declining in significance, therefore, is not only to argue that the life chances of blacks have less to do with race than with economic class affiliation, but also to maintain that racial conflict and competition in the economic sector—the most important historical factors in the subjugation of blacks—have been substantially reduced. However, it could be argued that the firm white resistance to public school desegregation, residential integration, and black control of central cities all indicate the unyielding importance of race in the United States. The argument could even be entertained that the impressive occupational gains of the black middle class are only temporary, and that as soon as affirmative action pressures are relieved, or as soon as the economy experiences a prolonged recession, industries will return to their old racial practices.

Both of these arguments are compelling if not altogether persuasive. Taking the latter contention first, there is little available evidence to suggest that the economic gains of privileged blacks will be reversed. Despite the fact that the recession of the early 1970s decreased job prospects for all educated workers, the more educated blacks continued to experience a faster rate of job advancement than their white counterparts. And although it is always possible that an economic disaster could produce racial competition for higher-paying jobs and white efforts to exclude talented blacks, it is difficult to entertain this idea as a real possibility in the face of the powerful political and social movement against job discrimination. At this point there is every reason to believe that talented and educated blacks, like talented and educated whites, will continue to enjoy the advantages and privileges of their class status.

My response to the first argument is not to deny the current racial antagonism in the sociopolitical order, but to suggest that such antagonism has far less effect on individual or group access to those opportunities and resources that are centrally important for life survival than antagonism in the economic sector. The factors that most severely affected black life chances in previous years were the racial oppression and antagonism in the economic sector. As race declined in importance in the economic sector, the Negro class structure became more differentiated and black life chances became increasingly a consequence of class affiliation.

Furthermore, it is even difficult to identify the form of racial contact in the sociopolitical order as the source of the current manifestations of conflict between lower-income blacks and whites, because neither the degree of racial competition between the have-nots, nor their structural relations in urban communities, nor their patterns of interaction constitute the ultimate source of present racial antagonism. The ultimate basis for current racial tension is the deleterious effect of basic structural changes in the modern American economy on black and white lower-income groups, changes that include uneven economic growth, increasing technology and automation, industry relocation, and labor market segmentation.

FIGHTING CLASS SUBORDINATION

The situation of marginality and redundancy created by the modern industrial society deleteriously affects all the poor, regardless of race. Underclass whites, Hispano Americans, and Native Americans are all victims, to a greater or lesser degree, of class subordination under advanced capitalism. It is true that blacks are disproportionately represented in the underclass population and that about one-third of the entire black population is in the underclass. But the significance of these facts has more to do with the historical consequences of racial oppression than with the current effects of race.

Although the percentage of blacks below the low-income level dropped steadily throughout the 1960s, one of the legacies of the racial oppression in previous years is the continued disproportionate black representation in the underclass. And since 1970 both poor whites and nonwhites have evidenced very little progress in their elevation from the ranks of the underclass. In the final analysis, therefore, the challenge of economic dislocation in the modern industrial society calls for public policy programs to attack inequality on a broad class front, policy programs—in other words—that go be- yond the limits of ethnic and racial discrimination by directly confronting the pervasive and destructive features of class subordination.

_____

NO

Charles V. Willie

THE INCLINING SIGNIFICANCE OF RACE

It is all a matter of perspective. From the perspective of the dominant people of power, inequality exists because of the personal inadequacies of those who are less fortunate. Varying degrees of fortune is the essence of the social stratification system in this nation. In America, it is the affluent rather than the poor who use social class theory to explain poverty. Moreover, they assert that poverty is not a function of institutional arrangements but a matter of individual capacities. From the perspective of the dominant people of power, the social stratification system in the United States is open and any who has the capacity can rise within it. This orientation toward individual mobility tends to mask the presence of opportunities that are institutionally based such as attending the "right" school, seeking employment with the "right" company or firm, and being of the "right" race. Also this orientation toward individual mobility tends to deny the presence of opposition and oppression that are connected with institutions. According to the perspective of the dominant people of power, opportunity and especially educational and economic opportunity is a function of merit.

William Julius Wilson has used the perspective of the dominant people of power in his article on "The Declining Significance of Race" that appeared in the January/February edition of *Society*. An individual, including a scholar in the social sciences, is free to use any perspective that he or she wishes to use. The tradition of friendly criticism in this field, however, supports the effort which I shall undertake in this commentary. My purpose is to make explicit that which is implicit so that others may assess the conclusions of Professor Wilson on the basis of the premises and the perspective of his analysis . . .

INCOME

First, let us look at income. As recently as 1975, the median income for white families was $14,268 compared with a median of $9,321 for blacks and other minority races. This means that blacks and other racial minorities received only two-thirds as much income as whites. At both ends of the income scale,

From "The Inclining Significance of Race," by Charles V. Willie, *Society*, vol. 15, no. 5, July/ August 1978, pp. 10, 12–15. Copyright © 1978 by Transaction, Inc. Reprinted by permission of Transaction, Inc.

the ratio of black to white income was about the same. Under $5,000 a year there was only 10.2 percent of the white families and individuals compared with 26.3 percent of the population of black families and individuals. Earning $25,000 a year and over in 1975, was 15.1 percent of the white population compared with 6.4 percent of the black population. The proportion of blacks who were very poor was two and one-half times greater than the proportion of whites who were very poor; and the proportion of whites who were most affluent was two and one-third times greater than the proportion of blacks with high incomes. There is not much of a difference in these income ratios by race for the poor and the affluent. In general, the proportion of high-income blacks is far less than what it would be if there was no racial discrimination. The 1977 report, *All Our Children*, by the Carnegie Council on Children of which Kenneth Keniston was senior author states that "90 percent of the income gap between blacks and whites is the result . . . of lower pay for blacks with comparable levels of education and experience." Despite this and other findings such as those presented by economist Herman Miller in his book *Rich Man, Poor Man*, Professor Wilson states that "many talented and educated blacks are now entering positions of prestige and influence at a rate comparable to or, in some situations, exceeding that of whites with equal qualifications."

In 1974, 15 percent of the white male population was of the professional or technical workers category compared with 9 percent of the male population of blacks and other minority races. This appeared to be a notable change relative to whites but it represented only an increase of 3 percentage points over the 6 percent of black and other minority males who were professionals 10 years earlier. Moreover, only 5 percent of the black and other racial minority males were managers and administrators in 1974 compared with 15 percent of all white employed males. In summary, 42 percent of the white male population was white collar in 1974 compared with 24 percent of the racial minority males in this nation. These data indicate that blacks have a long way to go before they catch up with whites in high-level occupations.

Moreover, a study by the Survey Research Center of the University of Michigan that was published in the *New York Times* February 26, 1978, reported that 61 percent of all blacks in a nationwide poll believed that whites either don't care whether or not blacks "get a break" or were actively trying to keep blacks down. It would appear that neither the sentiment of blacks nor the facts of the situation are in accord with the analysis of Professor Wilson and his claim that "class has become more important than race in determining black life chances."

The University of Michigan study also found that one out of every two white persons believed that "few blacks . . . miss out on jobs and promotions because of racial discrimination." This response is similar to the conclusion of Professor Wilson and is the reason why I stated earlier that his analysis was from the perspective of the dominant people of power.

EDUCATION

Second, let us look at what is happening to poor blacks to determine whether their circumstances are more a function of social class than of race. This analysis,

I believe, reveals a fundamental error in the analysis of Professor Wilson—an error no less serious than that committed by Daniel Patrick Moynihan and Christopher Jencks who made observations on whites and projected these upon blacks...

It is obvious that Professor Wilson has analyzed the job situation for affluent blacks. The census data that I reported earlier indicated that blacks were catching up with whites, relatively, so far as employment in the professions is concerned. While the proportion of white male professionals a decade ago was twice as great as the proportion of black and other minority male professionals, the proportion as late as 1974 was only two-thirds greater. On the basis of data like these, Professor Wilson states that "talented and educated blacks are experiencing unprecedented job opportunities in the growing government and corporate sectors." After analyzing the "job situation for the more privileged blacks," Professor Wilson projects these findings upon the poor and says "it would be difficult to argue that the plight of the black underclass is solely the consequence of racial oppression, that is, the explicit and overt efforts of whites to keep blacks subjugated. . . ."

While the facts cited earlier cast doubt upon the conclusion that talented blacks are experiencing "unprecedented job opportunities," even if one accepts the modest improvement for "talented blacks" as fact, it is inappropriate to project middle-class experience upon the underclass of blacks. This is precisely what Professor Wilson has done.

His assertion that "the black experience has moved historically from economic racial oppression experienced by virtually all blacks to economic subordination for the black underclass" can-

cels out racial discrimination as a key cause of poverty among blacks. If one assumes that there are not extraordinary biological differences between blacks and whites in the United States, then it is difficult to explain why the proportion of poor blacks with an annual income under $5,000 is two and one-half times greater than the proportion of poor whites. Among poor white youth and young adults the unemployment rate is higher for high school dropouts than for persons who graduated from high school but did not receive more education. Among blacks, however, the unemployment rate is high and is the same for high school dropouts and for those who graduated from high school but did not receive more education. Staying in high school seems not to make a difference for blacks so far as the risk of unemployment is concerned.

Among whites with only an elementary school education or less, 50 percent are likely to have jobs as service workers or laborers at the bottom of the occupational heap but 80 percent of black workers with this limited education are likely to find work only in these kinds of jobs. This was what Herman Miller found in his analysis of 1960 census data. These facts indicate that education alone cannot explain the disproportionate number of blacks in low-paying jobs. If the absence of education is the basis for limited upward mobility in the stratification system, why do whites with little education get better jobs than blacks?

Using 1968 data, Miller analyzed difference in median income for whites and blacks and other nonwhite minorities. He found that the difference for the races ranged from $880 for those who had completed grade school only to $2,469 for those who had attended or graduated from college. Median income by schooling not only differed by race but tended to widen between the racial groups with increase in education. On the bases of these findings, Miller said that "there is some justification for the feeling by Puerto Ricans, Negroes, and other minority groups that education does not do as much for them financially as it does for others." These findings Miller reported in the 1971 edition of his book, *Rich Man, Poor Man*, and they indicated that racial discrimination is a contributing factor to the occupational opportunities and income received by poor as well as affluent blacks.

RESIDENTIAL SEGREGATION

With reference to residential segregation which Professor Wilson wants to ignore as irrelevant, he has received modest support from the findings of Albert Simkus that were reported in the February 1978 edition of the *American Sociological Review* in an article entitled "Residential Segregation by Occupation and Race in Ten Urbanized Areas, 1950–1970," Simkus said that "historically, blacks with high incomes have been as highly or more highly segregated from whites with similar incomes than have low-income blacks." This fact became "slightly less true . . . by 1970." However, Simkus attributes the slight change to political rather than economic factors. Particularly singled out for credit is civil rights and housing legislation of the 1960s.

Simkus points out that the decrease in residential segregation of affluent blacks is beginning to catch up with the integrated residential areas that characterized lower-income blacks and whites in the past. Specifically, he said that "apart from the comparisons involving

nonwhite professionals, nonwhites and whites in the lowest occupational categories were still slightly less segregated than those in the higher categories."

Finally, I call attention to the fact that Professor Wilson's data are at variance with the clinical observations of other blacks. The unprecedented job opportunities simply have not been experienced by some talented and educated blacks. During the summer of 1977, the *New York Times* published an interview with Sanford Allen, a black violinist with the New York Philharmonic Orchestra. Allen announced his intention to resign from his position. He said that he was "simply tired of being a symbol." At that time, Allen was the only black who had been a member of the 133-year-old musical organization. He charged the more prestigious symphony orchestras of this nation, such as the Boston Symphony, the Chicago Symphony, and two or three others, with running a closed shop that excluded blacks. Allen joined the New York Philharmonic in 1962. During a decade and a half, no other blacks had been hired. A story like this one, of course, is clinical evidence and does not carry the same weight as research evidence systematically gathered. But such clinical evidence has been accumulated recently and deserves to be looked at carefully.

The response of white professionals to admissions policies by colleges and universities that are designed to reserve space for members of previously excluded racial populations in the first-year classes of professional schools is a case in point. The opposition to such practices indicates that talented and educated blacks are not being given access to privilege and power "at a rate comparable to or, in some situations, exceeding that of whites with equivalent qualifications" as

Professor Wilson claims. The opposition to special minority admissions programs is led by white professionals, not white hard-hat or blue-collar workers. This is further clinical evidence that race is not irrelevant and has not declined in significance for talented and educated blacks.

COUNTERHYPOTHESIS

Actually, I would like to introduce a counterhypothesis that the significance of race is increasing especially for middle-class blacks who, because of school desegregation and affirmative action and other integration programs, are coming into direct contact with whites for the first time for extended interaction.

My case studies of black families who have moved into racially integrated neighborhoods and racially integrated work situations indicate that race for some of these pioneers is a consuming experience. They seldom can get away from it. When special opportunities are created, such as in the admissions programs, the minorities who take advantage of them must constantly prove themselves. When a middle-class black has been accepted as Sanford Allen was in the Philharmonic, the issue then shifts to whether or not one is being used as a symbol. Try as hard as they may, middle-class blacks, especially middle-class blacks in racially integrated situations at this period in American history, are almost obsessed with race. Many have experienced this adaptation especially in residential and work situations.

Any obsession, including obsession with race, is painful. Freedom is circumscribed and options are delimited not because of physical segregation but because of the psychological situation. So painful is the experience of racial obsession that two extreme reactions are likely to occur. Middle-class blacks may attempt to deal with the obsession by capitulation—that is, by assuming everything is race-related, that all whites are racists, and that all events and circumstances must be evaluated first in terms of their racial implications. The other adaptation is denial, believing that race is irrelevant and insignificant even when there is clear and present evidence that is not. This is one of the personal consequences of a racist society for the oppressed as the old separatist system begins to crumble. The people who most severely experience the pain of dislocation due to the changing times are the racial minorities who are talented and educated and integrated, not those who are impoverished and isolated.

POSTSCRIPT

Is Racial Oppression Declining in America?

One theme running through Charles Willie's argument is that of black emotional suffering. He cites evidence that suggests that blacks *perceive* themselves as victims of white oppression. A logician would pounce on that. A *perception* of oppression does not by itself prove the *existence* of oppression. Whatever its logical difficulties, however, Willie's argument reveals the persistence of the racial issue in discussions of poverty and inequality. On the other hand, Wilson presents a strong argument that the trends in race relations are moving in the right direction.

The debate over the basic causes of inequalities between blacks and whites continues among black scholars and leaders. In 1978 William J. Wilson wrote *The Declining Significance of Race* (University of Chicago Press), which launched the debate. Somewhat earlier Nathan Glazer argued that the problems faced by blacks and other minorities were due to the effects of past not present discrimination (*Affirmative Discrimination: Ethnic Inequality and Public Policy*, Basic Books, 1975). The black whose works most challenge civil rights leaders is Thomas Sowell. In *Markets and Minorities* (Basic Books, 1981) he argued that blacks should take responsibility for their own success. In *Civil Rights: Rhetoric or Reality?* (Morrow 1984) he chides the civil rights movement. He calls on black leaders to stop asking for special treatment and instead challenge blacks to fight for basic rights, not entitlements. For a contrary view, look at Charles V. Willie's *Race, Ethnicity, and Socioeconomic Status: A Theoretical Analysis of Their Interrelationship* (General Hall, 1983).

For a dialogue that reveals the gulf between the perceptions of blacks and whites—or, between some blacks and some whites—see Margaret Mead and James Baldwin in *A Rap on Race* (Lippincott, 1971). At one point Mead accuses Baldwin of "going back into the past." Baldwin answers: "When I go downstairs out of this building I can be murdered for trying to get a cab. That is not the past. That's the present." For a black perspective that is sharply opposed to Baldwin's, see Thomas Sowell's *Ethnic America: A History* (Basic Books, 1981). A thoughtful exchange appeared in the *New York Times Magazine* on October 9, 1980; see "The Black Plight: Race or Class? A Debate Between Kenneth B. Clark and Carl Gershman," p. 22. For a more recent history of racial oppression, see *Oppression: A Socio-History of Black-White Relations in America* (Nelson-Hall, 1984), by Jonathan H. Turner et al.

ISSUE 10

Is Affirmative Action Reverse Discrimination?

YES: Glenn C. Loury, from "Beyond Civil Rights," *The New Republic* (October 7, 1985)

NO: Herman Schwartz, from "In Defense of Affirmative Action," *Dissent* (Fall 1984)

ISSUE SUMMARY

YES: Harvard professor Glenn Loury contends that insistence on "ill-suited" civil rights strategies makes it impossible for blacks to achieve full equality in American society.

NO: Law professor Herman Schwartz argues that we must somehow undo the cruel consequences of racism that still plague our society and its victims.

In America, equality is a political principle as basic as liberty. "All men are created equal" is the most famous phrase in the Declaration of Independence. More than half a century later, Alexis de Tocqueville examined democracy in America and concluded that its most essential ingredient was the equality of condition. Today we know that the "equality of condition" that de Tocqueville perceived did not exist for women, blacks, American Indians, and other racial minorities, nor for other disadvantaged social classes. Nevertheless, the ideal persisted. When slavery was abolished after the Civil War, the Constitution's newly ratified Fourteenth Amendment proclaimed: "No State shall . . . deny to any person within its jurisdiction the equal protection of the laws."

Equality has been a long time coming. For nearly a century after the freeing of the slaves, American blacks were denied equal protection by law in some states and by social practice nearly everywhere. One-third of the states and the national capital either permitted or compelled racially segregated schools, and segregation was achieved elsewhere through housing policy and social behavior. In 1954 the Supreme Court reversed a fifty-eight-year-old standard that had found "separate but equal" schools compatible with equal protection of the law. A unanimous Court in *Brown v. Board of Education* held that separate is *not* equal for the members of the discriminated-against group when the segregation "generates a feeling of inferiority as to their status in the community that may affect their hearts and minds in a way unlikely ever to be undone." The 1954 ruling on public elementary education has been extended to other areas of both governmental and private conduct, including housing and employment.

Even if judicial decisions and congressional statutes could end all segregation and racial discrimination, would we have achieved equality—or simply perpetuated the *status quo*? The black unemployment rate today is about twice that of whites. Disproportionately higher numbers of blacks experience poverty, brutality, broken homes, physical and mental illness, and early death, while disproportionately lower numbers of them have reached positions of affluence and prestige. It seems likely that much of this *de facto* inequality results from three hundred years of slavery and segregation. If we do no more than to cease this ill-treatment, have we done enough to end the injustices? No, say the proponents of "affirmative action."

The Supreme Court has considered the merits of affirmative action in four major cases: *Regents of the University of California v. Bakke* (1978), *United Steelworkers of America v. Weber* (1979), *Fullilove v. Klutznik* (1980), and *Firefighters v. Stotts* (1984). In the *Bakke* decision, a five-to-four majority agreed that Bakke, the white applicant to the medical school, had been wrongly excluded due to the school's affirmative action policy, but the majority did not agree that admission policies must be completely "color blind." Indeed, Justice Lewis Powell, whose opinion seemed to hold the balance in the case, specifically affirmed that race may be taken into account in considering a candidate's qualifications. In the *Weber* case, a five-to-two majority upheld an agreement between an aluminum plant and a union to establish a quota for blacks in admitting applicants to a special training program. In *Fullilove v. Klutznik*, a six-to-three majority upheld the constitutionality of a federal public works program requiring that ten percent of spending be reserved for minority contractors. Here, again, as in *Bakke*, the Court justices offered a variety of positions on affirmative action. Three justices upheld the program on the ground of congressional power, three wrote a separate opinion upholding it on broader grounds; two joined in a dissent based upon the doctrine of "color-blindness"; and one dissented on narrower grounds. In the more recent *Stotts* decision, the Court seemed to retreat from its earlier position in support of race-conscious remedies for racial imbalance. In a six-to-three decision, the Court ruled that federal courts may not order the firing of white employees who have more seniority than blacks simply for the purpose of saving the jobs of newly-hired blacks during a period of layoffs.

In the following selections, Professor Glenn C. Loury and writer Herman Schwartz debate the merits of affirmative action. In Loury's view, affirmative action only ends up demoralizing the people it was meant to serve, depriving them of a sense of accomplishment, while Schwartz maintains that it is an essential means of undoing the effects of racism in America.

YES

Glenn C. Loury

BEYOND CIVIL RIGHTS

There is today a great deal of serious discussion among black Americans concerning the problems confronting them. Many, if not most, people now concede that not all problems of blacks are due to discrimination, and that they cannot be remedied through civil rights strategies or racial politics. I would go even further: using civil rights strategies to address problems to which they are ill-suited thwarts more direct and effective action. Indeed, the broad application of these strategies to every case of differential achievement between blacks and whites threatens to make it impossible for blacks to achieve full equality in American society.

The civil rights approach has two essential aspects: first, the cause of a particular socioeconomic disparity is identified as a racial discrimination; and second, advocates seek such remedies for the disparity as the courts and administrative agencies provide under the law.

There are fundamental limitations on this approach deriving from our liberal political heritage. What can this strategy do about those important contractual relationships that profoundly affect one's social and economic status but in which racial discrimination is routinely practiced? Choice of marital partner is an obvious example. People discriminate here by race with a vengeance. A black woman does not have an opportunity equal to that of a white woman to become the wife of a given white man. Since white men are on the whole better off financially than black men, this racial inequality of opportunity has substantial monetary costs to black women. Yet surely it is to be hoped that the choice of husband or wife will always be beyond the reach of the law.

The example is not facetious. All sorts of voluntary associations—neighborhoods, friends, business partnerships—are the result of choices often influenced by racial criteria, but which lie beyond the reach of civil rights laws. A fair housing law cannot prevent a disgruntled white resident from moving away if his neighborhood becomes predominantly or even partly black. Busing for desegregation cannot prevent unhappy parents from sending their children to private schools. Withdrawal of university support for student clubs with discriminatory selection rules cannot prevent student cliques from forming along racial lines. And a vast majority of Americans would have it no other way.

As a result, the nondiscrimination mandate has not been allowed to interfere much with personal, private, and intimately social intercourse. Yet such exclusive social connections along group lines have important economic consequences. An extensive literature in economics and sociology documents the crucial importance of family and community background in determining a child's later success in life. Lacking the right "networks," blacks with the same innate abilities as whites wind up less successful. And the elimination of racial discrimination in the economic sphere—but not in patterns of social attachment—will probably not be enough to make up the difference. There are thus elemental limits on what one can hope to achieve through the application of civil rights strategies to what must of necessity be a restricted domain of personal interactions.

The civil rights strategy has generally been restricted to the domain of impersonal, public, and economic transactions such as jobs, credit, and housing. Even in these areas, the efficacy of this strategy can be questioned. The lagging economic condition of blacks is due in significant part to the nature of social life *within* poor black communities. After two decades of civil rights efforts, more than three-fourths of children in some inner-city ghettos are born out of wedlock; black high school dropout rates hover near 50 percent in Chicago and Detroit; two-fifths of murder victims in the country are blacks killed by other blacks; fewer black women graduate from college than give birth while in high school; more than two in five black children are dependent on public assistance. White America's lack of respect for blacks' civil rights cannot be blamed for all these sorry facts. This is not to deny that, in some basic sense, most of these difficulties are related to our history of racial oppression, but only to say that these problems have taken on a life of their own, and cannot be effectively reversed by civil rights policies.

Higher education is a case in point. In the not too distant past, blacks, Asians, and women faced severe obstacles to attending or teaching at American colleges and universities, especially at the most prestigious institutions. Even after black scholars studied at the great institutions, their only possibilities for employment were at the historically black colleges, where they faced large teaching loads and burdensome administrative duties. Their accomplishments were often acknowledged by their white peers only grudgingly, if at all.

Today opportunities for advanced education and academic careers for blacks abound. Major universities throughout the country are constantly searching for qualified black candidates to hire as professors, or to admit to study. Most state colleges and universities near black population centers have made a concerted effort to reach those in the inner city. Almost all institutions of higher learning admit blacks with lower grades or test scores than white students. There are special programs funded by private foundations to help blacks prepare for advanced study in medicine, economics, engineering, public policy, law, and other fields.

Yet, with all these opportunities (and despite improvement in some areas), the number of blacks advancing in the academic world is distressingly low. The percentage of college students who are black, after rising throughout the 1970s, has actually begun to decline. And though the proportion of doctorates granted to blacks has risen slightly over the last decade, a majority of black doctorates are still earned in the field of education. Despite constant pressure to hire black professors and strenuous efforts to recruit them, the percentage of blacks on elite university faculties has remained constant or fallen in the past decade.

Meanwhile, other groups traditionally excluded are making impressive gains. Asian-Americans, though less than two percent of the population, make up 6.6 percent of U.S. scientists with doctorates; they constitute 7.5 percent of the students at Yale, and nine percent at Stanford. The proportion of doctorates going to women has risen from less than one-seventh to nearly one-third in the last decade. Less than two percent of Harvard professors at all ranks are black, but more than 25 percent are women.

Now, it is entirely possible that blacks experience discrimination at these institutions. But as anyone who has spent time in an elite university community knows, these institutions are not racist in character, nor do they deny opportunities to blacks with outstanding qualifications. The case can be made that just the opposite is true—that these institutions are so anxious to raise the number of blacks in their ranks that they overlook deficiencies when making admissions or appointment decisions involving blacks.

One obvious reason for skepticism about discrimination as the cause of the problem here is the relatively poor academic performance of black high school and college students. Black performance on standardized college admissions test, though improving, still lags far behind whites. In 1982 there were only 205 blacks in the entire country who scored above 700 on the math component of the SAT. And, as Robert Klitgaard shows convincingly in his book *Choosing Elites*, post-admissions college performance by black students is less than that of whites, even when controlling for differences in high school grades and SAT scores. These differences in academic performance are not just limited to poor blacks, or to high school students. On the SAT exam, blacks from families with incomes in excess of $50,000 per year still scored 60 to 80 points below comparable whites. On the 1982 Graduate Record Exam, the gap between black and white students' average scores on the mathematics component of this test was 171 points. According to Klitgaard, black students entering law school in the late 1970s had median scores on the LSAT at the eighth percentile of all students' scores.

Such substantial differences in educational results are clearly a matter of great concern. Arguably, the government should be actively seeking to attenuate them. But it seems equally clear that this is not a civil rights matter that can be reversed by seeking out and changing someone's discriminatory behavior. Moreover, it is possible that great harm will be done if the problem is defined and pursued in those terms.

Take the controversy over the racial quotas at the Boston Latin School, the pride and joy of the city's public school system. It was founded before Harvard, in 1635, and it has been recognized ever since as a center of academic excellence. Boston Latin maintains its very high standards through a grueling program of study, including Latin, Greek, calculus, history, science, and the arts. Three hours of homework per night are typical. College admissions personnel acknowledge the excellence of this program; 95 percent of the class of 1985 will go to college.

The institution admits its students on the basis of their marks in primary school and performance on the Secondary School Admissions Test. In 1974, when Boston's public schools became subject to court-ordered desegregation, Judge Arthur Garrity considered closing Boston Latin, because the student population at the time was more than 90 percent white. In the end, a racial admissions quota was employed, requiring that 35 percent of the entering classes be black and Hispanic. Of the 2,245 students last year, over half were female, 57 percent white, 23 percent black, 14 percent Asian, and six percent Hispanic.

Historically the school has maintained standards through a policy of academic "survival of the fittest." Those who were unable to make it through the academic rigors simply transferred to another school. Thus, there has always been a high rate of attrition; it is now in the range of 30 percent to 40 percent. But today, unlike the pre-desegregation era, most of those who do not succeed at Boston Latin are minority students. Indeed, though approximately 35 percent of each entering class is black and Hispanic, only 16 percent of last year's senior class was. That is, for each non-Asian minority student who graduates from Latin, there is one who did not. The failure rate for whites is about half that. Some advocates of minority student interest have complained of discrimination, saying in effect that the school is not doing enough to assist those in academic difficulty. Yet surely one reason for

the poor performance of the black and Hispanic students is Judge Garrity's admissions quota. To be considered for admission, whites must score at the 70th percentile or higher on the admissions exam, while blacks and Hispanics need only score above the 50th percentile.

Recently Thomas Atkins, former general counsel of the NAACP, who has been representing the black plaintiffs in the Boston school desegregation lawsuit, which has been going on for ten years, proposed that the quota at Boston Latin be raised to roughly 50 percent black, 20 percent Hispanic and Asian, and 30 percent white—a reflection of the racial composition of the rest of Boston's public schools. Unless there were a significant increase in the size of the school, this could only be accomplished by doubling the number of blacks admitted while cutting white enrollment in half. This in turn, under plausible distributional assumptions, would require that the current difference of 20 points in the minimum test scores required of black and white students accepted be approximately doubled. Since the additional black students admitted would be less prepared than those admitted under the current quota, one could expect an even higher failure rate among minorities were this plan to be accepted. The likely consequence would be that more than three-fourths of those leaving Boston Latin without a degree would be blacks and Hispanics. It is also plausible to infer that such an action would profoundly alter, if not destroy, the academic climate in the school.

This is not simply an inappropriate use of civil rights methods, though it is surely that. It is an almost wanton moral surrender. By what logic of pedagogy can these students' difficulties be attributed to racism in view of the fact that the school system has been run by court order for over a decade? By what calculus of fairness can those claiming to be fighting for justice argue that outstanding white students, many from poor homes themselves (80 percent of Latin graduates require financial aid in college), should be denied the opportunity for this special education so that minority students who are not prepared for it may nonetheless enroll? Is there so little faith in the aptitude of the minority young people that the highest standards should not be held out for them? It would seem that the real problem here—a dearth of academically outstanding black high school students in Boston—is not amendable to rectification by court order.

Another example from the field of education illustrates the "opportunity costs" of the civil rights strategy. In 1977 the Ann Arbor public school system was sued by public interest lawyers on behalf of a group of black parents with children in the primary grades. The school system was accused of denying equal educational opportunity to these children. The problem was that the black students were not learning how to read at an acceptable rate, though the white youngsters were. The suit alleged that by failing to take into account in the teaching of reading to these children the fact that they spoke an identifiable, distinct dialect of the English language—Black English—the black students were denied equal educational opportunity. The lawsuit was successful.

As a result, in 1979 the court ordered that reading teachers in Ann Arbor be given special "sensitivity" training so that, while teaching standard English to these children, they might take into account the youngsters' culturally distinct patterns of speech. Ann Arbor's public school system has dutifully complied. A recent discussion of this case with local educators revealed that, as of six years after the initial court order, the disparity in reading achievement between blacks and whites in Ann Arbor persists at a level comparable to the one before the lawsuit was brought. It was their opinion that, though of enormous symbolic importance, the entire process had produced little in the way of positive educational impact on the students.

This is not intended as a condemnation of those who brought the suit, nor do I offer here any opinion on whether promotion of Black English is a good idea. What is of interest is the process by which the problem was defined, and out of which a remedy was sought. In effect, the parents of these children were approached by lawyers and educators active in civil rights, and urged to help their children learn to read by bringing this action. Literally thousands of hours went into conceiving and trying this case. Yet, in the end only a hollow, symbolic victory was won.

But it is quite possible that this line of attack on the problem caused other more viable strategies not to be pursued. For example, a campaign to tutor the first and second graders might have made an impact, giving them special attention and extra hours of study through the voluntary participation of those in Ann Arbor possessing the relevant skills. With roughly 35,000 students at the University of Michigan's Ann Arbor campus (a fair number of whom are black), it would have required that only a fraction of one percent of them spare an afternoon or evening once a week for there to be sufficient numbers to provide the needed services. There were at most only a few hundred poor black students in the primary grades experiencing reading difficulties. And, more than providing this needed aid for specific kids, such an undertaking would have helped to cultivate a more healthy relationship between the university and the town. It could have contributed to building a tradition of direct services that would be of more general value. But none of this happened, in part because the civil rights approach was almost reflexively embraced by the advocating parties concerned.

The danger to blacks of too broad a reliance on civil rights strategies can be subtle. It has become quite clear that affirmative action creates uncertain perceptions about the qualifications of those minorities who benefit from it. In an employment situation, for example, if it is known that different selection criteria are used for different races, and that the quality of performance on the job depends on how one did on the criteria of selection, then in the absence of other information, it is rational to expect lower performance from persons of the race that was preferentially favored in selection. Using race as a criterion of selection in employment, in other words, creates objective incentives for customers, coworkers, and others to take race into account after the employment decision has been made.

The broad use of race preference to treat all instances of "underrepresentation" also introduces uncertainty among the beneficiaries themselves. It undermines the ability of people confidently to assert, if only to themselves, that they are as good as their achievements would seem to suggest. It therefore undermines the extent to which the personal success of any one black can become the basis of guiding the behavior of other blacks. Fewer individuals in a group subject to such preferences return to their communities of origin to say, "I made it on my own, through hard work, self-application, and native ability, and so can you!" Moreover, it puts even the "best and brightest" of the favored group in the position of being supplicants of benevolent whites.

And this is not the end of the story. In order to defend such programs in the political arena—especially at the elite institutions—it becomes necessary to argue that almost no blacks could reach these heights without special favors. When there is internal disagreement among black intellectuals, for example, about the merits of affirmative action, critics of the policy are often attacked as being disingenuous, since (it is said) they clearly owe their own prominence to the very policy they criticize. The specific circumstances of the individual do not matter in this, for it is presumed that *all* blacks, whether directly or indirectly, are indebted to civil rights activity for their achievements. The consequence is a kind of "socialization" of the individual's success. The individual's effort to claim achievement for himself (and thus to secure the autonomy and legitimacy needed to deviate from group consensus, should that seem appropriate) is perceived as a kind of betrayal. There is nothing wrong, of course, with acknowledging the debt all blacks owe to those who fought and beat Jim Crow. There is everything wrong with a group's most accomplished persons feeling that the celebration of their personal attainment represents betrayal of their fellows.

In his recent, highly esteemed comparative history of slavery, *Slavery and Social Death*, sociologist Orlando Patterson defines slavery as the "permanent, violent domination of natally alienated and generally dishonored persons." Today's policy debates frequently focus on (or perhaps more accurately, appropriate) the American slave experience, especially the violent character of the institution, its brutalization of the Africans, and its destructive effects on social life among the slaves. Less attention is paid nowadays to the *dishonored* condition of the slave, and by extension, of the freedman. For Patterson this dishonoring was crucial. He sees as a common feature of slavery wherever it has occurred the parasitic phenomenon whereby masters derive honor and standing from their power over slaves, and the slaves suffer an extreme marginality by virtue of having no social existence except that mediated by their masters. Patterson rejects the "property in people" definition of slavery, arguing that relations of respect and standing among persons are also crucial. But if this is so, it follows that emancipation—the ending of the master's property claim—is not of itself sufficient to convert a slave (or his descendant) into a genuinely equal citizen. There remains the intractable problem of overcoming the historically generated "lack of honor" of the freedman.

This problem, in my judgment, remains with us. Its eventual resolution is made less likely by blacks' broad, permanent reliance on racial preferences as remedies for academic or occupational under-performance. A central theme in Afro-American political and intellectual history is the demand for respect—the struggle to gain inclusion within the civic community, to become coequal participants in the national enterprise. This is, of course, a problem that all immigrant groups also faced, and that most have overcome. But here, unlike some other areas of social life, it seems that the black population's slave origins, subsequent racist exclusion, and continued dependence on special favors from the majority uniquely exacerbates the problem.

Blacks continue to seek the respect of their fellow Americans. And yet it becomes increasingly clear that, to do so, black Americans cannot substitute judicial and legislative decree for what is to be won through the outstanding achievements of individual black persons. That is, neither the pity, nor the guilt, nor the coerced acquiescence in one's demands—all of which have been amply available to blacks over the last two decades—is sufficient. *For what ultimately is being sought is the freely conveyed respect of one's peers.* Assigning prestigious positions so as to secure a proper racial balance—this is a permanent, broadly practiced policy—seems fundamentally inconsistent with the attainment of this goal. It is a truth worth noting that not everything of value can be redistributed.

If in the psychological calculus by which people determine their satisfaction such status considerations of honor, dignity, and respect are important, then this observation places basic limits on the extent to which public policy can bring about genuine equality. This is especially so with respect to the policy of racially preferential treatment, because its use to "equalize" can actually destroy the good that is being sought on behalf of those initially unequal. It would seem that, where the high regard of others is being sought, there is no substitute for what is to be won through the unaided accomplishments of individual persons.

NO

Herman Schwartz

IN DEFENSE OF AFFIRMATIVE ACTION

The Reagan administration's assault on the rights of minorities and women has focused on the existing policy of affirmative action. This strategy may be shrewd politics but it is mean-spirited morally and insupportable legally. . . .

Affirmative action has been defined as "a public or private program designed to equalize hiring and admission opportunities for historically disadvantaged groups by taking into consideration those very characteristics which have been used to deny them equal treatment." The controversy swirls primarily around the use of numerical goals and timetables for hiring or promotion, for university admissions, and for other benefits. It is fueled by the powerful strain of individualism that runs through American history and belief.

It is a hard issue, about which reasonable people can differ. Insofar as affirmative action is designed to compensate the disadvantaged for past racism, sexism, and other discrimination, many understandably believe that today's society should not have to pay for their ancestors' sins. But somehow we must undo the cruel consequences of the racism and sexism that still plague us, both for the sake of the victims and to end the enormous human waste that costs society so much. Civil Rights Commission Chairman Pendleton has conceded that discrimination is not only still with us but is, as he put it, "rampant." As recently as January 1984, the dean of faculty at Amherst College wrote in the *New York Times:*

> In my contacts with a considerable range of academic institutions, I have become aware of pervasive residues of racism and sexism, even among those whose intentions and conscious beliefs are entirely nondiscriminatory. Indeed, I believe most of us are afflicted with such residues. Beyond the wrongs of the past are the wrongs of the present. Most discriminatory habits in academia are nonactionable; affirmative action goals are our only instrument for focusing sustained attention.

The plight of black America not only remains grave, but in many respects, it is getting worse. The black unemployment rate—21 percent in early 1983— is double that for whites and the gap continues to increase. For black

20- to 24-year-old males, the rate—an awful 30 percent—is almost triple that for whites; for black teenagers the rate approaches 50 percent. More than half of all black children under three years of age live in homes below the poverty line. The gap between white and black family income, which prior to the '70s had narrowed a bit, has steadily edged wider, so that black-family income is now only 55 percent of that of whites. Only 3 percent of the nation's lawyers and doctors are black and only 4 percent of its managers, but over 50 percent of its maids and garbage collectors. Black life expectancy is about six years less than that of whites; the black infant mortality rate is nearly double.

Although the situation for women, of all races, is not as bad, the average earnings of women still, at most, are only two-thirds of those of their male counterparts. And the economic condition of black women, who now head 41 percent of the 6.4 million black families, is particularly bad; a recent Wellesley study found that black women are not only suffering in the labor market, but they receive substantially less public assistance and child support than white women. The economic condition of female household heads of any race is just as deplorable: 90 percent of the 4 million single-parent homes are headed by women, and more than half are below the poverty line. Bureau of Labor Statistics data reveal that in 1983 women actually earned *less* than two-thirds of their male counterparts' salaries, and black women earned only 84 percent of the white female incomes. In his 1984 State of the Union address, President Reagan claimed dramatic gains for women during the 1983 recovery. A *Washington Post* analysis the next day charitably described his claims as "overstated," noting that the Bureau of Labor Statistics reports (on which the president relied) showed that "there was no breakthrough. The new jobs which the president cited included many in sales and office work, where women have always found work" and are paid little.

We must close these gaps so that we do not remain two nations, divided by race and gender. Although no one strategy can overcome the results of centuries of inequity, the use of goals and timetables in hiring and other benefit distribution programs has helped to make modest improvements. Studies in 1983 show, for example, that from 1974 to 1980 minority employment with employers subject to federal affirmative action requirements rose 20 percent, almost twice the increase elsewhere. Employment of women by covered contractors rose 15 percent, but only 2 percent among others. The number of black police officers nationwide rose from 24,000 in 1970 to 43,500 in 1980; that kind of increase in Detroit produced a sharp decline in citizen hostility toward the police and a concomitant increase in police efficiency. There were also large jumps in minority and female employment among firefighters, and sheet metal and electrical workers.

Few other remedies work as well or as quickly. As the New York City Corporation Counsel told the Supreme Court in the *Fullilove* case about the construction industry (before Mayor Edward Koch decided that affirmative action was an "abomination"), "less drastic means of attempting to eradicate and remedy discrimination have been attempted repeatedly and continuously over the past decade and a half. They have all failed."

What, then, is the basis for the assault on affirmative action?

Apart from the obvious political expediency and ideological reflex of this administration's unvarying conclusion that the "haves" deserve government help and the "have-nots" don't, President Reagan and his allies present two related arguments: (1) hiring and other distributional decisions should be made solely on the basis of individual merit; (2) racial preferences are always evil and will take us back to *Plessy vs. Ferguson* and worse.

Quoting Dr. Martin Luther King Jr., Thurgood Marshall, and Roy Wilkins to support the claim that anything other than total race neutrality is "discriminatory," Assistant Attorney General Reynolds warns that race consciousness will "creat[e] . . . a racial spoils system in America," "stifle the creative spirit," erect artificial barriers, and divide the society. It is, he says, unconstitutional, unlawful, and immoral.

Midge Decter, writing in the *Wall Street Journal* a few years ago, sympathized with black and female beneficiaries of affirmative action programs for the "self-doubts" and loss of "self-regard" that she is sure they suffer, "spiritually speaking," for their "unearned special privileges."

Whenever we take race into account to hand out benefits, declares Linda Chavez, the new executive director of the Reagan Civil Rights Commission, we "discriminate," "destroy[ing] the sense of self."

The legal position was stated by Morris Abram, in explaining why the reshaped Commission hastened to do Reagan's bidding at its very first meeting by withdrawing prior Commission approval of goals and timetables:

I do not need any further study of a principle that comes from the basic bedrock of the Constitution, in which the words say that every person in the land

shall be entitled to the equal protection of the law. Equal means equal. Equal does not mean you have separate lists of blacks and whites for promotion, any more than you have separate accommodations for blacks and whites for eating. Nothing will ultimately divide a society more than this kind of preference and this kind of reverse discrimination.

In short, any form of race preference is equivalent to racism.

All of this represents a nadir of "Newspeak," all too appropriate for this administration in Orwell's year. For it has not only persistently fought to curtail minority and women's rights in many contexts, but it has used "separate lists" based on color, sex, and ethnic origin whenever politically or otherwise useful.

For example, does anyone believe that blacks like Civil Rights Commission Chairman Clarence Pendleton or Equal Employment Opportunities Commission Chairman Clarence Thomas were picked because of the color of their eyes? Or that Linda Chavez Gersten was made the new executive director for reasons having nothing to do with the fact that her maiden and professional surname is Chavez?

Perhaps the most prominent recent example of affirmative action is President Reagan's selection of Sandra Day O'Connor for the Supreme Court. Obviously, she was on a "separate list," because on any unitary list this obscure lower-court state judge, with no federal experience and no national reputation, would never have come to mind as a plausible choice for the highest court. (Incidentally, despite Ms. Decter's, Mr. Reynolds's, and Ms. Chavez's concern about the loss of "self-regard" suffered by beneficiaries of such preferences, "spiritually speaking"

Justice O'Connor seems to be bearing her loss and spiritual pain quite easily.) And, like so many other beneficiaries of affirmative action given an opportunity that would otherwise be unavailable, she may perform well.

This is not to say that Reagan should not have chosen a woman. The appointment ended decades of shameful discrimination against women lawyers, discrimination still practiced by Reagan where the lower courts are concerned, since he has appointed very few female federal judges apart from Justice O'Connor—of 123 judgeships, Reagan has appointed no women to the courts of appeals and only 10 to the district benches. Of these judgeships, 86 percent went to white males. But the choice of Sandra O'Connor can be explained and justified only by the use of affirmative action and a separate list, not by some notion of neutral "individual merit" on a single list.

But is affirmative action constitutional and legal? Is its legal status, as Mr. Abram claims, so clear by virtue of principles drawn from the "basic bedrock of the Constitution" that no "further study" is necessary?

Yes, but not in the direction that he and this administration want to go. Affirmative action is indisputably constitutional. Not once but many times the Supreme Court has upheld the legality of considering race to remedy the wrongs of prejudice and discrimination. In 1977, for example, in *United Jewish Organizations vs. Carey,* the Supreme Court upheld a New York statute that "deliberately increased the nonwhite majorities in certain districts in order to enhance the opportunity for election of nonwhite representatives from those districts," even if it disadvantaged certain white Jewish

communities. Three members of the Court including Justice Rehnquist explained that "no racial slur or stigma with respect to whites or any other race" was involved. In the *Bakke* case, five members of the Court upheld the constitutionality of a state's favorable consideration of race as a factor in university admissions, four members would have sustained a fixed 16 percent quota. In *United Steelworkers of America vs. Weber,* a 5:2 majority held that private employers could set up a quota system with separate lists for selecting trainees for a newly created craft program. In *Fullilove vs. Klutznick,* six members of the Court led by Chief Justice Burger unequivocally upheld a congressional set-aside of 10 percent for minority contractors on federal public works programs.

All members of the present Court except for Justice O'Connor have passed on affirmative action in one or more of these four cases, and each has upheld it at one time or another. Although the decisions have been based on varying grounds, with many differing opinions, the legal consequence is clear: affirmative action is lawful under both the Constitution and the statutes. To nail the point home, the Court in January 1984 not once but *twice* rejected the Justice Department's effort to get it to reconsider the issue where affirmative action hiring plans are adopted by governmental bodies (the Detroit Police Department and the New York State Corrections system), an issue left open in *Weber,* which had involved a private employer.

The same result obtains on the lower-court levels. Despite the persistent efforts of Reagan's Justice Department, all the courts of appeals have unanimously and repeatedly continued to sustain hiring quotas.

Nor is this anything new. Mr. Reynolds told an audience of prelaw students in January 1984 that the Fourteenth Amendment was intended to bar taking race into account for any purpose at all, and to ensure race neutrality. "That was why we fought the Civil War," he once told the *New York Times.* If so, he knows something that the members of the 1865–66 Congress, who adopted that amendment and fought the war, did not.

Less than a month after Congress approved the Fourteenth Amendment in 1866 the very same Congress enacted eight laws exclusively for the freedman, granting preferential benefits regarding land, education, banking facilities, hospitals, and more. No comparable programs existed or were established for whites. And that Congress knew what it was doing. The racial preferences involved in those programs were vigorously debated with a vocal minority led by President Andrew Johnson, who argued that the preferences wrongly discriminated against whites.

All these governmental actions reflect the obvious point that, as Justice Harry Blackmun has said, "in order to get beyond racism, we must first take account of race. There is no other way." Warren Burger, our very conservative chief justice, had made the point even clearer in the prophetic commentary on this administration's efforts to get the courts to ignore race when trying to remedy the ravages of past discrimination. Striking down in 1971 a North Carolina statute that barred considerations of race in school assignments, the chief justice said:

The statute exploits an apparently neutral form to control school assignments' plans by directing that they be "color blind"; *that requirement, against the back-*

ground of segregation, would render illusory the promise of Brown. Just as the race of students must be considered in determining whether a constitutional violation has occurred so also must race be considered in formulating a remedy... *[color blindness] would deprive school authorities of the one tool [race consideration] absolutely essential to fulfillment of their constitutional obligation to eliminate existing dual school systems.* [Emphasis added.] . . .

But what of the morality of affirmative action? Does it amount to discrimination? Is it true, as Brian Weber's lawyer argued before the Supreme Court, that "you can't avoid discrimination by discriminating"? Will racially influenced hiring take us back to *Plessy vs. Ferguson,* as Pendleton and Reynolds assert? Were Martin Luther King, Jr., Thurgood Marshall, Roy Wilkins, and other black leaders against it?

Hardly. Indeed, it is hard to contain one's outrage at this perversion of what Dr. King, Justice Marshall, and others have said, at this manipulation of their often sorrow-laden eloquence, in order to deny a handful of jobs, school admissions, and other necessities for a decent life to a few disadvantaged blacks out of the many who still suffer from discrimination and would have few opportunities otherwise.

No one can honestly equate a remedial preference for a disadvantaged (and qualified) minority member with the brutality inflicted on blacks and other minorities by Jim Crow laws and practices. The preference may take away some benefits from some white men, but none of them is being beaten, lynched, denied the right to use a bathroom, a place to sleep or eat, being forced to take the dirtiest jobs or denied any work at all, forced to attend dilapidated and mind-killing schools, subjected to brutally unequal justice, or stigmatized as an inferior being.

Setting aside, after proof of discrimination, a few places a year for qualified minorities out of hundreds and perhaps thousands of employees, as in the Kaiser plant in the *Weber* case, or 16 medical-school places out of 100 as in *Bakke*, or 10 percent of federal public work contracts as in *Fullilove*, or even 50 percent of new hires for a few years as in some employment cases—this has nothing in common with the racism that was inflicted on helpless minorities, and it is a shameful insult to the memory of the tragic victims to lump together the two.

This administration claims that it does favor "affirmative action" of a kind: "employers should seek out and train minorities," Linda Chavez told a *Washington Post* interviewer. Apart from the preference involved in setting aside money for "seeking out" and "training" minorities (would this include preference in training programs like the *Weber* plan, whose legality Mr. Reynolds said was "wrongly decided"?), the proposed remedy is ineffectual—it just doesn't work. As the "old" Civil Rights Commission had reported, "By the end of the 1960s, enforcement officials realized that discernible indicators of progress were needed." Consequently, "goals and timetables" came into use. . . .

There are indeed problems with affirmative action, but not of the kind or magnitude that Messrs. Reynolds and Abram claim: problems about whether these programs work, whether they impose heavy burdens, how these burdens can be lightened, and the like. They are not the basis for charges that affirmative action is equivalent to racism and for perverting the words of Dr. King and others.

"Equal is equal" proclaims Morris Abram, and that's certainly true. But it is just as true that equal treatment of unequals perpetuates and aggravates inequality. And gross inequality is what we still have today. As William Coleman, secretary of transportation in the Ford administration, put it,

> For black Americans, racial equality is a tradition without a past. Perhaps, one day America will be color-blind. It takes an extraordinary ignorance of actual life in America today to believe that day has come. . . . [For blacks], there is another American "tradition"—one of slavery, segregation, bigotry, and injustice.

POSTSCRIPT

Is Affirmative Action Reverse Discrimination?

Much of the argument between Loury and Schwartz turns on the question of "color-blindness." To what extent should our laws be "colorblind"? During the 1950s and early 1960s, civil rights leaders were virtually unanimous on this point. "I have a dream," said Martin Luther King, "[that white and black people] will not be judged by the color of their skin but on the content of their character." This was the consensus view in 1963, but today Schwartz seems to be suggesting that the statement needs to be qualified. In order to *bring about* color-blindness, it may be necessary to become temporarily color-conscious. But for how long? And is there a danger that this temporary color-consciousness may become a permanent policy?

Robert M. O'Neil, in *Discriminating Against Discrimination* (Indiana, 1975), studied preferential admission to universities and supported preferential treatment without racial quotas. Those critical of this distinction hold that preferential treatment necessarily implies racial quotas, or at least race-consciousness. Another area that requires officials to focus upon race is that of busing, a policy of which Lina A. Gragli's *Disaster by Decree* (Cornell, 1976) is highly critical. The focus of Allan P. Sindler's *Bakke, DeFunis, and Minority Admissions* (Longman, 1978) is on affirmative action in higher education. Thomas N. Dayment estimates that the differences between black and white earnings will require half a century to decrease substantially (see "Racial Equity or Racial Equality," *Demography*, vol. 17, 1980, pp. 379–393).

Whatever the Supreme Court says today or in the future, it will not be easy to lay to rest the issue of affirmative action. There are few issues on which opposing sides are more intransigent. It appears as if there is no satisfactory "solution," and, at the moment, no compromise that can satisfy the passionate convictions on both issues.

PART 5

Political Economy

It often seems that political power and economic power are merged within a "power elite." Is this really the case? Two questions of public policy continue to be debated: is the size of our government creating problems, and what should the government do for people who cannot take care of themselves? These are important issues in a society that professes a dedication to democracy but prefers private actions to government actions.

Does an Elite Rule America?

Has American Government Gotten Too Big?

Does Welfare Do More Harm Than Good?

Capitol Bldg./K. Jewell

181

ISSUE 11
Does an Elite Rule America?

YES: G. William Domhoff, from *Who Rules America Now?* (Prentice-Hall, 1983)

NO: Andrew M. Greeley, from *Building Coalitions: American Politics in the 1970s* (Franklin Watts, 1974)

ISSUE SUMMARY

YES: Sociologist G. William Domhoff tries to demonstrate that the American upper class occupies a surprisingly large number of influential positions in society which enables it to rule America.
NO: Sociologist Andrew M. Greeley argues that there is no single, established center of power and points to the behavior of the system as evidence to support his view.

Since the framing of the United States Constitution in 1787, there have been periodic charges that America is controlled, or in imminent danger of being controlled, by a power elite. All representative government is necessarily government by elites (i.e., small, selective ruling groups), but those who raise the specter of a power elite are charging that America is run by an *unrepresentative* elite, one that is unaccountable to the majority of voters. Almost invariably it is pointed out that this elite is not just political but economic as well. Although all industrial societies have gradations of wealth, democracy is supposed to counter the weight of money with the weight of numbers. The basic contention of the elite-theorists, then, is not simply that there are rich and poor in America but that the very rich—or a small elite working in league with them—are making all the crucial decisions.

Fear of elitism has a long history in America. Richard Henry Lee, a signer of the Declaration of Independence, spoke for many "anti-federalists" who opposed ratification of the Constitution when he warned that the proposed charter shifted power away from the people and into the hands of the "aristocrats" and "moneyites," those who "avariciously grasp at all power and property." Long after these fears were more or less quieted, there still remained a residue of suspicion that the wealthy were manipulating the machinery of government for their own purposes. Before the Civil War, Jacksonian Democrats denounced the eastern merchants and bankers who, they charged, were usurping the power of the people. After the Civil War, a number of "radical" parties and movements revived this theme of anti-elitism. The ferment—which was brought about by the rise of industrial monopolies, government corruption, and economic hardship for western farmers—culminated in the founding of the People's party at the beginning of the 1890s. The Populists, as they were more commonly called, wanted economic and political reforms aimed at transferring power away from the rich and back to "the plain people." The populist assumption was that ordinary people had once possessed sovereign power in America, but that it had slipped away from them.

Since the 1930s, American radicalism has probably been more influenced by Marxism than by populism. Like populism, Marxism emphasizes the domination of America by the rich; unlike populism, Marxism does not look back with nostalgia on some golden age of democracy in America. Marxists believe America has always been dominated by wealth, though the domination has taken different forms at different periods. Marxists also differ from populists in that they stress the class basis of domination. Instead of seeing the problem of elitism as that of a conspiracy of a few evil men, Marxists view it more impersonally, as a tendency inherent in capitalism.

One of the best-developed arguments disputing the populist-Marxist thesis that America is ruled by an unrepresentative elite is the argument of *pluralism*. Pluralists admit that there are many elites in our society, for that is precisely their point: Because America contains so many groups, they contend, each has a tendency to counterbalance the power of the others. Thus, no group or coalition of groups can become an "establishment" in America.

Andrew Greeley, a priest and sociologist who teaches at the University of Arizona, argues the pluralist position in the following debate on elitism. On the other side, arguing the elitist thesis, is sociologist G. William Domhoff, who suggests that the upper class rules America because its members occupy a majority of the important positions in business and government.

YES

G. William Domhoff

THE ISSUE OF CLASS AND POWER IN AMERICA

Class and *power* are terms that make Americans a little uneasy, and concepts such as *ruling class* and *power elite* immediately put people on guard. The idea that a relatively fixed group of privileged people might dominate the economy and government goes against the American grain and the founding principles of the country. People may differ in their social levels, and some people may have more influence than others, but there can be no ruling class or power elite when power is constitutionally lodged in all the people, when there is democratic participation through elections and lobbying, and when the evidence of upward social mobility is everywhere apparent. If the question is asked, Who rules in the United States? the answer is likely to be in terms of interest groups, elected officials, and the people in general.

Contrary to this pluralistic view of power, it is the purpose of this book to present systematic evidence that suggests there is social upper class in the United States that is a ruling class by virtue of its dominant role in the economy and government. It will be shown that this ruling class is socially cohesive, has its basis in the large corporations and banks, plays a major role in shaping the social and political climate, and dominates the federal government through a variety of organizations and methods. . . .

[My] argument, although contrary to the pluralist theory of power so prevalent in the American social sciences, does not deny that everyone is equal before the law and that there are opportunities for social mobility. It does not deny that there is freedom of expression, open political participation, and public conflict over significant issues. Nor is the argument one that ignores fundamental changes in the United States over the centuries. It does not deny that the basic form of private property has evolved from personal ownership and partnerships to corporate stock ownership, that the basis of social cohesion has shifted in part from the family and church to schools and clubs, or that the responsibility for policy formation has transferred from informal caucuses and political parties to foundations, formal policy-planning groups, and think tanks. Indeed, to begin with the premise that the class system is an open and changing one, and the political system a democratic one, is to state the aim of the book more clearly, which is to demonstrate that a ruling class can continue to exist amid the conflict and change that are so apparent in American society.

Moreover, to claim that there is an upper class with enough power to be considered a ruling class does not imply that other levels of society are totally powerless. Domination does not mean total control, but the ability to set the terms under which other groups and classes must operate. Highly trained professionals with an interest in environmental and consumer issues have been able to couple their understanding of the legislative process with well-timed publicity to win governmental restrictions on some corporation practices. Wage and salary workers, when they are organized into unions, have been able to gain concessions on wages, hours, and working conditions. Even the most powerless of people, the very poor and those discriminated against, sometimes develop the capacity to disrupt the system through strikes, riots, or other forms of coercion, and there is evidence that such activities do bring about some redress of grievances, at least for a short time.

Most of all, there is also the fact that people can vote. Although one basic theme of [my argument] is a critique of the pluralistic notion that voting necessarily makes government responsive to the will of the majority, [I do] not deny that under certain circumstances the electorate has been able to place restraints on the actions of the power elite as a whole, or to determine which leaders within the power elite will have the greatest influence on policy. This is especially a possibility when there are disagreements within the ruling class, as has been pointed out by several political theorists in the past. . . .

THE CONTROL OF THE CORPORATE COMMUNITY

Most sectors of the American economy are dominated by a relative handful of large corporations. The corporations, in turn, are linked in a variety of ways to create a corporate community. At an economic level, the ties within the corporate community are manifested in ownership of common stock on the part of both families and other corporations, as well as in joint ventures among corporations and in the common sources of bank loans that most corporations share. At a more sociological level, the corporate community is joined together by the use of the same legal, accounting, and consulting firms and by the similar experiences of executives working in the bureaucratic structure of a large organization. Then too, the large corporations come together as a business community because they share the same values and goals—in particular, the profit motive. Finally, and not least, the common goals of the corporations lead them to have common enemies in the labor movement and middle-class reformers, which gives them a further sense of a shared identity.

[The purpose here is] to demonstrate that the most important corporations, commercial banks, investment banks, and law firms at the heart of this corporate community are controlled by members of the upper class and that the corporate community is therefore the primary financial basis for the upper class. Although information presented [previously] showed that upper class people are heavily involved in financial and business pursuits, such information does not demonstrate automatically that members of the upper class are leaders in the corporate community. It may be that they are involved in smaller businesses, less important sectors of the economy, or in less important positions in large corporations.

In fact, there are a great many pluralists among American social scientists who deny that members of the upper class have control positions within the corporation community. They believe that the growth of the corporation has led to the dispersal of stock ownership on the one hand and the rise in importance of highly trained professional managers with no class allegiance on the other. There has been a "breakup of family capitalism" in the often quoted words of sociologist Daniel Bell, a "separation of ownership and control," in the even more frequently cited words of lawyer A.A. Berle, Jr., and economist Gardner Means. According to this view, the upper class continues to exist as a high-status social group due to dividends from general stock ownership, but this upper class has lost its community of economic interest and its power now that its members no longer control major businesses. By way of contrast, managers of the large corporations are said to have power without property.

The idea that the upper class is cut off from a determinate role in the corporate community is one of the major objections to the claim that the upper class is a ruling class. In order to deal with this issue, [I] will present four types of information to show that (1) members of the upper class own a majority of all privately held corporate stock in the United States; (2) many large stockholders and stockholding families continue to be involved in the direction of major corporations; (3) members of the upper class are disproportionately represented on the boards of large corporations in general; and (4) the professional managers of middle-level origins who rise to the top of the corporations are assimilated into the upper class both socially and economically and share the values of upper class owners.

THE CONCENTRATION OF STOCK OWNERSHIP

It is often emphasized in advertising campaigns that there are many millions of stockholders in the United States. In the 1950s the New York Stock Exchange publicized the large number of stockholders by calling the system "people's capitalism," and in the 1960s and 1970s individual companies ran magazine and television advertising that included information on their tens of thousands of stockholders. During the late 1970s the stocks owned by pension funds were sometimes included in these claims, swelling the number of worker-owners higher than ever before. Management consultant Peter Drucker went so far as to say that the "unseen revolution" of pension fund socialism had brought to America "a more radical shift in ownership than Soviet communism," a claim that was pointed out to be quite inaccurate by economists and lawyers. A pension fund is only a promise to pay a certain amount of money to people of a certain age after certain number of years of work, not ownership of stock by workers by which they can reap the benefit of any appreciation in its value or exercise its voting power to affect corporate policy.

Whatever the actual number of stockholders, systematic studies show that most of them own very little stock. Robert Lampman's studies using the estate-multiplier method for six different years between 1922 and 1953 estimated that the top 1 percent of all adults held from 61.5 to 76 percent of all privately held stock. Using the same method, James D. Smith found the percentage to be 51 percent for the top 1 percent in 1969. Smith's work also demonstrates that stock is even more dramatically concentrated within the hands of a few thousand major owners. One-twentieth of 1 percent of American adults have one-fifth of the corporate stock, and 0.2 percent have one-third of it. Sociologist Maurice Zeitlin makes this concentration more graphic by pointing out that "the Rose Bowl's 104,696 seats would still be half empty if only every American who owns $1 million or more in corporate stock came to cheer." . . .

OWNERSHIP AND CONTROL

The control of a corporation, generally speaking, is demonstrated in three different ways. The first is the ability to replace top management. The second is the ability to maintain active involvement on the board of directors of the corporation. The third is the ability to have an influential part in major decisions concerning such matters as mergers, acquisitions, and large-scale changes in the growth and profit strategies of the corporation.

Except for the top several hundred publicly held corporations, there is every reason to believe that the relationship between ownership and control is very

close by these criteria. This is obviously the case for hundreds of very large corporations that are privately owned by a family or group of families. The size and extent of such corporations is often overlooked in discussions of the modern corporation. In 1976 *Forbes* estimated that there were over 350 such companies with sales above $100 million a year. Then, too, in some manufacturing industries that are less concentrated, such as printing, furniture, and clothing, privately held firms account for over two-thirds of sales, and privately held firms are even more important in such nonmanufacturing sectors as wholesaling, retailing, and construction. Moreover, the close relationship between ownership and control also holds for many large publicly held corporations that are just below the 200 or 300 largest firms; in most such firms, large percentages of stock are held by a few owners who also serve as directors and top managers. . . .

Family Ownership

Three different studies provide detailed evidence on the extent of family involvement in the largest American corporations. The factual information provided by these studies concerns the concentration of stock ownership in specific families and the number of people from these families who serve as corporate directors. In the past this information was sometimes looked upon as inconclusive by skeptics, who argued that the studies provided no evidence of family coordination. However, the work by Dunn, Schwartz, and others on family offices and holding companies greatly strengthens the possibility that these concentrations of stock can be used for control purposes.

The first of these studies, by political scientist Philip Burch, used both official documents and the informal—but often more informative—findings of the business press for the years 1950 to 1970 as its sources of information. Classifying companies as "probably" under family control if a family or group of families had 4 to 5 percent of the stock and longstanding representation on the board of directors, Burch concluded that, as of the mid-1960s, 40 percent of the top 300 industrials were probably under family control and that another 15 percent were "possibly" under family control.

Analyzing the more useful official records that became available in the 1970s, a team of researchers at Corporate Data Exchange, led by Stephen Abrecht and Michael Locker, provided detailed information on the major owners of most of the top 500 industrials for 1980. This study showed that significant individual and family ownership continues to exist for all but the very largest of corporations. Our classification of their findings reveals that one individual or family was a top stockholder, with at least 5 percent of the stock, in 44 percent of the 423 profiled corporations that were not controlled by other corporations or foreign interests. From two to four families held at least 5 percent of the stock and had representation on the board of directors in another 7 percent. The figures were much lower among the 50 largest, however, where only 17 percent of the 47 companies included in the study met our criteria of major family involvement.

These findings on the small percentage of the very largest industrials under individual or family control concur with those in a third study, that by economist Edward S. Herman, for the 200 largest corporations among all nonfinancial corporations for 1974–1975. Using slightly more stringent criteria than in our classification, and including public utilities that are highly unlikely to be controlled by families, he found that only 14 percent of the companies in his sample were under ownership control. There were another 7.5 percent where outside ownership was a significant influence. . . .

There have been numerous studies of the social class origins of the corporate executives who serve on boards of directors. These studies use varying criteria of class origin, but they most frequently focus on the occupation of the executive's father in making this determination. These studies show, as Michael Useem suggests in a detailed synthesis of work on the corporate elite, that "between 40% and 70% of all large corporation directors and managers were raised in business families, which comprised only a tiny fraction of the families of the era." . . .

In one of the most ambitious studies of corporate directors to date, political scientist Thomas R. Dye investigated the social origins of several thousand directors from the largest corporations of 1970. Using as his class indicators parental occupations as well as the parents' listing in the *Social Register*, attendance at a prestigious private school, and membership in upper-class clubs, Dye estimates that 30 percent of the corporate elite are upper class in origin. . . .

THE POWER ELITE AND GOVERNMENT

Members of the power elite directly involve themselves in the federal government through three basic processes, each of which plays a slightly different role in ensuring access to the White House,

Congress, and specific agencies, departments, and committees in the executive branch. Although some of the same people are involved in all three processes, most people specialize in one or two of the three processes. This is because each process requires slightly different knowledge, skills, and contacts. The three processes are:

1. The candidate selection process, through which members of the power elite attempt to influence electoral campaigns by means of campaign finances and favors to political candidates.

2. The special-interest process, through which specific individuals, corporations, and industrial sectors realize their narrow and short-run interests on taxes, subsides, and regulation in dealing with congressional committees, regulatory bodies, and executive departments.

3. The policy-making process, through which the general policies of the policy-planning network explained in the previous chapter are brought to the White House and Congress.

THE CANDIDATE-ELECTION PROCESS

The power elite involves itself in the candidate-selection process through the simple, direct, and often very unsubtle means of large campaign donations that far outweigh what other classes and groups can muster. Although the method of involvement is simple, the reason such a direct approach is possible requires a structural and historical understanding of why politics operate as they do in the United States. Only part of that understanding can be provided in this chapter, however. . . .

It is because the candidate-selection process in the American two-party system is so individualistic, and therefore dependent upon name recognition and personal image, that it can be in good part dominated by members of the power elite through the relatively simple and direct means of large campaign contributions. In the roles of both big donors and fund raisers, the same people who direct corporations and take part in policy groups play a central role in the careers of most politicians who advance beyond the local level in states of any size and consequence. "Recruitment of elective elites," concludes political scientist Walter D. Burnham, "remains closely associated, especially for the most important offices in the larger states, with the candidates' wealth or access to large campaign contributions."

The role of the wealthy donor and fund raiser seems to be especially crucial in the nomination phase of the process. . . .

The Results of the Candidate-Selection Process

What kinds of elected officials emerge from a political process that puts such great attention on campaign finance and media recognition? The answer is available from numerous studies. Politicians, especially those who hold the highest elective offices, are first of all people from the top 10 to 15 percent of the occupational and income ladders. Only a minority are from the upper class or corporate community, but in a majority of cases they share in common a business and legal background with members of the upper class.

Few twentieth-century Presidents have been from outside the very wealthiest circles. Theodore Roosevelt, William H.

Taft, Franklin D. Roosevelt, and John F. Kennedy were from upper-class backgrounds. Herbert Hoover, Jimmy Carter, and Ronald Reagan were millionaires before they became deeply involved in national politics. Lyndon B. Johnson was a millionaire several times over through his wife's land dealings and his use of political leverage to gain a lucrative television license in Austin. Even Richard M. Nixon was a rich man when he finally attained the presidency in 1968, after earning high salaries as a corporate lawyer between 1963 and 1968 due to his ability to open political doors for corporate clients.

Studies of the social backgrounds and occupations of members of Congress have consistently shown that they come from the highest levels of society and are involved in the business and legal communities. A study of the Congress for 1972 found that 66 percent of the senators and 74 percent of the representatives came from the 10 percent of families with business or professional occupations, and that virtually all of the senators and representatives were themselves professional people or former business executives. Twenty percent of the senators and 5 percent of a sample of representatives were members of the upper class. Only 5 percent of the senators had been farmers or ranchers; none had been blue-collar workers. Three percent of the representatives had been farmers or ranchers, and 3 percent had union backgrounds. A comparison of these findings with a study of the Senate in the mid-1950s and the House in the early 1940s showed that there had been very little change over that time span, except for a decrease in the number of farmers and a slight increase in the number of professionals and business executives. . . .

THE SPECIAL-INTEREST PROCESS

. . . The special-interest process is that aspect of business-government relations described by social scientists and journalists in their case studies and exposés. It is the process that was the target of the numerous investigations by consumer advocate Ralph Nader and his colleagues in the late 1960s and early 1970s, and it is constantly being scrutinized by other reform-minded groups as well. It is so well known, and so often lucrative to the corporate rich, that it is often taken as the sum and substance of policy making in Washington. Moreover, the conflicts that erupt within this process, occasionally pitting one corporate sector against another, reinforce the image of widely shared and fragmented power in America, including the image of a badly divided corporate community.

One of the finest summaries of the implications of the special-interest process is provided by political scientist Grant McConnell in his now-classic *Private Power and American Democracy*. After reviewing several decade of congressional investigations into lobbying, including half-hearted attempts to limit it, and numerous studies suggesting that, more often than not, regulatory agencies are "captured" by those they are supposed to regulate, he noted that "the record of exposure of this sort is one of almost tiresome repetition." He concludes, in an explicit rejection of the usual pluralist image, that the ability of special interests to dominate specific committees and agencies of concern to them has given these interests considerable isolation from any countervailing pressures from other sources:

The large extent of autonomy accorded to various fragments of government has gone far to isolate important matters of public policy from supposedly countervailing influences. Moreover, the picture of government as mediator among different interests is falsified to the extent that government itself is fragmented and the various fragments are beholden to particular interests.

However, as McConnell also points out, evidence on the power of special interests does not add up to power elite domination of government as a whole. It does not show that the many different sectors of the corporate community have an interest in larger issues, let alone the unity to evolve policies on such issues. Indeed, in McConnell's view the parts of government that deal with general issues that concern the nation as a whole, such as the presidency, are not controlled by a unified power elite: "These elites do not 'rule' in the sense of commanding the entire nation," he writes. "Quite the contrary, they tend to pursue a policy of noninvolvement in the large issues of statesmanship, save where such issues touch their own particular concerns."

In order to deal with the claim that the special interests do not come together to involve themselves in bigger policy issues, it is necessary to demonstrate how the policy-planning network described [previously] involves itself in government.

THE POLICY-MAKING PROCESS AND GOVERNMENT

The policy-making process is as little known and seldom studied as the special-interest process is highly visible and constantly written about. It appears to be as detached from day-to-day events as the special-interest process is completely immersed in them. It appears as concerned with fairness and the national interest as the special-interest processes seems biased and self-seeking. "Nonpartisan" and "objective" are its shibboleths, and many of its members show a mild disdain for lobbyists and trade associations. Compared with those who labor in the special-interest process, its members are much more likely to be from the "oldest" and wealthiest of families, the most prestigious of law schools and university institutes, and the highest levels of banks and corporations.

The perspectives developed in the organizations of the policy-planning network reach government in a variety of ways. On the most general level, their reports, news releases, and interviews are read by elected officials and their staffs, if not in their original form, then as they are summarized in the *Washington Post, New York Times*, and *Wall Street Journal*. Members of these organizations also testify before congressional committees and subcommittees that are writing legislation or preparing budget proposals. However, the most important involvements with government are more direct and formal in nature.

First, people from these organizations are regular members of the unpaid committees that advise specific departments of the executive branch on general policies. Second, they are prominent on the presidential commissions that have been appointed with regularity since World War II to make recommendations on a wide range of issues from foreign policy to highway construction. Third, they are members of two private organizations, the Business Council and the Business Roundtable, which are treated with the utmost respect and cordiality in Washington. Finally, they serve as informal advisors to the President in times of foreign-policy crisis, and they are appointed to government positions with a frequency far beyond what could be expected by chance. . . .

APPOINTMENTS TO GOVERNMENT

. . . Scholarly studies of cabinet appointments demonstrate in a more systematic way that the corporate community is highly overrepresented in government. However, those done by pluralists, though attesting to the presence of corporate officials in government, underestimate the actual extent of corporate involvement by placing lawyers in a separate category from businessmen even when their firms have major corporations as their clients. Fortunately, the work of sociologist Beth Mintz and political scientist Philip Burch reveals the full extent of corporate involvements.

The study of Mintz focused on the 205 individuals who served in presidential cabinets between 1897 and 1972. Defining her indicators of the "social elite" to include the 105 social clubs listed in the front of the *Social Register,* in addition to the *Social Register* itself and the schools and clubs outlined in the first chapter of this book, she found that 60 percent of the cabinet members were members of the upper class. Defining the "business elite" broadly in terms of service on at least one board of directors in any business corporation, or as membership in any corporation-oriented law firm, she also found that 78 percent were members of the business community. About half the cabinet officers were members of both the social and business elites as defined in this study. There were no differences in the overall percentages for Democratic and Republican administra-

tions, or for the years before and after 1933.

The exhaustive three-volume study by Burch covers cabinet officers, diplomats, and Supreme Court justices for every administration from George Washington through Jimmy Carter. It uses a more restricted definition than the Mintz study of what Burch calls the "economic elite," but it comes to similar conclusions except in the case of the New Deal administration of Franklin D. Roosevelt. For Burch, the economic elite are those who hold executive positions, directorships, or partnerships in a large corporation or law firm "at or around" the time of government appointment, or are from families with "considerable" wealth or top-level executives or director ties. What is considered to be a large corporation or law firm varies from generation to generation with the growth of the economy.

For the years 1789 to 1861, Burch concludes that 96 percent of the cabinet and diplomatic appointees were members of the economic elite, with a great many landowners, lawyers, and merchants in the group. From 1861 to 1933, the figure was 84 percent, with an increasing number of financiers and corporate lawyers. The figures in this era varied from a low of 57 percent for the Wilson years to a high of 90 percent for the McKinley-Roosevelt-Taft era. The overall percentage fell to 64 percent for the years 1933 to 1980, with only 47 percent of the appointees during the New Deal coming from the largest of corporations and law firms. The percentages for the last three eras in the study were about the same—63 percent for the Kennedy-Johnson years, 69 percent for the Nixon-Ford years, and 65 percent for the Carter administration. . . .

The general picture that emerges from this information on the overrepresentation of members of the corporate community and policy network in appointed governmental positions is that the highest levels of the executive branch, especially in the State, Defense, and Treasury departments, are interlocked constantly with the corporate community through the movement of executives and lawyers in and out of government. Although the same person is not in government and corporate positions at the same time, there is enough continuity for the relationship to be described as one of the "revolving interlocks." Corporate leaders sever their numerous directorships to serve in government for two or three years, then return to the corporate community in a same or different capacity. This system gives corporate officials temporary independence from the narrow concerns of their own companies and allows them to perform the more general roles they have learned in the policy-planning groups. However, it does not give them the time or inclination to become fully independent of the corporate community or to develop a perspective that includes the interests of other classes and groups. . . .

NO

Andrew M. Greeley

BUILDING COALITIONS

It is important that all of us who are concerned about politics realize that only on occasion can we legitimately blame a vague and shadowy "them" for our problems. Admittedly, it would be much easier if we could; then we could just sweep "them" out of office and replace them with some of "us." But one of the melancholy results of a democratic society in which power is widely diffused is that "they" turn out in the final analysis to be "we." . . .

There is a good deal to be said for the elitist viewpoint, and anyone who approaches American society with the naive notion that power is equally distributed in the population and that mere persuasive argumentation will mobilize the power in favor of social change is simply asking for trouble.

1. Some people have more power than others. The president of General Motors, for example, is likely to have more influence on decisions that are made in Washington than the assembly-line worker. The archbishop of Chicago is likewise going to have greater impact on what the Catholic Church does than the parish priest. Compared to Mayor Daley or County President George Dunne or Governor Walker or the president of the Chicago Board of Trade or of Marshall Field and Company or the *Chicago Sun-Times* I am relatively powerless about what happens in my native city. Indeed, a member of the United Steel Workers of America probably has more power than I do, because he is at least able to bring pressure on city events through his union that I am not able to bring because I lack some sort of intermediate pressure group standing between me and the city.

2. Because of the way power is distributed in American society, certain groups of men, either because of their position or because of the support they can command from large organizations, can have decisive power on specific issues, no matter what anyone else thinks. While it is rare that the combination of these powerful men can override the strongly felt convictions of a majority of the population, it is generally unnecessary for them to try. On most issues the majority of the population is relatively indifferent. Thus if the *Chicago Tribune* determines that there is to be a lakefront exposition hall named after their late beloved publisher, it is likely to succeed because it needs only the support of a few city leaders, and opposition to it is likely to be limited to a small segment of the population. A majority of Chicagoans probably

From *Building Coalitions: American Politics in the 1970s*, by Andrew M. Greeley (New York: Franklin Watts, Inc.). Copyright © 1974 by Andrew M. Greeley. Reprinted with the permission of the publisher, Franklin Watts, Inc.

don't care much one way or the other about the lakefront hall; if asked, they may be vaguely for it. It will be virtually impossible for the opposition to organize massive antagonism toward the idea among the general population.

3. Some extremely critical decisions are made in American society by a handful of men. For example, the decision to go ahead with the Bay of Pigs invasion and the subsequent decision to respond to the Russian intrusion of missiles into Cuba by a blockade were made by a handful of men in secret. So too, apparently, have most of the decisions in the Indochina war been made by a small group operating in secret. These men obviously do not make their decisions in complete isolation from the pressure of the wishes and opinions of the rest of society, and they also eventually run the risk of being ejected from political office if what they do displeases at least a majority of those who vote in an election. Nevertheless, most of us do not have much power in the making of foreign policy. Our influence on foreign policy is limited to what the political leadership thinks our limits of hostile response are and to our plebiscite on election day.

4. Well-organized pressure groups do exercise an influence on American society all out of proportion to the size of their membership and the representatives of their opinions. Even though there is strong national support for gun control legislation, for example, the National Rifle Association has been successful in limiting gun control laws and in punishing senators who have dared to push too vigorously against the association. This is but one example of an incredible number of pressure groups that zealously watch social events to make sure that the well-being of their members—judged, of course, by the professional staff of the organization—is not harmed by what goes on among the political leaders.

5. David Riesman and others have called these pressure groups (which run all the way from the United States Catholic Conference to the National Education Association and include the United Steelworkers of America, the American Chamber of Commerce, and a vast variety of other thoroughly reliable and respectable institutions) "veto groups," that is, their power is most effective in preventing things from happening than in causing them to happen. The American Medical Association, for example, has effectively vetoed national health insure for several decades, but it has not displayed much power in getting positive legislation for its own benefit. The veto groups may occasionally join forces with one another and rally around some common cause, but under normal circumstances they are much better at saying no than at saying yes.

6. But when all these concessions are made to the accuracy of the elitist analysis, one is still faced with the fact that they miss the most critical obstacle to social reform in the United States, and that obstacle is not the existence of an establishment but the relative nonexistence of one. To put the matter somewhat differently, it is the lack of concentration of power that is the real obstacle to social reform.

Let us take two examples. First of all, if there were an establishment of business, military, intellectual, and political leaders who did in fact exercise political control over the country, they would have gotten us out of the Vietnam war long before they did. The war was bad for business, bad for education, bad for government, bad for everyone in sight. It combined inflation with recession, alienated the youth, split the college campuses wide open, and had a rending effect on the whole fabric of American society. Furthermore, American business did not profit from the war, American political leaders did not profit from it (they generally lost elections because of it), and the American people, whose sons were killed, did not profit from it. Almost all the influential national journals were against it, and even the military muttered that it was trapped into the war by intellectual advisors of the president against their better judgment. Nevertheless, though it may have been desirable for all concerned to get us out of the war, there never existed a powerful establishment that could convene itself and announce that the war was over. The young people who vigorously demonstrated against the war were frustrated and angry because they could not communicate with the establishment to make it end the war. They might have considered the possibility that if there were an establishment, it certainly would have ended the war. The reason they can't communicate with an establishment is that there isn't one.

One can also take it as well established that the best way to cope with housing pressures in America's large cities is to distribute substantial segments of the black population in the suburban fringe that rings these large cities. Political leaders, business leaders, research experts, community leaders, virtually everyone would agree that the desegregation of the suburbs is absolutely essential for coping with problems of urban housing. Yet there does not exist in American society a group of men powerful enough to enforce such a decision over the collective opposition of all the suburban veto

groups. If there were an establishment with a base of power, we would certainly have blacks in the suburbs.

The implication of the previous paragraph is that an establishment should be capable of benign as well as malign activity. Many benign actions would be very much in the self-interest of any establishment worthy of the name. That these benign things do not get done is, I think, conclusive evidence that, alas, there is no establishment. Things would be much simpler and neater if there were.

Implicit in radical criticism of the establishment is the strategy that argues that if one replaced the existing establishment with a new one composed of radical elitists and representing "the people," then one could institute benign social reforms. Professor [C. Wright] Mills* was quite explicit about that. He did not so much advocate the abolition of the power elite as making it responsible—responsible to intellectuals. But obviously it could not be made responsible to all intellectuals, so Mills decided that the power elite should be responsible to those intellectuals who happened to have the same ideas on foreign policy that he did. The power elite, in other words, will become "responsible" when it is willing to do what C. Wright Mills and his colleagues tell it to do. On the whole, I am not sure I would have liked to be governed by Professor Mills or any of his successors. I very much doubt that we could have worked out an arrangement whereby they would have been willing to stand for reelection. It would be interesting to see what those critics of the establishment would do if they be-

---

*Late professor of sociology at Columbia University and author of The Power Elite (Oxford, 1956). —Eds.

came it. They would discover, of course, as do all government leaders, how limited their powers really are. They would probably suspect some sort of conspiracy on the part of shadowy forces still existing in the society bent on frustrating their noble plans. Like most other Jacobins before them, they would probably use force to destroy the conspiracy, only to discover that even force has its limitations as a means of effective government.

The most important obstacle to social change in the United States, then, is not the concentration of power but its diffusion. If power was concentrated sufficiently, those of us who wish for change would merely have to negotiate with those who hold the power and, if necessary, put pressure on them. But power is so widely diffused that, in many instances, there is no one to negotiate with and no one on whom to put pressure. American society has been organized from the beginning around two premises: (1) "The central guiding trend of American constitutional development has been the evolution of a political system in which all the active and legitimate groups in the population can make themselves heard at some crucial stage in the process of decision."* The second principle is a corollary of the first: (2) The larger society cannot ignore for very long what a given group considers to be its fundamental self-interest. No group, in other words, can be expected to assume the role of the permanent loser. . . .

One can fault this system of pluralism in two respects. First, one can say that it has failed according to its own principles; that certain disadvantaged groups

*Robert A. Dahl, *Preface to Democratic Theory* (Chicago: University of Chicago Press, 1956), p. 137.

are not given an adequate hearing or that society does not recognize its obligation to facilitate the development of political power in these groups. The criticism is certainly a valid one. The very nobility of the political ideal implied in American pluralism makes departures from it unfortunate and ugly, but if this is the only criticism one has to make, then the strategy is obvious: one must bargain to persuade the rest of society that its consensus must be broadened sufficiently to admit these other groups as valued and equal participants in the enterprise.

The second criticism is that given the complexities and difficulties of the modern world, the diffusion of power that exists in American society is dangerously inefficient. If one has to bargain with Polish surgeons, Latvian truckdrivers, red-necked farmers, Irish politicians, conservative black clergymen, Jewish garment makers, Swedish computer operators, Texas oil barons, Portuguese fishermen from Fall River, and cattle ranchers from Montana in order to win support for absolutely imperative social changes, then these changes will be delayed, perhaps for too long, while the evil and injustice continues. It is demeaning, degrading, and immoral to have to bargain for the elimination of clear and obvious injustice. Racism is obscene, war is obscene; both should go away without our having to bargain on the subject. A political system that distributes power so that bargaining is necessary to eliminate obscene immorality is in itself not merely inefficient but immoral. It is not proper that those who are moral and wise should be forced to negotiate with those who are immoral and stupid.

This is a logically and consistently coherent case; in effect, it advocates the abolition of the pluralistic bargaining, co-alition-forming polity that we currently have. It advocates taking the slack out of the political system and placing it in the hands of a ruling elite that would be both virtuous enough and powerful enough to accomplish quickly those social changes deemed urgent or imperative. One sup-poses that a strong case can be made for issues like pollution, population control, and racial injustice not to be made sub-ject to the bargaining process, that wise and virtuous ruling elites should enforce by legislation and by police power, if necessary, the regulations that cope with these problems. The issues are so critical that there is no time to bargain with those whose intelligence and sensitivity is so deficient that they cannot see how imperative it is that action be taken with utmost speed. One can, I say, make a convincing case for such a political sys-tem, but let it be clear that it is an elite-establishmentarian system with a ven-geance, that it bears no similarity to what normally has been considered democracy, that it is completely at odds with the Amer-ican political tradition, and completely objectionable to most Americans. . . .

If this model of American society is correct, the appropriate political strategy for those who wish to accomplish social change is not to tear down the establish-ment but rather to seek allies to form coalitions of various individuals and groups with some commonality of inter-est. These coalitions will represent an amassing of power that will be stronger than the power of those whose behavior we think is socially injurious. Thus, for example, a coalition was finally put to-gether to force both safety and antipollu-tion devices on the American automobile industry. It took a long time to put such a coalition together—indeed, much too long. Coalitions must be formed more rapidly if we are going to be able to cope with the critical problems that constantly arise in advanced industrial societies. The alternative to winning allies for one's cause is to impose it on the majority of one's fellow citizens whether they like it or not. Not only would this mean the end of political freedom, but it also might be extremely risky, because once we have begun to impose our will as a minority we run the risk that they may start counting noses and in full realization of our minority position, impose their will on us.

There was one thing clear in the sum-mer and fall of 1972. Practitioners of the New Politics were as capable of misusing power as were the "corrupt bosses" whom they supposedly replaced. It did not, however, appear that they were sub-stantially superior to the bosses in their capacity to use power intelligently. In-deed, a persuasive case could be made that as power brokers, the New Politi-cians were as inept as they were at every-thing else. Those who wish to rebuild the Democratic coalition can ill afford to be naive about the position of power in American society. Neither can they af-ford the naivete of raging against mythi-cal dragons like "the establishment." There may well be certain concentrations of power in American society that the reconstructed Democratic coalition will want to break up, but it must first amass for itself a sufficient concentration of po-litical power to be able to have a reason-able chance of winning an election and implementing its program. The builders of the new Democratic coalition must understand what their predecessors of 1972 apparently did not: One builds po-litical power not by excluding people but by including them.

POSTSCRIPT

Does an Elite Rule America?

The arguments of both Domhoff and Greeley raise questions. Greeley freely acknowledges that America is a society with gradations of power. Just as a parish priest does not have the same power as a bishop, so an ordinary citizen is less powerful than a political office-holder, or the assembly-line worker at General Motors less powerful than the corporate president. Does Greeley mean to suggest that hierarchy is inherent in all political relationships? What, then, becomes of the concept of popular sovereignty? As for Domhoff, his argument seems to turn upon the number of rich people from corporate backgrounds who serve in government. But is this really relevant? People in high office are generally well-to-do, and, in America, business is an important route to wealth. But if Domhoff has gone further, if he has demonstrated that the people who govern America are not only rich but alike in their political views, if those views are contrary to the views of the majority of Americans, and if the governing elites nevertheless enforce them upon the majority, then Domhoff's argument is very telling indeed. But has he demonstrated that? No doubt Ronald Reagan, Cyrus Vance, Zbigniew Brzezinski, and George McGovern would be startled to find themselves lumped into the same "power elite."

The literature of political science and sociology contains many confrontations between elite-theory and pluralism. In his refutation of elite theory, Greeley makes reference to C. Wright Mills' *The Power Elite* (Oxford, 1956), which is a classic statement of elite theory. As for pluralism, Greeley cites with approval Robert Dahl and David Riesman. Dahl's *Preface to Democratic Theory* (University of Chicago Press, 1969), *Who Governs?* (Yale, 1961), and *Dilemmas of Pluralist Democracy* (Yale, 1982) are elaborate defenses of the pluralistic thesis. Reisman's *The Lonely Crowd* (Yale, 1961) deals with a number of aspects of American society, including what he calls "veto groups." Political scientist Michael Parenti has written an American government textbook, *Democracy for the Few* (St. Martin's, 1980), based on the Domhofian thesis that our politics and government are dominated by rich corporate elites.

ISSUE 12

Has American Government Gotten Too Big?

YES: William Simon, from *A Time for Truth* (McGraw-Hill, 1978)

NO: John Kenneth Galbraith, from "The Social Consensus and the Conservative Onslaught," *Millenium Journal of International Studies* (Spring 1982)

ISSUE SUMMARY

Yes: Former Treasury Secretary William Simon argues that excessive government involvement in the economy abridges basic liberties and hurts the nation's productivity.

No: Economist John Kenneth Galbraith says that since public services are essential to those Americans who can't afford private services, the attack on "big government" is really an attack on the poor.

What is the purpose of government? The question has been asked and answered since ancient times. The answers have varied with the times. For the ancient Greeks and Romans, government was an instrument of glory, the means of making immortal the great words and deeds of statesmen. In the Middle Ages, government was supposed to be a servant of Christianity, a "protecter of the faith" against foreign and domestic enemies. By the seventeenth century, government was largely a vehicle of kingly ambition; through regulations, taxes, licenses, armies, swarms of officials, and a wide array of punishments, government was used to increase the power of kings and intimidate potential challengers.

Then came the eighteenth century, the Age of Enlightenment. For many of the leading thinkers of the time—from Adam Smith to Thomas Paine, from the "physiocrats" in France to Thomas Jefferson in America—government was not the solution but the problem, and the stronger the government, the greater the problem. "I own I am no friend of energetic government," Jefferson said, "it is always oppressive." Admittedly, government is necessary to keep people from killing and robbing each other. Thomas Paine said, "Government, like clothes, is the badge of lost innocence." But it is at best a necessary evil and should be kept as small as possible. Thus the famous maxim: "That government is best which governs least." Those who entertained such views were called "liberals," because they were committed to liberty as opposed to what they considered excessive government restraint. Their philosophy of government was summed up in the French expression *laissez-faire*, meaning "leave to be," or "leave alone." Government, they thought, should stay out of our lives as much as possible. Today, their philosophy is often called "classical liberalism," or "libertarianism," to distinguish it from modern liberalism.

Modern liberalism arrived in the 1930s. When Franklin Roosevelt was nominated for President by the Democratic party in 1932, the nation was caught up in the worst depression of its history. A quarter of the nation's work force was unemployed; everywhere there was idleness and despair and, in some places, outright starvation. In accepting the nomination, Roosevelt said: "I pledge you, I pledge myself, to a new deal for the American people." The "New Deal" was meant to fight the Depression by regulating business, stimulating the economy, and bringing welfare to the needy.

This new strain of liberalism opposed some forms of government regulation, especially the attempt to regulate speech, press, and religion. But in the economic sphere it openly supported government activism. Regulation of business, supervision of the economic sphere, public assistance to the poor: these were the hallmarks of "New Deal liberalism," a liberalism that rejected *laissez-faire* economics in favor of a more activist role of the state. Modern liberalism builds upon that tradition, expanding still further the size and scope of government.

The question is whether the activist role has gone too far. After all, the original insight of liberalism was that big government stifles freedom and creativity. Those who still cherish that insight (the "libertarians" or "classical liberals," sometimes called conservatives) say that modern liberalism is bringing us back to the bad old days of excessive government. True, the "big government" of the eighteenth century was much different than today's democratic government. It was government by kings and bishops and court intriguers, and it was motivated more by lust for power than by public spirit. Modern democratic government rests upon popular suffrage, so it cannot totally ignore people's needs. Moreover, our economic system has changed drastically since the eighteenth century. We are no longer a nation of small farms but of giant industrial firms wielding enormous power. The whole modern economy is complex and interdependent.

Even so, libertarians argue that government intervention must be kept to a minimum. In their view, *laissez-faire* is still the best way to ensure economic growth and preserve liberty. In the following selections, former Treasury Secretary William Simon develops that view, while economist John Kenneth Galbraith argues that it is unrealistic and out-of-date.

YES

William Simon

THE ROAD TO LIBERTY

. . . Normally in life, if one finds oneself in a situation where *all* known courses of action are destructive, one reassesses the premises which led to that situation. The premise to be questioned here is the degree of government intervention itself—the very competence of the state to function as a significant economic ruler. But to question that premise is to hurl oneself intellectually into a free market universe. And that the social democratic leaders will not do. A few may actually understand—as did the brilliant Chancellor Erhard in postwar Germany—that the solution to shortages, recession and unemployment, and an ominous decline in technological innovation is to dispense with most intervention and regulation and allow men to produce competitively in freedom. But they know that if they proposed this, they would be destroyed by the political intellectuals of their countries. . . .

What we need today in America is adherence to a set of broad guiding principles, not a thousand more technocratic adjustments. [I] shall not waste my time or yours with a set of legislative proposals. Instead, I will suggest a few of the most important general principles which I would like to see placed on the public agenda. They are actually the conclusions I have reached in the course of working on this book.

—The overriding principle to be revived in American political life is that which sets individual liberty as the highest political value—that value to which all other values are subordinate and that which, at all times, is to be given the highest "priority" in policy discussions.

—By the same token, there must be a conscious philosophical prejudice against any intervention by the state into our lives, for by definition such intervention abridges liberty. Whatever form it may take, state intervention in the private and productive lives of the citizenry must be presumed to be a negative, uncreative, and dangerous act, to be adopted only when its proponents provide overwhelming and incontrovertible evidence that the benefits to society of such intervention far outweigh the costs.

—The principle of "no taxation without representation" must again become a rallying cry of Americans. Only Congress represents American voters, and the process of transferring regulatory powers—which are a hidden power to tax—to unelected, uncontrollable, and unfireable bureaucrats must stop. The American voters, who pay the bills, must be in a position to know what is being economically inflicted on them and in a position to vote men out of office who assault their interests, as *the voters* define those interests. Which means that Congress should not pass bills creating programs that it cannot effectively oversee. The drive to demand scrupulous legislative oversight of our policing agencies, such as the CIA, is valid; it should be extended to *all* agencies of the government which are also, directly or indirectly, exercising police power.

—A critical principle which must be communicated forcefully to the American public is the inexorable interdependence of economic wealth and political liberty. Our citizens must learn that what keeps them prosperous is production and technological innovation. Their wealth emerges, not from government offices or politician's edicts, but only from that portion of the marketplace which is *free*. They must also be taught to understand the relationship among collectivism, centralized planning, and poverty so that every new generation of Americans need not naively receive the Marxist revelations afresh.

—Bureaucracies themselves should be assumed to be noxious, authoritarian parasites on society, with a tendency to augment their own size and power and to cultivate a parasitical clientele in all classes of society. Area after area of American life should be set free from their blind power drive. We commonly hear people call for a rollback of prices, often unaware that they are actually calling for the destruction of marginal businesses and the jobs they furnish. People must be taught to start calling for a rollback of the bureaucracy, where nothing will be lost but strangling regulation and where the gains will always take the form of liberty, productivity, and jobs.

—Productivity and the growth of productivity must be the *first* economic consideration at all times, not the last. That is the source of technological innovation, jobs and wealth. This means that profits needed for investment must be respected as a great social blessing, not as a social evil, and that the envy of the "rich" cannot be allowed to destroy a powerful economic system.

—The concept that "wealth is theft" must be repudiated. It now lurks, implicitly, in most of the political statements we hear. Wealth can indeed be stolen, but only *after* it has been produced, and the difference between stolen wealth and produced wealth is critical. If a man obtains money by fraud or by force, he is simply a criminal to be handled by the police and the courts. But if he has earned his income honorably, by the voluntary exchange of goods and services, he is not a criminal or a second-class citizen and should not be treated as such. A society taught to perceive producers as criminals will end up by destroying its productive processes.

—Conversely, the concept that the absence of money implies some sort of virtue should be repudiated. Poverty may result from honest misfortune, but it also may result from sloth, incompetence, and dishonesty. Again the distinction between deserving and undeserving poor is important. It is a virtue to assist those who are in acute need through no fault of their own, but it is folly to glamorize men simply because they are penniless. The crude linkage between wealth and evil, poverty and virtue is false, stupid, and of value only to demagogues, parasite, and criminals—indeed, the three groups that alone have profited from the linkage.

—Similarly, the view that government is virtuous and producers are evil is a piece of folly, and a nation which allows itself to be tacitly guided by these illusions must lose both its liberty and its wealth. Government has its proper functions, and consequently, there can be both good and bad governments. Producers as well can be honest and dishonest. Our political discourse can be rendered rational only when people are taught to make such discriminations.

—The "ethics" of egalitarianism must be repudiated. Achievers must not be penalized or parasites rewarded if we aspire to a healthy, productive, and ethical society. Able-bodied citizens must work to sustain their lives, and in a healthy economic system they should be enabled and encouraged to save for their old age. Clearly, so long as the government's irrational fiscal policies make this impossible, present commitments to pensions and Social Security must be maintained at all cost, for the bulk of the population has no other recourse. But as soon as is politically feasible—meaning, as soon as *production* becomes the nation's highest economic value—the contributions of able-bodied citizens to their own future pensions should be invested by them in far safer commercial institutions, where the sums can earn high interest without being squandered by politicians and bureaucrats. American citizens must be taught to wrest their life savings from the politicians if they are to know the comfort of genuine security.

—The American citizen must be made aware that today a relatively small group of people is proclaiming its purposes to be the will of the People. That elitist approach to government must be repudiated. There is no such thing as the People; it is a collectivist myth. There are only individual citizens with individual wills and individual purposes. There is only one social system that reflects this sovereignty of the individual: the free market, or capitalist, system, which means the sovereignty of the individual "vote" in the marketplace and the sovereignty of the individual vote in the political realm. That individual sovereignty is being destroyed in this country by our current political trends, and it is scarcely astonishing that individuals now feel "alienated" from their government. They are not just alienated from it; they have virtually been expelled from the governmental process, where only organized mobs prevail.

—The growing cynicism about democracy must be combated by explaining why it has become corrupted. People have been taught that if they can get together big enough gangs, they have the legal power to hijack other citizens' wealth, which means the power to hijack other people's efforts, energies, and lives. No decent society can function when men are given such power. A state does need funds, but a clear cutoff line must be established beyond which no political group or institution can confiscate a citizen's honorably earned property. The notion that one can differentiate between "property rights." and "human rights" is ignoble. One need merely see the appalling condition of "human rights" in nations where there are no "property rights" to understand why. This is just a manifestation of the socialist myth which imagines that one can keep men's minds free while enslaving their bodies.

These are some of the broad conclusions I have reached after four years in office. Essentially they are a set of guiding principles. America is foundering for the lack of principles; it is now guided by the belief that *unprincipled* action—for which the respectable name is "pragmatism"—is somehow superior. Such principles as I have listed do not represent dogma. There is, as I said, nothing arbitrary or dogmatic about the interlocking relationship between political and economic liberty. The history of every nation on earth demonstrates that relationship, and no economist known to me, including the theoreticians of interventionism and totalitarianism, denies this. If liberty is to be our highest political value, this set of broad principles follows consistently. . . .

It is often said by people who receive warnings about declining freedom in America that such a charge is preposterous, that there is no freer society on earth. That is true in one sense, but it is immensely deceptive. There has never been such freedom before in America to speak freely, indeed, to wag one's tongue in the hearing of an entire nation; to publish anything and everything, including the most scurrilous gossip; to take drugs and to prate to children about their alleged pleasures; to propagandize for bizarre sexual practices; to watch bloody and obscene entertainment. Conversely, compulsion rules the world of work. There has never been so little freedom before in America to plan, to save, to invest, to build, to produce, to invent, to hire, to fire, to resist coercive unionization, to exchange goods and services, to risk, to profit, to grow.

The strange fact is that Americans are constitutionally free today to do almost everything that our cultural tradition has previously held to be immoral and ob-

scene, while the police powers of the state are being invoked against almost every aspect of the productive process. Even more precisely, Americans today are left free by the state to engage in activities that could, for the most part, be carried on just as readily in prisons, insane asylums, and zoos. They are not left free by the state to pursue those activities which will give them *independence*.

That is not a coincidence. It is characteristic, in fact, of the contemporary collectivist, in both America and Europe, to clamor that freedom pertains exclusively to the verbal and emotional realms. It allows the egalitarian socialist the illusion that he is not trying to weave a noose for the throats of free men, and it renders him all the more dangerous to the credulous. It is difficult, indeed, to identify as a potential tyrant someone who is raising a righteous uproar over your right to fornicate in the streets. But in this as well, our contemporary "liberators" are not original. I transmit to you a warning by Professor Nisbet, professor of humanities at Columbia University, included in his essay "The New Despotism." He says something I consider vital for the contemporary citizen to know because it is the final reason for the invisibility surrounding the destruction of some of our most crucial liberties:

[M]ore often than not in history, license has been the prelude to exercises of extreme political coercion, which shortly reach all areas of a culture. . . . [V]ery commonly in ages when civil rights of one kind are in evidence—those pertaining to freedom of speech and thought in, say, theater, press and forum, with obscenity and libel laws correspondingly loosened—very real constrictions of individual liberty take place in other, more vital areas; political organization, voluntary association, property and the right to hold jobs . . . .

There are, after all, certain freedoms that are like circuses. Their very existence, so long as they are individual and enjoyed chiefly individually as by spectators, diverts men's minds from the loss of other, more fundamental social and economic and political rights.

A century ago, the liberties that now exist routinely on stage and screen, on printed page and canvas would have been unthinkable in America—and elsewhere in the West, for that matter, save in the most clandestine and limited of settings. But so would the limitations upon economic, professional, education and local liberties, to which we have by now become accustomed, have seemed equally unthinkable half a century ago. We enjoy the feeling of great freedom, of protection of our civil liberties, when we attend the theater, watch television, buy paperbacks. But all the while, we find ourselves living in circumstances of a spread of military, police and bureaucratic power that cannot help but have, that manifestly does have, profoundly erosive effect upon those economic, local and associative liberties that are by far the most vital to any free society.

From the point of view of any contemporary strategist or tactician of political power indulgence in the one kind of liberties must seem a very requisite to diminution of the other kind. We know it seemed that way to the Caesars and Napoleons of history. Such indulgence is but one more way of softening the impact of political power and of creating the illusion of individual freedom in a society grown steadily more centralized, collectivized and destructive of the diversity of allegiance, the autonomy of enterprise in all spheres and the spirit of spontaneous association that any genuinely free civilization requires.

I cite this for another reason. Like others whom I have quoted at length at several points in this book, Mr. Nisbet stands as a living illustration of what I mean by a counterintellectual. It is only the scholar with a profound understanding of the nature of liberty and the institutions on which it rests who can stand ultimate guard over American cultural life. It is only he who can offer the American citizen the authentic and profound choices that our political system and our press no longer offer him.

I do not mean to imply here that it is only on a lofty, scholarly level that the fight can be conducted, although it unquestionably must begin at that level. At any time and on any social level the individual can and should take action. I have done so in my realm, and you, too, can work for your liberty, immediately and with impact. . . .

Stop asking the government for "free" goods and services, however desirable and necessary they may seem to be. They are not free. They are simply extracted from the hide of your neighbors—and can be extracted only by force. If you would not confront your neighbor and demand his money at the point of a gun to solve every new problem that may appear in your life, you should not allow the government to do it for you. Be prepared to identify any politician who simultaneously demands your "sacrifices" and offers you "free services" for exactly what he is: an egalitarian demagogue. This one insight understood, this one discipline acted upon and taught by millions of Americans to others could do more to further freedom in American life than any other.

There is, of course, a minimum of government intervention needed to protect a society, particularly from all forms of physical aggression and from economic fraud and, more generally, to protect the citizen's liberty and constitutional rights. What that precise minimum is in terms of a percentage of the GNP I am not prepared to say, but I do know this: that a clear cutoff line, beyond which the government may not confiscate our property, must be sought and established if the government is not to invade every nook and cranny of our lives and if we are to be free and productive. It is with *our* money that the state destroys our freedom. It is not too soon to start the process of tightening the leash on the state on the individual level, above all, by refusing to be a parasite. In the lowest-income groups in our nation there are men and women too proud, too independent to accept welfare, even though it is higher than the wages they can earn. Surely such pride can be stimulated on the more affluent levels of our society. . . .

It is with a certain weariness that I anticipate the charge that I am one of those "unrealistic" conservatives who wishes to "turn back the clock." There is a good deal less to this criticism than meets the eye. History is not a determinist carpet rolling inexorably in the direction of collectivism, although an extraordinary number of people believe this to be the case. The truth is that it has unrolled gloriously in the opposite direction many times. Above all, the United States was born. There is nothing "historically inevitable" about the situation we are in. There is also nothing "realistic" in couseling people to adjust to that situation. That is equivalent to counseling them to adjust to financial collapse and the loss of freedom. Realism, in fact, requires the capacity to see beyond the tip of one's nose, to face intolerably unpleasant problems and to take the necessary steps to dominate future trends, not to be crushed passively beneath them.

The time plainly has come to act. And I would advise the socially nervous that if our contemporary "New Despots" prefer to conceive of themselves as "progressive" and denounce those of us who would fight for liberty as "reactionary," let them. Words do not determine reality. Indeed, if language and history are to be taken seriously, coercion is clearly reactionary, and liberty clearly progressive. In a world where 80 percent of all human beings still live under harrowing tyranny, a tyranny always rationalized in terms of the alleged benefits to a collectivist construct called the People, the American who chooses to fight for the sanctity of the individual has nothing for which to apologize.

One of the clearest measures of the disastrous change that has taken place in this country is the fact that today one must intellectually justify a passion for individual liberty and for limited government, as though it were some bizarre new idea. Yet angry as I get when I reflect on this, I know there is a reason for it. Seen in the full context of human history, individual liberty *is* a bizarre new idea. And an even more bizarre new idea is the free market—the discovery that allowing millions upon millions of individuals to pursue their material interests as they choose, with a minimum of interference by the state, will unleash an incredible and orderly outpouring of inventiveness and wealth. These twin ideas appeared, like a dizzying flare of light in the long night of tyranny that has been the history of the human race. That light has begun to fade because the short span of 200 years has not been long enough for most of our citizens to understand the extraordinary nature of freedom. I say this with genuine humility. I came to understand this late in life myself, inspired by a very special perspective: I was flying high over the land of one of the bloodiest tyrants on earth. But having understood it, I cannot let that light die out without a battle. . . .

NO

John Kenneth Galbraith

THE SOCIAL CONSENSUS AND THE CONSERVATIVE ONSLAUGHT

THE ECONOMIC AND SOCIAL CONSENSUS

In economic and social affairs we value controversy and take it for granted; it is both the essence of politics and its principal attraction as a modern spectator sport. This emphasis on controversy regularly keeps us from seeing how substantial, on occasion, can be the agreement on the broad framework of ideas and policies within which the political debate proceeds.

This has been the case with economic and social policy in the industrial countries since the Second World War. There has been a broad consensus which has extended to most Republicans and most Democrats in the United States, to both Christian Democrats and Social Democrats in Germany and Austria, to the Labour and Tory Parties in Britain, and to Liberals and Progressive Conservatives in Canada. In France, Italy, Switzerland and Scandinavia also, policies have generally been based on a consensus. Although the rhetoric in all countries has been diverse, the practical action has been broadly similar.

All governments in all of the industrial countries, although differing in individual emphasis, have agreed on three essential points. First, there must be macroeconomic management of the economy to minimise unemployment and inflation. This, particularly in the English-speaking countries, was the legacy of Keynes. Second, there must be action by governments to provide those services which, by their nature, are not available from the private sector, or on which, like moderate-cost housing, health care and urban transportation, the private economy defaults. Finally, there must be measures—unemployment insurance, old age pensions, medical insurance, environmental protection, job-safety and produce-safety regulation, and special welfare payments—to protect the individual from circumstances with which he or she, as an individual, cannot contend, and which may be seen as a smoothing and softening of the harsh edges of capitalism.

From "The Social Consensus and the Conservative Onslaught," by John Kenneth Galbraith, *Millenium Journal of International Studies*, Spring 1982. Copyright © 1982 by John Kenneth Galbraith. Reprinted by permission.

There is no accepted term for the consensus which these policies compromise. 'Keynesian' policy refers too narrowly to macroeconomic action; 'liberal' or 'social democratic' policy has too strong a political connotation for what has been embraced in practice by Dwight E. Eisenhower, Gerald Ford, Charles de Gaulle, Konrad Adenauer, Winston Churchill and Edward Heath. I will not try to devise a new term; instead I will refer to the broad macroeconomic, public-service and social welfare commitment as the economic and social consensus, or just 'the consensus.' It is the present attack on this consensus—notably in Mrs. Thatcher's government in Britain and by Ronald Reagan's government in the United States—that I wish to examine.

THE CONSERVATIVE CHALLENGE TO THE CONSENSUS

The ideas supporting the economic and social consensus have never been without challenge. Keynesian macroeconomic management of the economy, the first pillar of the consensus, was powerfully conservative in intent. It sought only to correct the most self-destructive feature of capitalism (the one Marx thought decisive), namely its tendency to produce recurrent and progressively more severe crisis or depression, while leaving the role of the market, the current distribution of income and all property rights unchallenged. Despite this, numerous conservatives, especially in the United States, for a long time equated Keynesian economics with subversion. There was discomfort among conservatives when, thirty years after Keynes's *General Theory*[1] was published and the policy it prescribed was tending visibly towards obsolescence, Richard Nixon, in an aberrant moment, was led to

say that all Americans, including Republicans, were Keynesians now. A reference to the welfare policies of the consensus—'the welfare state'—has always encountered a slightly disapproving mood; something expensive or debilitating, it was felt, was being done for George Bernard Shaw's undeserving poor. The need to compensate for the failures of capitalism through the provision of lower-cost housing, lower-income health care and mass transportation has been accepted in all countries; but, in the United States at least, not many have wanted to admit that this is an unavoidable form of socialism. In contrast, in all countries at all times there has been much mention of the cost of government, the level of taxes, the constraints of business regulation and the effect of these on economic incentives.

There has always been a likelihood, moreover, that an attack on the economic and social consensus would be taken to reflect the views of a larger section of the population than was actually the case, because a large share of all public comment comes from people of relatively high income, while the consensus is of greatest importance to those of lowest income. High social business and academic position gives access to television, radio, and the press, and those who are professionally engaged in the media are, themselves, relatively well off. It follows that the voice of economic advantage, being louder, regularly gets mistaken for the voice of the masses. Furthermore, since it is so interpreted by politicians, it has much the same effect on legislatures and legislation as a genuine shift of opinion.

In the last thirty-five years we have had many such shifts of opinion—all drastically to the right. Professor

Friedrich Hayek with his *Road to Serfdom;*[2] Senator Goldwater in 1964; the unpoor, non-black, distinctly unradical Dayton, Ohio housewife, the supposed archetype discovered by two American scholars; Vice President Spiro Agnew; George Wallace; and Enoch Powell in Britain—they were all, in their turn, seen to represent a growing new conservative mood, before being, each in his turn, rejected.

However, even if proper allowance is made for the dismal success, in the past, of conservative revival, it seems certain that there is now not only in the United States but in other industrial countries as well, an attack on the economic and social consensus that has a deeper substance. Mrs. Thatcher and Mr. Reagan have both won elections. Of course, much, if not most, of Mr. Reagan's success in 1980 must be attributed to President Carter's economists—to the macroeconomic management that combined a severe recession with severe inflation with a drastic slump in the housing industry with particular economic distress in the traditional Democratic industrial states, and all these in the year of the election. (Economists do some things with precision.) But *effective* macroeconomic management was one part of the consensus and, obviously, there is nothing wrong with the way it now functions.

THE CONSERVATIVE ONSLAUGHT

There is, indeed, substance to the conservative attack on the economic and social consensus, especially in Britain and the United States. It strikes at genuine points of vulnerability. This, however, is not true of all of the attack; some of it is merely a rejection of reality—or of compassion. The conservative onslaught we

now witness needs careful dissection and differentiation. . . .

THE SIMPLISTIC ATTACK

The *simplistic* attack, which is currently powerful in the United States, consists in a generalised assault on all the civilian services of modern government. Education, urban services and other conventional functions of government; government help to the unemployed, unemployable or otherwise economically incapable; public housing and health care; and the regulatory functions of government are all in the line of fire. People, in a now famous phrase, must be left free to choose.

In its elementary form this attack on the consensus holds that the services of government are the peculiar malignity of those who perform them; they are a burden foisted on the unwilling taxpayer by bureaucrats. One eloquent American spokesman for this view, Mr. William Simon, the former Secretary of the Treasury, has said that,

Bureaucrats should be assumed to be noxious, authoritarian parasites on society, with a tendency to augment their own size and power and to cultivate a parasitical clientele in all classes of society.[3]

There must, he has urged, 'be a conscious, philosophical prejudice against any intervention by the state into our lives.'[4] If public services are a foisted malignancy—if they are unrelated to need or function—it follows that they can be reduced more or less without limit and without significant social cost or suffering. This is implicit, even explicit, in the simplistic attack.

Other participants in this line of attack are, superficially at least, more sophisticated. Professor Arthur Laffer of the University of Southern California has supported the case with his now famous curve, which shows that when no taxes are levied, no revenue is raised, and that when taxes absorb all income, their yield, not surprisingly, is also zero. Taxes that are too high, as shown by a curve connecting these two points, have at some point a reduced aggregate yield. The Laffer Curve—which in its operative ranges is of purely freehand origin—has become, in turn, a general case against all taxes. Let there be large horizontal reductions, it is argued, and the resulting expansion of private output and income—for those who will believe anything—can be great enough to sustain public revenues at more or less the previous level. For the less gullible, the Laffer Curve still argues for a large reduction in the cost and role of the government.[5]

Another stronger attack on the public services comes from Professor Milton Friedman and his disciples. It holds that these services are relentlessly in conflict with liberty: the market accords to the individual the sovereignty of choice; the state, as it enlarges its services, curtails or impairs that choice—a cumulative and apocalyptic process. By its acceptance of a large service and protective role for the state, democracy commits itself to an irreversible descent into totalitarianism and to Communism. Professor Friedman is firm as to the prospect. He argues that,

> If we continue our present trend, and our free society is replaced by a collectivist society, the intellectuals who have done so much to drive us down this path will not be the ones who run the society; the prison, insane asylum, or the graveyard would be their fate.[6]

Against this trend he asks

shall we have the wisdom and the courage to change our course, to learn from experience, and to benefit from a 'rebirth of freedom'?[7]

I have called this attack on the social consensus simplistic: it could also be called rhetorical and, by the untactful, vacuous, because it depends almost wholly on passionate assertion and emotional response. No one, after reflection, can conclude that publicly rendered services are less urgently a part of the living standard than privately purchased ones—that clean water from the public sector is less needed than clean houses from the private sector, that good schools for the young are less important than good television sets. In most countries public services are not rendered with high efficiency, a point worthy of real concern. But no way has ever been found for seriously reducing outlays for either efficiently or inefficiently rendered services without affecting performance. Public bureaucracy has a dynamic of its own, but so does private bureaucracy. As road builders promote public highways and public educators promote public education, so private weapons firms promote weapons and other corporate bureaucracies promote tobacco, alcohol, toothpaste and cosmetics. This is the common tendency of organisation, as we have known since Max Weber. Good education, health care and law enforcement do not impair liberty or foretell authoritarianism. On the contrary, the entire experience of civilised societies is that these services are consistent with liberty and enlarge it. Professor Friedman's belief that liberty is measured, as currently in New York City, by the depth of the uncollected garbage is, as I have previously observed, deeply questionable.

Taxes on the affluent do reduce the freedom of those so taxed to spend their own money. 'An essential part of economic freedom is freedom to choose how to use our income.'[8] But, unemployment compensation, old-age pensions and other welfare payments serve even more specifically to increase the liberty of their recipients. That is because the difference for liberty between considerable income and a little less income can be slight; in contrast, the effect on liberty of the difference between *no* income and *some* income is always very, very great. It is the unfortunate habit of those who speak of the effect of government on freedom that they confine their concern to the loss of freedom for the affluent. All but invariably they omit to consider the way income creates freedom for the indigent.

The differential effect of taxes and public services on people of different income is something we must not disguise. Taxes in industrial countries are intended to be moderately progressive; in any case, they are paid in greatest absolute amount by people of middle income and above. Public services, in contrast, are most used by the poor. The affluent have access to private schools, while the poor must rely on public education. The rich have private golf courses and swimming pools; the poor depend on public parks and public recreation. Public transportation is most important

for the least affluent, as are public hospitals, public libraries and public housing, the services of the police and other municipal services. Unemployment and welfare benefits are important for those who have no other income, while they have no similar urgency for those who are otherwise provided.

We sometimes hesitate in these careful days to suggest an apposition of interest between the rich and the poor. One should not, it is felt, stir the embers of the class struggle. To encourage envy is uncouth, possibly even un-American or un-British. However, any general assault on the public services must be understood for what it is; it is an attack on the living standard of the poor. . . .

NOTES

1. John Maynard Keynes, *The General Theory of Employment Interest and Money* (London: Macmillan, 1936).

2. Fredrich von Hayek, *Road to Serfdom* (London: Routledge and Kegan Paul, 1944).

3. William Simon, *A Time for Truth* (New York: McGraw-Hill, 1978), p. 219.

4. *Ibid.*, p. 218.

5. Professor Laffer's inspired use of purely fortuitous hypotheses, it is only fair to note, has been a source of some discomfort to some of his more scrupulous academic colleagues.

6. Professor Friedman's foreword in William Simon, *op. cit.*, p. xiii.

7. Milton and Rose Friedman, *Free to Choose* (New York: Harcourt Brace Jovanovich, 1979), p. 7.

8. *Ibid.*, p. 65.

POSTSCRIPT

Has American Government Gotten Too Big?

"There is no such thing as the People," Simon insists, "it is a collectivist myth." Yet the United States Constitution begins, "We the People of the United States . . . " Does Simon think that our Constitution is based on a "collectivist myth"? Perhaps the question is unfair, because at the time the Constitution was written, the national government had little to do directly with the economy. Commercial activity was largely, to use Simon's words, the work of "individual citizens with individual wills and individual purposes." On the other hand, the Constitution left room for the growth of government, and a few of our Founders, such as Alexander Hamilton, actively promoted it. It is hard to say whether they would like the kind of "big government" we have today.

One of the best systematic treatments of the thesis argued by Simon is Milton Friedman's short classic, *Capitalism and Freedom* (University of Chicago, 1962). For more recent discussions of the theme, see Michael Novak, ed., *The Denigration of Capitalism: Six Points of View* (American Enterprise Institute, 1979). Galbraith develops his thesis at length in a number of works, especially *Economics and the Public Purpose* (Houghton Mifflin, 1973) and *The New Industrial State* (Houghton Mifflin, 1967).

Whether or not government has gotten too big may become a moot question. It is already clear that our huge budget deficits, coupled with our aversion to tax increases, are going to force cutbacks in government programs. The argument is starting to shift from *whether* to reduce government involvement to *where* to reduce it: in the military sphere or in the area of domestic welfare programs? Galbraith would cut the military and Simon would undoubtedly make most of his cuts in domestic spending. Their economic arguments are thus closely tied to their political assumptions and priorities.

213

ISSUE 13
Does Welfare
Do More Harm Than Good?

YES: **Charles Murray,** from *Losing Ground* (Basic Books, 1984)

NO: **Christopher Jencks,** from "How Poor Are the Poor," *The New York Review of Books* (May 9, 1985)

ISSUE SUMMARY

YES: Author Charles Murray outlines his contention that welfare programs can result in long-term dependency on the part of the poor.
NO: Social commentator Christopher Jencks argues that government aid programs are vital to meeting the needs of the poor.

Long before Ronald Reagan's campaign for office in 1980, "the welfare mess" had become a national issue. As far back as the Nixon administration, plans had been made to "reform" the system by various means, including the substitution of modest cash payments based upon a "negative income tax" for the crazy quilt pattern of services, commodities, checks, and in-kind payments provided by the existing welfare system. The Carter administration also tried to interest Congress in a "reform" plan that would simplify, though probably not reduce, welfare.

There is a backlash against welfare, often voiced in mean-spirited jibes such as "make the loafers work" and "I'm tired of paying them to breed." Such slogans ignore the fact that most people on welfare are not professional loafers, but women with dependent children or old or disabled persons. Petty fraud may not be uncommon, but "welfare queens" who cheat the system for spectacular sums are extremely rare. The overwhelming majority of people on welfare are those whose condition would become desperate if payments were cut off. Finally, to reassure those who worry about "breeding for dollars," there is no conclusive evidence that child support payments have anything to do with conception; the costs of raising childen far exceed the payments.

This does not mean that all objections to welfare can be dismissed as Scrooge-like grumblings. There does seem to be evidence that welfare can in some cases promote work "disincentives" (i.e., make it possible for a recipient to stay home instead of looking for a job). Benefits available in some states exceed what some recipients would earn after taxes, and the high rate at which welfare benefits are reduced as other income increases—the so-called "notches" in the payment scale—may mean that an additional dollar in earnings can result in more than a dollar loss in total income. Nor is it only in the economic sphere that the welfare system produces unintended effects. Of particular concern to sociologists were the experiments conducted during the 1970s in Seattle and Denver, in which poor families were supplied with guaranteed annual incomes. Family breakups then began to increase. The reasons for this phenomenon were not clear from the experiments, but some critics of welfare have hypothesized that guaranteed income may undermine the traditional "provider role" of husbands. Whether or not this hypothesis is true will require further testing, but it is noteworthy that during the same ten-year period in which welfare benefits leaped upward, the proportion of families headed by one parent nearly doubled. There are also some severe social costs of welfare that must be borne by the recipients themselves. In addition to the stigma of being on welfare, there is the constant threat of intrusion by government agents. The social workers charged with administering the program have a great deal of power over those who receive the benefits, and some of the provisions of the program can add more strain to an already shaky family situation.

What is to be done about welfare? Broadly speaking, the suggestions fall into three categories: (a) some say to *trim down* the program; (b) others advocate *monitoring* it carefully to make sure the truly needy are receiving a fair share of it. That may mean trimming the program in some areas while expanding it in others; (c) others favor outright *abolition* of welfare, except for the aged and the physically handicapped.

The "trim it" approach has been a central tenet in the philosophy of the Reagan administration. When Ronald Reagan first campaigned for office in 1980, he promised to "get government off our backs." His contention was that government welfare programs tend to stifle initiative, depress the economy, and do the poor more harm than good. After almost eight years in office, the President's conservative critics claimed that he had not really fulfilled his promises to trim welfare; his liberal critics claimed that he has indeed carried out his promises, with disastrous results.

The radical approach of abolishing welfare is advocated by writer Charles Murray. In the excerpt from his book *Losing Ground*, which we present here, Murray provides some of the reasons why he thinks welfare has deepened the problem of poverty rather than alleviated it. Professor Christopher Jencks, whose critique of Murray is presented here, agrees that our welfare system is flawed but points out that it has greatly reduced poverty, so he favors a more careful monitoring of the system.

YES

Charles Murray

LOSING GROUND

The complex story we shall unravel comes down to this:

Basic indicators of well-being took a turn for the worse in the 1960s, most consistently and most drastically for the poor. In some cases, earlier progress slowed; in other cases mild deterioration accelerated; in a few instances advance turned into retreat. The trendlines on many of the indicators are—literally—unbelievable to people who do not make a profession of following them.

The question is why. Why at that moment in history did so many basic trends in the quality of life *for the poor* go sour? Why did progress slow, stop, reverse?

The easy hypotheses—the economy, changes in demographics, the effects of Vietnam or Watergate or racism—fail as explanations. As often as not, taking them into account only increases the mystery.

Nor does the explanation lie in idiosyncratic failures of craft. It is not just that we sometimes administered good programs improperly, or that sound concepts sometimes were converted to operations incorrectly. It is not that a specific program, or a specific court ruling or act of Congress, was especially destructive. The error was strategic.

A government's social policy helps set the rules of the game—the stakes, the risks, the payoffs, the tradeoffs, and the strategies for making a living, raising a family, have fun, defining what "winning" and "success" mean. The more vulnerable a population and the fewer its independent resources, the more decisive is the effect of the rules imposed from above. The most compelling explanation for the marked shift in the fortunes of the poor is that they continued to respond, as they always had, to the world as they found it, but that we—meaning the not-poor and un-disadvantaged—had changed the rules of their world. Not of our world, just of theirs. The first effect of the new rules was to make it profitable for the poor to behave in the short term in ways that were destructive in the long term. Their second effect was to mask these long-term losses—to subsidize irretrievable mistakes. We tried to provide more for the poor and produced more poor instead. We tried to remove the barriers to escape from poverty, and inadvertently built a trap. . . .

POVERTY

Reducing poverty was the central objective of federal social programs during the reform period. Policymakers and legislators hoped for a variety of good things from the War on Poverty and OEO, the entitlements, and the widening population of eligible recipients. But, whatever else the programs were to accomplish, they were to put more money in the hands of poor people. They were to reduce poverty. . . .

The popular conception about poverty is that, at least on this one fundamental goal, the Great Society brought progress. The most widely shared view of history has it that the United States entered the 1960s with a large population of poor people—Harrington's "other America"—who had been bypassed by the prosperity of the Eisenhower years. The rich and the middle class had gained, but the poor had not. Then, after fits and starts during the Kennedy years, came the explosion of programs under Johnson. These programs were perhaps too ambitious, it is widely conceded, and perhaps the efforts were too helter-skelter. But most people seem to envision a plot in which dramatic improvement did not really get started until the programs of the Great Society took effect. . . .

The reality is that improvement was stopping, not starting, during that time. . . . Poverty did fall during the five Johnson years, from 18 percent of the population in 1964 to 13 percent in 1968, his last year in office, and the slope of the decrease was the steepest during this period. . . .

[The] Great Society reforms had very limited budgets through the Johnson administration. The real annual expenditures of the 1970s were far larger—by many orders of magnitude, for some of the programs—than expenditures in the sixties. Yet progress against poverty stopped in the seventies. The steep declines in poverty from 1964 to 1968 cannot glibly be linked with government antipoverty dollar expenditures. . . .

MAXIMIZING SHORT-TERM GAINS

When large numbers of people begin to behave differently from ways they behaved before, my first assumption is that they do so for good reason. [I] will apply this assumption to the trends of the 1960s and 1970s and suggest that it fits the facts.

Specifically, I will suggest that changes in incentives that occurred between 1960 and 1970 may be used to explain many of the trends we have been discussing. It is not necessary to invoke the *Zeitgeist* of the 1960s, or changes in the work ethic, or racial differences, or the complexities of postindustrial economies, in order to explain increasing unemployment among the young, increased dropout from the labor force, or higher rates of illegitimacy and welfare dependency. All were results that could have been predicted (indeed, in some instances were predicted) from the changes that social policy made in the rewards and penalties, carrots and sticks, that govern human behavior. All were rational responses to changes in the rules of the game of surviving and getting ahead. I will not argue that the responses were the right ones, only that they were rational. Even of our mistakes, we say: It seemed like a good idea at the time.

I begin with the proposition that all, poor and not-poor alike, use the same general calculus in arriving at decisions; only the exigencies are different. Poor people play with fewer chips and cannot wait as long for results. Therefore they tend to reach decisions that a more affluent person would not reach. The reformers of the 1960s were especially myopic about this, tending not only to assume that the poor and not-poor were alike in trying to maximize the goods in their lives (with which I agree), but also that, given the same package of benefits, the decision that seem reasonable to one would seem reasonable to the other. They failed to recognize that the behaviors that are "rational" are different at different economic levels. . . .

In the exercise we are about to conduct, it is important to suspend thoughts about how the world ought to work, about what the incentives should be. The objective is to establish what the incentives *are* (or were), and how they are likely to affect the calculations of a person who has few chips and little time. It is also important to put aside the distant view of long-term rewards that we, surveying the scene from above, know to be part of the ultimate truth of self-interest, and instead to examine the truth as it appears at ground level at the time decisions must be made.

Dramatis Personae

Our guides are a young couple—call them Harold and Phyllis. I deliberately make them unremarkable except for the bare fact of being poor. They are not of a special lower-class culture. They have no socialized propensities for "serial monogamy." They are not people we think of as "the type who are on welfare." They have just graduated from an average public school in an average American city. Neither of them is particularly industrious or indolent or dull. They are the children of low-income parents, are not motivated to go to college, and have no special vocational skills. Harold and Phyllis went together during their last year in high school and find themselves in a familiar predicament. She is pregnant.

They will have a child together. They will face the kinds of painful decisions that many young people have had to face. What will they decide? What will seem to them to be "rational" behavior?

We shall examine the options twice—first, as they were in 1960, then as they were only ten years later, in 1970. We shall ignore the turbulent social history of the intervening decade. We shall ignore our couple's whiteness or blackness. We simply shall ask: Given the extant system of rewards and punishments, what course of action makes sense?

Options in 1960

Harold's Calculations, Pre-Reform. Harold's parents have no money. Phyllis has no money. If Harold remains within the law, he has two choices: He can get a job, or he can try to get Phyllis to help support him.

Getting Phyllis to support him is intrinsically more attractive, but the possibilities are not promising. If Phyllis has the baby, she will qualify for $23 a week in AFDC ($63 in 1980 purchasing power). This is not enough to support the three of them. And, under the rules of AFDC, Phyllis will not be able to contribute more to the budget. If she gets a job, she will lose benefits on a dollar-for-dollar basis. There is in 1960 no way to make the AFDC payment part of a larger package.

Also, Harold and Phyllis will not be able to live together. AFDC regulations in 1960 prohibit benefits if there is "a man in the house." Apart from its psychic and sexual disadvantages, this regulation also means that Harold cannot benefit from Phyllis's weekly check. The amount cannot possibly be stretched across two households.

It follows that, completely apart from the moral stance of Harold, his parents, or society, it is not possible to use Phyllis for support. Whether or not he decides to stay with her, he will have to find a job.

The only job he can find is working the presses in a dry cleaning shop. It pays the rock-bottom minimum wage—$40 for a forty-hour week, or about $111 in the purchasing power of the 1980 dollar. It is not much of a living, not much of a job. There is no future in it, no career path. But it pays for food and shelter. And Harold has no choice.

The job turns out to be as tedious as he expected. It is hot in the laundry, and Harold in on his feet all day; he would much rather not stay there. But the consequences of leaving the job are intolerable. Unemployment Insurance will pay him only $20 ($56 in 1980 purchasing power). He stays at the laundry and vaguely hopes that something better will come along.

Phyllis's Calculations, Pre-Reform. Phyllis has three (legal) options: to support herself (either keeping the baby or giving it up for adoption); to go on AFDC (which means keeping the baby); or to marry Harold.

Other things being equal, supporting herself is the least attractive of these options. Like Harold, she can expect to find only menial minimum-wage employment. There is no intrinsic reason to take such a job.

The AFDC option is worth considering. The advantage is that it will enable her to keep the baby without having to work. The disadvantages are the ones that Harold perceives. The money is too little, and she is not permitted to supplement it. And Harold would not be permitted to be a live-in husband or father. If she tries to circumvent the rules and gets caught, she faces being cut off from any benefits for the foreseeable future.

If Phyllis thinks ahead, the economic attraction of AFDC might appear more enticing. The total benefits she will receive if she has several children may seem fairly large. If she were already on AFDC it might make sense to have more children. But, right now, setting up a household with Harold is by far the most sensible choice, even given the miserable wage he is making at the laundry.

Being married (as opposed to just living together) has no short-term economic implications. This is shown in the following table:

Harold employed?

| | Living Together | |
	Unmarried	Married
Yes	$111	$111
No	0	0

The choice of whether to get married is dependent primarily on noneconomic motivations, plus the economic advantages to Phyllis of having Harold legally responsible for the support of her and the baby.

Once the decision not to go on AFDC is made, a new option opens up. As long as Phyllis is not on AFDC, no penalty is attached to getting a part-time or full-time job.

Options in 1970

Harold's and Phyllis's namesakes just ten years later find themselves in the identical situation. Their parents have no money; he doesn't want to go to school any longer; she is pregnant; the only job he can get is in the back room of a dry cleaners. That much is unchanged from 1960.

Harold's Calculations, Post-Reform. Harold's options have changed considerably. If he were more clever or less honest (or, perhaps, just more aggressive), he would have even more new options. But since he is none of those things, the major changes in his calculations are limited to these:

First, the AFDC option. In 1960, he had three objections to letting Phyllis go on welfare: too little money, no way to supplement it, and having to live separately from his family. By 1970, all three objections have been removed.

Economically, the total package of AFDC and other welfare benefits has become comparable to working. Phyllis will get about $50 a week in cash ($106 in 1980 dollars) and another $11 in Food Stamps ($23 in 1980 dollars). She is eligible for substantial rent subsidies under the many federal housing programs, but only a minority of AFDC recipients use them, so we will omit housing from the package. She will get Medicaid. We assume that a year's worth of doctor's bills and medication for a mother and infant is likely to be more than $250 (many times that if there is even one major illness), and we therefore add $5 a week (1980 dollars) onto the package. Without bending or even being imaginative about the new regulations, without tapping

nearly all the possible sources of public support, and using conservative estimates in reaching a dollar total, the package of benefits available to Phyllis in a typical northern state has a purchasing power of about $134. This minimal package adds up to $23 more than the purchasing power of forty hours of work at a minimum-wage job ten years earlier, in 1960.

Also, the money can be supplemented. If Phyllis works, she can keep the first thirty dollars she makes. After that, her benefits are reduced by two dollars for every three additional dollars of income.

Harold has even greater flexibility. *As long as he is not legally responsible for the care of the child*—a crucial proviso—his income will not count against her eligibility for benefits. He is free to work when they need a little extra money to supplement their basic (welfare) income.

The third objection, being separated from Phyllis, has become irrelevant. By Supreme Court ruling, the presence of a man in the house of a single woman cannot be used as a reason to deny her benefits.

The old-fashioned solution of getting married and living off their earned income has become markedly inferior. Working a full forty-hour week in the dry-cleaning shop will pay Harold $64 ($136 in 1980 dollars) *before* Social Security and taxes are taken out. The bottom line is this: Harold can get married and work forty hours a week in a hot, tiresome job; or he can live with Phyllis and their baby without getting married, not work, and have more disposable income. From an economic point of view, getting married is dumb. From a noneconomic point of view, it involves him in a legal relationship that has no payoff for him. If he thinks he may sometime tire of Phyllis and fatherhood, the 1970 rules thus provide a further incentive for keeping the relationship off the books.

Phyllis's Calculations, Post-Reform. To keep the baby or give it up? To get married or not? What are the pros and cons?

Phyllis come from a poor family. They want her out of the house, just as she wants to get out of the house. If she gives up the baby for adoption (or, in some states by 1970, has a legal abortion), she will be expected to support herself; and, as in 1960, the only job she will be able to find is likely to be unattractive, with no security and a paycheck no larger than her baby would provide. *The only circumstance under which giving up the baby is rational is if she prefers any sort of job to having and caring for a baby.* It is commonly written that poor teenaged girls have babies so they will have someone to love them. This may be true for some. But one *need* not look for psychological explanations. Under the rules of 1970, it was rational on grounds of dollars and cents for a poor, unmarried woman who found herself to be pregnant to have and keep the baby even if she did not particularly want a child.

In Phyllis's case, the balance favors having the baby. What about getting married?

If Phyllis and Harold marry and he is employed, she will lose her AFDC benefits. His minimum wage job at the laundry will produce no more income than she can make, and, not insignificantly, he, not she, will have control of the check. In exchange for giving up this degree of independence, she gains no real security. Harold's job is not nearly as stable as the welfare system. And, should her marriage break up, she will not be able to count on residual benefits. Enforcement of payment of child support has fallen to near-zero in poor communities. In sum, marriage buys Phyllis nothing—not companionship she couldn't have otherwise, not financial security, not even increased income. In 1970, her child provides her with the economic insurance that a husband used to represent.

Against these penalties for getting married is the powerful positive inducement to remain single: Any money that Harold makes is added to their income without affecting her benefits as long as they remain unmarried. It is difficult to think of a good economic reason from Phyllis's viewpoint why marriage might be attractive.

Let us pause and update the table of economic choices, plugging in the values for 1970. Again, we assume that the two want to live together. Their maximum weekly incomes (ignoring payroll deductions and Harold's means-tested benefits) are:

Harold employed?

| | Living Together | |
	Unmarried	Married
Yes	$270	$136
No	$134	$134

The dominant cell for maximizing income is clearly "living together unmarried, Harold employed." If they for some reason do decide to get married and they live in a state that permits AFDC for families with unemployed fathers (as most of the industrial states do), they are about equally well off whether or not Harold is employed. Or, more precisely, they are about equally well off, in the short run, if Harold moves in and out of the labor market to conform to whatever local rules apply to maintaining eligibility. This is a distinction worth empha-sizing, . . . the changed rules do not en-courage permanent unemployment so much as they encourage periodic unem-ployment.

Harold and Phyllis take the economi-cally logical step—she has the baby, they live together without getting married, and Harold looks for a job to make some extra money. He finds the job at the laundry. It is just as unpleasant a job as it was in 1960, but the implications of per-severing are different. In 1970, unlike 1960, Harold's job is *not* his basic source of income. Thus, when the back room of the laundry has been too hot for too long, it becomes economically feasible and indeed reasonable to move in and out of the labor market. In 1980 dollars, Unemployment Insurance pays him $68 per week. As the sole means of support it is not an attractive sum. But added to Phyllis's package, the total is $202, which beats the heat of the presses. And, if it comes to it, Harold can survive even without the Unemployment payment. In 1970, Phyllis's welfare package is bring-ing in more real income than did a mini-mum-wage job in 1960.

Such is the story of Harold and Phyllis. They were put in a characteristically working-class situation. In 1960, the logic of their world led them to behave in traditional working-class ways. Ten years later, the logic of their world had changed and, lo and behold, they be-haved indistinguishably from "welfare types." What if we had hypothesized a more typical example—or ar least one that fits the stereotype? What if we had posited the lower-class and black cultural influences that are said to foster high illegitimacy rates and welfare depen-dency? The answer is that the same gen-eral logic would apply, but with even more power. When economic incentives are buttressed by social norms, the ef-fects on behavior are multiplied. But the main point is that the social factors are not necessary to explain behavior. There is no "breakdown of the work ethic" in this account of rational choices among alternatives. There is no shiftless irre-sponsibility. It makes no difference whether Harold is white or black. There is no need to invoke the spectres of cultural pathologies or inferior upbring-ing. The choices may be seen much more simply, much more naturally, as the be-havior of people responding to the real-ity of the world around them and making the decisions—the legal, ap-proved, and even encouraged deci-sions—that maximize their quality of life. . . .

A PROPOSAL
FOR PUBLIC WELFARE

I begin with the proposition that it is within our resources to do enormous good for some people quickly. We have available to us a program that would convert a large proportion of the youn-ger generation of hardcore unemployed into steady workers making a living wage. The same program would dras-tically reduce births to single teenage girls. It would reverse the trendline in the breakup of poor families. It would mea-surably increase the upward socio-economic mobility of poor families. These improvements would affect some millions of persons.

All these are results that have eluded the efforts of the social programs in-stalled since 1965, yet, from everything we know, there is no real question about whether they would occur under the program I propose. A wide variety of persuasive evidence from our own culture and around the world, from experimental data and longitudinal studies, from theory and practice, suggests that the program would achieve such results.

The proposed program, our final and most ambitious thought experiment, consists of scrapping the entire federal welfare and income-support structure for working-aged persons, including AFDC, Medicaid, Food Stamps, Unemployment Insurance, Worker's Compensation, subsidized housing, disability insurance, and the rest. I would leave the working-aged person with no recourse whatsoever except the job market, family members, friends, and public or private locally funded services. It is the Alexandrian solution: cut the knot, for there is no way to untie it.

It is difficult to examine such a proposal dispassionately. Those who dislike paying for welfare are for it without thinking. Others reflexively imagine bread lines and people starving in the streets. But as a means of gaining fresh perspective on the problem of effective reform, let us consider what this hypothetical society might look like.

A large majority of the population is unaffected. A surprising number of the huge American middle and working classes go from birth to grave without using any social welfare benefits until they receive their first Social Security check. Another portion of the population is technically affected, but the change in income is so small or so sporadic that it makes no difference in quality of life. A third group comprises persons who have to make new arrangements and behave in different ways. Sons and daughters who fail to find work continue to live with their parents or relatives or friends. Teenaged mothers have to rely on support from their parents or the father of the child and perhaps work as well. People laid off from work have to use their own savings or borrow from others to make do until the next job is found. All these changes involve great disruption in expectations and accustomed roles.

Along with the disruptions go other changes in behavior. Some parents do not want their young adult children continuing to live off their income, and become quite insistent about their children learning skills and getting jobs. This attitude is most prevalent among single mothers who have to depend most critically on the earning power of their offspring.

Parents tend to become upset at the prospect of a daughter's bringing home a baby that must be entirely supported on an already inadequate income. Some become so upset that they spend considerable parental energy avoiding such an eventuality. Potential fathers of such babies find themselves under more pressure not to cause such a problem, or to help with its solution if it occurs.

Adolescents who were not job-ready find they are job-ready after all. It turns out that they can work for low wages and accept the discipline of the workplace if the alternative is grim enough. After a few years, many—not all, but many—find that they have acquired salable skills, or that they are at the right place at the right time, or otherwise find that the original entry-level job has gradually been transformed into a secure job paying a decent wage. A few—not a lot, but a few—find that the process leads to affluence.

Perhaps the most rightful, deserved benefit goes to the much larger population of low-income families who have been doing things right all along and have been punished for it: the young man who has taken responsibility for his wife and child even though his friends with the same choice have called him a fool; the single mother who has worked full time and forfeited her right to welfare for very little extra money; the parents who have set an example for their children even as the rules of the game have taught their children that the example is outmoded. For these millions of people, the instantaneous result is that no one makes fun of them any longer. The longer-term result will be that they regain the status that is properly theirs. They will not only be the bedrock upon which the community is founded (which they always have been), they will be recognized as such. The process whereby they regain their position is not magical, but a matter of logic. When it becomes highly dysfunctional for a person to be dependent, status will accrue to being independent, and in fairly short order. Noneconomic rewards will once again reinforce the economic rewards of being a good parent and provider.

The prospective advantages are real and extremely plausible. In fact, if a government program of the traditional sort (one that would "do" something rather than simply get out of the way) could *as plausibly* promise these advantages, its passage would be a foregone conclusion. Congress, yearning for programs that are not retreads of failures, would be prepared to spend billions. Negative side-effects (as long as they were the traditionally acceptable negative side-effects) would be brushed aside as trivial in return for the benefits. For let me be quite clear: I am not suggesting that we dismantle income support for the working-aged to balance the budget or punish welfare cheats. I am hypothesizing, with

the advantage of powerful collateral evidence, that the lives of large numbers of poor people would be radically changed for the better.

There is, however, a fourth segment of the population yet to be considered, those who are pauperized by the withdrawal of government supports and unable to make alternate arrangements: the teenaged mother who has no one to turn to; the incapacitated or the inept who are thrown out of the house; those to whom economic conditions have brought long periods in which there is no work to be had; those with illnesses not covered by insurance. What of these situations?

The first resort if the network of local services. Poor communities in our hypothetical society are still dotted with storefront health clinics, emergency relief agencies, employment services, legal services. They depend for support on local taxes or local philanthropy, and the local taxpayers and philanthropists tend to scrutinize them rather closely. But, by the same token, they also receive considerably more resources than they formerly did. The dismantling of the federal services has poured tens of billions of dollars back into the private economy. Some of that money no doubt has been spent on Mercedes and summer homes on the Cape. But some has been spent on capital investments that generate new jobs. And some has been spent on increased local services to the poor, voluntarily or as decreed by the municipality. In many cities, the coverage provided by this network of agencies is more generous, more humane, more wisely distributed, and more effective in its results than the services formerly subsidized by the federal government.

But we must expect that a large number of people will fall between the cracks.

How might we go about trying to retain the advantages of a zero-level welfare system and still address the residual needs?

As we think about the nature of the population still in need, it becomes apparent that their basic problem in the vast majority of the cases is the lack of a job, and this problem is temporary. What they need is something to tide them over while finding a new place in the economy. So our first step is to re-install the Unemployment Insurance program in more or less its previous form. Properly administered, unemployment insurance makes sense. Even if it is restored with all the defects of current practice, the negative effects of Unemployment Insurance *alone* are relatively minor. Our objective is not to wipe out chicanery or to construct a theoretically unblemished system, but to meet legitimate human needs without doing more harm than good. Unemployment Insurance is one of the least harmful ways of contributing to such ends. Thus the system has been amended to take care of the victims of short-term swings in the economy.

Who is left? We are now down to the hardest of the hard core of the welfare-dependent. They have no jobs. They have been unable to find jobs (or have not tried to find jobs) for a longer period of time than the unemployment benefits cover. They have no families who will help. They have no friends who will help. For some reason, they cannot get help from local services or private charities except for the soup kitchen and a bed in the Salvation Army hall.

What will be the size of this population? We have never tried a zero-level federal welfare system under conditions of late-twentieth-century national wealth, so we cannot do more than speculate. But we may speculate. Let us ask of whom the population might consist and how they might fare.

For any category of "needy" we may name, we find ourselves driven to one of two lines of thought. Either the person is in a category that is going to be at the top of the list of services that localities vote for themselves, and at the top of the list of private services, or the person is in a category where help really is not all that essential or desirable. The burden of the conclusion is not that every single person will be taken care of, but that the extent of resources to deal with needs is likely to be very great—not based on wishful thinking, but on extrapolations from reality. . . .

NO

Christopher Jencks

HOW POOR ARE THE POOR?

From 1946 until 1964 the conservative politicians who dominated Congress thought that the federal government might be capable of transforming American society, but they saw this as a danger to be avoided at almost any cost. For the following twelve years the liberals who dominated Congress thought that the federal government should try to cure almost every ill Americans were heir to. After 1976 the political climate in Congress changed again. The idea that government action could solve—or even ameliorate— social problems became unfashionable, and federal spending was increasingly seen as waste. As a result, federal social-welfare spending, which had grown from 5 percent of the nation's gross national product in 1964 to 11 percent in 1976, has remained stuck at 11 percent since 1976.

Conservative politicians and writers are now trying to shift the prevailing view again, by arguing that federal programs are not just ineffective but positively harmful. The "problem," in this emerging view, is not only that federal programs cost a great deal of money that the citizenry would rather spend on video recorders and Caribbean vacations, but that such programs hurt the very people they are intended to help.

Losing Ground, by Charles Murray, is the most persuasive statement so far of this new variation on Social Darwinism. Murray is a former journalist who has also done contract research for the government and is now associated with the Manhattan Institute, which raises corporate money to support conservative authors such as George Gilder and Thomas Sowell. His name has been invoked repeatedly in Washington's current debates over the budget—not because he has provided new evidence on the effects of particular government programs, but because he is widely presumed to have proven that federal social policy as a whole made the poor worse off over the past twenty years. Murray's popularity is easy to understand. He writes clearly and eloquently. He cites many statistics, and he makes his statistics seem easy to understand. Most important of all, his argument provides moral legitimacy for budget cuts that many politicians want to make in order to reduce the federal deficit. . . .

In appraising this argument, we must, I believe, draw a sharp distinction between the material condition of the poor and their social, cultural, and moral condition. If we look at material conditions we find that, Murray notwithstanding, the position of poor people showed marked improvement after 1965, which is the year Murray selects as his "turning point." If we look at social, cultural, and moral indicators, the picture is far less encouraging. But since most federal programs are aimed at improving the material conditions of life, it is best to start with them. . . .

1

. . . Murray is right that, apart from health, the material condition of the poor improved faster from 1950 to 1965 than from 1965 to 1980. The most obvious explanation is that the economy turned sour after 1970. Inflation was rampant, output per worker increased very little, and unemployment began to edge upward. The real income of the median American family, which had risen by an average of 2.9 percent a year between 1950 and 1965, rose only 1.7 percent a year between 1965 and 1980. From 1950 to 1965 it took a 4.0 percent increase in median family income to lower net poverty by one percentage point. From 1965 to 1980, because of expanding social welfare spending, a 4.0 percent increase in median income lowered net poverty by 1.2 percent. Nonetheless, median income grew so much more slowly after 1965 that the decline in net poverty also slowed.

Murray rejects this argument. In his version of economic history the nation as a whole continued to prosper during the 1970s. The only problem, he claims, was that "the benefits of economic growth stopped trickling down to the poor." He supports this version of economic history with statistics showing that gross national product grew by 3.2 percent a year during the 1970s compared to 2.7 percent a year between 1953 and 1959. This is true, but irrelevant. The economy grew during the 1950s because output per worker was growing. It grew during the 1970s because the labor force was growing. The growth of the labor force reflected a rapid rise in the number of families dividing up the nation's economic output. GNP per household hardly grew at all after 1970.

But a question remains. [T]otal government spending on "social welfare" programs grew from 11.2 to 18.7 percent of GNP between 1965 and 1980. If all this money had been spent on the poor, poverty should have fallen to virtually zero. But "social welfare" spending is not mostly for the poor. It includes programs aimed primarily at the poor, like Medicaid and food stamps, but it also includes programs aimed primarily at the middle classes, like college loans and military pensions, and programs aimed at almost everybody, like medical research, public schools, and Social Security. In 1980, only a fifth of all "social welfare" spending was explicitly aimed at low-income families, and only a tenth was for programs providing cash, food, or housing to such families. [C]ash, food, and housing for the poor grew from 1.0 percent of GNP in 1965 to 2.0 percent in 1980. This was a large increase in absolute terms. But redistributing an extra 1.0 percent of GNP could hardly be expected to reduce poverty to zero.

A realistic assessment of what social policy accomplished between 1965 and 1980 must also take account of the fact that if all else had remained equal, demographic changes would have pushed the poverty rate up during these years, not down. [B]oth the number of people over sixty-five and the number living in families headed by women grew steadily from 1950 to 1980. We do not have poverty rates for these groups in 1950, but in 1960 the official rates were roughly 33 percent for the elderly and 45 percent of families headed by women. Since neither group includes many jobholders, economic growth does not move either group out of poverty fast. From 1960 to 1965, for example, economic growth lowered official poverty from 22 to 17 percent for the nation as a whole, but only lowered it from 33 to 31 percent among the elderly and from 45 to 42 percent among households headed by women.

When poverty became a major social issue during the mid-1960s, government assistance to both these groups was quite modest. In 1965 the typical retired person got only $184 a month from Social Security in 1980 dollars, and a large minority got nothing whatever. Only about a quarter of all families headed by women got benefits from Aid to Families with Dependent Children (AFDC), and benefits for a family of four averaged only $388 a month in 1980 dollars.

From 1965 to 1970 the AFDC system changed drastically. Welfare offices had to drop a wide range of restrictive regulations that had kept many women and children off the rolls. It became much easier to combine AFDC with employment, and benefit levels rose appreciably. As a result of these changes something like half of all persons in families headed by women appear to have been receiving AFDC by 1970.

But as the economy floundered in the 1970s legislators began to draw an increasingly sharp distinction between the "deserving" and the "undeserving" poor. The "deserving" poor were those whom legislators judged incapable of working, namely the elderly and the disabled. Despite their growing numbers, they got more and more help. By 1980 the average Social Security retirement check bought 50 percent more than it had in 1970, and official poverty among the elderly had fallen from 25 percent to 16 percent. Taking noncash benefits into account, the net poverty rate was lower for those over 65 than for those under 65 in 1980.

We have less precise data on the disabled, but we know their monthly benefits grew at the same rate as benefits for the elderly, and the percentage of the population receiving disability benefits also grew rapidly during the 1970s. Since we have no reason to suppose that the percentage of workers actually suffering from serious disabilities grew, it seems reasonable to suppose that a larger fraction of the disabled were getting benefits, and that poverty among the disabled fell as a result.

While legislators were increasingly generous to the "deserving" poor during the 1970s, they showed no such concern for the "undeserving poor." The undeserving poor were those who "ought" to work but were not doing so. They were mainly single mothers and marginally employable men whose unemployment benefits had run out—or who had never been eligible in the first place. Men whose unemployment benefits have run out usually get no federal benefits. Most states offer them token "general assistance," but it is seldom enough to live on. Data on this group is scanty.

Single mothers do better than unemployable men, because legislators are reluctant to let the children starve and cannot find a way of cutting benefits for mothers without cutting them for children as well. Nonetheless, the purchasing power (in 1980 dollars) of AFDC benefits for a family of four rose from $388 a month in 1965 to $435 in 1970. In addition, Congress made food stamps available to all low-income families after 1971. These were worth another $150 to a typical family of four. By 1972, the AFDC-food stamp "package" for a family of four was worth about $577 a month. Benefits did not keep up with inflation after 1972, however, and by 1980 the AFDC-food stamp package was worth only $495 a month. As a result, the welfare rolls grew no faster than the population after 1975, though the number of families headed by women continued to increase.

According to Murray, keeping women off the welfare tolls should have raised their incomes in the long run, since it should have pushed them into jobs where they would acquire the skills they need to better themselves. This did not happen. The official poverty rate in households headed by women remained essentially constant throughout the 1970s, at around 37 percent. Since the group at risk was growing, families headed by women accounted for a rising fraction of the poor.

Taken together, these data tell a story very different from the one Murray tells in *Losing Ground*. First, contrary to what Murray claims, "net" poverty declined almost as fast after 1965 as it had before. Second, the decline in poverty after 1965, unlike the decline before 1965, occurred despite unfavorable economic conditions, and depended to a great extent on government efforts to help the poor. Third, the groups that benefited from this "generous revolution," as Murray

rightly calls it, were precisely the groups that legislators hoped would benefit, notably the aged and the disabled. The groups that did not benefit were the ones that legislators did not especially want to help. Fourth, these improvements took place despite demographic changes that would ordinarily have made things worse. Given the difficulties, legislators should, I think, look back on their efforts to improve the material conditions of poor people's lives with some pride.

2

Up to this point I have treated demographic change as if it were entirely beyond human control, like the weather. According to Murray, however, what I have labeled "demographic change" was a predictable byproduct of government policy. Murray does not, it is true, address the role of government in keeping old people alive longer. But he does argue that changes in social policy, particularly the welfare system, were responsible for the increase in families headed by women after 1965. Since this argument recurs in all conservative attacks on the welfare system, and since scholarly research supports it in certain respects, it deserves a fair hearing.

Murray illustrates his argument with an imaginary Pennsylvania couple named Harold and Phyllis. They are young, poorly educated, and unmarried. Phyllis is also pregnant. The question is whether she should marry Harold. Murray first examines her situation in 1960. If Phyllis does not marry Harold, she can get the equivalent of about $70 a week in 1984 money from AFDC. She cannot supplement her welfare benefits by working, and on $70 a week she cannot live by herself. Nor can she live with Harold, since the welfare agency checks up on her living arrangements, and if she is living with a man she is no longer eligible for AFDC. Thus if Phyllis doesn't marry Harold she will have to live with her parents or put her baby up for adoption. If Phyllis does marry Harold, and he gets a minimum-wage job, they will have the equivalent of $124 a week today. This isn't much, but it is more than $70. Furthermore, if Phyllis is not on AFDC she may be able to work herself, particularly if her mother will help look after her baby. Unless Harold is a complete loser, Phyllis is likely to marry Harold if he asks.

Now the scene shifts to 1970. The Supreme Court has struck down the "man in the house" rule, so Phyllis no longer has to choose between Harold and AFDC. She can have both. According to Murray, if Phyllis does not marry Harold and he does not acknowledge that he is the father of their child, Harold's income will not "count" when the local welfare department decides whether Phyllis is eligible for AFDC, food stamps, and Medicaid. This means she can get paid to stay home with her child while Harold goes out to work, but only so long as she doesn't marry Harold. Furthermore, the value of her welfare "package" is now roughly the same as what Harold or she could earn at a minimum-wage job. Remaining eligible for welfare is thus more important than it was in 1960, as well as being easier. From Phyllis's viewpoint marrying Harold is now quite costly.

While the story of Harold and Phyllis makes persuasive reading, it is misleading in several respects. First, it is not quite true, as Murray claims, that "any money that Harold makes is added to their income without affecting her benefits as long as they remain unmarried." If Phyllis is living with Harold, and Harold

is helping to support her and her child, the law requires her to report Harold's contributions when she fills out her "need assessment" form. What has changed since 1960 is not Phyllis's legal obligation to report Harold's contribution but the likelihood that she will be caught if she lies. Federal guidelines issued in 1965 now prohibit "midnight raids" to determine whether Phyllis is living with Harold. Furthermore, even if Phyllis concedes that she lives with Harold, she can deny that he pays the bills and the welfare department must then prove her a liar. Still, Phyllis must perjure herself, and there is always some chance she will be caught.

The second problem with the Harold and Phyllis story is that Murray's account of Harold's motives is not plausible. In 1960, according to Murray, Harold marries Phyllis and takes a job paying the minimum wage because he "has no choice." But the Harolds of this world have always had a choice. Harold can announce that Phyllis is a slut and that the baby is not his. He can tell Phyllis to get an illegal abortion. He can join the army. Harold's parents may insist that he do his duty by Phyllis, but then again they may blame her for leading him astray. If Harold cared only about improving his standard of living, as Murray suggests, he would not have married Phyllis in 1960.

According to Murray, Harold is less likely to marry Phyllis in 1970 than in 1960 because, with the demise of the "man in the house" rule and with higher benefits, Harold can get Phyllis to support him. But unless Harold works, Phyllis has no incentive either to marry him or to let him live off her meager check, even if she shares her bed with him occasionally. If Harold *does* work, and all he cares about is having money in his pocket, he is better off on his own than he is sharing his check with Phyllis and their baby. From an economic viewpoint, in short, Harold's calculations are much the same in 1970 as in 1960. Marrying Phyllis will still lower his standard of living. The main thing that has changed since 1960 is that Harold's friends and relatives are less likely to think he "ought" to marry Phyllis.

This brings us to the central difficulty in Murray's story. Since Harold is unlikely to want to support Phyllis and their child, and since Phyllis is equally unlikely to want to support Harold, the usual outcome is that they go their separate ways. At this point Phyllis has three choices: get rid of the baby (through adoption or abortion), keep the baby and continue to live with her parents, or keep the baby and set up housekeeping on her own. If she keeps the baby she usually decides to stay with her parents. In 1975 three-quarters of all first-time unwed mothers lived with their parents during the first year after the birth of their baby. (No room for Harold here.) Indeed, half of all unmarried mothers under twenty-four lived with their parents in 1975—and this included divorced and separated mothers as well as those who had never been married.

If Phyllis expects to go on living with her parents, she is not likely to worry much about how big her AFDC check will be. Phyllis has never had a child and she has never had any money. She is used to her mother's paying the rent and putting food on the table. Like most children she is likely to assume that this arrangement can continue until she finds an arrangement she prefers. In the short run, having a child will allow her to leave school (if she has not done so already) without having to work. It will also mean changing a lot of diapers, but Phyllis may well expect her mother to help with that. Indeed, from Phyllis's viewpoint having a child may look rather like having another little brother or sister. If it brings in some money, so much the better, but if she expects to live with her parents money is likely to be far less important to her than her parents' attitude toward illegitimacy. That is the main thing that changed for her between 1960 and 1970.

Systematic efforts at assessing the impact of AFDC benefits on illegitimacy rates support my version of the Harold and Phyllis story rather than Murray's. The level of a state's AFDC benefits has no measurable effect on its rate of illegitimacy. In 1984, AFDC benefits for a family of four ranged from $120 a month in Mississippi to $676 a month in New York. David Ellwood and Mary Jo Bane recently completed a meticulous analysis of the way such variation affects illegitimate births. In general, states with high benefits have *less* illegitimacy than states with low ones, even after we adjust for differences in race, region, education, income, urbanization, and the like. This may be because high illegitimacy rates make legislators reluctant to raise welfare benefits.

To get around this difficulty, Ellwood and Bane asked whether a change in a state's AFDC benefits led to a change in its illegitimacy rate. They found no consistent effect. Nor did high benefits widen the disparity in illegitimate births between women with a high probability of getting AFDC—teen-agers, nonwhites, high school dropouts—and women with a low probability of getting AFDC.

What about the fact that Phyllis can now live with Harold (or at least sleep with him) without losing her benefits? Doesn't this discourage marriage and thus increase illegitimacy? Perhaps. [Data show] that illegitimacy has risen at a steadily accelerating rate since 1950. There is no special "blip" in the late 1960s, when midnight raids stopped and the "man in the house" rules passed into history. Nor is there consistent evidence that illegitimacy increased faster among probable AFDC recipients than among women in general.

Murray's explanation of the rise in illegitimacy thus seems to have at least three flaws. First, most mothers of illegitimate children initially live with their parents, not their lovers, so AFDC rules are not very relevant. Second, the trend in illegitimacy is not well correlated with the trend in AFDC benefits or with rule changes. Third, illegitimacy rose among movie stars and college graduates as well as welfare mothers. All this suggests that both the rise of illegitimacy and the liberalization of AFDC reflect broader changes in attitudes toward sex, law, and privacy, and that they had little direct effect on each other.

But while AFDC does not seem to affect the number of unwed mothers, as Murray claims, it does affect family arrangements in other ways. Ellwood and Bane found, for example, that benefit levels had a dramatic effect on the living arrangements of single mothers. If benefits are low, single mothers have trouble maintaining a separate household and are likely to live with their relatives—usually their parents. If benefits rise, single mothers are more likely to maintain their own households.

Higher AFDC benefits also appear to increase the divorce rate. Ellwood and Bane's work suggests, for example, that if the typical state had paid a family of four only $180 a month in 1980 instead of $350, the number of divorced women would have fallen by a tenth. This might be partly because divorced women remarry more hastily in states with very low benefits. But if AFDC pays enough for a woman to live on, she is also more likely to leave her husband. The Seattle-Denver "income maintenance" experiments, which Murray discusses at length, found the same pattern. . . .

Shorn of rhetoric, then, the "empirical" case against the welfare system comes to this. First, high AFDC benefits allow single mothers to set up their own households. Second, high AFDC benefits allow mothers to end bad marriages. Third, high benefits may make divorced mothers more cautious about remarrying. All these "costs" strike me as benefits. . . .

3

. . . Murray's conviction that getting checks from the government is always bad for people is complemented by his conviction that working is always good for them, at least in the long run. Since many people do not recognize that working is in their long-run interest, Murray assumes such people must be forced to do what is good for them. Harold, for example, would rather loaf than take an exhausting, poorly paid job in a laundry. To prevent Harold from indulging his self-destructive preference for loafing, we must make loafing financially impossible. America did this quite effectively until the 1960s. Then we allegedly made it easier for him to qualify for unemployment compensation, so he was more likely to quit his job whenever he got fed up. We also made it easier for him to live off Phyllis's AFDC check. Once Harold had tasted the pleasures of indolence, he found them addictive, like smoking, so he never acquired either the skills or the self-discipline he would have needed to hold a decent job and support a family. By trying to help we therefore did him irreparable harm.

While I share Murray's enthusiasm for work, I cannot see much evidence that changes in government programs significantly affected men's willingness to work during the 1960s. When we look at the unemployed, for example, we find that about half of all unemployed workers were getting unemployment benefits in 1960. The figure was virtually identical in both 1970 and 1980. Thus while the rules governing unemployment compensation did change, the changes did not make joblessness more attractive economically. Murray is quite right that dropping the man-in-the-house rule made it easier for Harold to live off Phyllis's AFDC check. But there is no evidence that his contributed to rising unemployment. Since black women receive about half of all AFDC money, Murray's argument implies that as AFDC rules became more liberal and benefits rose in the late 1960s, unemployment should have risen among young black men. Yet Murray's own data show that such men's unemployment rates fell during the late 1960s. Murray's argument also implies that young black men's unemployment rate should have fallen in the 1970s, when the purchasing power of AFDC benefits was falling. In fact, their unemployment rates rose. . . .

4

While Murray's claim that helping the poor is really bad for them is indefensible, his criticism of the ways in which government tried to help the poor from 1965 to 1980 still raises a number of issues that defenders of these programs need to face. Any successful social policy must strike a balance between collective compassion and individual responsibility. The social policies of the late 1960s and 1970s did not strike this balance very well. They vacillated unpredictably between the two ideals in ways that neither Americans nor any other people could live with over the long run. This vacillation played a major role in the backlash against government efforts to "do good." Murray's rhetoric of individual responsibility and self-sufficiency is not the basis for a social policy that would be politically acceptable over the long run either, but it provides a useful starting point for rethinking where we went wrong.

One chapter of *Losing Ground* is titled "The Destruction of Status Rewards"— not a happy phrase, but a descriptive one. The message is simple. If we want to promote virtue, we have to reward it. The social policies that prevailed from 1964 to 1980 often seemed to reward vice instead. They did not, of course, reward vice for its own sake. But if you set out to help people who are in trouble, you almost inevitably find that most of them are to some extent responsible for their present troubles. Few victims are completely innocent. Helping those who are not doing their best to help themselves poses extraordinarily difficult moral and political problems.

Phyllis, for example, turns to AFDC after she has left Harold. Her cousin Sharon, whose husband has left her, works forty hours a week in the same laundry where Harold worked. If we help Phyllis very much, she will end up better off than Sharon. This will not do. Almost all of us believe it is "better" for people to work than not to work. This means we also believe those who work should end up "better off" then those who do not work. . . .

The AFDC revolution of the 1960s sometimes left Sharon worse off than Phyllis. In 1970, for example, Sharon's minimum-wage job paid $275 a month if she worked forty hours every week and was never laid off. Once her employer deducted Social Security and taxes she was unlikely to take home more than $250 a month. Meanwhile, the median state (Oregon) paid Phyllis and her three children $225 a month, and nine states paid her more than $300 a month. This comparison is somewhat misleading in one respect, however. By 1970 Sharon could also get AFDC benefits to supplement her earnings in the laundry. Under the "thirty and a third" rule, adopted in 1967, local welfare agencies had to ignore the first $30 of Sharon's monthly earnings plus a third of what she earned beyond $30 when they computed her need for AFDC. . . .

Yet while Murray claims to be concerned about rewarding virtue, he seems only interested in doing this if it does not cost the taxpayer anything. Instead of endorsing the "thirty and a third" rule, for example, on the grounds that it rewarded work, he lumps it with all the other undesirable changes that contrib-

uted to the growth of the AFDC rolls during the late 1960s. . . .

The difficulty of helping the needy without rewarding indolence or folly recurs when we try to provide "second chances." America was a "second chance" for many of our ancestors, and it remains more committed to the idea that people can change their ways than any other society I know. But we cannot give too many second chances without undermining people's motivation to do well the first time around. In most countries, for example, students work hard in secondary school because they must do well on the exams given at the end of secondary school in order to get a desirable job or go on to a university. In America, plenty of colleges accept students who have learned nothing whatever in high school, including those who score near the bottom on the SAT. Is it any wonder that Americans learn less in high school than their counterparts in other industrial countries? . . .

The problem of "second chances" is intimately related to the larger problem of maintaining respect for the rules governing rewards and punishments in American society. As Murray rightly emphasizes, no society can survive if it allows people to violate its rules with impunity on the grounds that the system is at fault. . . .

POSTSCRIPT

Does Welfare Do More Harm Than Good?

The welfare debate in this issue has been argued in rational terms. In the public arena, however, it is entangled in emotional language, and rational discussion seems impossible. One side accuses the other of being heartless. The other side responds with anecdotes about "welfare queens." The only way a genuine public dialogue can begin is to de-escalate the rhetoric.

A little candor on both sides might help. Surely all rational Americans accept the fact that there are genuinely needy people. In many cases, these people do not have families to help them, and private charity is limited. They need public assistance. At the same time, we have to recognize that public assistance carries with it a cost—not merely the immediate dollar cost of the programs, but cost in terms of its effect on self-respect and work incentives. This, according to Murray, is the central defect of our welfare system. Jencks defends the record of achievement of welfare against Murray's attack even while fully agreeing with Murray's point that welfare should not undermine work incentives.

The American welfare system is often criticized for being both stingy and too free with tax monies. Socialist Michael Harrington's opinion in *The Other America* (Macmillan, 1962) is that the system is ungenerous. Harrington's latest preachment against what he considers the heartless treatment of the poor in America is *The New American Poverty* (Holt, 1984). After analyzing its history and structure, Sar A. Levitan and Clifford M. Johnson conclude that the current welfare system is a fairly rational and necessary response to emerging societal needs (*Beyond the Safety Net: Reviving the Promise of Opportunity in America*, Ballinger, 1984).

Writers who criticize the welfare program for going too far include Martin Anderson, *Welfare* (Hoover Institution, 1977), and Charles Hobbs, *The Welfare Industry* (Heritage Foundation, 1978). Neil Gilbert acknowledges in *Capitalism and the Welfare State* (Yale, 1983) that the welfare system is overextended, but points out that this is largely because much of the money goes into the pockets of middle-class service providers and middle-class recipients. An excellent review of some of the current debates on the welfare system from several viewpoints is presented in the January/February 1986 issue of *Society*. A work which should be examined to understand the psychology of the recipients of welfare, especially those who are poor, is Leonard Goodwin's *Causes and Cures of Welfare: New Evidence on the Social Psychology of the Poor* (Lexington, 1983). He explodes the myth that welfare recipients do not want to work and argues that welfare creates less dependency than is commonly supposed.

UN Photo/Jane Schreibman

PART 6

Social Control and the Protection of Society

One of the most basic functions of a social structure is to protect its members. But what constitutes a threat? Those whose life-styles are outside the norm? Criminals? Immigrants? How do we respond as a society? With tolerance? With force? And are some solutions potentially more destructive than the dangers they seek to thwart?

Are Homosexual Relations Deviant?

Is Incapacitation the Answer to the Crime Problem?

Should Immigration Be More Limited?

Is Nuclear Deterrence Irrational?

ISSUE 14
Are Homosexual Relations Deviant?

YES: Robert Gordis, from *Love and Sex* (Farrar, Straus and Giroux, 1978)

NO: Jeannine Gramick, from "Homosexuality and Bisexuality are Just as Natural and Normal as Heterosexual Behavior and Relations," in *Taking Sides: Clashing Views on Controversial Issues in Human Sexuality* (Dushkin, 1986)

ISSUE SUMMARY

YES: Robert Gordis, biblical professor at the Jewish Theological Seminary, argues that homosexuality is contrary to the natural sexual programming of the human species and should be considered an abnormality or illness.

NO: Jeannine Gramick, a Catholic nun who works with homosexuals, argues that homosexuality is natural and normal by pointing to its prevalence in human history and the fact that most homosexuals are born with a homosexual orientation.

In Sioux Falls, South Dakota, on May 12, 1979, Randy Rohl and Grady Quinn made headlines. They were the first acknowledged homosexual couple ever to receive permission from their high school principal to attend the prom together. The National Gay Task Force heralded the event as a great moment in the history of human rights. What the voters of Sioux Falls thought of it nobody knows for certain; no one asked them. However, if their views were like those of the voters in Dade County, Florida, St. Paul, Minnesota, Eugene, Oregon, Wichita, Kansas, and Houston, Texas, they probably were not very enthusiastic about the decision. Voters in those areas were asked to approve resolutions specifically banning discrimination against people because of "sexual preference," and the voters overwhelmingly rejected the resolutions.

Yet the attitude of Americans toward gay rights is really quite ambiguous. On the one hand are the long string of defeats for gay rights resolutions on public referenda and the public opinion polls that show people don't want their children supervised by homosexuals in day care centers or taught sex education by homosexual teachers. On the other hand are public opinion poll results showing that Americans oppose the punishment of people for homosexual behavior, the election and reelection of public officials who support gay liberation, and defeat of referendum resolutions (such as one in California in 1978) that would ban the hiring of homosexuals in public schools. If behind the apparent inconsistency on "gay rights" there is a thread of consistency, it is this: Americans believe in minding their own business, and are thus opposed to penalizing people for what they do in private; at the same time, Americans persist in viewing homosexual behavior as wrong, and they are thus unwilling either to elevate it to the status of a civil right or to expose their children to its promotion.

Public uneasiness concerning homosexuality may have increased in recent years because of AIDS (Acquired Immune Deficiency Syndrome). AIDS is caused by a virus transmitted through the exchange of bodily fluids, primarily in sexual activity and intravenous drug use. Since 1981 when the first case of AIDS was diagnosed, the majority of its victims have been homosexuals. And because AIDS is fatal in all cases and because there remains much that is unknown about the disease and how it may be spread, the dread of AIDS may unleash many prejudices and fears, including homophobia.

Sexual acts between members of the same sex are usually classified as "deviant" by sociologists. The term "deviant" carries with it at least two sets of meanings. For sociologists, "deviance" simply means behavior that radically departs from the norm *in a given society*. Thus, for a man to get down on one knee and kiss the hand of a woman he has just met (unless he is drunk or joking) is deviant behavior in the America of the 1980s; it would not be deviant in the court of Louis XIV. That does not mean that there is anything at all immoral or "wrong" about it. It just means that is a departure from our particular social norms and expectations. And that is the way sociologists use the term—in a non-normative and relative sense. For the average American, however, "deviant" often connotes more; it carries the sense of "sick" and "evil."

In the selections that follow Jeannine Gramick attacks the view that homosexuality is sick or immoral, while acknowledging that it departs from what society morally approves. She argues that homosexuality has been quite prevalent in human history and for many homosexuals it is largely genetically determined and not a matter of choice. Hence discrimination against them is unjust. Robert Gordis condemns past persecutions of homosexuals but argues that homosexuality is an abnormality or illness like alcoholism. It should be treated with understanding, and homosexuals should be given their full rights, but their life-styles should not be granted the same value and legitimacy as heterosexuality.

YES

Robert Gordis

HOMOSEXUALITY IS NOT ON A PAR WITH HETEROSEXUAL RELATIONS

Nowhere else is the confrontation between the classical religious tradition and emerging contemporary attitudes sharper than with regard to homosexuality. Biblical law and biblical life are completely at one in condemning the practice. The sexual codes in the Torah describe male homosexuality as an "abomination" punishable with death like other major infractions of the moral code, such as incest and sexual contact with animals (Lev. 18:22; 20:13).

The practice is clearly regarded as worse than rape, as is evident from an incident narrated in Chapter 19 of Genesis. Two strangers, who are actually angels sent by the Lord to survey the sinful city of Sodom, are given hospitality by Lot, Abraham's nephew. When the townsmen hear of the strangers in their midst, they besiege Lot's house and demand that he turn the wayfarers over to them for homosexual abuse. Horrified at this breach of the ancient custom of hospitality, Lot offers instead to send out his two virgin daughters to the mob to do with as they wish. When the mob refuses the offer and tries to storm the door of Lot's house, it becomes clear that the city is beyond hope, and its destruction is decreed by God.

A similar tragic incident, going back to an early, lawless period shortly after the conquest of the land, is reported in Chapter 19 of the Book of Judges. A traveler passing through the town of Gibeah in Benjamin is denied hospitality by the townspeople. Only one old man gives lodging and food to the stranger, his concubine, and his animals. When the Benjaminites learn that the stranger is being housed among them, they gather and demand that he be handed over to them for sexual purposes. The host remonstrates with them in vain, offering to turn over his daughter and his guest's concubine to satisfy their lust. When the mob does not desist, the guest takes his concubine and pushes her out of doors. They rape her and abuse her all night and leave her lifeless body on the threshold. The book of Judges goes on to narrate the punishment visited upon the Benjaminites, leading to the virtual extinction of that tribe from the household of Israel.

There are many instances where rabbinic law has modified biblical attitudes in the direction of greater leniency, but this is not true of homosexuality. Here the attitude remains strongly negative, though the practice receives relatively little attention in the Talmud, probably because the rabbis believed that "Jews are not suspected of committing homosexuality and buggery."

This persistent feeling of revulsion toward homosexuality was nourished by a variety of historical causes. During the biblical period, the fertility cults that were widespread throughout the Middle East included intercourse with sacred male prostitutes at the pagan temples. From the Canaanites these practices, along with idolatry in general, penetrated into the religious practices of the Hebrews during the early days of the Davidic kingdom. These functionaries were finally banished from the precincts of the Temple, but only after repeated and determined efforts by several Judean kings, Asa, Jehoshaphat, and Josiah.

During the Greco-Roman era and beyond, the opposition to homosexuality by Jewish rabbinic leadership was a reaction to its widespread presence in the ancient world, where it was furthered and encouraged by pagan society and religion. Homosexual liaisons played a significant role in the social and cultural life of the ancient Greeks and Romans. Indirect evidence of the strong hold that homosexuality had on the Greco-Roman world is to be found in Paul's Epistle to the Romans. In the strongest of terms he castigates homosexuality as "dishonorable" and "unnatural." That he places homosexuality at the head of a list of offenses would suggest that the practice was widespread. It is also noteworthy that he first levels his attack against the

women and only then turns to the men as "likewise" engaging in these "shameless acts." (1:26, 27)

This negative attitude toward homosexuality has been maintained by Jewish tradition to the present time. It regards homosexuals as flouting the will of the Creator, who fashioned men and women with different anatomical endowments and with correspondingly distinct roles to play in the sexual process.

All these objections to homosexuality in Judaism were intensified in Christianity because of several additional factors. Most of the converts to the early Christian Church were former pagans who had been exposed to the presence of homosexual practices in their previous environment. Paul, as well as the Church after him, therefore felt it incumbent to attack the practice with all the power at his command. Moreover, as we have seen, classical Christianity was basically unhappy with the sexual component of human nature in general. It had to concede that sexual contact was legitimate, first because the instinct cannot be successfully suppressed by most men and women and, second, because it is essential for procreation. Since this last factor is obviously lacking in homosexual activity, there is no justification for yielding to "unnatural lust."

In sum, both Judaism and Christianity, in spite of differences in their approach to sex, have regarded homosexuality as a violation of God's will and a perversion of nature.

The subsequent weakening of religion and the growth of secularism in the Western world did little to reduce the sense of hostility toward homosexuality. The new emphasis on the cultivation of the body and the development of athletics in the modern period underscored the goal that men should be men. Nowhere is masculinity revealed more unmistakably than in sexual potency. Psychoanalytic theory, particularly in its classical Freudian formulation, saw male and female sexuality as the fundamental element in the human personality, which, when diverted from "normal" channels, becomes the source of psychological and physical trauma. In this respect as well, homosexuality ran counter to the values of the age. As a result of all these factors, as well as vestiges of the religious approach, homosexuality continued to engender feelings of revulsion going beyond the bonds of rational response.

Perhaps the most sensational manifestation of this reaction came at the end of the nineteenth century. In 1895, the brilliant and gifted English dramatist and poet Oscar Wilde was prosecuted by the Crown for having homosexual relations with Lord Alfred Douglas. Wilde was convicted, imprisoned for two years, and emerged from this experience a man physically broken and creatively ruined.

Wilde is by no means the only example of talent or genius to be found among homosexuals. More or less plausibly, many distinguished figures of the past and the present have been described as homosexuals. It is likely that lesbianism is as common as male homosexuality, but it is felt to be less offensive because its manifestations seem less blatant.

The hostility of society to homosexuals is reflected in the statute books. Homosexual behavior is treated as a crime in China and the Soviet Union; in the United States, homosexual soliciting is a criminal act. To be sure, such laws have often not been enforced in this country, particularly in the recent past.

By and large, the penalties accorded to homosexuals have been social and eco-nomic rather than legal. Homosexuals have been driven underground and have had to suffer all the psychological traumas associated with a closet existence. They have been forced to deny their desires and to pretend to interests and feelings not their own. Always there is the human propensity to cruelty, of which the twentieth century has made us painfully aware. Add to it the negative attitude toward homosexuals in the religious tradition and in secular law and you have a moral base for flagrant discrimination and hostility toward homosexuals in housing and employment.

The alleged effeminacy in dress and demeanor of homosexuals has been the butt of ridicule and scorn in public and in private, on the printed page, the radio, television, the screen, and the stage. This in spite of the alleged high percentage of homosexuals in the artistic, literary, and entertainment worlds.

Only within the past two decades has the public attitude begun to change. The general weakening of traditional religion has diminished the influence of biblical and post-biblical teaching on the subject. In addition, sexual experience without regard to procreation has increasingly been accepted and glorified as a good in itself, if not as the *summum bonum* of existence. Hence, homosexuality has lost some of the horror it conjured up in earlier generations. Above all, in our age, the drive for new and exciting experiences, however untried and even dangerous they may be, has led to new patterns of sexual conduct, like sexual communes and wife-swapping, not to speak of various forms of perversion. Advocates of homosexuality have, therefore, felt free to argue that they are simply practicing an equally legitimate life style, a variant pattern to the dominant heterosexuality of our culture. Some have maintained that 10 percent of the population are homosexual, a figure that can neither be demonstrated nor disproved.

Substantial success has already crowned the efforts of the various organizations in the gay liberation movement to remove [discrimination] in employment and housing from homosexuals, in the United States. In France, Italy, Sweden, Denmark, Switzerland, Mexico, and Uruguay, the practice has long been decriminalized. Great Britain took the same step in 1967 and Canada in 1969.

What approach toward homosexuality should modern religion sanction and modern society adopt? No excuse can or should be offered for the cruelty that traditional attitudes toward the practice have engendered in the past. Nevertheless, the classical viewpoint of Judaism and Christianity, that homosexual conduct is "unnatural," cannot be dismissed out of hand.

Here a brief theological digression is called for. That the goal of the universe and, by that token, the purpose of existence are veiled from man has been the conviction of thinkers in every age. Koheleth in the Bible and the medieval philosopher Maimonides are at one with the Hasidic teacher Rabbi Bunam of Pshysha, who found his beloved disciple Enoch in tears. The rabbi asked him, "Why are you weeping?" and Enoch answered, "Am I not a creature of this world, and am I not made with eyes and heart and all limbs, and yet I do not know for what purpose I was created and what good I am in the world." "Fool!" said Rabbi Bunam. "I also go around thus."

Nevertheless, we may perhaps catch a slight glimpse of the purpose of the Creator, or, if secular terms be preferred, the direction and goal of the life process in the universe. The lowest creatures in the evolutionary ladder, the single-cell organisms, multiply by fission, the splitting of the cell into two equal parts. As a result, each of the two new beings possesses exactly the same attributes as the parent, no more, no less, no change. Only with the emergence of multicellular organisms does bisexuality appear on the evolutionary ladder. Fission is now replaced by bisexual reproduction, which becomes the universal pattern. This fundamental change seems to indicate that the Author of life has intended the life process to be not a perpetually static repetition of the old but a dynamic adventure, with new combinations of attributes constantly emerging through the interaction of a male and a female producing a new organism different from both its parents. It therefore follows that, in purely secular biological terms, homosexuality is an aberration from the norm, a violation of the law of nature.

It may be objected that since man is not merely a creature of nature and is free to modify his environment and perhaps even his heredity, what is natural is not the sole touchstone of what is right for man. There is, however, good reason for believing that homosexuality is a violation not only of nature but of human nature as well. No attribute is more characteristic of humanity than the gift of speech. Language is probably the greatest intellectual achievement of primitive man. Imbedded in the structure of all languages is gender, a recognition of bisexuality, which, by extension, is applied to every object in the real world. Gender remains basic to language and to thought for the most sophisticated of moderns.

For later stages of human development, it may be noted that no society has made homosexuality its basic or even its preferred pattern of sexual conduct. This is true even of predatory groups that could have replenished their ranks through captives taken in war.

Transposed into theological language, heterosexuality is the will of God. It therefore follows that homosexuality is a violation of His will, for which the traditional term is "sin." The concept of sin in general may seem outmoded to modern ears and, in any event, too harsh a term to apply to homosexuality. But the etymology of the Hebrew word *het*, like its Greek counterpart, *hamartia*, is derived from marksmanship and means "missing the mark," as has already been noted. Sin means a turning aside from the right path that can and should be followed. Consequently the Hebrew's *teshubbah*, generally translated as "repentance," means "returning" to the right road.

Judgments and attitudes aside, what are the facts about homosexuality? In spite of the vast interest in the phenomenon, very little is really known about its origin and nature or any possible treatment. Modern psychologists may be correct in believing that latent homosexual tendencies are to be found in most people. If this is true, it would seem that homosexual patterns of behavior become dominant for some men and women because they are stimulated by personal contact with homosexuals. If, therefore, homosexuality is culturally induced, it would be a flagrant example of a conscious and often conscienceless distortion of normal human nature.

On the other hand, homosexuality may be the product of a genetic disturbance. In this case, it must be regarded as a biological abnormality. Whether the practice is the result of heredity or of environment, or of both, intensive research is needed to discover the etiology of homosexuality and then to search for a remedy, or at least for methods of treatment.

For centuries, society, abetted by religion, has been guilty of condemning as a sin and punishing as a crime what should have been recognized as an illness. In fact, physical illness in general was regarded as a Divine visitation, a punishment for sins for which the sufferer himself was responsible. This attitude is not altogether dead today. Recently, the president of a mammoth bank in New York demonstrated that he is obviously afflicted with massive spiritual myopia. He declared that physical illness is a crime against society committed by those who are ill, and that therefore society has no obligation to provide medical care and other social services to the sick poor.

If homosexuality is an abnormality or an illness, as has been maintained, a parallel to our problem in several respects may be found in alcoholism. So long as the alcoholic was regarded as an incorrigible sinner, little progress was made in curing this major malady. It is only in our day, when alcoholism is being recognized as a disease, probably genetic in origin though socially stimulated, that genuine progress has begun to be made overcoming it.

The analogy is helpful in another respect as well. Experts are agreed that the will to recover, as expressed in total abstinence, which is encouraged by such programs as Alcoholics Anonymous, plays an indispensable role in the treatment of alcohol addiction. It is also known that only a fraction of all alcoholics, somewhere between one third and one half of all patients who undergo treatment, recover fully or substantially.

At the present level of our knowledge, the percentage of homosexuals who can be "rehabilitated" is almost surely lower than that of alcoholics. To a substantial degree, this is due to the varying attitudes of contemporary society toward two phenomena. While alcoholism is universally recognized as a liability, homosexuality is often defended as a normal life style, a legitimate alternate pattern to heterosexuality. The gay liberation movement has vigorously opposed the older traditional view of homosexuality as a sin. It is not more kindly disposed to the more modern concept of homosexuality as an illness. It uses every available means to propagate the idea that homosexuality is an entirely proper life style.

Nevertheless, if we are not to fall prey to the old prejudice or to succumb to the new fashion, we must insist that homosexuality is not normal. To the extent that men and women cannot control their homosexual desires, they are suffering from an illness like any other physical disability. To the degree that they can hold the impulse in rein and fail to do so, they are committing a sin, a violation of the will of God or, in secular terms, an aberration from the norm.

However, a basic caution is in order. Ignorant as we are of the etiology of the disorder, we are in no position to determine to which category a given act belongs. Hence, homosexual activity, when carried on by adults in private and violating no one's wishes and desires, should be decriminalized on the statute books. The practice belongs to the rabbinic category of an act that is "free from legal punishment (by human agency), but forbidden." The homosexual in contemporary society has a just claim to be free from legal penalties and social disabilities.

Yet there are some critical areas where blanket removal of all restrictions against homosexuals may be unwise. Such a decision should be reached without panic or prejudice, on the basis of a careful investigation of all the relevant factors. Sensing the widespread erosion of conventional moral standards everywhere, homosexual groups are pressing for much more than freedom from discrimination and harassment. They are demanding that homosexuality be recognized as a legitimate and normal alternative to heterosexuality.

Some Christian theologians, troubled by the tragic and undeniable fact that Western society has been grievously lacking in compassion for homosexuals, have attempted to give a Christian justification for homosexuality. One Catholic writer explains away the biblical condemnations of homosexual practices as "Old Testament legalism." A Protestant theologian takes his point of departure from the Christian doctrine that salvation is directed to all mankind, so that all human beings are equally sinful in the eyes of God. He, therefore, leaps to the non sequitur that "no human condition or life style is intrinsically *justified* or righteous—neither heterosexuality nor homosexuality, closed nor open marriage, celibacy nor profligacy." He proceeds to express doubts as to whether the family centeredness of contemporary Christianity can be justified theologically, since both Jesus and Paul were suspicious of family ties! He concludes that there are three life styles open to men and women intrinsically equal in moral validity: marriage, celibacy, and homosexuality.

The lengths to which sympathetic souls may be led are evident in the secular sphere as well. In fact, like the generous Irishman who was asked, "Isn't one man as good as another?" and answered, "Sure, and a whole lot better, too," some advocates have argued that homosexuality is not merely as good as heterosexuality but better, since it avoids the possibility of increasing the population! The same logic would lead to the conclusion that sterility is healthier and more beneficial than fecundity.

It is perhaps a sign of the times that a recent radio broadcast referred to a sadomasochist liberation movement, which calls itself the Til Eulenspiegel Society. This group, whose size was not indicated, demands "equal rights" for the practice of sexual perversion, including such forms as flagellation and sodomy, which, they insist, are also legitimate alternatives.

Having mastered the modern art of lobbying, homosexuals carried on a campaign among the members of the American Psychological Association and, in 1974, succeeded in having homosexuality removed from the list of abnormal patterns of behavior. An effort is being made in some quarters to reverse the ruling of the American Psychological Association. The argument advanced by gay liberation groups is that homosexuals are basically healthy, well-adjusted individuals who do not seek medical or psychiatric treatment because they do not need it. Spokesmen for homosexuality, aware of the widespread frustration and unhappiness with conventional marriages, have urged the claim. In a growing number of cases, homosexuals have asked the clergy to officiate at homosexual "marriages." No comparative study is available of either the permanence of homosexual unions or of the quality of life of homosexual couples.

On the other hand, testimony has been advanced to show that the self-acceptance and satisfaction with life ex-pressed by many homosexuals is often only a facade for resignation and despair, all the more hopeless because it cannot find channels of expression. In their youth, it has been maintained, homosexuals have suffered from rejection and unhappiness, which are integral to their condition. In adult life, they continue to experience conflict, anguish, and pain which they deny even to themselves. It has also been argued that the growing militant assertion of "gay pride," coupled with the A.P.A. declaration that homosexuality is normal human behavior on the one hand and the generally negative attitude of society on the other, has intensified their unhappiness. That there is so much heat and so little light demonstrates only how slight is the authentic scientific knowledge available on this important issue. . . .

As is so frequently the case, truth and justice in this troubled area lie, not with the extremes, but with the center position. We can no longer accept the traditional religious reaction to homosexuality as a horror and an abomination. On the other hand, the fashionable doctrine being propagated in our time—that it is an alternate life style of equal value and legitimacy—must be decisively rejected. Homosexuality is an abnormality, an illness which, like any other, varies in intensity with different individuals. Until more efficacious means are discovered for dealing with their problem, homosexuals deserve the same inalienable rights as do all their fellow human beings—freedom from harassment and discrimination before the law and in society.

There can be no question that homosexuals are entitled to more than justice before the law. It is not enough merely to remove the various kinds of legal disability and overt hostility to which they have long been subjected. Whatever evaluation is placed upon their condition, be it moral, medical, or psychological, they are human beings, our brothers and sisters, who deserve compassion and love from their fellow men and, above all, from their brothers in kinship and in faith.

NO

Sr. Jeannine Gramick

HOMOSEXUALITY AND BISEXUALITY ARE JUST AS NATURAL AND NORMAL AS HETEROSEXUAL BEHAVIOR AND RELATIONS

For the last 15 years I have worked in church ministry for lesbian and gay Catholics. Much of the time has been devoted to providing educational opportunities for heterosexual people to discuss the sensitive topic of homosexuality in a calm, reasoned and impassioned way. When I have met resistance from well-meaning heterosexual people to accepting homosexual individuals as persons, the bottom line has usually been, "But homosexuality is just unnatural." I try to pursue the conversation in a reasoned manner by asking them to explain their statement and to define, as best they can, what they mean by the words "unnatural" and "natural."

Over the years, their explanations and definitions have been varied. I am convinced that people have unconsciously absorbed from the dominant culture a deep-seated feeling of antipathy toward homosexuality for which they have tried, usually unsuccessfully, to provide a semblance of rational argument. For a good part of my adult life, I also unquestioningly assumed that homosexuality was unnatural. But from meeting thousands of lesbian and gay people over the years, from reading reliable research in the field, and from reflecting on what it means to be natural, I am now convinced that homosexual and bisexual feelings and behaviors are just as natural as heterosexual ones.

In the pages which follow, I shall present some of the reasons or arguments I have heard on both sides of the question. I shall examine what it means to be "natural" and, in so doing, shall draw upon historical, anthropological, psychological, and biological evidence. That the main stumbling block to my argument comes from theological and philosophical discourse demonstrates to me that these disciplines either have failed to keep abreast of scientific developments or have willfully ignored current findings in order to legitimate a preconceived notion of divine intent for the human order.

How can I say that bisexual and homosexual feelings are as natural as heterosexual ones? What does it mean to be "natural"? Let us consider the definition of the word from various disciplines.

HISTORY

Goethe once wrote that homosexuality and bisexuality can be considered natural because they are as old as the human race itself. Some people, such as Goethe, would say that something is natural if it has existed and continues to exist over time and place. This is a definition of "natural" which I have heard among a number of professors in academic circles.

Historical knowledge would certainly affirm Goethe's belief. It is fairly well-known that particular societies at different historical times socially approved of homosexual and bisexual liaisons. Between the eighth and second centuries before the Christian era, Greek art and literature assumed that virtually everyone responded at different times both to homosexual and to heterosexual stimuli. Such an attitude was implicit in the non-philosophical writings as well as in the philosophy of the time. In Plato's *Symposium*, the guests at a dinner party take turns delivering speeches in praise of Eros, the god of love. Most of the examples used by the speakers are homosexual. In expounding his own view of eros in the work, Plato describes a male responding to the beauty of another male, and not to a female, as the starting point of his philosophical understanding of ideal beauty. Probably because homosexual relations were so commonly accepted, Plutarch, another Greek writer, in his *Dialogue on Love*, had to argue passionately in defense of the naturalness of heterosexual love.

The historian A.L. Rowse has documented numerous cases of homosexual persons throughout history. Let us consider only a relatively few of these. The famous twelfth century English king, Richard the Lionhearted, seems to have been bisexual, though obviously preferring the company of his male minstrel. The coronation festivities of the fourteenth century English king, Edward II, were almost halted by Edward's conspicuous attentions for Piers Gaveston, his constant male companion whom, historians say, "he adored." When the powerful barons murdered his beloved Gaveston, the king could only take the body to his own foundation, grieve intensely and pray for his loved one's soul. From his passionate love letters to a fellow monk and from his close male attachments, historians believe that the medieval scholar Erasmus was also homosexually oriented.

The Renaissance genius, Leonardo da Vinci, wrote that heterosexual intercourse was "so ugly that, if it were not for the beauty of faces and the liberation of the spirit, the species would lose its humanity," i.e., the human race would cease to propagate. At age 24, the reserved and aristocratic da Vinci was accused of having sex with a 17-year-old male and imprisoned for two months. More withdrawn and mysterious than ever after his release, da Vinci engaged a "graceful and beautiful," irresistible youth as an apprentice and taught him to paint. Although the youth stole from his master as well as from his master's clients, da Vinci overlooked his faults because of his strong attachment to the youth. As with other tragic love stories, the man left da Vinci but the master painter was to find happiness in the devotion of another man who remained faithful to him until da Vinci's death.

Although he was da Vinci's contemporary, Michelangelo Buonarotti could not have been more unlike da Vinci in temperament and personality. While Leonardo was calm, courteous and an introvert, Michelangelo was abrupt, aggressive, impatient; the two men disliked each other. Unmarried like da Vinci, Michelangelo was dominated by the nude male body in his sculptures, paintings, and drawings. His preference for males was well known during his lifetime although there is no documentation concerning his sexual practice. After his death his love poems to Cavalieri, who became the passion of his life, were altered so that they appeared to be addressed to a woman.

Although a host of eminent historical figures were homosexual, most of those known to us are male because most of our religious, literary and political information has been written by men about men and for other men to read. Only in more modern times have women produced historical records of themselves. Despite this significant handicap, historical data do indicate that lesbian women have existed, though certainly more hidden, throughout the ages. The word lesbian derives from the ancient Greek poetess Sappho who lived on the island of Lesbos with her community of female admirers. . . .

ANTHROPOLOGY

Not only have bisexual and homosexual individuals existed at all times throughout history, but they have also existed in almost all cultures which anthropologists have studied. In those cultures where homosexuality or bisexuality has not been observed, anthropologists point out that language and communication problems may have obscured evidence of them. Moreover, those societies in which no homosexual behavior is evident are very sparsely populated ones, such as the Alorese in the mountains of Timor. We would expect that in such close knit groupings it would be difficult for individuals to engage in relationships disapproved of by the group.

Not only were bisexual and homosexual practices condoned and even encouraged among the ancient Greeks and Romans, but also the ancient Celts, Scandinavians, Egyptians, Etruscans, Cretans, Carthagenians, and Sumerians accepted same-sex behavior. The greatest approval of homosexuality in ancient times came from the lands surrounding the Tigris-Euphrates and the Nile Rivers and the Mediterranean Sea. With the exception of the Hebrews and perhaps the Assyrians, the ancient cultures of the Mediterranean did not restrain the homosexual instincts of their people.

In the past, the Far East also tolerated homosexuality and bisexuality. From ancient to modern times same-sex behavior has been acceptable in China and Japan. In China, where male brothels were common, boys were trained for prostitution by their parents. In Japan during the feudal period, male homosexual love was considered more "manly" than heterosexual love. Male geishas in teahouses were prevalent until the middle of the nineteenth century and still existed until they were suppressed at the end of World War II by the American occupation forces. Today homosexuality and bisexuality in both Japan and China remain more hidden. . . .

In some cultures homosexuality is identified with sex-role stereotyping. Among the Koniag of Alaska, the Largo of East Africa, the Tanala of Madagascar, and the Chukchee of Siberia, some males are raised from early childhood to perform female tasks and to dress as females. Known as the "berdache," such a male often becomes the "wife" of an important man in the community and lives with him, but the berdache may have heterosexual affairs with a mistress and father children. The berdache often enjoys a considerable amount of social prestige and assumes a position of power in the community. He usually becomes a shaman, a kind of priest, medicine man or religious figure, who is believed to possess supernatural powers which may be transmitted by sexual relations.

An example of socially expected and approved bisexuality involving a large segment of the male population is found among the Siwans of Africa. Both married and unmarried men are expected to have bisexual affairs and those males who do not engage in same-sex behavior are considered odd. In a number of cultures, such as the Keraki of New Guinea and the Kiwai, homosexual behavior is sanctioned as part of male puberty rites. In a detailed study of cultural data from 76 societies, 64% of the cultures surveyed approved of some form of homosexual behavior and considered it normal and socially acceptable for at least some members of the community.

So it seems to be clear from historical and anthropological data that homosexuality is natural if "natural" is defined to be existence over time and place. But there are other ways to consider the meaning of the word "natural."

PSYCHOLOGY

A second approach involves what is psychologically instinctive. From a psychological perspective an action is considered natural if it originates from an impulse or drive; an involuntary want or need coming from within an organism is natural to that organism. If such an instinctive urge is not impeded, an individual will seek to satisfy the inclination.

A substantial minority of human beings have an instinctive tendency to fulfill same-sex desires. The sex drive itself is innate and instinctive. In most people, this sex drive is directed primarily toward the same gender; for still others, their sexual attractions are equally strong in intensity and frequency toward both genders. As a conservative estimate, approximately 7% of women and 15% of men are strictly bisexual or predominantly or exclusively homosexual in orientation and behavior.

Until the last decade or so, thousands of lesbian and gay persons sought out psychiatrists and other therapists to help them to change their same-sex feelings. Unfortunately, thousands of these individuals wasted their time and money as the experts now believe that a change in orientation, i.e., in desire and attraction, is not possible.

The helping professions have failed in their long attempt to reverse sexual behavior in homosexual people. For example, Masters and Johnson presented only one actual case of reversion or conversion to heterosexual functioning among 54 male subjects, and this individual was identified as bisexual at the outset. In another study of 106 homosexual men, only 29 became exclusively heterosexual in behavior and this change was not known to have lasted beyond two years. More than half of these men were initially bisexual and most of the subjects required 350 or more hours of therapy. Thus, even with a high degree of motivation, an expenditure of much time and money, and an existing predisposition to bisexuality, the possibility of actually altering behavior is extremely low, costly, time consuming and short lived.

These reports concern alteration of sexual behavior. There is not known documentation of permanent alteration of same-sex feelings, attractions and desires. If it is virtually impossible to modify a homosexual orientation, then these same-sex feelings must be very deeply ingrained in the person's psychological makeup.

The psychologist Frank A. Beach once claimed, "Various social goals and ethical laws are violated by the homosexual individual [and, we may add, the bisexual one], but to describe [such] behavior as 'unnatural' is to depart from strict accuracy." While same-sex genital behavior may indeed be the natural psychological result of same-sex love and attractions, strong social sanctions imposed in many cultures have frequently inhibited such innate responses to same-sex stimuli and have conditioned people to respond to heterosexual stimuli. Despite strong social taboos, countless individuals persist in expressing these desires and feelings of love for their own gender. If, as some would claim, only heterosexuality is psychologically natural, i.e., instinctively imprinted within an individual's personality structure, how can heterosexuality be obliterated or obscured in millions and millions of people? If, then, "natural" is defined as that which is instinctive and freely acted on without restraint, same-sex feelings and attractions do indeed seem to be quite natural for a significant proportion of the human population.

BIOLOGY

A third definition of natural is illustrated in such phrases as "laws of nature,"

"naturalist," and "natural history." What is congruent or consistent with the "laws of nature" is deemed natural. This approach to nature involves a study of non-living phenomena, plants and animals. From this perspective, a given characteristic is "natural" for human beings if it is in accordance with their animal heritage.

What is needed is an application of animal data to human behavior. In research on the sexual behavior of species below the human, homosexual activity appears frequently in infrahuman primates, such as apes, monkeys and baboons especially as they approach adulthood, although this may not be exclusive in many cases. Only recently have scientific studies been conducted to observe same-sex behavior among sub-primate mammals. These studies indicate that homosexual behavior appears in lower mammals, frequently among domestic stock such as sheep, cattle, horses, pigs and rabbits.

There is some preliminary evidence that aquatic species may have a higher psychological status than such terrestrial animals as dogs, cats, cows, and horses, and that they may consequently form stronger relational attachments. One story is related about two male porpoises who formed a very close attachment with each other after several months. One of the porpoises was removed from the tank and then returned after a three week separation. Their reunion was described as follows:

"No doubt could exist that the two recognized each other, and for several hours they swam side by side rushing frenziedly through the water, and on several occasions they leaped completely out of the water. For several days, the two males were inseparable and neither paid any attention to the female."

Examples of homosexuality have been found even among the nonmammalian species. Any two male or female pigeons will engage in same-sex behavior when placed together. Phylogenetic data indicate that same-sex behavior becomes both more common and more complex as one ascends the evolutionary scale. Innate homosexual behavioral patterns are not exclusively human phenomena but are definitely consonant with the human's mammalian background. As such, they are natural in the biological sense.

THEOLOGY

A fourth meaning for the term "natural" will often be given by religious persons, but primarily in discussions about sexuality. Traditional religious arguments maintain that there are necessary links between marriage and sexual intercourse and between intercourse and biological generation. The classic explanation hinges on the Stoic exultation of natural law. Between the fifteenth and nineteenth centuries most theologians writing on sexuality divided sexual sins into two categories: those in accordance with nature (i.e., open to procreation) and those contrary to nature (i.e., inhibiting procreation). Thus anal and oral intercourse, masturbation, bestiality, coitus interruptus, and intercourse during pregnancy were considered unnatural; adultery, fornication, and rape were considered sinful but natural.

Religious adherents would refer to biology, often in contradictory ways to substantiate their arguments. At times the term natural was equated with animal behavior when, for example, Thomas Aquinas considered contraception "against nature, for even beasts look for offspring." Yet, at other times, nature was described as what was different from animals, when, for example, the position in human intercourse of the woman beneath the man was thought to be natural because any other position was comparable to "brute animals." Like the early Church Fathers, the scholastic theologians selectively chose their analogies of what was natural in order to reinforce views already held.

Frequently the theological argument is accompanied by explanations regarding the physiological purpose or function of bodily parts. A functional argument goes something like this: God intends that the necessary purpose of the sexual organs is reproduction. Since homosexual activity cannot result in procreation, such acts are contrary to God's intent and are thus unnatural.

The hidden assumption of human ability to know divine intent with certitude can certainly be challenged. How can humans know God's will with moral certainty and without reference to reason and logic? When appeals are made to divine revelation, who decides and interprets revelation?

An obvious function of the genital organs is reproduction. But to maintain that a particular bodily organ serves only one purpose or must serve a certain specified purpose seems provincial at best. In the human evolutionary development, hands serve as a means of grasping, not of walking. Yet who would object that hands be used in conveying greetings or other messages with emotional content because such actions are contrary to the nature of hands? Would anyone deny that the mouth, whose primary function is food ingestion, has another and socially more aesthetic function of verbal communication?

If other parts of the body may serve multiple purposes, why is it that the sexual parts may not? To claim, as some have, that the sexual parts are not morally equal to other parts of the body and are of special value because they involve the generation of life betrays a lack of appreciation for other bodily parts and systems, all of which likewise contribute to life. Placing a hierarchy of value on bodily parts leads to an idolatry or sacralization of some parts. Would proponents of a theology which maintains that there is a single or special purpose of sexual parts refuse to admit that another function of the penis is demonstrated in the biological process of elimination of urine?

Many sexual moralists today acknowledge more than one purpose of human intercourse. They differentiate between the reproductive and unitive functions of sexual intercourse and maintain that the two functions need not be present simultaneously in every genital act in order to render the action ethically responsible. In fact, they point out that concern about the modern world's population explosion and about a reasonable care and stewardship of the earth's resources challenge traditional notions of the meaning of sexuality. They thus liberate God from being controlled by a rigid and predetermined view of reality.

A similar theological case is often made by appealing to the structure of the human body: God intends heterosexuality because the male and female sexual parts "fit." As the vagina is an obvious receptacle for the penis, any use of the male sexual organ other than for the deposit of semen in the vagina is believed to be unnatural. An examination of the male and female bodies in which the parts manifestly "fit" shows the truth to be self-evident. Although axioms require no demonstration, such reasoning illustrates an argument by limitation or restriction. The fact that one

form of linkage is obvious and rather common does not render alternative ways "unnatural." Because human genitalia fit together in one way does not preclude other ways of sexual union.

Underlying these philosophical and theological approaches is a definition of nature as that which makes an object what it essentially or actually is or what God intends it to be. The key question, of course, is "What is the divine purpose?" Do such arguments merely interpret human preference and prejudice as God's will?

Along with divine intent, one must also examine human motives to determine whether insistence on the unnaturalness of homosexuality, or even other sexual acts, is merely a reflection of an unconscious desire to legitimate the existing social order. Unfortunately, the expression of same-sex feelings and desires is often perceived as some kind of threat to the heterosexual structure. Unexamined cultural assumptions influence human perceptions and judgments; what is conveniently regarded as natural is often an expression of a deep-seated cultural bias. Appeals to God's intent are at least questionable and can lead to such absurd deductions as "If God wanted human beings to fly, God would have given them wings. Therefore, the airplane is unnatural." While the faith of those who hold these positions cannot be questioned, their interpretation of human sexuality and divine intent regarding sexual expression certainly can and should be.

CONTEMPORARY VIEWS

A current understanding of nature is one which is dynamic and constantly in flux. Aristotle taught that fire by its nature moved away from the center of the universe. When science demonstrated the Copernican theory in which the earth was no longer viewed as the central planetary body, the Aristotelian concept of the nature of fire was revised. Similarly, the ancient Greeks believed that every earthly object was composed of earth, air, water, or fire. But a deeper understanding of physics and chemistry demanded a more sophisticated explanation of the nature of any object in the universe. As species of living objects themselves are gradually being transformed by evolution, the human perception of such objects' nature is constantly adapting and in need of revision. Even slight variations in successive generations of a species influence the constantly developing human understanding of nature.

Unless rigid or static, a construct of human nature which was popular 500 years before the Christian era or 1300 years after is not identical to a contemporary perception of human nature which can incorporate scientific advancement and current data from the behavioral sciences. Accurate knowledge regarding human reproduction was not discovered until after 1875. Basing their philosophical and theological arguments in the context of the biology of their day, religious leaders of the past cannot be faulted for an understandably limited analysis of human sexuality. But with the quantum leaps that have been achieved in biology, psychology and sociology, the twentieth century mind must subject traditional religious arguments about nature to more thorough and critical analyses. Today's personalist interpretation of human nature is not bound by a static view reminiscent of Freud's "biology is destiny" but rather is struggling to free itself from biological imperatives.

CONCLUSION

When all the rational debate is over concerning what is natural and what is unnatural about human sexuality, what many people, perhaps subconsciously, mean is that same-sex attraction is not experienced by the majority of people. This may indeed be the case since Kinsey's figures indicate that approximately 72% of females and 76% of males are exclusively heterosexual in feelings and behaviors; i.e., they experience not even minimal same-sex attractions or fantasies. These percentages may be somewhat higher than actual fact since they were computed almost 40 years ago when people were less willing to acknowledge their same-sex feelings.

If North American society tolerated a gay or lesbian lifestyle, I believe that it would be highly likely that the incidence of bisexuality and homosexuality would become more visible. This would not result from supposed mass conversions of confirmed heterosexual individuals to homosexuality; rather, people would feel freer to express the homosexual or bisexual feelings they already have. Since there is evidence that in societies that condone bisexual and homosexual behavior a heterosexual lifestyle is still predominant, one can reasonably conclude that not everyone would engage in predominantly homosexual behavior.

The majority can, and often does, reveal its prejudice and intolerance for diversity. Because the majority of individuals feel, react or believe one way, must all persons do so? As long as the minority group does not harm or infringe on the majority lifestyle, the two should be able to coexist peacefully. The sociologist Becker who has written considerably about the societal outsider states, "Social groups create deviance by making the rules whose infraction constitutes deviance, and by applying those rules to particular people and labelling them as outsiders."

I harbor a cherished hope that all peoples in the human family may live together as true brothers and sisters. Only when the dominant majority in each culture accords proper respect for the rights and dignity of the racial, ethnic, sexual, economic and religious minorities in its midst can we hope to have a truly free and just society. Only when our unspoken fears and insecurities are recognized and our unnamed ignorance and biases erased, can we work collaboratively in realizing the fullness of the exciting human project upon the earth.

POSTSCRIPT

Are Homosexual Relations Deviant?

What is deviance? According to the *Encyclopedic Dictionary of Sociology*, Third Edition (Dushkin, 1986) it is ". . . behavior that is contrary to the standards of conduct or social expectations of a given group or society." If the issue of homosexuality is simply a matter of definition it can be settled quickly. Homosexuality is deviant but is seen as less deviant as it becomes more tolerated by society. The real issue, however, is how should homosexual behavior be treated by society? Since just and effective treatment requires, in part, an understanding of the nature of homosexuality, its origins must be explored. Is it biologically determined? Is it a result of early childhood experiences or observations? To what extent is homosexuality something that people choose or reject? The answers to these questions may affect our views on how natural homosexuality is. Gramick presents historical, anthropological, psychological, biological, and theological arguments for the naturalness of homosexuality. Gordis argues from theology, language, and biological design that it is unnatural and abnormal. Edgar Gregersen (*Sexual Practices: The Story of Human Sexuality*, Franklin Watts, 1982) complicates the debate by showing that homophilia (sexual activity between adult men who otherwise have conventional masculine roles) is historically and anthropologically very rare and is found almost exclusively in industrial societies.

A number of studies have surveyed the habits and "life-styles" of homosexuals. In *The Gay Report: Lesbians and Gay Men Speak Out* (Summit Books, 1979), Karla Jay and Allen Young provide the results of a survey of some 5,000 male and female homosexuals. In *Homosexualities: a Study of Diversity Among Men and Women* (Simon and Schuster, 1978), Alan P. Bell and Martin Weinberg study the way homosexuals cope with living. Thomas S. Weinberg studies the processes by which men develop and maintain a homosexual identity in *Gay Men, Gay Selves: The Social Construction of Homosexual Identities* (Irvington, 1983). Laud Humphreys' *Out of the Closets: The Society of Homosexual Liberation* (Prentice Hall, 1972) provides a history of the "gay liberation" movement.

"Gay liberation" implies an analogy to "black liberation" and "women's liberation." Yet there are obvious differences. One is that women and blacks have been discriminated against for what they *are* rather than for what they *do*. Skin color and gender are biological facts, while sexual preference involves behavior that has been considered immoral and unnatural in the West since the fall of Rome. (In Western culture it has never been considered immoral or unnatural to be black or female.) Do these differences invalidate the analogy between "gay liberation" and the civil rights and feminist movements? That is a question that invites debate.

ISSUE 15
Is Incapacitation
the Answer to the Crime Problem?

YES: James Q. Wilson, from *Thinking About Crime* (Basic Books, 1975)

NO: David L. Bazelon, from "Solving the Nightmare of Street Crime" *USA Today Magazine* (January 1982)

ISSUE SUMMARY

YES: James Q. Wilson argues that imprisoning everyone convicted of a serious offense for several years would greatly reduce these crimes. He contends that incapacitation is the one policy that works.
NO: Judge David L. Bazelon discusses the moral and financial costs of the incapacitation approach and argues that society must attack the brutal social and economic conditions that are the root causes of street crime.

Not a day passes in America without reports of murder, rape, or other violent crimes. As crime has mushroomed, public indignation has intensified—particularly when spectacular cases have been brought to light about paroled convicts committing new felonies, light sentences being handed down for serious crimes, and cases being thrown out of court on legal technicalities. Over the past decade or so, there has been a dramatic increase in the number of Americans who think that the authorities should be "tougher" on criminals. To take one prominent example: While a majority of Americans in the 1960s favored the abolition of the death penalty, today more than seventy percent favor its use in some cases.

Even in the intellectual community, there has been a turnaround. When George Wallace and others raised the issue of "law and order" at the end of the 1960s, the term was called "a code word for racism" in academic and literary circles. This is understandable because Wallace *had* previously identified himself with white racism. Nevertheless, the fact that the largest number of crime *victims* come from the black community should have given pause to anyone who would identify lenience toward criminals with benevolence to blacks.

The attitude toward crime that was popular in academic circles during the 1960s might be briefly summarized under two headings: the prevention of crime and the treatment of criminals.

To prevent crime, it was contended, government must do more than rely upon police, courts, and jails. It must do something about "the underlying social roots" of crime, especially poverty and racism. Once these roots are severed, it was assumed, crime would begin to fade away or at least cease to be a major social problem.

The prescription for treating criminals followed much the same logic. The word "punishment" was avoided in favor of "treatment" or "rehabilitation," for the purpose was not to inflict pain or to "pay back" the criminal but to bring about a change in his behavior. If that could be done by lenient treatment—by short prison terms, by education, counseling, and above all by understanding people who have suffered abuse since childhood—then so much the better.

By the late 1970s, the intellectual community itself showed signs that it was reassessing its outlook toward crime. Harvard professor James Q. Wilson's views on crime became widely respected in universities and in the mass media. Wilson stresses the need for "realism." It may be that some day all poverty and social injustice will cease to exist, says Wilson, but until that day arrives we had better keep criminals off the streets. He maintains that crime can be significantly reduced here and now simply by "incapacitating" (incarcerating) dangerous offenders. Wilson also takes a dim view of the prospects for "rehabilitating" criminals in prison. In his view, statistics prove that the question of whether a criminal goes back to crime after release does not depend upon what kind of prison he has gone to but rather his own personal characteristics. In other words, Wilson believes, it is unlikely that even the most enlightened prison system can rehabilitate a hardened criminal.

David L. Bazelon admits that incapacitation is a short-term solution to street crime that delivers some results. He points out, however, its high financial and moral costs, explaining that the United States already imprisons a larger proportion of its citizens than all other developed nations, except the U.S.S.R. A three-fold increase in the prison population will not make a significant dent in the rate of serious crimes, maintains Bazelon, and the needed new prisons will cost many billions of dollars. More importantly, he says, the incapacitation approach assumes that convicted offenders will continue to commit crimes and in effect punishes them for future misdeeds. Bazelon's approach raises serious questions concerning individual justice. He believes the only satisfactory answer is to attack the social and economic conditions that are the root causes of street crime; others, such as Wilson, argue for more immediate action. These two competing approaches are illustrated in the following selections.

YES

James Q. Wilson

THINKING ABOUT CRIME

The average citizen hardly needs to be persuaded that crimes will be committed more frequently if, other things being equal, crime becomes more profitable than other ways of spending one's time. Accordingly, the average citizen thinks it obvious that one major reason why crime has increased is that people have discovered they can get away with it. By the same token, a good way to reduce crime is to make its consequences to the would-be offender more costly (by making penalties swifter, more certain, or more severe), or to make alternatives to crime more attractive (by increasing the availability and pay of legitimate jobs), or both.

These citizens may be surprised to learn that social scientists who study crime are deeply divided over the correctness of such views. While some scholars, especially economists, believe that the decision to become a criminal can be explained in much the same way as we explain the decision to become a carpenter or to buy a car, other scholars, especially sociologists, contend that the popular view is wrong—crime rates do not go up because would-be criminals have little fear of arrest, and will not come down just because society decides to get tough on criminals.

This debate over the way the costs and benefits of crime affect crime rates is usually called a debate over deterrence—a debate, that is, over the efficacy (and perhaps even the propriety) of trying to prevent crime by making would-be offenders fearful of punishment. But the theory of human nature that supports the idea of deterrence—the theory that people respond to the penalties associated with crime—also assumes that people will take jobs in preference to crime if the jobs are more attractive. In both cases, we are saying that would-be offenders are rational and that they respond to their perception of the costs and benefits attached to alternative courses of action. When we use the word "deterrence," we are calling attention to only the cost side of the equation. No word in common scientific usage calls attention to the benefit side of the equation, though perhaps "inducement" might serve.

The reason scholars disagree about deterrence is that the consequences of committing a crime, unlike the consequences of shopping around for the best price on a given automobile, are complicated by delay, uncertainty, and ignorance. In addition, some scholars contend that many crimes are committed by persons who are so impulsive, irrational, or abnormal that even if delay, uncertainty, or ignorance were not attached to the consequences of criminality, we would still have a lot of crime.

Imagine a young man walking down the street at night with nothing on his mind but a desire for good times and high living. Suddenly he sees a little old lady standing alone on a dark corner, stuffing the proceeds of her recently cashed Social Security check into her purse. Nobody else is in view. If the young man steals the purse, he gets the money immediately. The costs of taking it are uncertain—the odds are at least ten to one that the police will not catch a robber, and even if he is caught, the odds are very good that he will not go to prison, unless he has a long record. On the average, no more than three felonies out of a hundred result in the imprisonment of the offender. In addition, whatever penalty may come his way will come only after a long delay—in some jurisdictions, a year or more might be needed to complete the court disposition of the offender, assuming he is caught in the first place. Moreover, this young man might, in his ignorance of how the world works, think the odds against being caught are even greater than they are, or that delays in the court proceedings might result in a reduction or avoidance of punishment.

Compounding the problem of delay and uncertainty is the fact that society cannot feasibly increase by more than a modest amount the likelihood of arrest, and though it can to some degree increase the probability and severity of prison sentences for those who are caught, it cannot do so drastically, by, for example, summarily executing all convicted robbers, or even by sentencing all robbers to twenty-year prison terms. Some scholars note a further complication: the young man may be incapable of assessing the risks of crime. How, they ask, is he to know his chances of being caught and punished? And even if he does know, perhaps he is driven by uncontrollable impulses to snatch purses whatever the risks.

As if all this were not bad enough, the principal method by which scholars have attempted to measure the effect of deterrence on crime has involved using data about aggregates of people (entire cities, counties, states, and even nations) rather than about individuals. In a typical study, the rate at which, say, robbery is committed in each state is "explained" by means of a statistical procedure in which the analyst takes into account both the socioeconomic features of each state that might affect the supply of robbers (for example, the percentage of persons with low incomes, the unemployment rate, the population density of the big cities, the proportion of the population made up of young males) and the operation of the criminal-justice system of each state as it attempts to cope with robbery (for example, the probability of being caught and the length of the average prison term for robbery). . . .

The best analysis of [problems] in statistical studies of deterrence is to be found in a 1978 report of the Panel on Research on Deterrent and Incapacitative Effects, which was set up by the National Research Council (an arm of the National Academy of Sciences). That panel, chaired by Alfred Blumstein, of Carnegie-Mellon University, concluded that the available statistical evidence (as of 1978) did not warrant any strong conclusions about the extent to which differences among states or cities in the probability of punishment might alter deterrent effect. The panel (of which I was a member) noted that "the evidence certainly favors a proposition supporting deterrence more than it favors one asserting that deterrence is absent," but urged "scientific caution" in interpreting this evidence.

Other criticisms of deterrence research, generally along the same lines as those of the panel, have led some commentators to declare that "deterrence doesn't work," and that we may now get on with the task of investing in those programs, such as job-creation and income maintenance, that *will* have an effect on crime. Such a conclusion is, to put it mildly, premature.

One way to compensate for errors in official statistics relating to crime rates is to consider other measures of crime, in particular reports gathered by Bureau of the Census interviewers from citizens who have been victims of crime. While these victim surveys have problems of their own (such as the forgetfulness of citizens), they are not the same problems as those that affect police reports of crime. Thus, if we obtain essentially the same findings about the effect of sanctions on crime from studies that use victim data as we do from studies that use police data, our confidence in these findings is strengthened. Studies of this sort have been done by Itzhak Goldberg, at Stanford, and by Barbara Boland and myself, and the results are quite consistent with those from research based on police reports. As sanctions become more likely, both sets of data suggest, crime becomes less common.

It is possible, as some critics of deterrence say, that rising crime rates swamp the criminal-justice system, so that a negative statistical association between, say, rates of theft and the chances of going to prison for theft may mean not that a decline in imprisonment is causing theft to increase but rather that a rise in theft is causing imprisonment to become less likely. This might occur particularly with respect to less serious crimes, such as shoplifting or petty larceny; indeed, the proportion of prisoners who are shoplifters or petty thieves has gone down over the past two decades. But it is hard to imagine that the criminal-justice system would respond to an increase in murder or armed robbery by letting some murderers or armed robbers off with no punishment. Convicted murderers are as likely to go to prison today as they were twenty years ago. Moreover, the deterrent effect of prison on serious crimes like murder and robbery was apparently as great in 1940 or 1950, when these crimes were much less common, as it is today, suggesting that swamping has not occurred.

Still more support for the proposition that variations in sanctions affect crime can be found in the very best studies of deterrence—those that manage to avoid the statistical errors described above. In 1977, Alfred Blumstein and Daniel Nagin published a study of the relationship between draft evasion and the penalties imposed for draft evasion in each of the states. After controlling for the socioeconomic characteristics of the states, they found that the higher the probability of conviction for draft evasion, the lower the evasion rates. This is an especially strong finding, because the study is largely immune to the problems associated with other analyses of deterrence.

Draft evasion is more accurately measured than street crimes, and draft-evasion cases could not have swamped the federal courts in which they were tried, in part because such cases made up only a small fraction (about 7 percent) of the workload of these courts, and in part because federal authorities had instructed the prosecutors to give high priority to these cases. For all these reasons, Blumstein and Nagin felt they could safely conclude that draft evasion is deterrable.

White-collar crime can also be deterred. In the late 1970s, Michael Block, Fred Nold, and J.G. Sidak, then at Stanford, investigated the effect of enforcing the antitrust laws on the price of bread in the bakery business. When the government filed a price-fixing complaint against colluding bakery firms, and when those firms also faced the possibility of private suits claiming treble damages for this price-fixing, the collusion ended and the price of bread fell.

Another way of testing whether deterrence works is to look not at differences among states or firms at one point in time but at changes in the nation as a whole over a long period of time. Historical data on the criminal-justice system in America are so spotty that such research is difficult to do here, but it is not at all difficult in England, where the data are excellent. Kenneth I. Wolpin, of Yale, analyzed changes in crime rates and in various parts of the criminal-justice system (the chances of being arrested, convicted, and punished) for the period 1894 to 1967, and concluded that changes in the probability of being punished seemed to cause changes in the crime rate. He offered reasons for believing that this causal connection could not be explained away by the argument that the criminal-justice system was being swamped.

Given what we are trying to measure—changes in the behavior of a small number of hard-to-observe persons who are responding to delayed and uncertain penalties—we will never be entirely sure that our statistical manipulations have proved that deterrence works. What is impressive is that so many (but not all) studies using such different methods come to similar conclusions. More such evidence can be found in studies of the death penalty. Though the evidence as to whether capital punishment deters crime is quite ambiguous, most of the studies find that the chances of being imprisoned for murder do seem to affect the murder rate. Even after wading through all this, the skeptical reader may remain unconvinced. Considering the difficulties of any aggregate statistical analysis, that is understandable. But, as we shall shortly see, the evidence from certain social experiments reinforces the statistical studies. . . .

Two well-known changes in sentencing practices are the so-called Rockefeller drug laws in New York and the Bartley-Fox gun law in Massachusetts. In 1973, New York State revised its criminal statutes relating to drug trafficking in an attempt to make more severe and more certain the penalties for the sale and possession of heroin (the law affecting other drugs was changed as well, but the focus of the effort—and the most severe penalties—were reserved for heroin). The major pushers—those who sold an ounce or more of heroin—would be liable for a minimum prison term of fifteen years and the possibility of life imprisonment. But the law had some loopholes. Someone who had sold an ounce could plea bargain the charges against him down, but no lower than to a charge that would entail a mandatory one-year minimum prison sentence. Police informants could get probation instead of prison, and persons under the age of sixteen were exempt from the mandatory sentences. A provision that was made part of some amendments passed in 1975 exempted from the law persons aged sixteen to eighteen. A group was formed to evaluate the effect of this law. The authors of its report, issued in 1977, found no evidence that the law had reduced the availability of heroin on the streets of New York City or reduced the kinds of property crime often committed by drug users. Of course, it is almost impossible to measure directly the amount of an illegal drug in circulation, or to observe the illicit transactions between dealers and users, but a good deal of circumstantial evidence, gathered by the study group, suggests that no large changes occurred. The number of deaths from narcotics overdoses did not change markedly, nor did admissions to drug-treatment programs or the price and purity of heroin available for sale on the street (as inferred from buys of heroin made by undercover narcotics agents).

The explanation for this disappointing experience, in the opinion of the study group, was that difficulties in administering the law weakened its deterrent power, with the result that most offenders and would-be offenders did not experience any significantly higher risk of apprehension and punishment. There was no increase in the number of arrests, and a slight decline in the proportion of indictments resulting in conviction. Offsetting this was a higher probability that a person convicted would go to prison. The net effect was that the probability of imprisonment for arrested drug dealers did not change as a result of the law—it was about one imprisonment per nine

arrests both before and after passage of the law. On the other hand, the sentences received by those who did go to prison were more severe. Before the law was passed, only 3 percent of persons imprisoned for selling an ounce or more of heroin received a sentence of three years or more. After the law went into effect, 22 percent received such sentences. Perhaps because sentences became more severe, more accused persons demanded trials instead of pleading guilty; as a result, the time needed to dispose of the average drug case nearly doubled.

Does the experience under the Rockefeller law disprove the claim that deterrence works? The answer is no, but that is chiefly because deterrence theory wasn't satisfactorily tested. If "deterrence" means changing behavior by increasing either the certainty or the swiftness of punishment, then the Rockefeller law, as it was administered, could not have deterred behavior, because it made no change in the certainty of punishment and actually reduced its swiftness. If, on the other hand, "deterrence" means changing behavior by increasing the severity of punishment, then deterrence did not work in this case. What we mainly want to know, however, is whether heroin trafficking could have been reduced *if* the penalties associated with it had been imposed more quickly and in a higher proportion of cases.

Severity may prove to be the enemy of certainty and speed. As penalties get tougher, defendants and their lawyers have a greater incentive to slow down the process, and those judges who, for private reasons, resist heavy sentences for drug dealing may use their discretionary powers to decline indictment, accept plea bargains, grant continuances, and modify penalties in ways that reduce the certainty and the celerity of punishment. The group that evaluated the Rockefeller law suggested that reducing severity in favor of certainty might create the only real possibility for testing the deterrent effect of changes in sentences.

The Bartley-Fox gun law in Massachusetts was administered and evaluated in ways that avoided some of the problems of the Rockefeller drug laws. In 1974, the Massachusetts legislature amended the law that had long required a license for a person carrying a handgun, by stipulating that a violation of this law would entail a mandatory penalty of one year in prison, which sentence could not be reduced by probation or parole or by judicial finagling. When the law went into effect, in April of 1975, various efforts were made to evaluate both the compliance of the criminal-justice system with it and the law's impact on crimes involving handguns. James A. Beha, II, then at the Harvard Law School, traced the application of the law for eighteen months, and concluded that, despite widespread predictions to the contrary, the police, prosecutors, and judges were not evading the law. As in New York, more persons asked for trials, and delays in disposition apparently increased, but in Massachusetts, by contrast with the experience in New York, the probability of punishment increased for those arrested. Beha estimated in 1977 (at a time when not all the early arrests had yet worked their way through the system) that prison sentences were being imposed five times more frequently on persons arrested for illegally carrying firearms than had been true before the law was passed. Owing to some combination of the heavy publicity given to the Bartley-Fox law and the real increase in the risk of imprisonment facing persons arrested

while carrying a firearm without a license, the casual carrying of firearms seems to have decreased. This was the view expressed to interviewers by participants in the system, including persons being held in jail, and it was buttressed by a sharp drop in the proportion of drug dealers arrested by the Boston Police who, at the time of their arrest, were found to be carrying firearms. . . .

Deterrence and job-creation are not different anti-crime strategies; they are two sides of the same strategy. The former increases the costs of crime; the latter enhances the benefits of alternatives to criminal behavior. The usefulness of each depends on the assumption that we are dealing with a reasonably rational potential offender.

Let us return to our original example. The young man is still yearning for the money necessary to enjoy some high living. Let us assume that he considers finding a job. He knows he will have to look for one; this will take time. Assuming he gets one, he will have to wait even longer to obtain his first paycheck. But he knows that young men have difficulty finding their first jobs, especially in inner-city neighborhoods such as his. Moreover, he cannot be certain that the job he might get would provide benefits that exceed the costs. Working forty hours a week as a messenger, a dishwasher, or a busboy might not seem worth the sacrifice in time, effort, and reputation on the street corner that it entails. The young man may be wrong about all this, but if he is ignorant of the true risks of crime, he is probably just as ignorant of the true benefits of alternatives to crime.

Compounding the problems of delay, uncertainty, and ignorance is the fact that society cannot feasibly make more than modest changes in the employment prospects of young men. Job-creation takes a long time, when it can be done at all, and many of the jobs created will go to the "wrong" (i.e., not criminally inclined) persons; thus, unemployment rates among the young will not vary greatly among states and will change only slowly over time. And if we wish to see differences in unemployment rates (or income levels) affect crime, we must estimate those effects by exactly the same statistical techniques we use to estimate the effect of criminal-justice sanctions.

The problem of measurement error arises because we do not know with much accuracy the unemployment rate among youths by city or state. Much depends on who is looking for work and how hard, how we count students who are looking only for part-time jobs, and whether we can distinguish between people out of work for a long period and those who happen to be between jobs at the moment. Again, since inaccuracies in these data vary from place to place, we will obtain biased results.

The problem of omitted factors is also real, as is evident in a frequently cited study done in 1976 by Harvey Brenner, of Johns Hopkins University. He suggested that between 1940 and 1973, increases in the unemployment rate led to increases in the homicide rate. But he omitted from his analysis any measure of changes in the certainty or the severity of sentences for murder, factors that other scholars have found to have a strong effect on homicide.

Finally, the relationship between crime and unemployment (or poverty) is probably complex, not simple. For example, in a statistical study that manages to overcome the problems already mentioned, we might discover that as unemployment rates go up, crime rates go up. One's natural instinct would be to interpret this as meaning that rising unemployment causes rising crime. But rising crime might as easily cause rising unemployment. If young men examining the world about them conclude that crimes pays more than work—that, for instance, stealing cars is more profitable than washing them—they may then leave their jobs in favor of crime. Some young men find dealing in drugs more attractive than nine-to-five jobs, but, technically, they are "unemployed."

Perhaps both crime and unemployment are the results of some common underlying cause. In 1964, the unemployment rate for black men aged twenty to twenty-four was 12.6 percent; by 1978, it was 20 percent. During the same period, crime rates, in particular those involving young black men, went up. Among the several possible explanations are the changes that have occurred where so many young blacks live, in the inner parts of large cities. One such change is the movement out of the inner cities of both jobs and the social infrastructure that is manned by adult members of the middle class. The departure of jobs led to increased unemployment; the departure of the middle class led to lessened social control and hence to more crime. If we knew more than we now know, we would probably discover that all three relationships are working simultaneously: for some persons, unemployment leads to crime; for others, crime leads to unemployment; and for still others, social disintegration or personal inadequacy leads to both crime and unemployment. . . .

The hope, widespread in the 1960s, that job-creation and job-training programs would solve many social problems, including crime, led to countless efforts both to prevent crime by supplying jobs to crime-prone youths and to reduce crime among convicted offenders by supplying them with better job opportunities after their release from prison. One preventive program was the Neighborhood Youth Corps, which gave to poor young persons jobs during the afternoons and evenings and all day during the summer. An evaluation of the results of such programs among poor blacks in Cincinnati and Detroit found no evidence that participation in the Youth Crops had any effect on the proportion of enrollees who came into contact with the police. Essentially the same gloomy conclusion was reached by the authors of a survey of a large number of delinquency-prevention programs, though they reported a few glimmers of hope that certain programs might provide some benefits to some persons. For example, persons who had gone through a Job Corps program that featured intensive remedial education and job training in a residential camp were apparently less likely to be arrested six months after finishing their training than a control group. . . .

The best and most recent effort to identify the link between employment and crime was the "supported-work" program of the Manpower Demonstration Research Corporation (MDRC). In ten locations around the country, MDRC randomly assigned four kinds of people with employment problems to special workshops or to control groups. The four categories were long-term welfare (Aid to Families with Dependent Children) recipients, school dropouts, former drug addicts, and ex-convicts. The workshops provided employment in unskilled jobs

supplemented by training in job-related personal skills. The unique feature of the program was that all the participants in a given work setting were people with problems; thus the difficulties experienced by persons with chronic unemployment problems when they find themselves competing with persons who are successful job-seekers and jobholders were minimized. Moreover, the workshops were led by sympathetic supervisors (often themselves ex-addicts or ex-convicts), who gradually increased the level of expected performance until, after a year or so, the trainees were able to go out into the regular job market on their own. This government-subsidized work in a supportive environment, coupled with training in personal skills, was the most ambitious effort of all we have examined to get persons with chronic problems into the labor force. Unlike vocational training in prison, supported work provided real jobs in the civilian world, and training directly related to what one was paid to do. Unlike work-release programs, supported work did not immediately place the ex-convict in the civilian job market to sink or swim on his own.

Welfare recipients and ex-addicts benefited from supported work, but ex-convicts and youthful school dropouts did not. Over a twenty-seven-month observation period, the school dropouts in the project were arrested as frequently as the school dropouts in the control group, and the ex-offenders in the project were arrested *more* frequently (seventeen more arrests per 100 persons) than ex-offenders in the control group.

The clear implication, I think, of the supported-work project—and of all the studies to which I have referred—is that unemployment and other economic factors may be well be connected with criminality, but the connection is not a simple one. If, as some people assume, "unemployment causes crime," then simply providing jobs to would-be criminals or to convicted criminals would reduce their propensity to commit crimes. We have very little evidence that this is true, at least for the kinds of persons helped by MDRC. Whether crime rates would go down if dropouts and ex-convicts held on to their jobs we cannot say, because, as the supported-work project clearly showed, within a year and a half after entering the program, the dropouts and ex-convicts were no more likely to be employed than those who had never entered the program at all—despite the great and compassionate efforts made on their behalf. Help, training, and jobs may make a difference for some persons—the young and criminally inexperienced dropout; the older, "burned-out" ex-addict; the more mature (over age thirty-five) ex-convict. But ex-addicts, middle-aged ex-cons, and inexperienced youths do not commit most of the crimes that worry us. These are committed by the young chronic offender. . . .

Some may agree with me but still feel that we should spend more heavily on one side or the other of the cost-benefit equation. At countless scholarly gatherings, I have heard learned persons examine closely any evidence purporting to show the deterrent effect of sanctions, but accept with scarcely a blink the theory that crime is caused by a "lack of opportunities." Perhaps they feel that since the evidence on both propositions is equivocal, it does less harm to believe in—and invest in—the "benign" (i.e., job-creation) program. That is surely wrong. If we try to make the penalties for crime swifter and more certain, and it should turn out that deterrence does not work, then we have merely increased the risks facing persons who are guilty of crimes in any event. If we fail to increase the certainty and swiftness of penalties, and it should turn out that deterrence *does* work, then we have needlessly increased the risk of being victimized for many innocent persons. . . .

But we cannot achieve large reductions in crime rates by making sanctions very swift or very certain or by making jobs very abundant, because things other than the fear of punishment or the desire for jobs affect the minds of offenders, and because while we say we want a speedy, fair, and efficient criminal-justice system, we want other things more.

The behavior of most of us is affected by even small (and possibly illusory) changes in the costs attached to it. We are easily deterred by a crackdown on drunk driving, especially if it is highly publicized, and our willingness to take chances when filling out our tax returns is influenced by how likely we think an audit may be. Why, then, should we not see big changes in the crime rates when we make our laws tougher?

The answer is not that, unlike the rest of us, burglars, muggers, and assaulters are irrational. I am struck by the account given in Sally Engle Merry's book, *Urban Danger*, of her extended interviews with youthful offenders in a big-city neighborhood she observed for a year and a half. She found that these young men had a sophisticated, pragmatic view of their criminal enterprises, even though they were neither "white-collar" criminals nor highly professional burglars. They distinguished carefully between affluent and less-affluent targets, spoke knowledgeably about the chances of being caught in one part of the district as opposed to another, understood that some citizens were less likely to call the police than others, knew which offenses were most and which were least likely to lead to arrest and prosecution, and had formed a judgment about what kinds of stories the judges would or would not believe. Though many committed crimes opportunistically, or in retaliation for what they took to be the hostile attitudes of certain neighbors, they were neither so impulsive nor so emotional as to be unaware of, or indifferent to, the consequences of their actions. . . .

Chronic offenders may attach little or no importance to the loss of reputation that comes from being arrested; in certain circles, they may feel that an arrest has enhanced their reputation. They may attach a low value to the alleged benefits of a legitimate job, because it requires punctuality, deferential behavior, and a forty-hour week, all in exchange for no more money than they can earn in three or four burglaries carried out at their leisure. These values are not acquired merely by trying crime and comparing its benefits with those of non-criminal behavior; if that were all that was involved, far more of us would be criminals. These preferences are shaped by personal temperament, early familial experiences, and contacts with street-corner peers—by character-forming processes that occur in intimate settings, produce lasting effects, and are hard to change.

Whereas the drinking driver, the casual tax cheat, or the would-be draft evader, having conventional preferences, responds quickly to small changes in socially determined risks, the chronic offender seems to respond only to changes in risks that are sufficiently great to offset the large benefits he associates with

crime and the low value he assigns to having a decent reputation. Changing risks to that degree is not impossible, but changing those risks permanently and for large numbers of persons is neither easy nor inexpensive, especially since (as we saw in Wayne County, with the felony firearm statute, and in New York, with the Rockefeller drug law) some members of the criminal-justice system resist programs of this kind.

One third of all robberies committed in the United States are committed in the six largest cities, even though they contain only 8 percent of the nation's population. The conditions of the criminal-justice system in those cities range from poor to disastrous. *The New York Times* recently described one day in New York City's criminal courts. Nearly 4,000 cases came up on that day; each received, on the average, a three-minute hearing from one of seventy overworked judges. Fewer than one case in two hundred resulted in a trial. Three quarters of the summons issued in the city are ignored; 3.7 million unanswered summonses now fill the courts' files. It is possible that some measure of rough justice results from all this—that the most serious offenders are dealt with adequately, and the trivial or nonexistent penalties (other than inconvenience) imposed upon minor offenders do not contribute to the production of more chronic offenders. In short, these chaotic courts may not, as the *Times* described them, constitute a "system in collapse." But could such a system reduce the production of chronic offenders by increasing the swiftness, certainty, or severity of penalties for minor offenders? Could it take more seriously spouse assaults where the victim is reluctant to testify? Or monitor more closely the behavior of persons placed on probation on the condition that they perform community service or make restitution to their victims? Or weigh more carefully the sentences given to serious offenders, so as to maximize the crime-reduction potential of those sentences? It seems most unlikely. And yet, doing some or all of these things is exactly what is required by any plan to reduce crime by improving deterrence. For reasons best known to state legislators who talk tough about crime but appropriate too little money for a big-city court system to cope properly with lawbreakers, the struggle against street crime that has supposedly been going on for the last decade or so is in large measure a symbolic crusade.

I have written at length elsewhere about the obstacles that prevent more than small, planned changes in the criminal-justice system. Given the modest effect that changes will have on the observable behavior of chronic offenders, we may want to supplement improvements in the criminal-justice system with programs that would reduce the causes of crime. When I published the first edition of *Thinking About Crime*, in 1975, I argued that a free society lacked the capacity to alter the root causes of crime, since they were almost surely to be found in the character-forming processes that go on in the family. The principal rejoinder to that argument was that these root causes could be found instead in the objective economic conditions confronting the offender. Labor-market or community conditions may indeed have some effect on the crime rate, but since I first wrote, the evidence has mounted that this effect is modest and hard to measure and that devising programs— even such extraordinary programs as supported work—that will have much

impact on repeat offenders or school dropouts is exceptionally difficult.

By contrast, a steadily growing body of evidence suggests that the family affects criminality and that its effect, at least for serious offenders, is lasting. Beginning with the research of Sheldon and Eleanor Glueck in Boston during the 1930s and 1940s, and continuing with the work of Lee Robins, William and Joan McCord, and Travis Hirschi in this country, Donald West and David Farrington in England, Lea Pulkinnen in Finland, Dan Olweus in Norway, and many others, we now have available an impressive number of studies that, taken together, support the following view: Some combination of constitutional traits and early family experiences accounts for more of the variation among young persons in their serious criminality than any other factors, and serious misconduct that appears relatively early in life tends to persist into adulthood. What happens on the street corner, in the school, or in the job market can still make a difference, but it will not be as influential as what has gone before.

If criminals are rational persons with values different from those of the rest of us, then it stands to reason that temperament and family experiences, which most shape values, will have the greatest effect on crime, and that perceived costs and benefits will have a lesser impact. For example, in a society where people cannot be under continuous official surveillance, the pleasure I take in hitting people is likely to have a greater effect on my behavior than the occasional intervention of some person in a blue uniform who objects to my hitting others and sets in motion a lengthy and uncertain process that may or may not result in my being punished for doing the hitting.

In a sense, the radical critics of America are correct. If you wish to make a big difference in crime rates, you must make a fundamental change in society. But what they propose to put in place of existing institutions, to the extent that they propose anything at all except angry rhetoric, would leave us yearning for the good old days when our crime rate may have been higher but our freedom was intact.

There are, of course, ways of reorganizing a society other than along the authoritarian lines of radical Marxism. One can imagine living in a society in which the shared values of the people, reinforced by the operation of religious, educational, and communal organizations concerned with character formation, would produce a citizenry less criminal than ours is now without diminishing to any significant degree the political liberties we cherish. Indeed, we can do more than imagine it; we can recall it. During the latter half of the nineteenth century, we managed in this country to keep our crime rate lower than it might have been in the face of extensive urbanization, rapid industrialization, large-scale immigration, and the widening of class differences. We did this, as I have argued elsewhere ("Crime and American Culture," *The Public Interest*, Winter, 1982), by investing heavily in various systems of impulse control through revival movements, temperance societies, uplift organizations, and moral education—investments that were based on and gave effect to a widespread view that self-restraint was a fundamental element of character.

These efforts were designed to protect (and, where necessary, to replace) the family, by institutionalizing familial virtues in society at large. The efforts weakened as the moral consensus on which they were based decayed: self-expression began to rival self-control as a core human value, at first among young, well-educated persons, and eventually among persons of every station. Child-rearing methods, school curricula, social fashions, and intellectual tendencies began to exalt rights over duties, spontaneity over loyalty, tolerance over conformity, and authenticity over convention.

The criminal-justice system of the nineteenth century was probably no swifter or more certain in its operations than the system of today, at least in the large cities, and the economy was even more subject to booms and busts than anything we have known since the 1930s. The police were primitively organized and slow to respond, plea bargaining was then, as now, rife in the criminal courts, prisons were overcrowded and nontherapeutic, and protection against the vicissitudes of the labor market was haphazard or nonexistent. Yet these larger social processes may have had a greater effect on crime rates then than they do today, because then, unlike now, they were working in concert with social sentiments: society condemned those whom the police arrested, the judge convicted, or the labor market ignored. Shame magnified the effect of punishment, and perhaps was its most important part.

Today, we are forced to act as if the degree of crime control that was once obtained by the joint effect of intimate social processes and larger social institutions can be achieved by the latter alone. It is as if we hope to find in some combination of swift and certain penalties and abundant economic opportunities a substitute for discordant homes, secularized churches, intimidated schools, and an

272 / 15. IS INCAPACITATION THE ANSWER TO CRIME?

ethos of individual self-expression. We are not likely to succeed.

Nor are we likely to reproduce, by plan, an older ethos or its accompanying array of voluntary associations and social movements. And, since we should not abandon essential political liberties, our crime-control efforts for the most part will have to proceed on the assumption—shaky as it is—that the things we can change, at least marginally, will make a significant difference. We must act as if swifter and more certain sanctions and better opportunities will improve matters. Up to a point, I think, they will, but in reaching for that point we must be prepared for modest gains uncertainly measured and expensively priced.

Brighter prospects may lie ahead. By 1990, about half a million fewer eighteen-year-old males will be living in this country than were living here in 1979. As everyone knows, young males commit proportionately more crimes than older ones. Since it is the case in general that about 6 percent of young males become chronic offenders, we will in 1990 have 30,000 fewer eighteen-year-old chronic offenders; if each chronic offender commits ten offenses (a conservative estimate) per year, we will have a third of a million fewer crimes from this age group alone. But other things may happen as well as the change in numbers. A lasting drop in the birthrate will mean that the number of children per family will remain low, easing the parental problem of supervision. A less youthful society may be less likely to celebrate a "youth culture," with its attendant emphasis on unfettered self-expression. A society less attuned to youth may find it can more easily re-assert traditional values and may be more influenced by the otherwise marginal effects of improvements in the efficiency of the criminal-justice system and the operation of the labor market. Natural and powerful demographic forces, rather than the deliberate re-establishment of an older culture, may increase the values of those few policy tools with which a free society can protect itself. In the meantime, justice requires that we use those tools, because penalizing wrong conduct and rewarding good conduct are right policies in themselves, whatever effect they may have.

NO

David L. Bazelon

SOLVING THE NIGHTMARE
OF STREET CRIME

The nightmare of street crime is slowly paralyzing American society. Across the nation, terrified people have altered their lifestyles, purchasing guns and doubling locks to protect their families against the rampant violence outside their doors. After seething for years, public anxiety is now boiling over in a desperate search for answers. Our leaders are reacting to these public demands. In New York, Gov. Hugh Carey proposed the hiring or more police officers and prosecutors; in California, Attorney General Deukmejian has asked the legislature for immediate adoption of a package of new law enforcement bills.

A recent address by the Chief Justice of the United States has helped to place this crisis high on the public agenda. Speaking before the American Bar Association in February, Chief Justice Warren Burger described ours as an "impotent society," suffering a "reign of terror" in its streets and homes. The time has come, he declared, to commit vast social resources to the attack on crime—a priority comparable to the national defense.

Some have questioned whether a sitting Chief Justice should advocate sweeping changes in the criminal justice system and others have challenged his particular prescriptions, but I believe the prestige of his office has focused the nation's attention on issues critical to our future. We should welcome this opportunity to begin a thoughtful and constructive debate about our national nightmare.

In this debate, public concern is sure to generate facile sloganeering by politicians and professionals alike. It would be easy to convert this new urgency into a mandate for a "quick fix." The far-harder task is to marshall that energy toward examining the painful realities and agonizing choices we face. Criminologists can help make our choices the product of an informed, rational, and morally sensitive strategy. As citizens and as human beings, they have a special responsibility to contribute their skills, experience, and knowledge to keep the debate about crime as free of polemics and unexamined assumptions as possible.

From "Solving the Nightmare of Street Crime," by David Bazelon, USA Today Magazine, Society for the Advancement of Education, January 1982. Copyright © 1982 by the Society for the Advancement of Education. Reprinted by permission.

I would like to outline some avenues of inquiry worthy of exploration. I offer no programs, no answers. After 31 years on the bench, I can say with confidence that we can never deal intelligently and humanely with crime until we face the realities behind it. First, we must carefully identify the problem that so terrorizes America. Second, we should seek to understand the conditions that breed those crimes of violence. Finally, we should take a close look at both the short- and long-term alternatives for dealing with the problem.

TYPES OF CRIMES AND WHO COMMITS THEM

A reasoned analysis must begin by asking: What is it that has our society in such a state of fear? Politicians, journalists, and criminal justice professionals who should know better speak rather generally about "crime in America" without specifying exactly what they mean. There are, in fact several distinct types of crimes and people who commit them.

Consider white-collar crime. This category embraces activities ranging from shoplifting to tax fraud to political corruption. It is undoubtedly a phenomenon of the gravest concern, costing society untold billions of dollars—far more than street crime. To the extent that such crimes appear to go unpunished, they breed disrespect for law and cynicism about our criminal justice institutions. Yet, as costly and corrosive as such crimes are, they do not instill the kind of fear reflected in the recent explosion of public concern. White-collar crimes, after all, are committed by the middle and upper classes, by "[p]eople who look like one's next-door neighbor," as sociologist Charles Silberman puts it. These people

do not, by and large, threaten our physical safety or the sanctity of our homes.

Nor do the perpetrators of organized crime. After all, hired guns largely kill each other. The average citizen need not lock his doors in fear that he may be the object of gang warfare. Organized crime unquestionably does contribute to street crime—the most obvious connection is drugs—but organized crime has certainly not produced the recent hysteria.

Nor do crimes of passion cause us to bolt our doors so firmly at night. That would be like locking the fox *inside* the chicken coop. Clearly, it is the random assault of *street* crime—the muggings, rapes, purse snatchings, and knifings that plague city life—which puts us all in such mortal fear for our property and lives.

Once we focus on the kind of crime we fear, the second step in a constructive analysis is to identify those people who commit it. This is no pleasant task. The real roots of crime are associated with a constellation of suffering so hideous that, as a society, we can not bear to look it in the face. Yet, we can never hope to understand street crime unless we summon the courage to look as the ugly realities behind it. Nobody questions that street criminals typically come from the bottom of the socioeconomic ladder —from among the ignorant, the ill-educated, and the unemployed, and the unemployable. A recent National Institute of Justice study confirms that our prison population is disproportionately black and young. The offenders that give city dwellers nightmares come from an underclass of brutal social and economic deprivation. Urban League president Vernon Jordan calls them America's "boat people without boats."

It is no great mystery why some of these people turn to crime. They are born into families struggling to survive, if they have families at all. They are raised in deteriorating, overcrowded housing. They lack adequate nutrition and health care. They are subjected to prejudice and educated in unresponsive schools. They are denied the sense of order, purpose, and self-esteem that makes law-abiding citizens. With nothing to preserve and nothing to lose, they turn to crime for economic survival, a sense of excitement and accomplishment, and an outlet for frustration, desperation, and rage.

Listen to the words of a 15-year-old ghetto youth:

> In Brooklyn you fall into one of two categories when you start growing up.... First, there's the minority of the minority, the "ducks" or suckers. These are the kids who go to school every day. They even want to go to college. Imagine that! School after high school! . . . They're wasting their lives waiting for a dream that won't come true.
>
> The ducks are usually the ones getting beat up on by the majority group— the "hard rocks." If you're a real hard rock you have no worries, no cares. Getting high is as easy as breathing. You just rip off some duck. You don't bother going to school, it's not necessary. You just live with your mom until you get a job—that should be any time a job comes looking for you. Why should you bother to go looking for it? Even your parents can't find work.
>
> Hard rocks do what they want to do when they want to do it. When a hard rock goes to prison it builds up his reputation. He develops a bravado that's like a long sad joke. But it's all lies and excuses. It's a hustle to keep ahead of the fact that he's going nowhere. . . .

This, then, is the face behind the mask we call "the crime problem."

Having identified the kind of crime that causes public anxiety and the kind of people who commit it, we can now consider some alternative responses. For purpose of analysis, we can divide the alternatives into two types. The first set, which enjoys the greatest currency in the political arena today, consists of short-term proposals. They proceed from our universally acknowledged need to protect ourselves *immediately* from the menace of crime. These kinds of prescriptions are endorsed by many good people in high places, including the Chief Justice of the United States and the Mayor of New York. The short-term proposals rely principally on deterrence and incapacitation as means of controlling the symptoms of our national disease. The second, more long-term proposals seek to attack the root causes of crime. Both of these approaches have great costs as well as benefits that must be carefully understood and weighed before we set our course.

DETERRENCE

Let us first examine the short-run proposals. Deterrence has always been intuitively attractive. The recent spate of prescriptions underscores the popularity of this theory and have taken many forms. The Chief Justice says we must provide "swift and certain consequences" for criminal behavior. The California Attorney General advocates mandatory prison terms for certain kinds of crimes. New York Mayor Edward Koch favors harsher sentences including the death penalty. Former U.S. Attorney Whitney North Seymour, Jr., contends that tougher prosecution is necessary. Each of these proposals is premised on Harvard University Prof. James Q. Wilson's theory that, "if the expected cost of crime goes up without a corresponding increase in the expected benefits, then the would-be criminal—unless he or she is among that small fraction of criminals who are utterly irrational—engages in less crime." To the same effect, Wayne State Prof. Ralph Slovenko wrote in a letter to the editor of *The New York Times* that, since "[p]rofits are tax-free and penalties are minimal," those who violate the law are "criminals by choice."

This "rational man" theory of crime is quite plausible with respect to certain kinds of criminals. I can believe that those who have alternatives to crime can indeed be dissuaded from choosing the lawless path if the price is made high enough. If the Abscam episode accomplished nothing else, it induced some potentially corrupt politicians to forebear from taking bribes—at least where there might be cameras around. In fact, white-collar offenders may be so susceptible to deterrence that punishment is superfluous. The fellow country-club members of a corporate embezzler whose life is ruined in a storm of publicity may not need to actually see him go to jail in order to be deterred.

However, the white-collar criminal is *not* the object of these deterrence proposals. Seymour says his proposals are aimed at "the hoodlums and ruffians who are making life in our cit[ies] a nightmare for many citizens"; in other words, at the "hard rocks." Can *these* kinds of criminals be effectively deterred? Diana Gordon, Executive Vice Pres. of the National Council on Crime and Delinquency, points out that the threat of prison may be a meaningless deterrent to one whose urban environment is itself a prison; and as our 15-year-old ghetto resident informs us, "[w]hen a hard rock goes to prison it builds up his reputation."

Common sense is confirmed by experience. New York's highly touted Rockefeller drug law did not produce a decrease in heroin use. In fact, it was actually followed by an increase in property crimes associated with heroin users. Nor is the New York situation unique. Since 1965, the average time served in Federal prison has *risen* from 18 to 30 months. Yet, crime continues to rise unabated.

Even the high priest of deterrence, Prof. Wilson, recognizes the limits of this theory. Although many bandy about his name in support of get-tough proposals, Wilson suggests that the *severity* of punishment has little deterrent effect. Indeed, "the more severe the penalty, the more unlikely that it will be imposed." The benefits of deterrence, according to Wilson, lie only in *certainty* of punishment.

How can we increase that certainty? The *Miranda* rule, the right to seek collateral review, and even the time to prepare for trial have all come under attack in the name of "swift and certain" punishment. These trial and appellate safeguards reflect our fundamental commitment to the presumption of innocence. Before we trade them away, we must know what we are getting in return. From an exhaustive review of the evidence, Silberman concluded that "criminal courts generally *do* an effective job of separating the innocent from the guilty; most of those who should be convicted are convicted, and most of those who should be punished are punished." Today, we prosecute, convict, and incarcerate a larger proportion of those arrested for felonies than we did 50 years ago; yet, the crime rate continues to rise. Clearly, the uncertainty about punishment derives from the great unlikelihood of *arrest*. For every 100 crimes committed, only six persons will be arrested. Thus, sacrificing the constitutional protections of those charged with crime will do little to deter the "hard rocks."

What must we do to achieve certainty of arrest sufficient to have an impact on crime? I asked my good friend, Maurice Cullinane, the former Chief of Police of the District of Columbia, about this. He presided over a force with far more policemen per capita than any other in the country, and that is aside from the several thousand park, Capitol, and other Federal police visible all over Washington. Chief Cullinane told me that, in order to deter street crime to any significant degree, he would have to amass an enormous concentration of patrolmen in one particular area. Only then might the physical presence of a policemen on virtually every block possibly keep crime under control. Of course, crime suppressed in one neighborhood would burgeon in other, unguarded parts of the city. Before we can endorse certainty of arrest as an effective deterrent, we must consider whether we could tolerate the kind of police state it might require.

We need to know much more about the precise costs of an effective program of deterrence before we can dismiss the recent proposals. At the present time, however, the case for deterrence has not been convincingly made. After a comprehensive review of the literature, a panel of the National Academy of Sciences concluded:

Despite the intensity of the research effort, the empirical evidence is still not sufficient for providing a rigorous confirmation of the existence of a deterrent effect. . . . Policy makers in the criminal justice system are done a disservice if they are left with the impression that the empirical evidence, which they themselves are frequently unable to evaluate, strongly supports the deterrence hypothesis.

INCAPACITATION

A more realistic rationale put forth for short-term proposals, in my opinion, is incapacitation. This politely named theory has become the new aim of corrections. No one who has been in an American prison can seriously adhere to the ideal of rehabilitation, and more and more of us have come to suspect the futility of deterrence. The new theory of incapacitation essentially translates as lock the bastards up. At least then they will pose no threat to us while incarcerated. Incapacitation takes many forms: preventive detention, isolation of "career criminals," and stricter parole release requirements.

This notion has something to be said for it. We *must* do something to protect ourselves immediately so that we may "live to fight another day." Thus, the swift and tough route is appealing—get the attackers off the street forthwith; put them away fast and long so that the threat they pose to our daily lives can be neutralized.

A thorough commitment to this policy might indeed make our streets somewhat safer, but at what price? Consider first the cost in dollars. Today, even without an avowed commitment to incapacitation, we already imprison a larger proportion of our citizens than any other industrialized nation in the world, except Russia and South Africa. This dubious honor has cost us dearly. A soon-to-be published survey by the Department of Justice's National Institute of Justice reports that the 1972-78 period saw a 54 percent increase in the population of state prisons. The survey predicts that demand for prison space will continue to outstrip capacity. It has been conservatively estimated that we need $8-10,000,000,000 immediately for construction just to close the gap that exists *now.*

Embarking on a national policy of incapacitation would require much more than closing the gap. One study has estimated that, in New York, a 264 percent increase in state imprisonment would be required to reduce serious crime by only 10 percent! Diana Gordon has worked out the financial requirements for this kind of incapacitation program. In New York alone, it would cost about $3,000,000,000 just to construct the additional cells necessary and probably another $1,000,000,000 each year to operate them. The public must be made aware of the extraordinary financial costs of a genuine incapacitation policy.

In addition, there are significant non-monetary costs. Incapacitation rests on the assumption that convicted offenders would continue to commit crimes if not kept in prison, but can we determine in advance which offenders would in fact repeat and which would not? We simply do not know enough about the "hard rocks" to decide who to warehouse, and for how long. It has been estimated that, to be sure of identifying one potential criminal, we would have to include as many as eight people who would not offend. Thus, to obtain the benefits of incapacitation, we might have to incarcerate a substantial number of people who would have led a blameless life if released. A policy of sentencing individuals based on crimes not yet committed would therefore raise serious doubts about our dedication to the presumption of innocence. The thought of having to choose between immediate safety and sacred constitutional values is frightening.

Nor can there be any comfort that the grave moral and financial costs of incapacitation will only be temporary. Even as we put one generation of offenders behind bars, another set of "hard rocks" will emerge from the hopeless subculture of our ghettos, ready to follow the model set by their fathers and brothers. Unless we intend to keep every criminal and potential criminal in prison *forever*, we must acknowledge the futility of expecting them to behave when they get out. As journalist Tom Wicker recently observed, "to send them to the overcrowded, underfunded, inadequately staffed and policed prisons of America would negate [the] purpose; because more, and more frightening, criminals come out of these schools of crime and violence than go into them." Merely providing inmates with educational and counseling services would do little good "when they return to a society largely unwilling to hire them." We should not fool ourselves that the "hard rocks" will emerge from the cesspools of American prisons willing or able to conduct law-abiding lives.

Incapacitation, then, must be recognized as an extraordinarily costly and risky policy. To meaningfully affect crime, it might require a garrison state. This is not to deny that our "clear and present danger" must be addressed immediately. Still, reason and good faith require us to consider alternatives to a program of endlessly warehousing succeeding generations of human beings.

ATTACKING
THE ROOT CAUSES OF CRIME

A more long-term response to crime is to attack its root causes. This approach also offers no decisive balance of costs and benefits. The unique advantage of a successful attack on the roots of crime would be the promise of *enduring* social tranquility. If we can first break the cycle of suffering which breeds crime, we could turn it to our advantage. We would achieve more than "damage control." Our nation could begin to tap the resources of those we now fear. Instead of a police or garrison state, ours would then be a social order rooted in the will and hearts of our people. We would achieve criminal justice by pursuing social justice.

However, like the short-term solutions, this path would involve substantial risks and uncertainties. The root causes of crime are, of course, far more complex and insidious than simple poverty. After all, the vast majority of the poor commit no crime. Our existing knowledge suggests that the roots of street crime lie in poverty *plus*—plus prejudice, plus poor housing, plus inadequate education, plus insufficient food and medical care, and, perhaps most importantly, plus a bad family environment or no family at all.

Accepting the full implications of what we know about street crime might require us to provide every family with the means to create the kind of home all human beings need. It might require us to afford the job opportunities that pose for some the only meaningful alternatives to violence. It would assure all children a constructive education, a decent place to live, and proper pre- and postnatal nutrition. It would seek to provide those children of inadequate family environments with proper day care or foster care. More fundamentally, it would seek to eradicate racism and prejudice.

Such an attack on the roots of crime would obviously be an extremely long and expensive process. Before we can determine which programs offer the greatest promise, we must face what we know about the crime and build on previous efforts to attack its root causes.

More importantly, a genuine commitment to attacking the roots of crime might force us to reconsider our entire social and economic structure. Like the short-term approach, this might conflict with other deeply held values. Can we break the cycle at crime's roots without invading the social sphere of the ghetto? Would this require the state to impose its values on the young? If we really want a lasting solution to crime, can we afford not to?

In short, any approach we take to crime presents attractive benefits and frightening risks. None of our choices offers a cheap or easy solution. Analysis takes us this far. As I have repeatedly emphasized, we can not choose which difficult path to take without facing the realities of street crime. Obviously, we can not deter those whom we do not understand. Nor can we make a rational assessment of incapacitation without knowing how many we will have to incapacitate and for how long. Finally, of course, we can not evaluate the long-term approach without some idea of its specific strategies and their various costs.

A constructive and fruitful debate about the best means of solving the nightmare of street crime is long overdue. The public's fear of crime cries out for a response and our leaders have made it a national priority, but we can never hope to achieve a just and lasting solution to crime without first facing the realities that underlie it. Emerson said, "God offers to every mind its choice between truth and repose." Truth will not come easy. It will take patience and the strength to put aside emotional reactions. If we do not strive for truth, this nation and all it stands for is bound to enjoy only a brief, false, and dangerous repose.

POSTSCRIPT

Is Incapacitation the Answer to the Crime Problem?

If realism is the criterion for choosing policy options, Wilson's case is the stronger. Bazelon himself allows that incapacitation is a realistic short-term solution, though he argues that it is too costly and produces unsatisfactory long-term results. Bazelon's major argument is a moral one. He criticizes the incapacitation approach as inhumane, dangerous to civil liberties, and hypocritical. Criminals may be errant humans, he says, but they are humans and should be treated with compassion. He sees the incapacitation approach as expressing a revengeful attitude of "lock the low-lifes up," and believes this attitude is unbecoming to a civilized society. The rehabilitation of criminals—not their punishment—should be our goal, even if its accomplishment is very difficult, maintains Bazelon, adding that the incapacitation approach also threatens the civil liberties upon which this society stands. He believes that it is unfortunate that our civil liberties, which are among our proudest possessions, increase the difficulty of putting criminals behind bars. But he emphasizes that we must not weaken these rights in trying to solve the crime problem. Finally, Bazelon contends that the incapacitation approach treats the criminal as the only guilty party and that a more enlightened view recognizes the contributions of blocked opportunities, slum environments, broken families, and social pressures that are in conflict with legitimate values.

It should be pointed out that Wilson shares many of Bazelon's concerns but still sees the incapacitation approach as necessary under present circumstances. On this issue, as on many other issues, hard choices must be made between conflicting values.

A number of other studies explore the pros and cons of "law and order." In *Crime in America* (Simon and Schuster, 1971) former Attorney General Ramsey Clark takes a position in many ways similar to Bazelon's. Hans Zeisel in *The Limits of Law Enforcement* (University of Chicago Press, 1983) argues that the criminal justice system can do little to effectively reduce crime. His emphasis is on increasing protection from crime and attacking its root causes in the conditions of poverty. On the other side, Andrew Von Hirsch's *Doing Justice* (Hill and Wang, 1976) is critical of the Bazelon philosophy.

The issue of deterrence is hotly debated by authors Ernest van den Haag and John P. Conrad in their book on the ultimate in deterrence punishment,

The Death Penalty: A Debate (Plenum Press, 1983). Graeme Newman presents an extreme position on punishment in advocating electric shocks and whippings in *Just and Painful: A Case for the Corporal Punishment of Criminals* (Macmillan, 1983).

A revival of biological explanations of crime is occurring along with some shocking proposals such as sterilization and abortion when the wrong genes are detected in adults or fetuses (see Lawrence Taylor, *Born to Crime: The Genetic Causes of Criminal Behavior,* Greenwood Press, 1984). A more sophisticated and less shocking discussion is presented by James Q. Wilson and Richard Harstein in *Crime and Human Nature* (Simon and Schuster, 1985).

ISSUE 16

Should Immigration Be More Limited?

YES: Gary Imhoff, from "Sovereignty and Security: Immigration Today,"
The Humanist (September/October 1986)

NO: Julian L. Simon, from "Don't Close Our Border," *Newsweek* (February
27, 1984)

ISSUE SUMMARY

YES: Author Gary Imhoff argues that excessive immigration poses serious
dangers to Americans and undermines the sovereignty of our nation.
NO: Professor Julian Simon contends that immigration, which he considers
modest by previous standards, invigorates and enriches our nation.

During the U.S.-Soviet summit meeting in Washington in December of 1987,
Gennadi Gerasimov, the chief spokesman for the Soviet delegation, was
asked by an American reporter why the Soviet Union won't let Jews
emigrate. He deflected the question by turning the tables on the questioner:
"I could say what about Mexican immigration to this country, what about the
wetbacks? When the United States wants Jewish emigration from our
country, it's for the brain power. But what about the wetbacks? You don't
want to let them in." In his reply, Gerasimov ignored the important
distinction between not wanting to let people in and refusing to let them out.
Nevertheless, his statement was accurate in one respect: many Americans
worry about unrestricted immigration and will support measures aimed at
controlling the flow of immigrants—including Mexican immigrants. A recent
Roper poll showed that nine out of ten Americans want illegal immmigration
stopped, and eight out of ten want even legal immigration cut back.

Such attitudes may not be justified, but they ought to be understandable.
Over the past twenty-five years there has been a startling growth in
immigration. This has resulted in part from the liberalization of our immigration laws during the 1960s. Before then, at least since the 1920s, immigration
was seldom much higher than 150,000 per year. But by 1978, annual
immigration was more than 600,000, and it has increased every year since
then. And this is counting only legal immigrants. The number of illegal
(undocumented) aliens entering this country is obviously hard to estimate,
but the fraction of the total caught every year offers evidence that the
numbers have exploded.

Most of the new immigrants come from Third World countries. The largest
percentages of immigrants now come from Mexico, the Philippines, Korea,
and the Caribbean. They come here to flee tyranny and war. They come to

join relatives who have already arrived. Above all, they come because America is one of the few islands of affluence in a global sea of poverty; here they could earn five to ten times what they earn in their home countries. The question for Americans, is what will be the effect of this new flood of immigrants.

Some see the new immigration as a threat to our nation's future. Environmentalists focus on the danger of overcrowding. Since immigration now accounts for one-half of all U.S. population growth, they argue that unrestricted immigration is starting to put pressure on our limited resources. Others worry about the crime problem among some immigrant groups. Some labor leaders worry that the new immigrants may take jobs from American workers and force down wages by working for low salaries. Other Americans are concerned about the impact of the new immigration on schools and social services. The Supreme Court has ruled that the children of illegal immigrants are entitled to public education, and legal immigrants (and those granted amnesty) may also apply for welfare payments. Finally, there are concerns about the cultural effects of unrestricted immigration. Will America's common language and culture be overwhelmed?

Supporters of the new immigration argue that these fears are unjustified. America has traditionally been the land of immigrants, and our immigrants have brought strength, energy, and productivity to this country. The ancestors of Jefferson, Washington, and Franklin were immigrants, and so were the Irish, Italians, Chinese, Germans, and Slavs who built this country into one of the most prosperous on earth. If these historic immigrants helped make America great, the defenders of immigration ask, why shouldn't our new immigrants help make it greater? Their skin color and languages may be different, but they have the same energy and grit, the same devotion to thrift and hard work, that earlier immigrants possessed. Indeed, they may already by putting as much into America as they are getting out of it. They are upgrading marginal neighborhoods, opening up new businesses, taking jobs that no one else would take, paying taxes, and moving up the economic ladder.

In recent years supporters and critics of the new immigration have clashed with each other in Congress as legislators argued the merits of the so-called Simpson-Mazzoli bill. Named after its sponsors, Wyoming Senator Alan Simpson and Kentucky congressman Romano Mazzoli, the bill was aimed at reducing illegal immigration by making it a crime to employ anyone who lacked proper identification. The bill had a stormy four-year passage through Congress; the Senate approved it twice but it met considerable resistance in the House. Finally, in much-modified form (which included amnesty for illegal immigrants already here), it became law in 1986.

In the following selections, author Gary Imhoff focuses on the dangers of the new immigration, while economist Julian Simon—who wrote his article while the Simpson-Mazzoli bill was still being debated—debunks what he considers to be the unfairly critical myths about the new immigrants.

YES

Gary Imhoff

SOVEREIGNTY AND SECURITY: IMMIGRATION TODAY

Over the past two decades, legal immigration gradually doubled in annual volume and illegal immigration skyrocketed. As that growth has occurred, Americans have rediscovered massive immigration as an issue in this country's economic and resource security and in its cultural sovereignty. But it is still taboo to examine the relationship between large-scale immigration—particularly uncontrolled, illegal immigration—and America's national and political security. Is there, in fact, any relationship between illegal immigration and the security of the United States?

In the context of today's immigration debate, it is necessary to return to first principles and to reestablish the legitimacy of national sovereignty. What is a nation? What constitutes a nation, what legitimizes it, and what are its powers? How are relations between nations to be regulated and controlled? Does the United States have the right to control and limit immigration from other countries?

It would surprise most people that such questions even need to be asked. But, over the past few years, congressional and public debates over the Simpson-Mazzoli Immigration Reform and Control Act have made it obvious that some of the Act's opponents doubt the value and importance of the very sovereignty of the United States. Some groups believe it is an open question whether or not the United States has any right to limit immigration, to control its borders, or to define who is and is not a member of its polity. Some groups question the need to distinguish between American citizens and aliens. These groups, to one extent or another, believe that aliens should have the right to enter the United States at will, to remain here indefinitely, and, while here, to receive all the rights and benefits of American citizens.

At heart, what these groups are calling into question is the legitimacy of the nation itself. They are saying that the United States has no right to define itself as an independent nation, that the people of the United States have no right to declare their sovereignty over this country, that there is no right to bar the free passage of the peoples of the world into this country over the

From "Sovereignty and Security: Immigration Today," by Gary Imhoff, *The Humanist*, September/October 1986. Reprinted by permission.

border of the United States, and that no legitimate distinction in laws or rights can be made between citizens of the United States and any other people. They are exploiting the immigration problem, denying this country's right to control immigration, on behalf of a larger agenda that includes the casting of doubt on the very foundation of international political organization: the nation-state.

What, then, is the nation, and why has the existence of nations become the center of political controversy? According to Roger Scruton's *Dictionary of Political Thought*, a nation is a "sovereign state with political autonomy and settled territory." But a nation also consists of a people with a common language and common customs "who recognize common interests and a common need for a single sovereign."

Not every state or country, in other words, is a nation; Czechoslovakia, with its antagonistic nationality groups, for example, is not. Not every nation is yet a single state; Germany, politically divided into East and West, is not. Nationalism, as a political theory, holds that nations and states work best when they are congruent. Nationalism advocates the people's conscious identity of territorial integrity, common language, customs, and culture. Its "motive is to find some binding force between people that is stronger than any revocable agreement to be governed, wider that any merely personal affection, and sufficiently public to lend itself to the foundation of political institutions and laws," according to Scruton. Nationalism envisions the nation to be, at its best, a voluntary association.

Sovereignty is the authority and power of the state. External sovereignty is the authority of the state to deal with other states as the agent for the nation, for its people. Internal sovereignty is the state's legal and coercive power to rule within its territory and to command the society under its government.

Political thought during the American Revolution, and the U.S. Constitution which resulted, were particularly innovative on the subject of sovereignty. America invested power in the people; the people and the Constitution are sovereign. Neither the executive nor the legislature nor the courts are sovereign—they derive all their power from the people and the Constitution. This was the political innovation which modernized and legitimized the institution of the nation and brought about the spread of nationalism. Henceforth, nationhood was sought not just to unify a people who shared a common culture and interests but also to invest those people with the ultimate authority in their government. Nationalism, embodying both the unity of a people and their accession to power, was the focus of all progressive movements.

But, today, many argue that nationalism is simply an outdated and dangerous political philosophy and that nationalism in the United States stems from nothing more than prejudice and ethnocentrism. How the political theory of nationalism is denigrated may be seen in a typical introductory political science textbook, Brian R. Nelson's *Western Political Thought: From Socrates to the Age of Ideology:*

> Nationalism posits the nation-state as the supreme value, and asserts that the individual ought to subordinate his moral judgment to the dictates of the nation. . . .
> Nationalism is a uniquely important ideology, not only because of its influ-

ence, but because it has profoundly subverted the theoretical integrity of each of the other major ideological systems of thought.

This view of nationalism is wittily expressed by Mel Brooks, as the Two-Thousand-Year-Old Man, when he sings what he says was the first national anthem: "Hooray for Cave 327. To hell with all the rest." Nationalism, in short, is nothing more than an excuse for centralizing and expanding power; it is built on xenophobia and it is best expressed by war.

By taking an open-door position on immigration, the advocates of globalism express both their distaste for American nationhood and their contempt for national sovereignty. If a nation is the legitimate expression of a community's sense of its common culture and interests, then it is incumbent upon that nation to regulate its immigration and to protect its borders. Immigration control is inherently part of the nation's sovereignty. As Aristide Zolberg wrote, "It has been universally acknowledged ever since the state system arose in its modern form that, under the law of nations, the right to regulate entry is a fundamental concomitant of sovereignty."

Controlling immigration is an important part of the nation's larger responsibility to define its members and to make meaningful distinctions between citizens and aliens. A good expression of this responsibility can be found in the Supreme Court's decision in the case of *Cabell v. Chavez-Salido*. In upholding California's exclusion of resident aliens from the occupation of peace officer, the Court accepted the state's argument that, "although citizenship is not a relevant ground for the distribution of economic benefits, it is a relevant ground for determining membership in the political community." Justice Byron White held in the Court's decision that "the exclusion of aliens from governmental process is not a deficiency in the democratic system but a necessary consequence of the community's process of self-definition."

If the nation is a community, then membership in the community is a joint voluntary compact. The right to emigrate, which is fundamental in a free society, does not confer upon an individual the right to immigrate into another country. Indeed, it turns the concept of freedom and free association on its head to say that an individual's right to emigrate implies an absolute right for one to compel any nation or community of which one is not a member to admit him or her. Switzerland need not allow me to settle within its borders simply because I desire to live there. Unless they choose to do so, the Swiss are not required to admit me even if I have been mistreated and persecuted in my country of origin. The compact between a community and an individual must be mutually voluntary.

On the other hand, if the state is nothing more than an illegitimate and artificial construct, then controls over foreign immigration are the least justifiable of the state's laws. If a nation is simply an association of convenience, then no nation has any good excuse for excluding any individual simply because he or she happened to be born outside of its arbitrary borders. Immigration restriction is nothing more than nativism and prejudice.

Nativism and prejudice are exactly the terms under which the history of American immigration control and restriction has been rewritten. One of the blessings of the human mind is that dangers, like pains, seem unreal once we are past them. But forgetting the reality of dangers means that we are often tempted to dismiss them. That is why liberal historians such as Oscar Handlin, John Higham, and Barbara Miller Solomon, who wrote in the 1950s and 1960s—two generations after massive immigration to the United States was brought under control and after the problems it caused were long solved—were able to disregard the economic and social arguments presented by the earlier generations who fought for limiting immigration. That is also why they were able to portray these earlier advocates of immigration control—most of whom were drawn from the ranks of the liberal and progressive movements, the abolitionists, the unionists, the suffragettes, the muckrakers, the pioneers of the public schools, the opponents of corruption in city government machines, the founders of settlement houses—as motivated solely by racism and nativism. That is why they were able to portray massive immigration itself as causing no real problems and to portray immigrants' crime, poverty, slums, lack of education, and, most importantly, their economic competition with black and white native workers as being caused solely by the inhospitality, prejudice, and grudging acceptance accorded them by native-born Americans.

That is also why they were able to downplay the history of political violence by immigrant groups and why modern Americans find it difficult to remember and apply the long history of violence to today's situation. Migration streams have historically included violent elements. Just a few examples are the Molly Maguires of the Pennsylvania coal fields, the radical agitators of the Workingmen's Party (new immigrants from Europe who beat up and killed new immigrants from China), the migrant railroad workers who struck violently in 1877, the organizers of the 1863 New York Draft Riots, the Germans and German Americans who committed sabotage in the United States fairly regularly during 1915 and 1918, and the German and Italian anarchists who conducted forty years of bombings and assassinations. The Tong wars did happen; they are not romantic fiction. Victor and Brett De Bary Nee, in *Longtime, Californ'*, their history of San Francisco's Chinatown, seek to downplay the image of widespread Tong violence with the reassurance that there were never more than three thousand armed Tong warriors in the United States. For comparison, there have never been more than five thousand armed rebels in El Salvador, and they have succeeded in creating a disturbance of some note. The peace of a society is fragile, and small numbers of people determined to break the peace can succeed to a remarkable degree.

The American anarchists proved that. The anarchists were a predominantly immigrant movement; they were active in the United States for four decades, from 1880 to 1920, and they were notable more for their terrorism than for their political idealism. Today, it is hard for us to envision the importance the anarchists had as terrorists. It is common to focus upon only the excesses of American city police forces and of the Department of Justice in combatting anarchism. And it must be admitted that the Haymarket Riot was a police riot; the fairness of the trial of Sacco and Vanzetti was subject to many questions; and the repression of anarchist writers and speakers, the denial of their First Amendment rights, was outrageous. The Immigration and Nationality Act's exclusion of anarchists seems a quaint, though un-American, discrimination against a noble political theory. But the Department of Justice and the cities' police forces were fighting a danger that was real. Johann Most's pamphlet of instructions on how to construct dynamite bombs and when to use them was more than just a nationally distributed bestseller; it was an operational manual, and it was put into operation.

Compare the effect that the Weathermen had on American society to that of the anarchists. There were never more than a handful of Weathermen, a few dozen, and yet they instilled fear into the entire nation. There were tens of thousands of anarchists, hundreds of whom belonged to an inner circle that was dedicated to violence. Their movement lasted not for a few brief years but for decades. Anarchists assassinated a president and several local city officials and businessmen; they bombed factories and transportation and engaged in numerous robberies and murders to finance their cause.

An article by Amitai Etzioni appeared in the *Washington Post* on December 11, 1985. Entitled "America Is Unsecured," it said in part:

> Nobody, in my experience, mentions that able-bodied spies and terrorists may cross the Rio Grande at least with the same ease as maids seeking household work in the North. Indeed, it seems it would be quite easy to march a small division into the United States, every night, for quite a while. (People who feel that I am exaggerating should note: this is happening now, only the "divisions" want to work rather than to foment trouble.) . . . The United States is more than an open country: it is an unsecured one. It displays an attitude that mixes "we are invulnerable" with a rhetoric about the need to improve security, but a deep-seated distaste for what improving public safety entails.

What was perhaps most interesting about Professor Etzioni's article was the reaction it inspired: there was widespread denial that it could happen here and outrage that the possibility could be discussed. Our arrogant assumption of our own invulnerability, based upon our ignorance and misreading of history, has made us scorn the importance of immigration control to the security of our nation's sovereignty.

Guarding a country's borders is a single, seamless job. The borders cannot remain open to illegal immigration and still be guarded against smuggling and terrorists. Smugglers, criminals, foreign agents, and other sharks swim in the same sea with schools of illegal immigrants. Even those who believe that illegal immigration is a benign and beneficent institution cannot, I believe, design a net that will catch only the dangerous fish.

Yet, making that simple statement attracts charges of nativism and racism. After all, it cannot happen here. Even a hint that uncontrolled borders and unrestricted illegal immigration may facilitate terrorism, even when the suggestion is made as mildly and reasonably as in Professor Etzioni's article, draws such a hostile reaction. Terrorists may use dynamite, but raising the issue of terrorism by immigrants is playing with dynamite. Questioning the patriotism or suggesting the subversive tendencies of even a small portion of immigrants could, it is claimed, endanger the remarkable generosity and tolerance with which Americans treat both legal and illegal immigrants. Questioning the patriotism of even a few of the immigrants or raising doubts about their ultimate loyalty only, it is said, gives aid and comfort to nativism.

But it is exactly these difficult questions, these questions which are forbidden to be raised, that are most dangerous for us to ignore. Twenty years ago, Daniel Moynihan said that the rising rate of broken black families was going to create serious social problems and that the issue should be addressed by the government. He was vilified; it was said that even to mention the problem was to give aid and comfort to racists, if not to be racist. It was said that the best thing would be for our government and society to ignore the issue. We did. We let it become a crisis. We let it grow until it was impossible to ignore any longer, until well-intentioned, responsible people could envision no reasonable, moderate steps that could begin to solve it.

Our knowledge about the relationship between illegal immigration and national security is now at an early stage. We know a lot less about it than Mr. Moynihan knew about the black family. We are in a state of less than blissful ignorance about the criminals and the government agents in the Mariel boatlift, about the smugglers and the bandits in the "normal" flow, and about the agents of hostile governments and hostile revolutionary movements from other countries. We need only remember our floundering inability in 1979 and 1980 to locate Iranian nationals in this country to recognize our unpreparedness. It is time for us to face the issue directly and to study the issue of immigration and security. This coun-

try needs to determine what the extent of the problem is and how immigration can be prevented from ever again becoming a security crisis in the United States.

As a first step, the government should survey its own resources to determine what its various agencies know about the current extent of the problem. The immigration subcommittees of the House and Senate could hold hearings and get reports from the Federal Bureau of Investigation, the Central Intelligence Agency, the Defense Intelligence Agency, the Drug Enforcement Agency, the Immigration and Naturalization Service, the State Department, the President's Commission on Organized Crime, and local police forces on what information already exists within these agencies about the security aspects of illegal immigration. Or the INS could begin such a survey on its own, although the Reagan administration, like all the administrations since Eisenhower's, places such a low priority on the INS that a report by that agency would not be likely to lead to any action. Whichever route is taken, this country should choose knowledge over deliberate ignorance.

This may be the advice given to Pandora: "Come on, aren't you curious about what's in the box?" But the myth of Pandora is the truth of a backward society in which knowledge and change are dangerous and ignorance is safety. In the modern world, while we acknowledge the risks of gaining knowledge, we know that knowledge leads to a deeper security.

NO

Julian L. Simon

DON'T CLOSE OUR BORDERS

Many Americans think of immigrants as the tired and poor. And too many believe that they live on welfare or that they displace natives from scarce jobs by accepting low wages. These complaints and others will be heard as Congress tries to secure this country's borders by way of the Simpson-Mazzoli bill. The proposed law includes amnesty for longtime illegal immigrants, sanctions against those who hire them and a national identity card, but its main impact would be to reduce the total number of illegal and legal immigrants into the United States.

Opponents of immigration believe they are guarding their own economic interests when they argue that immigrants damage our pocketbooks and our environment. But recent research shows that many of their beliefs are dead wrong and are based on myth.

Myth 1. *The United States is being flooded by Mexican illegals.* Leonard Chapman, then the commissioner of the Immigration and Naturalization Service, first scared us in the 1970s with an estimate that up to 12 million people were illegally in this country. It was just a guess, but now ingenious statisticians using a variety of methods report that the total number of illegals is almost certainly below 6 million, and may be only 3.5 to 5 million. Furthermore, the number of illegals in the country overstates the number of Mexicans who intend to remain permanently, leaving perhaps 1.3 million Mexican illegals—certainly not a large number by any economic test, and far less than the scare figures promulgated earlier.

Myth 2. *Illegal and legal immigrants abuse welfare and government services.* Study after study shows that small proportions of illegals use government services: free medical, 5 percent; unemployment insurance, 4; food stamps, 1; welfare payments, 1; child schooling, 4. Illegals are afraid of being caught if they apply for welfare. Practically none receive social security, the costliest service of all, but 77 percent pay social security taxes, and 73 percent have federal taxes withheld.

In an analysis of Census Bureau data I conducted for the Select Commission on Immigration and Refugee Policy, I found that, aside from social security and Medicare, immigrant families average about the same level of welfare services as do citizens. When programs for the elderly are included, immigrant families use far *less* public funds than do natives. During the first five years in the United States, the average immigrant family receives $1,404 (in 1975 dollars) in welfare compared with $2,279 received by a native family. The receipts become equal in later years, but when immigrants retire, their own children contribute to their support and so they place no new or delayed burdens upon the tax system.

Immigrants also pay more than their share of taxes. Within three to five years, immigrant-family earnings reach and pass those of the average American family. The tax and welfare data together indicate that, on balance, immigrants contribute to the public coffers an average of $1,300 or more each year that family is in the United States.

Myth 3. *Immigration is high.* An article in the prestigious journal *Foreign Affairs* states that "immigration and refugee flows to the United States in the late 1970s were at or near the highest levels ever experienced." This is just wrong even in absolute terms. There were 800,000 immigrants in 1980—the most recent high—yet near the turn of the century and for six years, immigration topped the million mark. The burden of absorbing it was, in fact, greater then. Between 1901 and 1910, immigrants constituted 9.6 percent of the population: between 1961 and 1970, they were only 1.6 percent. Or consider this. In 1910, 14.6 percent of the population was foreign-born. In 1970 only 4.7 percent had been born abroad, or less than 1 person in 20, including those who had come many years ago. Amazingly, this "country of

immigrants," as the politicians often put it, has a smaller share of foreign-borns than more "homogeneous" countries like Great Britain, Sweden, Switzerland, France, Australia and Canada.

Myth 4. *Immigrants are "huddled masses"—uneducated and unskilled.* The central economic fact now, as it has been throughout U.S. history—is that, in contrast to the rapidly aging U.S. population, immigrants tend to arrive in their 20s and 30s when they are physically and mentally vigorous and in the prime of their work life. On average, they have about as much education as do natives, and did so even at the turn of the century. Immigrants also tend to be unusually self-reliant and innovative: they have the courage and the belief in themselves that is necessary for the awesome challenge of changing one's culture and language.

Myth 5. *Immigrants cause native unemployment.* This has always been the major fear. If the number of jobs is fixed and immigrants occupy some jobs, then there are fewer jobs for natives. This overlooks the dynamic that immigrants create jobs as well as take them. Their purchases increase the demand for labor, leading to new hires. They frequently open small businesses that are a main source of new jobs.

Experiments conducted by INS show little, if any, damage to citizens even in the few areas where immigrants—legal and illegal—concentrate: in the restaurant and hotel industries. Most Americans, having better alternatives (including welfare programs), do not accept these jobs on the conditions offered.

On balance, immigrants are far from a drag on the economy. As workers, consumers, entrepreneurs and taxpayers, they invigorate it and contribute healthy economic benefits. By increasing the work force, they also help solve our social security problem. Immigrants tend to come at the start of their work lives but when they retire and collect social security, they typically have raised children who are then contributing taxes to the system.

This country needs more, not fewer, immigrants. The U.S. birthrate is low and our future work force is shrinking. By opening our doors we will not only do good but the evidence indicates we will also do well.

_____

POSTSCRIPT

Should Immigration Be More Limited?

Imhoff and Simon do not really disagree on the facts; instead, they present different sets of facts. Simon notes that there are not as many immigrants as some fear and that the immigrants are making important economic contributions. Imhoff does not dispute those assertions but focuses on the need to preserve our identity as a nation and worries about the chaos that can be caused by even a few troublemakers. Perhaps there is a basis here for agreement. If new immigrants can be brought securely within the American tradition—perhaps by a carefully designed program of "Americanization"—then Imhoff's worries might be set at rest. This was done before, and with considerable success, with the great waves of European immigrants who came here at the turn of the century. The complaint about this "melting pot" approach is that it destroyed ethnic identities and made immigrants ashamed of being "foreign." This may or may not be a price worth paying to avoid the dangers cited by Imhoff.

One of the most thoughtful and comprehensive discussions of the effects of the new immigration is the extensive article by James M. Fallows in *The Atlantic Monthly* of November 1983 entitled, "Immigration: How It's Affecting Us." Charles Keely's U.S. Immigration Policy Analysis (Population Council, 1979), traces what he terms the "ambivalent" history of American immigration policy through the 1970s. Thomas Kessner and Betty Caroli, in *Today's Immigrants, Their Stories* (Oxford, 1981), offer an array of narratives based on firsthand accounts of both legal and illegal immigrants from various countries. The entire Spring 1982 issue of *Law and Contemporary Problems* is devoted to U.S. immigration policy. It consists of a variety of essays, written from many viewpoints, all of them rich in content.

At the base of the Statue of Liberty is the famous poem by Emma Lazarus: "Give me your tired, your poor, your huddled masses yearning to breathe free . . ." Many nations of the world seem only too happy to oblige. Perhaps in the long run those nations will be poorer, and we will be richer, because of the population transfer. It has happened before. But right now many Americans seem to agree with Senator Alan Simpson's view that America has become "the patsy of the earth." Whether that is a fair assessment remains to be seen.

ISSUE 17
Is Nuclear Deterrence Irrational?

YES: Jonathan Schell, from *The Fate of the Earth* (Knopf, 1982)

NO: Charles Krauthammer, from "The Real Way to Prevent Nuclear War," *The New Republic* (April 28, 1982)

ISSUE SUMMARY

YES: In arguing for an end to the nuclear arms race, Jonathan Schell, staff writer for the *New Yorker*, offers a view of the consequences of nuclear war and its implications for the human race and the earth itself.

NO: Charles Krauthammer, senior editor of the *New Republic*, does not dispute the terror of nuclear war but argues that this very balance of terror is what prevents war from occurring.

Since the destructive powers of the atom were unleashed on the Japanese cities of Hiroshima and Nagasaki in 1945, it has become increasingly apparent that humans now possess weapons that are radically different from any others in history. Previously, the destructive force of weapons—from slings and catapults to high-explosive bombs—could be limited to target populations. One could hit the enemy, then take reasonable measures to limit destruction if the enemy hit back. But that basic feature of warfare has been changed by the advent of nuclear weapons. The moment hydrogen warheads begin exploding on a large scale, it becomes impossible to predict the final outcome. By the same token, it becomes exceedingly difficult to place any limits upon the destruction caused by these weapons. If the Soviet Union and the United States ever become involved in a full-scale nuclear exchange, both countries would suffer such losses that they would probably cease to exist as political entities. Nor is this all: The nuclear winter and the radioactive fallout from such a war would threaten the populations of countries not involved in it and might even threaten the ecological structure of the planet.

In the debate over the doctrine of nuclear deterrence, both sides generally accept the above arguments. The debate is not over whether nuclear war would cause horrible devastation; the debate turns upon the question of how to prevent such a war.

Some writers and activists believe the way to prevent nuclear war is to stop "saber-rattling." They say that American political leaders who insist on talking tough, continuing arms build-ups, and increasing military spending generate an atmosphere of confrontation that makes it difficult to compromise or even negotiate with the Soviets. These activists maintain that the Soviet leaders may be suspicious, crude, and even shrill at times, but they are rational enough to respond to genuine peace initiatives. The proponents of this position point out that the initiatives could take a variety of forms, from the de-escalation of cold war rhetoric to the willingness to forego new weapon production and deployment. If the West, and particularly the United States, could only bring itself to start the process, contend these advocates, there is every prospect that the U.S.S.R. would respond in kind.

Those who defend the doctrine of nuclear deterrence argue that the former position stems from a naive view of the Soviet Union's leadership. Its leadership, they contend, is inherently expansionist and is deterred not by good will but by the threat of counterforce. They maintain that the reason there has been no nuclear war during the forty years of cold war between the Soviet Union and the United States is not in spite of but *because* of America's nuclear arsenal and its willingness to use it. All along the Soviets have known that if they were to commit major aggression against the United States or a close ally, they would risk nuclear retaliation, argue these pro-nuclear advocates. They believe it follows that the real danger of nuclear war stems not from America's nuclear armaments or its resolve but from those whose actions may tempt the Soviets to believe that they can commit aggression with impunity. Any nuclear arms agreement with the Soviets must not jeopardize our nuclear deterrence.

There are replies to the above rebuttal. There are also replies to the replies, and so on. The reader can find many of the competing arguments in the selections that follow. Author Jonathan Schell depicts the kind of nightmare that would follow from a massive nuclear exchange and suggests that the philosophy of MAD (Mutually Assured Destruction) well deserves the acronym. Editor Charles Krauthammer argues that it is precisely the balance of terror that prevents nuclear war from occurring.

YES

Jonathan Schell

THE CHOICE

. . . One way to begin to grasp the destructive power of present-day nuclear weapons is to describe the consequences of the detonation of a one-megaton bomb, which possesses eighty times the explosive power of the Hiroshima bomb, on a large city, such as New York. Burst some eighty-five hundred feet above the Empire State Building, a one-megaton bomb would gut or flatten almost every building between Battery Park and 125th Street, or within a radius of four and four-tenths miles, or in an area of sixty-one square miles, and would heavily damage buildings between the northern tip of Staten Island and the George Washington Bridge, or within a radius of about eight miles, or in an area of about two hundred square miles. A conventional explosive delivers a swift shock, like a slap, to whatever it hits, but the blast wave of a sizable nuclear weapon endures for several seconds and "can surround and destroy whole buildings" (Glasstone). People, of course, would be picked up and hurled away from the blast along with the rest of the debris. Within the sixty-one square miles, the walls, roofs, and floors of any buildings that had not been flattened would be collapsed, and the people and furniture inside would be swept down onto the street. (Technically, this zone would be hit by various overpressures of at least five pounds per square inch. Overpressure is defined as the pressure in excess of normal atmospheric pressure.) As far away as ten miles from ground zero, pieces of glass and other sharp objects would be hurled about by the blast wave at lethal velocities. In Hiroshima, where buildings were low and, outside the center of the city, were often constructed of light materials, injuries from falling buildings were often minor. But in New York, where the buildings are tall and are constructed of heavy materials, the physical collapse of the city would certainly kill millions of people. The streets of New York are narrow ravines running between the high walls of the city's buildings. In a nuclear attack, the walls would fall and the ravines would fill up. The people in the buildings would fall to the street with the debris of the buildings, and the people in the street would be crushed by this avalanche of people and buildings. At a distance of two miles or so from ground zero, winds would reach four hundred miles an hour, and another two miles away they would reach a hundred and eighty miles an hour. Meanwhile, the fireball would be growing, until it was more than a mile wide, and rocketing upward, to a height of over six miles. For ten seconds, it would broil the city below. Anyone caught in the open within nine miles of ground zero would receive third-degree burns and would probably be killed; closer to the explosion, people would be charred and killed instantly. From Greenwich Village up to Central Park, the heat would be great enough to melt metal and glass. Readily inflammable materials, such as newspapers and dry leaves, would ignite in all five boroughs (though in only a small part of Staten Island) and west to the Passaic River, in New Jersey, within a radius of about nine and a half miles from ground zero, thereby creating an area of more than two hundred and eighty square miles in which mass fires were likely to break out.

If it were possible (as it would not be) for someone to stand at Fifth Avenue and Seventy-second Street (about two miles from ground zero) without being instantly killed, he would see the following sequence of events. A dazzling white light from the fireball would illumine the scene, continuing for perhaps thirty seconds. Simultaneously, searing heat would ignite everything flammable and start to melt windows, cars, buses, lampposts, and everything else made of metal or glass. People in the street would immediately catch fire, and would shortly be reduced to heavily charred corpses. About five seconds after the light appeared, the blast wave would strike, laden with the debris of a now nonexistent midtown. Some buildings might be crushed, as though a giant fist had squeezed them on all sides, and others might be picked up off their foundations and whirled uptown with the other debris. On the far side of Central Park, the West Side skyline would fall from south to north. The four-hundred-mile-an-hour wind would blow from south to north, die down after a few seconds, and then blow in the reverse direction with diminished intensity. While these things were happening, the fireball would be burning in the sky for the ten seconds of the thermal pulse. Soon huge, thick clouds of dust and smoke would envelop the scene, and as the mushroom cloud rushed overhead (it would have a diameter of about twelve miles) the light from the sun would be blotted out, and day would turn to night. Within minutes, fires, ignited both by the thermal pulse and by broken gas mains, tanks of gas and oil, and the like, would begin to spread in the darkness, and a strong, steady wind would begin to blow in the direction of the blast. As at Hiroshima, a whirlwind might be produced, which would sweep through the ruins and radioactive rain, generated under the meteorological conditions created by the blast, might fall. Before long, the individual fires would coalesce into a mass fire, which, depending largely on the winds, would become either a conflagration or a firestorm. In a conflagration, prevailing winds spread a wall of fire as far as there is any combustible material to sustain it; in a firestorm, a vertical updraft caused by the fire itself sucks the surrounding air in toward a central point, and the fires therefore converge in a single fire of extreme heat. A mass fire of either kind renders shelters useless by burning up all the oxygen in the air and creating toxic gases, so that anyone inside the shelters is asphyxiated, and also by heating the ground to such high temperatures that the shelters turn, in effect, into ovens, cremating the people inside them. In Dresden, several days after the firestorm raised there by Allied conventional bombing,the interiors of some bomb shelters were still so hot that when they were opened the inrushing air caused the contents to burst into flame. Only those who had fled their shelters when the bombing started had any chance of surviving. (It is difficult to predict in a particular situation which form the fires will take. In actual experience, Hiroshima suffered a firestorm and Nagasaki suffered a conflagration.)

In this vast theatre of physical effects, all the scenes of agony and death that took place at Hiroshima would again take place, but now involving millions of people rather than hundreds of thousands. Like the people of Hiroshima, the people of New York would be burned, battered, crushed, and irradiated in every conceivable way. The city and its people would be mingled in a smoldering heap. And then, as the fires started, the survivors (most of whom would be on the periphery of the explosion) would be driven to abandon to the flames those family members and other people who were unable to flee, or else to die with them. Before long, while the ruins burned, the processions of injured, mute people would begin their slow progress out of the outskirts of the devastated zone. However, this time a much smaller proportion of the population than at Hiroshima would have a chance of escaping. In general, as the size of the area of devastation increases, the possibilities for escape decrease. When the devastated area is relatively small, as it was at Hiroshima, people who are not incapacitated will have a good chance of escaping to safety before the fires coalesce into a mass fire. But when the devastated area is great, as it would be after the detonation of a megaton bomb, and fires are springing up at a distance of nine and a half miles from ground zero, and when what used to be the streets are piled high with burning rubble, and the day (if the attack occurs in the daytime) has grown impenetrably dark, there is little chance that anyone who is not on the very edge of the devastated area will be able to make his way to safety. In New York, most people would die wherever the blast found them, or not very far from there.

If instead of being burst in the air the bomb were burst on or near the ground in the vicinity of the Empire State Building, the overpressure would be very much greater near the center of the blast area but the range hit by a minimum of five pounds per square inch of overpressure would be less. The range of the thermal pulse would be about the same as that of the air burst. The fireball would be almost two miles across, and would engulf midtown Manhattan from Greenwich Village nearly to Central Park. Very little is known about what would happen to a city that was inside a fireball, but one would expect a good deal of what was there to be first pulverized and then melted or vaporized. Any human beings in the area would be reduced to smoke and ashes; they would simply disappear. A crater roughly three blocks in diameter and two hundred feet deep would open up. In addition, heavy radioactive fallout would be created as dust and debris from the city rose with the mushroom cloud and then fell back to the ground. Fallout would begin to drop almost immediately, contaminating the ground beneath the cloud with levels of radiation many times lethal doses, and quickly killing anyone who might have survived the blast wave and the thermal pulse and might now be attempting an escape; it is difficult to believe that there would be appreciable survival of the people of the city after a megaton ground burst. And for the next twenty-four hours or so more fallout would descend downwind from the blast, in a plume whose direction and length would depend on the speed and the direction of the wind that happened to be blowing at the time of the attack. If the wind was blowing at fifteen miles an hour, fallout of lethal intensity would descend in a plume about a hundred and fifty miles long and as much as fifteen miles wide. Fallout that was sublethal but could still cause serious illness would extend another hundred and fifty miles downwind. Exposure to radioactivity in human beings is measured in units called rems—an acronym for "roentgen equivalent in man." The roentgen is a standard measurement of gamma- and X-ray radiation, and the expression "equivalent in man" indicates that an adjustment has been made to take into account the differences in the degree of biological damage that is caused by radiation of different types. Many of the kinds of harm done to human beings by radiation—for example, the incidence of cancer and of genetic damage—depend on the dose accumulated over many years; but radiation sickness, capable of causing death, results from an "acute" dose, received in a period of anything from a few seconds to several days. Because almost ninety per cent of the so-called "infinite-time dose" of radiation from fallout—that is, the dose from a given quantity of fallout that one would receive if one lived for many thousands of years—is emitted in the first week, the one-week accumulated dose is often used as a convenient measure for calculating the immediate harm from fallout. Doses in the thousands of rems, which could be expected throughout the city, would attack the central nervous system and would bring about death within a few hours. Doses of around a thousand rems, which would be delivered some tens of miles downwind from the blast, would kill within two weeks everyone who was exposed to them. Doses of around five hundred rems, which would be delivered as far as a hundred and fifty miles downwind (given a wind speed of fifteen miles per hour), would kill half of all exposed able-bodied young adults. At this level of exposure, radiation sickness proceeds in the three stages observed at Hiroshima. The plume of lethal fallout could descend, depending on the direction of the wind, on other parts of New York State and parts of New Jersey, Pennsylvania, Delaware, Maryland, Connecticut, Massachusetts, Rhode Island, Vermont, and New Hampshire, killing additional millions of people. The circumstances in heavily contaminated areas, in which millions of people were all declining together, over a period of weeks, toward painful deaths, are ones that, like so many of the consequences of nuclear explosions, have never been experienced. . . .

The central proposition of the deterrence doctrine—the piece of logic on which the world theoretically depends to see the sun rise tomorrow—is that a nuclear holocaust can best be prevented if each nuclear power, or bloc of powers, holds in readiness a nuclear force with which it "credibly" threatens to destroy the entire society of any attacker, even after suffering the worst possible "first strike" that the attacker can launch. Robert McNamara, who served as Secretary of Defense for seven years under Presidents Kennedy and Johnson, defined the policy, in his book *The Essence of Security*, published in 1968, in the following terms: "Assured destruction is the very essence of the whole deterrence concept. We must possess an actual assured-destruction capability, and that capability also must be credible. The point is that a potential aggressor must believe that our assured-destruction capability is in fact actual, and that our will to use it in retaliation to an attack is in fact unwavering." Thus, deterrence "means the certainty of suicide to the aggressor, not merely to his military forces, but to his society as a whole." Let us picture what is going on here. There are two possible eventualities: success of the strategy or its failure. If it succeeds, both sides are frozen into inaction by fear of retaliation by the other side. If it fails, one side annihilates the other, and then the leaders of the second side annihilate the "society as a whole" of the attacker, and the earth as a whole suffers the consequences of a full-scale holocaust, which might include the extinction of man. In point of fact, neither the United States nor the Soviet Union has ever adopted the "mutual-assured-destruction" doctrine in pure form; other aims, such as attempting to reduce the damage of the adversary's nuclear attack and increasing the capacity for destroying the nuclear forces of the adversary, have been mixed in. Nevertheless, underlying these deviations the concept of deterring a first strike by preserving the capacity for a devastating second strike has remained constant. The strategists of deterrence have addressed the chief issue in any sane policy in a nuclear-armed world—the issue of survival—and have come up with this answer: Salvation from extinction by nuclear weapons is to be found in the nuclear weapons themselves. The possession of nuclear weapons by the great powers, it is believed, will prevent the use of nuclear weapons by those same powers. Or, to put it more accurately, the threat of their use by those powers will prevent their use. Or, in the words of Bernard Brodie, a pioneer in nuclear strategy, in *The Absolute Weapon: Atomic Power and World Order*, a book published in 1946: "Thus far, the chief purpose of our military establishment has been to win wars. From now on its chief purpose must be to avert them. It can have almost no other useful purpose." Or, in the classic, broad formulation of Winston Churchill, in a speech to the House of Commons in 1955: "Safety will be the sturdy child of terror, and survival the twin brother of annihilation."

This doctrine, in its detailed as well as its more general formulations, is diagrammatic of the world's failure to come to terms with the nuclear predicament. In it, two irreconcilable purposes clash. The first purpose is to permit the survival of the species, and this is expressed in the doctrine's aim of frightening everybody into holding back from using nuclear weapons at all; the second purpose is to serve national ends, and this is expressed in the doctrine's permitting the defense of one's nation and its interests by threatening to use nuclear weapons. The strategists are pleased to call this clash of two opposing purposes in one doctrine a paradox, but in actuality it is a contradiction. We cannot both threaten ourselves with something and hope to avoid that same thing by making the threat—both intend to do something and intend not to do it. the head-on contradiction between these aims has set up a crosscurrent of tension within the policies of each superpower. The "safety" that Churchill mentions may be emphasized at one moment, and at the next moment it is the "terror" that comes to the fore. And since the deterrence doctrine pairs the safety and the terror, and makes the former depend on the latter, the world is never quite sure from day to day which one is in the ascendant—if, indeed the distinction can be maintained in the first place. All that the world can know for certain is that at any moment the fireballs may arrive. I have said that we do not have two earths, one to blow up experimentally and the other to live on; nor do we have two souls, one for reacting to daily life and the other for reacting to the peril to all life. But neither do we have two wills, one with which we can intend to destroy our species and the other with which we can intend to save ourselves. Ultimately, we must all live together with one soul and one will on our one earth.

. . . The policy of deterrence does not contemplate doing anything in defense of the homeland; it only promises that if the homeland is annihilated the aggressor's homeland will be annihilated, too. In fact, the policy goes further than this: it positively requires that each side leave its population open to attack, and make no serious effort to protect it. This requirement follows from the basic logic of deterrence, which is that safety is "the sturdy child of terror." According to this logic, the safety can be only as great as the terror is, and the terror therefore has to be kept relentless. If it were to be diminished—by, for example, building bomb shelters that protected some significant part of the population—then safety would be diminished, too, because the protected side might be

tempted to launch a holocaust, in the belief that it could "win" the hostilities. That is why in nuclear strategy "destruction" must, perversely, be "assured," as though our aim were to destroy, and not to save, mankind.

In strategic terms, the requirement that the terror be perfected, and never allowed to deteriorate toward safety, translates into the requirement that the retaliatory force of both sides be guaranteed—first, by making sure that the retaliatory weapons cannot be destroyed in a first strike, and, second, by making sure that the society of the attacking power *can* be destroyed in the second strike. And since in this upside-down scheme of things the two sides will suffer equally no matter which one opens the hostilities, each side actually has an interest in maintaining its adversary's retaliatory forces as well as its own. For the most dangerous of all the configurations of forces is that in which one side appears to have the ability to destroy the nuclear forces of the other in a first strike. Then not only is the stronger side theoretically tempted to launch hostilities but—what is probably far more dangerous—the other side, fearful of completely losing its forces, might, in a crisis, feel compelled to launch the first strike itself. If on either side the population becomes relatively safe from attack or the retaliatory strike becomes vulnerable to attack, the temptation to launch a first strike is created, and "stability"—the leading virtue of any nuclear balance of power—is lost. As Thomas Schelling, the economist and noted nuclear theorist, has put it, in *The Strategy of Conflict*, a book published in 1960, once instability is introduced on either side, both sides may reason as follows: "He, thinking I was about to kill him in self-defense, was about to kill me in self-defense, so I had to kill him in self-defense." Under deterrence, military "superiority" is therefore as dangerous to the side that possesses it as it is to the side that is supposedly threatened by it. (According to this logic, the United States should have heaved a sigh of relief when the Soviet Union reached nuclear parity with it, for then stability was achieved.) All these conclusions follow from the deterrence doctrine, yet they run so consistently counter to the far simpler, more familiar, and emotionally comprehensible logic of traditional military thinking—not to mention instinct and plain common sense, which rebel against any such notion as "assuring" our own annihilation—that we should not be surprised when we find that the deterrence doctrine is constantly under challenge from traditional doctrine, no matter how glaringly at odds with the facts traditional doctrine may be. The hard-won gains of deterrence, such as they are, are repeatedly threatened by a recrudescence of the old desire for victory, for national defense in the old sense, and for military superiority, even though every one of these goals not only would add nothing to our security but, if it should be pursued far enough, would undermine the precarious safety that the deterrence doctrine tries to provide.

If the virtue of the deterrence policy lies in its acceptance of the basic fact of life in the nuclear world—that a holocaust will bring annihilation to both sides, and possibly the extinction of man as well—its defect lies in the strategic construct that it erects on the foundation of that fact. For if we try to guarantee our safety by threatening ourselves with doom, then we have to mean the threat; but if we mean it, then we are actually planning to do, in some circumstance or

other, that which we categorically must never do and are supposedly trying to prevent—namely, extinguish ourselves. This is the circularity at the core of the nuclear-deterrence doctrine; we seek to avoid our self-extinction by threatening to perform the act. According to this logic, it is almost as though if we stopped threatening ourselves with extinction, then extinction would occur. . . .

Yet the deterrence policy in itself is clearly not the deepest source of our difficulty. Rather, as we have seen, it is only a piece of repair work on the immeasurably more deeply entrenched system of national sovereignty. People do not want deterrence for its own sake; indeed, they hardly know what it is, and tend to shun the whole subject. They want the national sovereignty that deterrence promises to preserve. National sovereignty lies at the very core of the political issues that the peril of extinction forces upon us. Sovereignty is the "reality" that the "realists" counsel us to accept as inevitable, referring to any alternative as "unrealistic" or "utopian." If the argument about nuclear weapons is to be conducted in good faith, then just as those who favor the deterrence policy (not to speak of traditional military doctrine) must in all honesty admit that their scheme contemplates the extinction of man in the name of protecting national sovereignty, so must those who favor complete nuclear and conventional disarmament, as I do, admit that their recommendation is inconsistent with national sovereignty; to pretend otherwise would be to evade the political question that is central to the nuclear predicament. The terms of the deal that the world has now struck with itself must be made clear. On the one side stand human life and the terrestrial creation. On the other side stands a particular organization of human life—the system of independent, sovereign nation-states. Our choice so far has been to preserve that political organization of human life at the cost of risking all human life. . . . But must we embrace nihilism? Is there nothing we can do? I do not believe so. Indeed, if we admit the reality of the basic terms of the nuclear predicament—that present levels of global armament are great enough to possibly extinguish the species if a holocaust should occur; that in extinction every human purpose would be lost; that because once the species has been extinguished there will be no second chance, and the game will be over for all time; that therefore this possibility must be dealt with morally and politically as though it were a certainty; and that either by accident or by design a holocaust can occur at any second—then, whatever political views we may hold on other matters, we are driven almost inescapably to take action to rid the world of nuclear arms. Just as we have chosen to live in the system of sovereign states, we can choose to live in some other system. To do so would, of course, be unprecedented, and in many ways frightening, even truly perilous, but it is by no means impossible. Our present system and the institutions that make it up are the debris of history. They have become inimical to life, and must be swept away. They constitute a noose around the neck of mankind, threatening to choke off the human future, but we can cut the noose and break free. To suppose otherwise would be to set up a false, fictitious fate, molded out of our own weaknesses and our own alterable decisions. We are indeed fated by our acquisition of the basic knowledge of physics to live for the rest of time with the knowledge of how to destroy ourselves. But we are not for that reason fated to destroy ourselves. We can choose to live. . . .

In supposing for a moment that the world had found a political means of making international decisions, I made a very large supposition indeed—one that encompasses something close to the whole work of resolving the nuclear predicament, for, once a political solution has been found, disarmament becomes a merely technical matter, which should present no special difficulties. And yet simply to recognize that the task is at bottom political, and that only a political solution can prepare the way for full disarmament and real safety for the species, is in itself important. The recognition calls attention to the fact that disarmament in isolation from political change cannot proceed very far. It alerts us to the fact that when someone proposes, as President Carter did in his Inaugural Address, to aim at ridding the world of nuclear weapons, there is an immense obstacle that has to be faced and surmounted. For the world, in freeing itself of one burden, the peril of extinction, must inevitably shoulder another: it must assume fully responsibility for settling human differences peacefully. Moreover, this recognition forces us to acknowledge that nuclear disarmament cannot occur if conventional arms are left in place, since as long as nations defend themselves with arms of any kind they will be fully sovereign, and as long as they are fully sovereign they will be at liberty to build nuclear weapons if they so choose. And if we assume that wars do break out and some nations find themselves facing defeat in the conventional arena, then the reappearance of nuclear arms, which would prevent such defeat, becomes a strong likelihood.

What nation, once having entrusted its fortunes to the force of arms, would permit itself to be conquered by an enemy when the means of driving him back, perhaps with a mere threat, was on hand? And how safe can the world be while nations threaten one another's existence with violence and retain for themselves the sovereign right to build whatever weapons they choose to build? This vision of an international life that in the military sphere is restricted to the pre-nuclear world is, in fact, thoroughly implausible. If we are serious about nuclear disarmament—the minimum technical requirement for real safety from extinction—then we must accept conventional disarmament as well, and this means disarmament not just of nuclear powers but of all powers, for the present nuclear powers are hardly likely to throw away their conventional arms while nonnuclear powers hold on to theirs. But if we accept both nuclear and conventional disarmament, then we are speaking of revolutionizing the politics of the earth. The goals of the political revolution are defined by those of the nuclear revolution. We must lay down our arms, relinquish sovereignty, and found a political system for the peaceful settlement of international disputes.

The tasks we face is to find a means of political action that will permit human beings to pursue any end for the rest of time. We are asked to replace the mechanism by which political decisions, whatever they may be, are reached. In sum, the task is nothing less than to reinvent politics: to reinvent the world. However, extinction will not wait for us to reinvent the world. . . .

Two paths lie before us. One leads to death, the other to life. If we choose the first path—if we numbly refuse to acknowledge the nearness of extinction, all the while increasing our preparations to bring it about—then we in effect become the allies of death, and in everything we do our attachment to life will weaken; our vision, blinded to the abyss that has opened at our feet, will dim and grow confused; our will, discouraged by the thought of trying to build on such a precarious foundation anything that is meant to last, will slacken; and we will sink into stupefaction, as though we were gradually weaning ourselves from life in preparation for the end. On the other hand, if we reject our doom, and bend our efforts toward survival—if we arouse ourselves to the peril and act to forestall it, making ourselves the allies of life—then the anesthetic fog will lift: our vision, no longer straining not to see the obvious, will sharpen; our will, finding secure ground to build on, will be restored; and we will take full and clear possession of life again. One day—and it is hard to believe that it will not be soon—we will make our choice. Either we will sink into the final coma and end it all or, as I trust and believe, we will awaken to the truth of our peril, a truth as great as life itself, and, like a person who has swallowed a lethal poison but shakes off his stupor at the last moment and vomits the poison up, we will break through the layers of our denials, put aside our faint-hearted excuses, and rise up to cleanse the earth of nuclear weapons.

NO

Charles Krauthammer

HOW TO PREVENT NUCLEAR WAR

"Safety will be the sturdy child of terror, and survival the twin brother of annihilation." That was Winston Churchill's description of what he called "the balance of terror." Each superpower has the ability to incinerate the defenseless population of the other many times over, each refrains from attacking because it fears retaliation in kind; each knows that aggression is tantamount to suicide. That is deterrence. Sometimes deterrence is called MAD, mutual assured destruction. By whatever name, deterrence has prevented the outbreak of nuclear war, indeed any war, between the United States and the Soviet Union for a generation.

Living in a world of deterrence is very uncomfortable. Every American and Soviet city dweller knows that he is targeted for destruction by nuclear weapons five thousand miles away. But the physical danger is only part of the problem. The world of deterrence is a world of paradoxes. Weapons are built in order never to be used. Weapons purely for defense of helpless populations, like the antiballistic missile systems, become the greatest threat to peace. Weapons aimed at people lessen the risk of war; weapons aimed at weapons, increase it.

The strains of living in such a world are enormous. A vast antinuclear movement is now rising in the U.S., animated principally by weariness and revulsion with this arrangement. Why now? Ronald Reagan is much of the answer. He helped defeat the SALT II treaty before his election, and has been reluctant to engage the Soviets in strategic arms talks since. For the first time in more than a decade, the U.S. and the Soviet Union are not engaged in negotiations to control strategic nuclear weapons. Worse, Mr. Reagan and some of his advisers have spoken in frighteningly offhand ways about "limited nuclear war" and nuclear warning shots. The Carter Administration's mobile MX plan played a part, too. It appeared such an enormously cumbersome and expensive contrivance that people began to wonder if the experts had not lost touch with reality. So millions of Americans have decided it is time for them to take the problem into their own hands, and an antinuclear grass-roots crusade has emerged.

Like all crusades, it has its bible: Jonathan Schell's just published *The Fate of the Earth* and its banner: "the freeze." Recently it even acquired an auxiliary brigade, four members of the American foreign policy establishment who opened a wholly new front by calling for a U.S. renunciation of any first use of nuclear weapons. The bible, the banner, and the brigade approach the nuclear dilemma from different directions, but they all challenge the established doctrines of deterrence. The brigade wants to limit deterrence; the freeze proponents want to ignore it; and Jonathan Schell wants to abolish it. Each deserves the closest scrutiny.

Jonathan Schell flatly rejects deterrence. That is the source of his originality. Otherwise his three-part thesis is unremarkable. Part I restates, albeit elegantly, the awful details of a nuclear holocaust, and concludes it would lead to the extinction of the human race. (That is the view of some scientists, though not of the National Academy of Sciences' study which Schell used in reaching many of his conclusions.) Part II, an interminable rumination of the meaning of human extinction, comes to the unsurprising conclusion that extinction would be monstrous.

"From the foregoing it follows," Schell writes, after delivering his message in a reiterative style that constitutes its own kind of overkill, "that there can be no justification for extinguishing mankind." The real interest in Schell's book lies in Part III, "The Choice." Here he argues that traditional approaches to nuclear peril, like strategic arms limitation treaties, are mere gestures, aspirin given to a dying patient. He argues that deterrence is a logical fraud because the leaders of a country that had sustained a first strike would have no reason to retaliate, indeed, no country in whose name to retaliate.

What Schell refuses to acknowledge is that any potential aggressor would be deterred—and for over thirty years has been deterred—from striking first because he must anticipate not only the logical responses of the victim, but all possible human responses. Revenge, for example, is one motive to launch a second strike. Paul Warnke, President Carter's arms control chief, gives another. He argues that "our moral commitment" would "require that the leaders who had perpetrated this enormity not be allowed to inherit the earth and bend its people to their will." Soviet leaders reading Warnke (a nuclear dove and a supporter of the freeze) are highly unlikely to calculate that a first strike would meet with no response because that would be "illogical." Furthermore, no one knows what would happen in the confused, unimaginably strained atmosphere of a nuclear crisis. To act—to attack—under the assumption that the other side is constrained to follow purely "logical" courses of action is itself totally illogical. It is precisely because of these calculations that nuclear deterrence has succeeded in preventing nuclear war. That is not to say that deterrence can never fail, but the argument from history is a powerful one. An even more powerful one is the absence of an alternative.

Not that Schell shies away from providing one: a world graced by total disarmament (nuclear and conventional), the abolition of violence, the eradication of national boundaries, the renunciation of sovereignty, and the founding of a new world political order for the peaceful settlement of international disputes. How does he propose to bring this about? That is a detail he could not work into his 231-page treatise. That "awesome, urgent task," he graciously concedes, "I have left to others."

Although he does not explain how we are to bring about a lion-and-lamb scenario which even Isaiah had the audacity only to predict and not to mandate, he does give us a clue as to what the operating principle of his post-messianic world will be. Here we come directly to the critical center of Schell's thinking, to the force that not only underlies his passion today but will save mankind tomorrow—fear. In his world, Schell writes, "Fear would no longer dictate particular decisions, such as whether or not the Soviet Union might place missiles in Cuba; rather, it would be a moving force behind the establishment of a new system by which every decision was made. And, having dictated the foundation of the system, it would stand guard over it forever after, guaranteeing that the species did not slide back toward anarchy and doom." I have my doubts.

Fear is not just the saving principle of Schell's new world order; it is the animating force behind a new mass movement—the freeze campaign. The movement demands a mutual halt in the development, production, and deployment of all nuclear weapons, "because," as the campaign slogan puts it, "no one wants a nuclear war." Like Schell, freeze proponents are deeply concerned, and rightly so, about the prospect of living in a world in which we have the capacity to blow ourselves to bits at any moment. The freeze crusade has enlisted hundreds of thousands of Americans by showing what happens if the Sword of Damocles ever drops. Thus the graphic stills of Hiroshima victims and the maps with concentric circles radiating from ground zero in everyone's hometown. Schell recognizes that removing this sword requires renunciation not just of overkill, but of minimal deterrence, of the simple capacity to destroy the other side *once*. But very few freeze proponents advocate reducing levels below "suffi-

ciency," because they recognize that in a pre-messianic world this would destabilize the nuclear balance and increase the chances of war. Under a freeze—indeed, under even the most radical of arms proposals, such as former Ambassador George Kennan's proposal to cut nuclear levels in half—the superpowers would still retain the capacity for the total destruction of the other society. Insofar as people support the freeze because they can't stand the thought of being a target of Soviet missiles, they have joined the wrong movement. The freeze offers no solution to that problem. They should be with Jonathan Schell's total disarmament movement, working on the "awesome, urgent task" of remaking human nature.

Some might argue that there is another way, short of universal brotherhood, to remove the Sword of Damocles. That is unilateral disarmament. But quite apart from the fact that such a move would mean the surrender of our values, it would do little to secure our survival. The historical record does not support the proposition that helplessness is a guarantee of safety. There has been one nuclear war on record; in it a nonnuclear Japan lost Hiroshima and Nagasaki. So far there has been only one biological war, the one going on today in Laos and Cambodia. These weapons, now used against helpless tribesmen, were never used against American troops fighting the same Vietnamese forces in the same place. The Hmong, unlike the Americans, lack the capacity to retaliate in kind.

The freeze is not unilateralist, nor do many of its advocates reject deterrence. They say they reject overkill. "Enough is enough," they say. "Why waste billions on useless weapons if all they will do, as Churchill said, is to make the rubble bounce?" (It is sometimes also argued, somewhat anomalously, that having useless, rubble-bouncing weapons is at the same time dangerous.)

The problem is that in their zeal to curb overkill, freeze advocates ignore the requirements of deterrence and, in particular, the requirement for survivability of the deterrent. Our weapons must be able to withstand a first strike and penetrate Soviet defenses in a retaliatory strike (and vice versa). If either side finds the survivability of its weapons systems declining, the world becomes less safe. In an international crisis, each side, particularly the more vulnerable side, has incentive to strike first: the invulnerable side to use its advantage, the vulnerable side to strike before it is too late.

What would happen under a freeze? The U.S. retaliatory capacity depends on the three legs of its strategic triad: the land-based ICBMs, the bomber force, and submarines. Because of the increasing accuracy, power, and numbers of Soviet missiles, the U.S. land-based missile force will soon become vulnerable to a first strike. (It is precisely to eliminate that vulnerability that President Carter proposed hiding the MX in multiple shelters, a scheme now abandoned.) That leaves the bomber and submarine forces. The bomber force consists of aging B-52s that are increasingly vulnerable to attack while still on the ground, and to being shot down while trying to penetrate Soviet air space. Hence President Carter's decision to deploy air-launched cruise missiles, which would be better able to penetrate Soviet defenses and would allow the B-52s to remain outside Soviet air space. The freeze proposal would prevent deployment of these missiles. It would also prevent production and development of a new bomber, either the B-1 or the Stealth, which would be better able to elude destruction on the ground and Soviet defenses in the air. Note that

the B-1 or the Stealth would not be any more destructive than the B-52. They would not make the rubble bounce any higher. They would simply be more likely to get the target, and therefore present the Soviets with a very good reason never to launch a first strike.

That leaves the submarine force, which the U.S. is now in the process of modernizing to make more survivable. The new Tridents are quieter than existing subs, and because they have longer-range missiles they can hide in larger areas of the ocean. The freeze would stop their deployment.

The freeze, a proposal devised for its simplicity, does not deal very well with paradox. It is one of the paradoxes of deterrence that defensive weapons (the ABM, for example) can be more destabilizing and therefore more dangerous to peace than offensive weapons. The freeze fixates on nuclear weapons because they are not necessarily more destabilizing. As former Under Secretary of the Navy James Woolsey points out, the freeze does nothing to prevent nonnuclear antisubmarine and antiaircraft advances, which weaken deterrence. But it does prevent modernization of nuclear systems designed for survivability, which enhances deterrence.

What exactly does it mean to say that if survivability declines, war becomes more likely? One quick fix for a vulnerable deterrent is to adopt a policy of launch-on-warning: as soon as we detect enemy missiles leaving their silos, we launch our missiles before they can be destroyed. (Some officials unsuccessfully urged President Carter to adopt launch-on-warning as an alternative to building the mobile MX.) But this creates a hair-trigger situation, where the time for the world's most important decision is not a matter of minutes but of seconds, too short to check out a faulty radar reading or a misinterpretation of data. That's the price of ignoring the deterrence.

This analysis looks simply at what would happen if the freeze were already a reality. But however fervently American citizens may wish it, they cannot vote a "mutual verifiable freeze" into existence. Unfortunately, that must be negotiated with the Soviets. And bad as a freeze would be as an end point, it would be worse as a U.S. negotiating position—which is exactly what it would be if, say, the Kennedy-Hatfield amendment were adopted. First, it is certain to delay other arms control initiatives. The freeze appeals to American voters because of its simplicity, but a mutual freeze would involve complex negotiations with the Soviets. What exactly would be frozen? At what stage? How would it be verified? The production, stockpiling, and qualitative upgrading of nuclear weapons cannot be detected by satellite, and the Russians have always refused on-site inspection. That problem alone turns the freeze into either a nonstarter or a source of interminable negotiation.

Ironically, there does exist an arms control proposal which, though very complicated, poorly understood by the American people, and unsuited for two-hour ratification by town meetings, is very well understood by the Soviets: SALT II. They have already signed it. If the aim of the freeze movement is a quick, simple, bold move in arms control that would allow us to proceed to real reductions, then the answer is not a freeze, but SALT II. Representative Les Aspin has already pointed out with dismay the American penchant for reinventing the arms control wheel every four years. In 1977 President Carter rejected the Vladivostok Accords negoti-

ated by President Ford and proposed drastic reductions instead. The Soviets rejected his proposal out of hand. It took more than two years to renegotiate SALT II on the original lines of Vladivostok. President Reagan in turn rejected SALT II and called for as yet unspecified START talks. The freeze proponents are doing precisely the same thing. It simply makes no sense to propose a freeze that would require years of negotiations when SALT II is at hand, has already been approved by the Soviets, and could be adjusted in small details and ratified quickly. Of course, SALT is not as catchy a slogan as the freeze. But it is certainly a better, quicker, and more serious path to arms control.

Another aim of the freeze campaign is to move to real reductions. But to arm a U.S. negotiating team with a freeze offer is to ensure that it will have no leverage with which to bargain the Soviets into reductions. We will have unilaterally announced our willingness to forgo all our modernization programs, like the Trident, the cruise missile, and the Stealth bomber. The theory is that this gesture will elicit from the Soviets a more conciliatory negotiating position. The theory is in conflict with history. The Soviets do not have a good record of responding to unilateral gestures. At the Glassboro Summit in 1967, President Johnson tried to interest Premier Kosygin in ABM negotiations. Kosygin demurred. A year later, the Senate defeated an amendment to deny funds for an American ABM system. Three days later Soviet Foreign Minister Andrei Gromyko announced the Soviets' willingness to negotiate arms control. Eventually they agreed to an almost total ban on ABMs. We are using the same strategy today in Geneva, offering systems that we propose to build as bargaining chips. We offer to forgo deployment of the Pershing II and ground-launched cruise missiles in Europe if the Soviets dismantle their SS-20s. Under a freeze, our position in Geneva would collapse and the SS-20s would remain in place. (Brezhnev calls *that* arrangement a freeze.) In strategic arms talks, any attempts on our part to, say, bargain away one of our new systems against the Soviets' destabilizing silo-killing ICMBs would fail.

The freeze is not a plan; it is a sentiment. (Montana's proposed freeze resolution, for example, opposes "the production, development and deployment of nuclear weapons by any nation." It will unfortunately not be binding on President Zia of Pakistan.) The freeze reflects the deeply felt and wholly laudable wish of millions of Americans that something be done to control nuclear weapons. But when taken seriously as a plan, the freeze continually fails on its own terms. It seeks safety, but would jeopardize deterrence; it seeks quick action, but would delay arms control; it seeks real reductions, but removes any leverage we might have to bring them about.

Finally, it mistakes the most likely cause of an outbreak of nuclear war. In its fixation on numbers, the freeze assumes that somehow high weapons levels *in themselves* make war more likely. True, an uncontrolled arms race breeds suspicion between the superpowers and can increase the risk of war, but arms control measures (like SALT I or II) can allow higher levels, and still decrease the risk of building confidence on both sides and letting each know precisely what the other is doing. If nuclear war even comes, it most likely will be not because the weapons fire themselves, but because some national leader, in order to preserve some national interest, orders them fired. When did we come closest to nu-

clear war in the last thirty-six years? In October 1962, when President Kennedy decided to threaten Khrushchev with war unless he obeyed our ultimatum on the Cuban missiles. In 1962 the level of nuclear arms was much lower than it is today. And when was the chance of nuclear war smallest? Probably at the height of detente, during the Appolo-Soyuz love fest, when U.S.-Soviet relations were good, even though each side had the capacity for multiple overkill.

The absolute level of nuclear weapons is only one factor, and a relatively small one at that, in determining the likelihood of nuclear war breaking out. (It is certainly less important than the balance of vulnerabilities on each side, i.e., the stability of deterrence.) The most likely source of nuclear war is from a regional conflict between the superpowers, where one or the other has important interests but finds itself at a conventional disadvantage. That is the American situation today in Europe and in the Persian Gulf. To prevent the Soviets from taking advantage of their superiority in conventional arms, the U.S. has reserved the option of using nuclear weapons to respond to a nonnuclear Soviet attack. This policy of extending nuclear deterrence to conventional conflicts has kept the peace. But it is dangerous. It blurs the line between conventional and nuclear war, and by threatening "limited" nuclear war it opens the door to a nuclear holocaust, since no one knows whether a limited nuclear war can be kept limited. The most effective way to eliminate that danger, and thus eliminate the greatest risk of nuclear war, is to make this kind of extended deterrence unnecessary: to right the conventional balance by radically bolstering allied forces, particularly on the West European frontier. NATO could then deter a conventional attack without having to threaten to wage nuclear war.

One of Schell's dictums is that compared to the peril of a nuclear holocaust, all other human values pale into insignificance, indeed, lose their meaning because they lose their context. If the antinuclear crusaders really believe that, they should be clamoring for increased conventional forces to reduce the European imbalance. They aren't. The reason is that the freeze crusade, which springs from deeply felt antiwar and antiarmament sentiments, is not comfortable with the thought that preventing nuclear way may require a radically enlarged conventional defense. Furthermore, one of the major appeals of the antinuclear movement is the promise to halt the economic drain caused by "useless" nuclear weapons and to redirect resources to human needs. But a shift away from strategic to conventional weapons would be very expensive. Our reliance on nuclear weapons—and the current conventional balance in Europe—results in large part from a desire to *reduce* defense spending. In the 1950s we decided to buy defense in Europe on the cheap. Rather than match the vast armies and tank forces of the Warsaw Pact, we decided to go nuclear, because, as John Foster Dulles put it, it offered "more bang for the buck."

But the European defense balance has become more unstable since Dulles's day. In the 1950s the U.S. threatened "massive retaliation." If the Soviets crossed into Western Europe, we would attack the Russian homeland with a strategic nuclear strike. When the Russians acquired the same capacity against the U.S., that threat lost its credibility. The Kennedy Administration adopted a new policy of "flexible response," a euphemism for a limited nuclear war. Under the new doctrine, the U.S. reserved the right to use

theater nuclear weapons on the battlefield to thwart a conventional Soviet attack. That has been our policy ever since. (Ronald Reagan did not invent it, although he has the habit of throwing it around more casually and publicly than other Presidents.) This doctrine has troubled many Americans, but as long as the U.S. was not prepared to challenge the Soviet conventional superiority in Europe, nor prepared to abandon its European allies, there seemed no other choice.

Enter the auxiliary brigade of the antinuclear movement: four former high Administration officials, two of whom, under President Kennedy, gave us "limited nuclear war" (Robert McNamara and McGeorge Bundy); one of whom gave us "containment" (George Kennan); and one of whom gave us SALT I (Gerard Smith). Two weeks ago they opened an entirely new front in the crusade. They called for the adoption of a "no-first-use" policy on nuclear weapons. It was a renunciation of "flexible response" and of "extended deterrence." (They would retain extended deterrence in one restricted sense: as a retaliation for a Soviet *nuclear* attack on Western Europe, an unlikely possibility since the Soviets are prepared to renounce first use, and since with their conventional advantage they have no reason to attack with nuclear weapons.)

The problem with folding our nuclear umbrella, as the four wise men themselves acknowledged, is that, unaccompanied by conventional rearmament, it means the end of the Western alliance and the abandonment in particular of West Germany to Soviet intimidation and blackmail. The other problem with a no-first-use policy is that it might paradoxically increase the chances of nuclear war. Today a war between the U.S. and

312 / 17. IS NUCLEAR DETERRENCE IRRATIONAL?

the Soviets is deterred at its origin: since even the slightest conventional conflict between them carries the threat of escalating into a nuclear one, neither happens. The no-first-use policy moves the "firebreak" from the line dividing war from peace to the line dividing conventional war from nuclear war. It trades the increased chance of conventional war (because now less dangerous and more "thinkable") for a decreased chance of such a war becoming nuclear. But no one can guarantee that *in extremis*, faced with a massive Soviet invasion of Western Europe, the U.S. would stick to its no-first-use pledge. Thus, by making a European war thinkable, this policy could, whatever its intentions, lead to a nuclear war.

Unless, that is, we have the conventional forces to preserve the original firebreak between war and peace. Thus, to prevent both political and (possibly) nuclear calamity, a no-first-use pledge must be accompanied, indeed preceded, by a serious conventional build-up of Western forces on the European frontier. The problem with McNamara et al. is that although they acknowledge this need, they treat it very casually—certainly with nothing like the urgency with which they call for abandoning extended deterrence. They speak only vaguely of the need for "review" and "study" of conventional military needs, of whether the political will exists in the West for such a build-up, and of "whether we Americans have a durable and effective answer to our military manpower needs in the present all-volunteer active and reserve forces" (they cannot quite bring themselves to say the word "draft"). Their eagerness to be the first off the blocks with a no-first-use policy is obvious. Their reluctance to urge on their antinuclear allies the only responsible and

safe (and costly) means of achieving it is lamentable. The result of their highly publicized, grossly unbalanced proposal is predictable: another support in the complex and highly vulnerable structure of deterrence has been weakened. The world will be no safer for it.

Despite the prophesies of Schell, the pandering of the freeze-riding politicians, and the posturing of the four wise men—and the good intentions of millions of concerned Americans caught up in the antinuclear maelstrom—there is no need to reinvent nuclear policy. There *is a* need for arms control: SALT II is the best transition to real reductions. There *is a* need to avoid limited nuclear war: rebuilding our conventional strength and perhaps reintroducing the draft would reduce that risk. These proposals are neither new nor exciting. Unlike Schell's crusade, they don't promise to restore "the wholeness and meaning of life." They don't suggest that "the passion and will that we need to save ourselves would flood into our lives. Then the walls of indifference, inertia, and coldness that now isolate each of us from others, and all of us from the past and future generations, would melt, like snow in the spring." They don't promise to set right "our disordered instinctual life." That is because working to reduce the chances of nuclear war is not an exercise in psychotherapy. It is not a romance. It is mundane work in pursuit of mundane objectives: a modest program of nuclear modernization, SALT II, and a bigger conventional defense. These measures will not cure anomie, but will help to maintain deterrence, that difficult abstraction on which our values and our safety depend.

POSTSCRIPT

Is Nuclear Deterrence Irrational?

Both sides agree that nuclear deterrence is undesirable. The debate is over the feasibility and desirability of the alternatives to nuclear deterrence. The alternatives to nuclear deterrence, according to Krauthammer, are either a massive build up of U.S. conventional weapons or Soviet influence over large portions of the earth. The alternative for Schell is for nations to relinquish national sovereignty and to build an international system for the peaceful settlement of international disputes. In Schell's later book, *The Abolition* (Knopf, 1984) he loses hope in the feasibility of a world government to enforce a ban on nuclear weapons. Nevertheless, he preaches the abolition of all nuclear weapons on the basis that it clearly is in everyone's best interest. The organization, Ground Zero, also advocates the abolition of nuclear weapons in *Nuclear War: What's in It for You?* (Pocket Books, 1982), and so does Solly Zuckerman in *Nuclear Illusion and Reality* (Viking, 1982). On the other side, the Harvard Nuclear Study Group's *Living with Nuclear Weapons* (Harvard University Press, 1983) argues that disarmament does not eliminate the causes of war or even the means to wage it. American nuclear policy of deterrence is vigorously defended in Norman Podhoretz's *The Present Danger* (Simon and Schuster, 1980) and General Maxwell Taylor's *Precarious Security* (Norton, 1976).

In recent years, some writers have argued that technology may provide the alternative. If we develop devices in outer space to destroy incoming Soviet missiles, then we would not need to rely on the strategy of massive deterrence. The proponents of this concept call it the "high frontier" strategy. Its early stages, they say, could be put in place with existing technology in a few years, though its final form would require more research and development. President Ronald Reagan alluded to this high frontier strategy in 1983, in an address that the press dubbed his "Star Wars speech." The critics of high frontier suggest that it would be exorbitantly expensive, would escalate the arms race, and probably would not work. Nevertheless, the idea may be worth exploring, if only because it offers an alternative to the either-or dilemma with which we now seem to be faced. The definitive presentation of the high frontier strategy is by General Daniel Graham, former Deputy Director of the CIA, in *High Frontier: A Strategy for National Survival* (Tom Doherty Associates, 1983).

PART 7

The Future: Population/ Environment/Society

Because we have been able to overcome the limitations of our natural environment through technology, we are now witnessing explosive population growth. Is this necessarily a terrible prospect? Are there sufficient resources to allow for human population growth into the future? What will be the social responses to increased pressure for resources? And just what is happening to those resources? These are questions of global concern that affect us individually as well. Closer to home, we ask where America's economy, and thus our current way of life, is headed.

Is the World Threatened by a
  Population Bomb?

Is the Environmnent Improving?

Is America Headed for an Economic
  Bust?

ISSUE 18

Is the World Threatened by a Population Bomb?

YES: Steven Mumford, from "Population Growth and Global Security," *Humanist* (January/February 1981)

NO: Julian L. Simon, from "World Population Growth," *Atlantic Monthly* (August 1981)

ISSUE SUMMARY

YES: Steven Mumford, an expert in population studies, makes his case that population over-growth is the most serious threat to our lives and security.
NO: Economist Julian Simon defends his optimistic view that increased population will make greater opportunities available to future generations.

In 1968 Paul Ehrlich wrote *The Population Bomb* (Ballantine), which stated that overpopulation was the major problem facing mankind and that population had to be controlled or the human race might cause the collapse of the global ecosystem and its own destruction. Since 1968, many voices have joined Ehrlich's, and many have joined the organization that he founded, Zero Population Growth (ZPG). Back in 1970, Ehrlich explained why he thought the death of the world was imminent.

> Because the human population of the planet is about five times too large, and we're managing to support all these people—at today's level of misery—only by spending our capital, burning our fossil fuels, dispersing our mineral resources and turning our fresh water into salt water. We have not only overpopulated but overstretched our environment. We are poisoning the ecological systems of the earth—systems upon which we are ultimately dependent for all of our food, for all of our oxygen and for all of our waste disposal.

Let us review the population growth rates past, present, and future. At about 0 A.D., the world had about one-quarter billion people. It took about 1650 years to double this number to one-half billion and two hundred years to double the world population again to one billion by 1850. The next doubling took only about eighty years, and the last doubling time about forty-five years (from two billion in 1930 to about four billion in 1975). The world population may double again to eight billion some time between 2010 and 2020. It is easy to keep multiplying by twos until one gets to standing-room-only densities, but obviously population must stop growing in the next century or two.

When and at what level will population stop growing? The ZPG advocates say population must stop growing now or we may overshoot the carrying capacity of the earth's ecosystem and cause the death of much of the race. In the 1970 article cited above, Ehrlich stated that the world population should eventually be reduced "to an absolute maximum of 500,000,000." The research team headed by Dennis Meadows, which produced the "Limits to Growth" study on the basis of a complicated world systems model, estimated a population/environment long-term equilibrium at around three billion people. *The Global 2000 Report to the President* (Government Printing Office, 1980) came to roughly the same conclusion as National Academy of Sciences study eleven years earlier: that about ten billion people could live on this earth in a measure of comfort, or else thirty billion could be provided for without ecosystem collapse, but at the barest of subsistence and without freedoms. Herman Kahn sees no reason why fifteen billion could not live on this planet in luxury forever (Herman Kahn et al., *The Next 200 Years*, Morrow, 1976). He predicts, however, that the environmental movement will lead to changes that will level population growth off at ten billion (*World Economic Development*, Morrow, 1979). Robert Katz (*A Giant in the Earth*, 1973) thinks that fifteen billion is too small to get the full benefits of the economic and synergistic effects of high population. He says that one hundred billion is a more ideal population because the additional geniuses, scientists, and engineers would improve the world's science and technology many-fold and life would be on a much higher plane. So what is the ideal population size? Ehrlich says one half billion, and Katz says one hundred billion. Ehrlich looks at the effect of population on the environment; Katz looks at what people contribute to their society.

In the selections that follow, Steven Mumford sounds the alarm on the dangers of current rates of population growth. He is a scientist with the International Fertility Research Program who passionately believes that population growth not only causes famines and migration but also is a very serious threat to national security. Julian Simon, an economic demographer, sets out to deflate the arguments of those who project geometric growth rates into the future and then predict catastrophes. He points to the economic benefits of population growth and couples it with reassurances that population growth will slow down.

YES

Steven Mumford

POPULATION GROWTH AND SECURITY

In the past three decades, a new threat to international and domestic security has emerged: uncontrolled world population movements, compounded by a global natural resource interdependence. If current growth rates continue, the inevitability of widespread social and political instability by the year 2000 makes population growth the most serious threat—a threat more often recognized than acknowledged. . . .

REDEFINING NATIONAL SECURITY

Americans would like to forget that their national security is the foundation for the freedoms and privileges that they cherish. Freedom of political activity, of personal expression, and of the press cannot be realized in the absence of national security. But what do we mean by that?. . . .

It has become increasingly apparent that to the long-standing interest in military affairs and defense policy must be added topics that affect national security in less obvious but increasingly important ways: energy resources, availability of industrial raw materials, the diffusion of military technology, chronic unemployment, and food production. In this rapidly changing environment, one overwhelming factor underlying these issues remains: global population growth.

Two of the most significant changes in history have occurred since 1945. The first is a drastic decrease in worldwide death rates without a concomitant decrease in birth rates. The second is the sharply increased dependence of affluent nations upon the less affluent nations as suppliers of industrial raw materials.

The world added a fourth billion to its population in a mere fifteen years (1960-1975), and from 1976-2000 it will be adding an additional 2.5 billion. To avert catastrophic food shortages, world food production must increase by 43 percent in the next two decades. This will not occur automatically. Many agriculturists believe a 20 percent increase in food production is a more realistic hope—one percent per year. If we have only a 20 percent increase in

From "Population Growth and Global Security," by Steven Mumford, *The Humanist*, January/February 1981. Reprinted by permission.

food production in the next twenty years, we will have a shortfall equal to the total food requirements of one billion people—one third of the world's presently underfed developing world population beyond the existing (1980) shortfall. The International Food Policy Research Institute predicts that even by 1990 the world food deficit will be 120 to 140 million metric tons per year—the total food requirements of 660 to 770 million people calculated using the current Indian average of 400 pounds of grain per capita per year. The realistic possibility that hunger may cause widespread disruption of social organization makes world population growth a serious security issue.

Ninety percent of the world's population growth occurs in the developing world, where growth rates are 2 percent or more per year. It is in the countries of the developing world that the disparity between food production and population growth is the greatest. Hunger-induced social disorganization will cause some nations to lose their domestic stability and internal cohesion. As the security of a nation slips away, surrounding nations will have to be concerned not only with their own diminishing per capita food production but also with the migration of hungry people from neighboring countries. Alternatively, a weakened social fabric may easily result in incremental decreases in food supplies. A catastrophic spiral is thereby set in motion.

Witness Cambodia. Initially, the Pol Pot government deliberately took steps to destroy the existing social organization. Fewer crops were planted, harvested, and distributed; the result was great hunger. Continuing civil strife further reduced food production, and hunger became more widespread. Then, hunger itself hastened social disorganiz-

ation; both contributed to increased civil strife and damaged the infrastructure of the agricultural system. With each growing season, fewer and fewer crops were planted and hunger increased. Seed stocks were eaten, and fuel needed for food production became less available; draft animals and breeding stocks were slaughtered. By 1979 only a small portion of the food produced just five years earlier was harvested. Social organization has been completely shattered. The millions of deaths due to starvation and the large number of violent deaths are direct results of the destruction of social organization. Hunger did not initiate the devastation in Cambodia, but it has obviously exacerbated its impact. . . .

ACKNOWLEDGING THE PROBLEM: AMERICAN LEADERSHIP

An acknowledgement that world population growth is a serious threat to the security of all nations, including the United States, is essential if the population problem is to be dealt with successfully. Massive assistance in a population control effort should not be at the expense of the people of the developing world; rather, it is in everybody's self interest to achieve mutual benefits.

Norman Borlaug, father of the green revolution, never looked to his revolution as the solution to the food problem. Rather, he felt that it would buy perhaps an additional fifteen or twenty years, during which the brakes could be applied to population growth. The year 1968 marked the beginning of his revolution. Twelve of those years have now passed, and we have essentially wasted this purchase. In fact, the total impact of the deliberate attempts of governments, excluding China, to achieve population growth control has postponed the scenario described above for only a matter of months. To gain twelve months, population growth control efforts would have to prevent eighty million births—a number that has taken us more than ten years to achieve. Obviously, the present approach is just not working.

Reason dictates that we not attempt to manage this problem with less than an adequate commitment, and only after world population growth is acknowledged by the United States and other countries to be a serious security threat will adequate allocations be forthcoming and a solution attainable. The United States made the political, moral, and economic commitment to win World War II. Today, it allocates more than one-fourth of its defense budget each year specifically to counter the Russian threat. Arresting population growth requires an enormous effort and a highly complex solution. The exact cost is unknown, but costs comparable to those expended by the United States and the USSR to counter the perceived threats to their respective national security cannot be discounted.

The United States has as much at stake as any other nation if the current laissez faire approach to the solution of this extremely complex problem continues. Most countries, expecting the United States to be the leader, have delegated responsibility to us. If the United States does not accept the challenge, the year 2000 will find a world with a billion or more people than it would have had otherwise.

In general, the United States should adopt laws and policies similar to or similar in effect to those of Hong Kong, Singapore, and the People's Republic of China. Unfortunately, few, if any, nations will follow these governments in elimination of pronatalistic laws and policies and in the institution of antinatalistic ones. However, many countries would follow the United States if it boldly instituted these changes.

Pronatalistic forces, who encourage births, must be stopped. We must adopt the antinatalistic policies that we are suggesting for rapidly growing developing countries. All government policies and laws encouraging childbirth must be changed. All tax incentives for having children must be eliminated, as well as any remaining welfare incentives. Teenage childbearing must be eliminated, and childbearing before the mid-twenties strongly discouraged to lengthen the time between generations. Childless and one-child families must be encouraged....

LOOKING INTO THE FUTURE

Failure to acknowledge that population growth threatens persons and nations calls attention to a number of somber scenarios. Those few aspects discussed below provide some indication of the profound challenges we can expect, from family to federal government. Our procrastination in confronting the problem will probably be expensive and the price will increase with each year of continued delay.

There could be great impingement on our personal life-style. As we procrastinate, the degree of regimentation that we will encounter as the demand for food, fuel, and other resources outstrips shrinking supplies will grow rapidly. This continued delay brings us closer and closer to a society similar to George Orwell's *1984*. The People's Republic of China is a highly regimented society regulated in order to manage effectively a population that had outstripped the resources of the land. To maintain social organization—and to avoid chaos in China—very strict regimentation had to be imposed to drive maximum benefit from scarce resources. Our refusal to respond to the threat of overpopulation is bringing us dangerously close to such a highly regimented society because our resource base is shrinking. The longer we procrastinate, the more strict and the more extensive will be the regimentation.

The great influx of aliens attempting illegal immigration could have a profound impact on American life. The requirement of carrying a national identification card at all times could be imposed. Anti-terrorist activities may force a sharp retreat in the promotion of civil rights. An increased police/domestic military presence to counter terrorist and other criminal activities by underemployed illegal aliens will be more evident. An expansion in our Coast Guard service is most likely. Money spent to halt the flow, apprehend, and deport illegal aliens will be one of the largest expenditures in the U.S. budget. The money spent will include the estimated $161 billion that will be needed over the next twenty years for apprehension, detention, processing, and deportation of [an] estimated 161 million illegal aliens. . . .

The American military establishment will undergo profound changes. For example, its size may drastically increase in response to increasing global insecurity. Soldiers will be asked to fight to ensure the continued supply of materials essential to the survival of Americans and to maintain domestic order.

This is but a sample of the consequences due to our refusal to acknowledge population growth as a security threat. This acknowledgment must occur before an adequate political, economic, and moral commitment will be forthcoming. As our supplies of resources shrink, as social disorganization increases, and as we become concerned with mere survival, the freedoms that Americans have enjoyed for so long will vanish one by one.

CONCLUSION

This essay has not described a world population growth control program. Presently no one knows the specifics of a successful program; no one has ever seriously outlined the appropriate financial commitment (admittedly an expensive one). There is a frightening lack of respect for the world population problem. Likewise, there is no clear respect for an appropriate response. I would suggest that we are talking about a Marshall Plan or something similar to our space program. Ultimately, it could run in the $30 billion per year range.

The ease with which people assume that the future will be a simple extension of the past, despite the two significant historical changes of unprecedented world population growth and increased American political and economic dependence on the developing world, may be the single greatest danger that we face in the coming decades. We simply cannot make this assumption. At a minimum, our national leaders should address the issue; it needs to become a key item in our national policy agenda.

The inevitability of widespread social and political chaos in the face of continued unprecedented 2 percent growth for the next two decades makes population growth the single greatest threat to world peace. Strategically, acknowledgment of this new threat is a must if an adequate political, moral, and economic commitment to action is to be forthcoming. The effective opposition to population growth control activities by the Roman Catholic church has clearly been the single greatest deterrent. This is a political issue that needs to be overcome, hopefully with the help of Catholics themselves. It is fair to say that using the teachings of the church, the Vatican has effectively thwarted the development of and successful implementation of population policies worldwide with the exception of the People's Republic of China. Because of its global geopolitical presence, its economic capabilities, and the strength of its democratic institutions, the only nation capable of successfully addressing that barrier is the United States.

In the face of continued inaction, the scenarios described earlier will become a reality. We should prefer a massive effort that later proves to be unnecessary (but yet had the worldwide side effects of improved food production, nutritional status, maternal and child health, literacy, advancement of women's rights, environment, and security) to a lesser effort that later proves to be totally inadequate. . . .

NO

Julian L. Simon

PEOPLE ARE THE ULTIMATE RESOURCE

Every schoolchild seems to "know" that the natural environment is deteriorating and that food is in increasingly short supply. The children's books leave no doubt that population size and growth are the villains. In the *Golden Stamp Book of Earth and Ecology* we read: "If the population continues to explode, many people will starve. About half of the world's population is underfed now, with many approaching starvation. . . . All of the major environmental problems can be traced to people—more specifically, to too many people." But these facts, which are reported to children with so much assurance, are either unproven or wrong.

The demographic facts, to the extent that they are known, are indeed frightening, at first glance. The human population appears to be expanding with self-generated natural force at an exponential rate, restrained only by starvation and disease. It seems that, without some drastic intervention to check this geometric growth, there will soon be "standing room only." . . .

The idea of "natural breeding," "natural fertility," or "untrammeled copulation" has been buttressed by experiments in animal ecology, which some biologists say can serve as models of human population growth. The analogies that have been proposed include John B. Calhoun's famous observations of Norwegian rats in a pen, the putative behavior of flies in a bottle or of germs in a bucket, and the proclivities of meadow mice and cotton rats—creatures that keep multiplying until they die for lack of substance. But as Malthus himself acknowledged in the revised edition of his *Essay on Population*, human beings are very different from flies or rats. When faced with a bottle-like situation, people are capable of foresight and may abstain from having children for "fear of misery." That is, people can choose a level of fertility to fit the resources that will be available. Malthus wrote, "Impelled to the increase of his species by an equally powerful instinct, reason interrupts his career, and asks him whether he may not bring beings into the world, for whom he cannot provide the means of support. . . ."

From "World Population Growth," by Julian L. Simon, *The Atlantic Monthly*, August 1981. Excerpt from *The Ultimate Resource*, by Julian L. Simon (New Jersey: Princeton University Press). Copyright © 1981 by Julian L. Simon. Reprinted by permission of Princeton University Press.

Income has a decisive effect on population. Along with a temporary jump in fertility as income rises in poor countries come a fall in child mortality, because of better nutrition, better sanitation, and better health care (though in the twentieth century mortality has declined in some poor countries without a rise in income.) As people see that fewer births are necessary to achieve a given family size, they adjust fertility downward. Increased income also brings education and contraception within reach of more people, makes children more expensive to raise, and perhaps influences the desire to have children. It usually initiates a trend toward city living; in the city, children cost more and produce less income for the family than they do in the country.

The process by which these effects of economic development reduce fertility in the long run is called the "demographic transition." We see clearly in the excellent historical data for Sweden that the deathrate began to fall *before* the birthrate fell. We can see the same relationship between income and birthrate in many other countries. At present, the birthrate is far below replacement—that is, below zero population growth—for a number of the largest countries in Europe. Fertility has been falling in many developing countries as well. For example, the birthrate per thousand people declined in Cuba and Singapore from 1965 to 1975 by 40 percent; in Hong Kong by 36 percent; in South Korea by 32 percent; in Costa Rica by 29 percent; in Taiwan by 20 percent; in China by 24 percent; in India by 16 percent. I think we can be reasonably sure that the European pattern of demographic transition is being repeated now in other parts of the world as mortality falls and income rises. . . .

Although no one knows what population size or rate of growth the future holds in store, one often hears that zero population growth, or ZPG, is the only tolerable state. Classical economic theory bolsters this conviction. It purports to show that population growth inevitably reduces the standard of living. The heart of all economic theory of population, from Malthus to *The Limits to Growth*, can be stated in a single sentence: The more people using a stock of resources, the lower the income per person, if all else remains equal. This proposition derives from what economists have called the law of diminishing returns. Two men cannot use the same tool, or farm the same piece of land, without producing less than they would if they did not have to share. A related idea is that two people cannot nourish themselves as well as one person can from a given stock of food. The age distribution that results from a high birthrate reinforces this effect: the number of children in proportion to workers will be larger. Also, the more children women have, the less chance they have to work outside the home, so the work force is diminished further.

According to this reasoning, both sheer numbers of people and the age distribution that occurs in the process of getting to the higher numbers ought to have the effect of a smaller per capita product. But the evidence does not confirm the conventional theory. It suggests that population growth almost certainly does not hinder, and perhaps even helps, economic growth.

According to this reasoning, both sheer numbers of people and the age of distribution that occurs in the process of getting to the higher numbers ought to have the effect of a smaller per capita product. But the evidence does not confirm the conventional theory. It suggests that population growth almost certainly does not hinder, and perhaps even helps, economic growth.

One piece of historical evidence is the concurrent explosion of population and economic development in Europe from 1650 onward. Further evidence comes from a comparison of the rates of population growth and output per capita in those developed countries for which data are available for the past century. No strong relationship between the two variables appears. For example, population has grown six times faster in the United States than in France, but the rate of increase in output per capita has been about the same. The populations of Great Britain and Norway grew at the same pace for the past century, but the rate of Norway's output per capita was about a third faster. Australia, on the other hand, had a very fast rate of population growth, but its rate of increase in output per capita was quite slow.

Studies of recent rates of population growth and economic growth are another source of evidence. In less-developed countries, per capita income has been growing as fast as or faster than in the developed countries, according to a World Bank survey for the years 1950 to 1975, despite the fact that population has grown faster in developing countries than in developed countries.

Such evidence does not show that fast population growth in developed countries *increases* per capita income. But it does contradict the belief that population growth inevitably *decreases* economic growth. The lack of a cause-and-effect relationship between population and economic growth has a number of explanations, as follows:

• People make special efforts when they perceive a special need. For example, American fathers work extra, the equivalent of two to five weeks a year, for each additional child. In the long run, this yearly 4 to 10 percent increase in work may fully (or more than fully) balance the temporary loss of labor by the mother. (The other side of this coin is that people may slack off when population growth slows and demand lessens.)

• The larger proportion of young people in the labor force which results from population growth has advantages. Young workers produce more in relation to what they consume than older workers, largely because the older workers receive increases in pay with seniority, regardless of productivity. And because each generation enters the labor force with more education than the previous generation, the average worker becomes more and more knowledgeable.

• Population growth creates business opportunities and facilitates change. It makes expansion investment and new ventures more attractive, by reducing risk and by increasing total demand. For example, if housing is overbuilt or excess capacity is created in an industry, a growing population can take up the slack and remedy the error.

• More job opportunities and more young people working mean that there will be more mobility within the labor force. And mobility greatly enhances the efficient allocation of resources: the best matching of people to jobs.

• Population growth promotes "economies of scale": the greater efficiency of larger-scale production. Through this mechanism, the more people, the larger the market, and therefore the greater the need for bigger and more efficient machinery, division of labor, and improved transportation and communication. Hollis

B. Chenery, an economist, compared manufacturing in less-developed countries and found that, all else being equal, if one country is twice as populous as another, output per worker is 20 percent larger. It is an established economic truth that the faster an industry grows, the faster its efficiency improves. One study, which compared the output of selected industries in the U.S. with the output of those same industries in the United Kingdom and Canada, showed that if you quadruple the size of an industry, you may expect to double the output per worker and per unit of capital employed. This should hold true for the developed world in general.

A larger population also provides economies of scale for many expensive social investments that would not be profitable otherwise—for example, railroads, irrigation systems, and ports. And public services, such as fire protection, can also be provided at lower cost per person when the population is larger.

All of the explanations just summarized have economic force, but the most important benefit that population growth confers on an economy is that people increase the stock of useful knowledge. It is your mind that matters economically, as much as or more than your mouth or hands. In the long run, the contributions people make to knowledge are great enough to overcome all the costs of population growth. This is a strong statement, but the evidence for it seems strong as well.

The importance of technological knowledge has clearly emerged in two famous studies, by Robert Solow in 1957 and by Edward Denison in 1962. Using different methods, both calculated the extent to which the growth of physical capital and of the labor force could ac-count for economic growth in the U.S. Denison made the same calculations for Europe. They found that even after capital and labor are allowed for, much of the economic growth cannot be explained by any factor other than improvement in technological practice (including improved organization). Economies of scale as a result of larger factories do not appear to be very important from this point of view, though technology improves more rapidly in large, fast-growing industries than in small, slow-growing ones. This improvement in productivity doesn't come for free; much of it is bought with investments in research and development. But that does not alter its importance.

What is the connection between innovation and population size and growth? Since ideas come from people, it seems reasonable that the number of improvements depends on the number of people using their heads. This is not a new idea. William Petty wrote in 1683 that "it is more likely that one ingenious curious man may rather be found out amongst 4 millions than 400 persons." Hans Bethe, who won the Nobel Prize for physics in 1967, has said that the prospects for nuclear fusion would be rosier if the population of scientists were larger. Bethe said, "Money is not the limiting factor. . . . Progress is limited rather by the availability of highly trained workers."

Even a casual consideration of history shows that as population has grown in the last century, there have been many more discoveries and a faster rate of growth in productivity than in previous centuries. In prehistoric times, progress was agonizingly slow. For example, whereas routinely we develop new materials—say, plastics and metals—millennia passed between the invention of copper metallurgy and of iron metallurgy. If population had been larger, technological discoveries would surely have come along faster. Ancient Greece and Rome have often been suggested as examples contrary to this line of reasoning. Therefore, I plotted the numbers of great discoveries, as recorded by historians of science who have made such lists, against Greek and Roman populations in various centuries. This comparison showed that an increase in population or its rate of growth (or both) was associated with an increase in scientific activity, and population decline with a decrease.

In modern times, there is some fairly strong evidence to confirm the positive effect of population growth on science and technology: in countries at the same level of income, scientific output is proportional to population size. For example, the standard of living in the U.S. and in Sweden is roughly the same, but the U.S. is much larger than Sweden and it produces much more scientific knowledge. A consideration of the references used in Swedish and U.S. scientific papers and of the number of patented processes that Sweden licenses from the U.S. bears this out.

Why isn't populous India a prosperous and advanced country? I have not argued that a large population will by itself overcome all the other variables in a society—its climate, culture, history, political structure. I have said only that there is no evidence to prove that a large population *creates* poverty and underdevelopment. India is poor and underdeveloped for many reasons, and it might be even more so if it had a smaller population. The proper comparison is not India and the United States but India and other poor countries, and the fact is that India has one of the largest scientific establishments in the Third World—perhaps in part because of its large population.

It cannot be emphasized too strongly that "technological and scientific advance" does not mean only sophisticated research, and geniuses are not the only source of knowledge. Much technological advance come from people who are neither well-educated nor well-paid: the dispatcher who develops a slightly better way of deploying the taxis in his ten-taxi fleet, the shipper who discovers that garbage cans make excellent cheap containers, the supermarket manager who finds a way to display more merchandise in a given space, the clerk who finds a quicker way to stamp prices on cans, and so on.

Population growth spurs the adoption of existing technology as well as the invention of new technology. This has been well documented in agriculture, where people turn to successively more "advanced" but more laborious methods of getting food as population density increases—methods that may have been known but were ignored because they weren't needed. For example, hunting and gathering—which require very few hours of work a week to provide a full diet—give way to migratory slash-and-burn agriculture, and that yields to settled, long-fallow agriculture, and that to short-fallow agriculture. Eventually fertilizer, irrigation, and multiple cropping are adopted. Though each stage initially requires more labor than the one before, the end point is a more efficient and productive system.

This phenomenon also explains why the advance of civilization is not a race between technology and population, each progressing independently of the other. Contrary to the Malthusian view, there is no direct link between each food-increasing invention and increased production of food. Some inventions, such as a better calendar for planting, may be adopted as soon as they prove successful, because they will increase production with no more labor. Others, such as settled agriculture or irrigated multicropping, require more labor, and thus will not be adopted until there is demand.

The fact that people learn by doing is a key to the improvement of productivity in particular industries, and in the economies of nations. The idea is simple: the bigger the population, the more of everything that is produced. With a greater volume come more chances for people to improve their skills and to devise better methods. Industrial engineers have understood this process for many decades, but economists first grasped its importance when they examined the production of airplanes during World War II. They discovered that when twice as many airplanes are produced, the labor required per plane is reduced by 20 percent. That is, if the first airplane requires 1,000 units of labor, the second will require 800 units, and so on, though after some time the gains from increased effi-

ciency level off. Similar "progress ratios" describe the production of lathes, machine tools, textile machines, and ships. The effect of learning by doing can also be seen in the progressive reduction in price of new consumer devices in the years following their introduction to the market—room air-conditioners and color television sets, for example. . . .

In the short run, all resources are limited: the pulpwood that went into making this magazine, the pages the magazine will allow me, and the attention the reader will devote to what I say. The longer run, however, is a different story. The standard of living has risen along with the size of the world's population since the beginning of recorded time. There is no convincing economic reason why these trends toward a better life should not continue indefinitely. Adding more people causes problems, but people are also the means to solve these problems. The main fuel to speed the world's progress is our stock of knowledge, and the brake is our lack of imagination. The ultimate resource is people—skilled, spirited, and hopeful people—who will exert their wills and imaginations for their own benefit, and so, inevitably, for the benefit of us all.

POSTSCRIPT

Is the World Threatened by a Population Bomb?

Simon may be right that population growth over the long run will contribute to economic growth and technological development, but will the masses of poor people be better off? Improvement may occur in terms of national averages, even while the poor sink into deeper misery. Back in 1974 the Food and Agricultural Organization of the United Nations estimated that there were about five hundred million malnourished people in the world (UN, World Food Conference, "Assessment of the World Food Situation, Present and Future," 1974). These figures have been extensively debated, but the figure of half a billion is still commonly used. The point to note, however, is that there are many poor regions of the world where malnourishment is widespread. In these areas, population growth puts greater strain on hard-pressed resources, resulting in more malnourishment and starvation. Outside these areas, population growth may have largely beneficial effects, as Simon points out, or may cause widespread social and political instability, as Mumford points out.

The recent *Global 200 Report to the President* concludes:

> Rapid growth in world population will hardly have altered by 2000. The world's population will grow from 4 billion in 1975 to 6.35 billion in 2000, an increase of more than 50 percent. The rate of growth will slow only marginally, from 1.8 percent a year to 1.7 percent. In terms of sheer numbers, population will be growing faster in 2000 than it is today, with 100 million people added each year compared with 75 million in 1975. Ninety percent of the growth will occur in the poorest countries.

This same report projects an even greater percent increase in world food production but acknowledges that most will go to the rich food countries. Per capita food consumption in much of South Asia and Africa will actually decline below present inadequate levels.

For an optimistic assessment of the world population situation see Julian L. Simon, "World Food Supplies," *The Atlantic Monthly* (July 1981) and *The Ultimate Resource* (Princeton University, 1981) as well as Marylin Chou and David P. Harman, Jr., eds., *Critical Food Issues of the Eighties* (Pergamon, 1979). For a pessimistic assessment see Erik P. Eckholm, *Losing Ground: Environmental Stress and World Food Prospects* (Norton, 1976) and Paul R. Ehrlich et al., *Ecoscience: Population, Resources, Environment* (Freeman, 1977). For an in-between assessment, see Philip M. Hauser, ed., *World Population and Development* (Syracuse University Press, 1979); and National Academy of Sciences, *Supporting Papers: World Food and Nutrition Study* (Washington, DC, 1977).

ISSUE 19
Is the Environment Improving?

YES: Julian L. Simon, from "Life on Earth Is Getting Better, Not Worse," *The Futurist* August 1983)

NO: Lester R. Brown and Sandra L. Postel, from "Thresholds of Change," *The Futurist* (September/October 1987)

ISSUE SUMMARY

YES: Economist Julian Simon reviews several indicators of improving environmental conditions for human life.

NO: Lester R. Brown and Sandra L. Postel, president and senior researcher respectively at the Worldwatch Institute, argue that many of the earth's natural systems have become seriously destabilized in environmentally destructive ways. Some of these systems are beyond the point where they can be corrected or restabilized at acceptable levels.

The literature on socioeconomic development in the 1960s was based on the belief in material progress for everyone. It largely ignored the environment and presumed that raw materials would not be a problem. All societies would get richer because all societies were investing in new machinery and technology that would improve productivity and increase wealth. Some of the poor countries were having trouble developing because their values were not supportive of modernization and they lacked the social, political, and economic organization or psychological attitudes conducive to growth. It was believed that if these social and psychological defects could be overcome by a modernizing elite, and ten percent of the gross national product could be devoted to capital formation for at least three decades, then that society would take off into self-sustained growth just as industrial societies had done decades earlier (see Walt W. Rostow, *The Stages of Economic Growth*, Cambridge University Press, 1960). After take-off, growth would be self-sustaining—i.e., would continue for the foreseeable future.

In the 1970s an intellectual revolution occurred. Suddenly, the deeply entrenched idea of progress came under attack by environmentalists. By the end of the 1960s, Rachel Carson's *Silent Spring* (Alfred A. Knopf, 1962) had worked its way into the public's consciousness. Carson's book traced the noticeable loss of birds to the use of pesticides. Her book made the middle and upper classes in the United States realize that pollution affected complex ecological systems in ways that put even the wealthy at risk—that deteriorating ecosystems affect everyone.

Many of the environmentalists sounded apocalyptic. Paul Ehrlich wrote *Population Bomb* (Ballantine Books, 1968), which pointed out all of the possible evils and problems that further population pressures on the environment might cause. In 1967 William and Paul Paddock wrote *Famine 1975* (Little, Brown & Co., 1967) to warn of coming food shortages in many of the poor regions of the world. Increasing numbers of people became aware of the gloomy predictions, but most people trusted that technological developments and numerous private and government responses would prevent catastrophes and continue the growth of prosperity.

In 1973 the Arab members of OPEC (Organization of Petroleum Exporting Countries) cut off oil supplies to the United States and Western Europe because of their relationships to Israel. Quickly, gas lines emerged and conservation policies were passed. The major United States policy was the national fifty-five miles per hour speed limit, which conserved very little oil. Europe instituted more stringent measures and confronted serious scarcities for the first time since World War II. The lesson of the oil embargo was that scarcity lies close at hand and that industrial societies are vulnerable to cut-offs of vital resources.

Currently the major proponent of the optimistic view is Julian Simon. In the article that follows he argues that the environment is becoming more beneficent for man because pollution is decreasing, resources are becoming more available, average food consumption levels are improving, few species are becoming extinct, and people are living longer. The picture that Simon presents suggests that the concerns of environmentalists are largely fanciful fears and that current environmental trends are healthy. Environmentalists Lester R. Brown and Sandra L. Postel are leading spokespersons for the pessimistic view. They argue for the need to radically change the mode of agricultural and industrial production and the wasteful life-styles of consumers to save the world from very real dangers of ecocatastrophes.

YES

Julian L. Simon

LIFE ON EARTH
IS GETTING BETTER, NOT WORSE

If we lift our gaze from the frightening daily headlines and look instead at wide-ranging scientific data as well as the evidence of our senses, we shall see that economic life in the United States and the rest of the world has been getting better rather than worse during recent centuries and decades. There is, moreover, no persuasive reason to believe that these trends will not continue indefinitely.

But first: I am *not* saying that all is well everywhere, and I do not predict that all will be rosy in the future. Children are hungry and sick; people live out lives of physical or intellectual poverty, with little opportunity for improvement; war or some new pollution may finish us. What I *am* saying is that for most relevant economic matters I have checked, aggregate trends are improving rather than deteriorating. Also, I do not say that a better future will happen automatically or without effort. It will happen because men and women will use muscle and mind to struggle with problems that they will probably overcome, as they have in the past.

LONGER AND HEALTHIER LIVES

Life cannot be good unless you are alive. Plentiful resources and a clean environment have little value unless we and others are alive to enjoy them. The fact that your chances of living through any given age now are much better than in earlier times must therefore mean that life has gotten better. In France, for example, female life expectancy at birth rose from under 30 years in the 1740s to 75 years in the 1960s. And this trend has not yet run its course. The increases have been rapid in recent years in the United States: a 2.1-year gain between 1970 and 1976 versus a 0.8-year gain in the entire decade of the 1960s. This pattern is now being repeated in the poorer countries of the world as they improve their economic lot. Life expectancy at birth in low-income countries rose from an average of 35.2 years in 1950 to 49.9 years in

From "Life on Earth Is Getting Better, Not Worse," by Julian L. Simon, *The Futurist*, August 1983. Reprinted with permission from *The Futurist*, published by the World Future Society, 4916 St. Elmo Avenue, Bethesda, MD 20814.

1978, a much bigger jump than the rise from 66.0 to 73.5 years in the industrialized countries.

The threat of our loved ones dying greatly affects our assessment of the quality of our lives. Infant mortality is a reasonable measure of child mortality generally. In Europe in the eighteenth and nineteenth centuries, 200 or more children of each thousand died during their first year. As late as 1900, infant mortality was 200 per 1000 or higher in Spain, Russia, Hungary, and even Germany. Now it is about 15 per 1000 or less in a great many countries.

Health has improved, too. The incidence of both chronic and acute conditions has declined. While a perceived "epidemic" of cancer indicates to some a drop in the quality of life, the data show no increase in cancer except for deaths due to smoking-caused lung cancer. As Philip Handler, president of the National Academy of Sciences, said:

> The United States is not suffering an "epidemic of cancer," it is experiencing an "epidemic of life"—in that an even greater fraction of the population survives to the advanced ages at which cancer has always been prevalent. The overall, age-corrected incidence of cancer has not been increasing; it has been declining slowly for some years.

ABATING POLLUTION

About pollution now: The main air pollutants—particulates and sulfur dioxide—have declined since 1960 and 1970 respectively, the periods for which there is data in the U.S. The Environmental Protection Agency's Pollutant Standard Index, which takes into account all the most important air pollutants, shows that the number of days rated "unhealthful" has declined steadily since the index's inauguration in 1974. And the proportion of monitoring sites in the U.S. having good drinking water has greatly increased since record-keeping began in 1961.

Pollution in the less-developed countries is a different, though not necessarily discouraging, story. No worldwide pollution data are available. Nevertheless, it is reasonable to assume that pollution of various kinds has increased as poor countries have gotten somewhat less poor. Industrial pollution rises along with new factories. The same is true of consumer pollution—junked cars, plastic wrappers, and such oddments as the hundreds of discarded antibiotics vials I saw on the ground in an isolated Iranian village. Such industrial wastes do not exist in the poorest preindustrial countries. And in the early stages of development, countries and people are not ready to pay for clean-up operations. But further increases in income almost surely will bring about pollution abatement, just as increases in income in the United States have provided the wherewithal for better garbage collection and cleaner air and water.

THE MYTH OF FINITE RESOURCES

Though natural resources are a smaller part of the economy with every succeeding year, they are still important, and their availability causes grave concern to many. Yet, measured by cost or price, the scarcity of all raw materials except lumber and oil has been *decreasing* rather than increasing over the long run. . . .

Perhaps surprisingly, oil also shows downward cost trend in the long run. The price rise in the 1970s was purely political; the cost of producing a barrel of oil in the Persian Gulf is still only perhaps 15 to 25 cents.

There is no reason to believe that the supply of energy is finite, or that the price will not continue its long-run decrease. This statement may sound less preposterous if you consider that for a quantity to be finite it must be measurable. The future supply of oil includes what we usually think of as oil, plus the oil that can be produced from shale, tar sands, and coal. It also includes the oil from plants that we grow, whose key input is sunlight. So the measure of the future oil supply must therefore be at least as large as the sun's 7 billion or so years of future life. And it may include other suns whose energy might be exploited in the future. Even if you believe that one can in principle measure the energy from suns that will be available in the future—a belief that requires a lot of confidence that the knowledge of the physical world we have developed in the past century will not be superseded in the next 7 billion years, plus the belief that the universe is not expanding—this measurement would hardly be relevant for any practical contemporary decision making.

Energy provides a good example of the process by which resources become more abundant and hence cheaper. Seventeenth-century England was full of alarm at an impending energy shortage due to the country's deforestation for firewood. People feared a scarcity of fuel for both heating and the vital iron industry. This impending scarcity led inventors and businessmen to develop coal.

Then, in the mid-1800s, the English came to worry about an impending coal crisis. The great English economist William Stanley Jevons calculated then that a shortage of coal would surely bring England's industry to a standstill by 1900; he carefully assessed that oil could never make a decisive difference. But spurred by the impending scarcity of coal (and of whale oil, whose story comes next), ingenious and profit-minded people developed oil into a more desirable fuel than coal ever was. And today England exports both coal and oil.

Another strand in the story: Because of increased demand due to population growth and increased income, the price of whale oil used in lamps jumped in the 1840s. Then the Civil War pushed it even higher, leading to a whale oil "crisis." The resulting high price provided an incentive for imaginative and enterprising people to discover and produce substitutes. First came oil from rapeseed, olives, linseed, and pine trees. Then inventors learned how to get coal oil from coal, which became a flourishing industry. Other ingenious persons produced kerosene from the rock oil that seeped to the surface. Kerosene was so desirable a product that its price rose from 75 cents to $2 a gallon, which stimulated enterprisers to increase its supply. Finally, Edwin L. Drake sunk his famous oil well in Titusville, Pennsylvania. Learning how to refine the oil took a while, but in a few years there were hundreds of small refiners in the U.S. Soon the bottom dropped out of the whale oil market: the price fell from $2.50 or more a gallon at its peak around 1866 to well below a dollar.

Lumber has been cited as an exception to the general resource story of falling costs. For decades in the U.S., farmers clearing land disposed of trees as a nuisance. As lumber came to be more a commercial crop and a good for builders and railroad men, its price rose. For some time, resource economists expected the price to hit a plateau and then follow the course of other raw materials as the transition to a commercial crop would be completed. There was evidence consistent with this view in the increase, rather than the popularly supposed decrease, in the tree stock in the U.S., yet for some time the price did not fall. But now that expectation seems finally to have been realized as prices of lumber have fallen to a fourth of their peak in the late 1970s.

MORE FOOD FOR MORE PEOPLE

Food is an especially important resource, and the evidence indicates that its supply is increasing despite rising population. The long-run prices of food relative to wages, and even relative to consumer goods, are down. Famine deaths have decreased in the past century even in absolute terms, let alone relative to the much larger population, a special boon for poor countries. Per person food production in the world is up over the last 30 years and more. And there are no data showing that the people at the bottom of the income distribution have fared worse, or have failed to share in the general improvement, as the average has improved. Africa's food production per capita is down, but that clearly stems from governmental blunders with price controls, subsidies, farm collectivization, and other institutional problems.

There is, of course a food-production problem in the U.S. today: too much production. Prices are falling due to high productivity, falling consumer demand for meat in the U.S., and increased foreign competition in such crops as soybeans. In response to the farmers' complaints, the government will now foot an unprecedentedly heavy bill for keeping vast amounts of acreage out of production.

THE DISAPPEARING-SPECIES SCARE

Many are alarmed that the earth is losing large numbers of its species. For example, the *Global 2000 Report to the President* says: "Extinctions of plant and animal species will increase dramatically. Hundreds of thousands of species—perhaps as many as 20 percent of all species on earth—will be irretrievably lost as their habitats vanish, especially in tropical forests," by the year 2000.

The available facts, however, are not consistent with the level of concern expressed in *Global 2000*, nor do they warrant the various policies suggested to deal with the purported dangers.

The *Global 2000* projection is based upon a report by contributor Thomas Lovejoy, who estimates that between 437,000 and 1,875,000 extinctions will occur out of a present estimated total of 3 to 10 million species. Lovejoy's estimate is based on a linear relationship running from 0% species extinguished at 0% tropical forest cleared, to about 95% extinguished at 100% tropical forest cleared. (The main source of differences in the range of estimated losses is the range of 3 to 10 million species in the overall estimate.)

The basis of any useful projection must be a body of experience collected under a range of conditions that encompass the expected conditions, or that can reasonably be extrapolated to the expected conditions. But none of Lovejoy's references seems to contain any scientifically impressive body of experience.

A projected drop in the amount of tropical forests underlines Lovejoy's projection of species losses in the future. Yet to connect these two events as Lovejoy has done requires systematic evidence relating an amount of tropical forest removed to a rate of species reduction. Neither *Global 2000* nor any of the other sources I checked give such empirical evidence. If there is not better evidence for Lovejoy's projected rates, one could extrapolate almost any rate one chooses for the year 2000. Until more of the facts are in, we need not undertake alarmist protection policies. Rather, we need other sorts of data to estimate extinction rates and decide on policy. None of this is to say that we need not worry about endangered species. The planet's flora and fauna constitute a valuable natural endowment; we must guard them as we do our other physical and social assets. But we should also strive for a clear, unbiased view of this set of assets in order to make the best possible judgments about how much time and money to spend guarding them, in a world where this valuable activity must compete with other valuable activities, including the preservation of other assets and human life.

MORE WEALTH FROM LESS WORK

One of the great trends of economic history is the shortening of the workweek coupled with increasing income. A shorter workweek represents an increase in one's freedom to dispose of that most treasured possession—time—as one wishes. In the U.S., the decline was from about 60 hours per week in 1870 to less than 40 hours at present. This benign trend is true for an array of countries in which the length of the workweek shows an inverse relationship with income.

With respect to progress in income generally, the most straightforward and meaningful index is the proportion of persons in the labor force working in agriculture. In 1800, the percentage in the U.S. was 73.6%, whereas in 1980 the proportion was 2.7%. That is, relative to population size, only $\frac{1}{25}$ as many persons today are working in agriculture as in 1800. This suggests that the effort that produced one bushel of grain or one loaf of bread in 1800 will now produce the bushel of grain plus what 24 other bushels will buy in other goods, which is equivalent to an increase in income by a factor of 25.

Income in less-developed countries has not reached nearly so high a level as in the more-developed countries, by definition. But it would be utterly wrong to think that income in less-developed countries has stagnated rather than risen. In fact, income per person has increased at a proportional rate at least as fast, or faster, in less-developed than in more-developed countries since World War II.

THE ULTIMATE RESOURCE

What explains the enhancement of our material life in the face of supposed limits to growth? I offer an extended answer in my recent book, *The Ultimate Resource* (1981). In short, the source of our increased economic blessings is the human mind, and, all other things being equal, when there are more people, there are more productive minds. Productivity increases come directly from the additional minds that develop productive new ideas, as well as indirectly from the impact upon industrial productivity of the additional demand for goods. That is, population growth in the form of babies or immigrants helps in the long run to raise the standard of living because it brings increased productivity. Immigrants are the best deal of all because they usually migrate when they are young and strong; in the U.S., they contribute more in taxes to the public coffers than they take out in welfare services.

In the short run, of course, additional people mean lower income for other people because children must be fed and housed by their parents, and educated and equipped partly by the community. Even immigrants are a burden for a brief time until they find jobs. But after the children grow up and enter the work force, and contribute to the support of others as well as increasing productivity, their net effect upon others becomes positive. Over their lifetimes they are a boon to others.

I hope you will now agree that the long-run outlook is for a more abundant material life rather than for increased scarcity, in the U.S. and in the world as a whole. Of course, such progress does not come about automatically. And my message certainly is not one of complacency. In this I agree with the doomsayers—that our world needs the best efforts of all humanity to improve our lot. I part company with them in that they expect us to come to a bad end despite the efforts we make, whereas I expect a continuation of successful efforts. Their message is self-fulfilling because if you expect inexorable natural limits to stymie your efforts you are likely to feel resigned and give up. But if you recognize the possibility—indeed, the probability—of success, you can tap large reserves of energy and enthusiasm. Energy and enthusiasm, together with the human mind and spirit, constitute our solid hope for the economic future, just as they have been our salvation in ages past. With these forces at work, we will leave a richer, safer, and more beautiful world to our descendants, just as our ancestors improved the world that they bestowed upon us.

NO

Lester R. Brown
and Sandra L. Postel

THRESHOLDS OF CHANGE

Daily news events remind us that our relationship with the earth and its natural systems is changing, often in ways we do not understand.

In May 1985, a British research team reported findings of a sharp decline in the level of atmospheric ozone over Antarctica. This "hole" in the earth's protective shield of ozone sent waves of concern throughout the international scientific community. In late July 1986, scientists studying the effect of rising atmospheric levels of carbon dioxide and other "greenhouse gases" published evidence that the predicted global warming has begun. And recently, biologists at a forum on biodiversity warned of a forthcoming wave of mass extinction driven by human activities—one that would approach the magnitude of that which wiped out the dinosaurs and half of all other extant species some 65 million years ago.

These changes in atmospheric chemistry, global temperature, and the abundance of living species reflect the crossing of key thresholds in natural systems, crossings that may impair the earth's capacity to sustain an ever-growing human population. A frustrating paradox is emerging. Efforts to improve living standards are themselves beginning to threaten the health of the global economy. The very notion of progress begs for redefinition in light of the intolerable consequences unfolding as a result of its pursuit.

The breaching of many thresholds has occurred inadvertently from advances in technology and growth in human numbers. Corporations manufacturing the family of chemicals known as chlorofluorocarbons, for example, surely did not intend for these compounds to deplete the ozone layer. Their goal was to produce efficient refrigerants, a practical propellant for aerosol spray cans, and a chemical agent for making foam products. Nonetheless, the accumulation of chlorofluorocarbons in the atmosphere threatens to subject all forms of life to damaging doses of ultraviolet radiation, a threat that will take on new urgency if scientists determine that chlorofluorocarbons play a role in the periodic depletion of the ozone layer over Antarctica.

Other trends of the mid-1980s also call into question the viability of our path toward economic progress. World agriculture is producing surpluses,

From "Thresholds of Change," by Lester R. Brown and Sandra L. Postel, *The Futurist*, September/October 1987. Adapted from *State of the World 1987* by Lester R. Brown et al. Copyright © 1987, Worldwatch Institute. Reprinted by permission.

but for the wrong reasons. A portion of today's surplus is being produced only by diminishing the agricultural resource base—for example, by plowing highly erodible land and overdrafting underground water supplies.

Burgeoning populations in many urban areas are overtaxing local water sources, fuel supplies, and waste-disposal capacities, crossing natural thresholds and translating directly into economic costs. Resource demands in numerous cities already exceed the limits of local supplies, whether it be water in Tucson and Mexico City or firewood in Hyderabad. Especially in Third World areas experiencing unprecedented rates of urbanization, these imbalances will frustrate efforts to improve living standards.

A sustainable society satisfies its needs without diminishing the prospects of the next generation. By many measures, contemporary society fails to meet this criterion. Questions of ecological sustainability are arising on every continent. The scale of human activities has begun to threaten the habitability of the earth itself. Nothing short of fundamental adjustments in population and energy policies will stave off the host of costly changes now unfolding, changes that could overwhelm our long-standing efforts to improve the human condition.

ENERGY, ENVIRONMENT, AND THE ECONOMY

When this century began, scarcely one life-span ago, world population numbered 1.6 billion. Assuming an average per capita income of $400 per year (1986 dollars), the gross world product was $640 billion, just slightly more than France's 1986 national product of $550 billion. Over the next half century, world population grew by nearly a billion, bringing the total to 2.5 billion. Modest progress in raising per capita income brought the gross world product to roughly $3 trillion in 1950.

Though impressive by historical standards, this growth was dwarfed by what followed. Between 1950 and 1986, human numbers doubled to nearly 5 billion, expanding as much during these 36 years as during the preceding few million. Per capita income also roughly doubled, pushing the gross world product to over $13 trillion. Within a generation, the global output of goods and services quadrupled. A variety of technological advances aided this expansion, but none compares with the growth in fossil-fuel use. Between 1950 and 1986, world fossil-fuel consumption also increased fourfold, paralleling the growth in the global economy.

Resource constraints on global economic expansion emerged from time to time throughout the century. But a combination of advancing technology and cheap energy repeatedly pushed them back. As opportunities for adding new cropland diminished, for example, energy was widely substituted for land in boosting food production. After mid-century, relatively little new land was brought under the plow in most regions, yet global crop output expanded even faster than before. World agriculture made a smooth transition from expanding cropland area to raising yields and even picked up the pace of food production in doing so.

Economic growth became the central goal of governments everywhere. Regardless of ideology or stage of development, all sought similar ends — an expansion of their economies and improvements in living standards. Though the gains achieved were far from equally distributed, the world as a whole experienced remarkable economic progress.

While the global economy has expanded continuously, the natural systems that support it have not. Economist Herman Daly suggests that, "as the economy grows beyond its present physical scale, it may increase costs faster than benefits and initiate an era of uneconomic growth which impoverishes rather than enriches." In essence, Daly points to an economic threshold with profound implications. As currently pursued, economic activity could be approaching a level where further growth in the gross world product costs more than it is worth.

The negative side effects of this century's twentyfold expansion of economic activity are now becoming inescapable. Whether through spreading forest damage, a changing climate, or eroding soils, the pursuit of short-term economic growth at the environment's expense will exact a price. As the natural systems that underpin economies deteriorate, actions that make good sense environmentally will begin to converge with those that make good sense economically. But will that convergence occur before irreversible changes unfold?

CROSSING NATURAL THRESHOLDS

Sometimes a natural threshold can be defined fairly precisely, and the consequences of breaching that threshold can be known with a reasonable degree of certainty. If wood harvesting exceeds annual forest growth, for example, the volume of standing timber will diminish, and it will do so at a rate directly tied to how much the sustainable yield has been exceeded. Similarly, in a fishery, if the annual fish catch exceeds the rate of replacement, the stock of fish will gradually dwindle.

With many of the natural systems now at risk, however, thresholds are not well defined. Exactly how systems respond to threshold crossings is not well understood, so the consequences of crossing a threshold are largely incalculable. Moreover, threshold effects are now appearing in systems of continental and global scale.

For example, the onset of forest damage in the early 1980s took West German scientists by surprise, despite West Germany's long tradition of meticulous forest management. In 1982, rough estimates showed that 8% of the nation's trees had suffered some damage. Just one year later, a thorough survey showed that 34% of West Germany's trees were yellowing and losing foliage. And by the summer of 1984, the share of unhealthy trees had climbed to 50%. Something had tipped the balance within forest systems, triggering widespread decline.

Scientists believe that pollutants from the burning of fossil fuels are behind the spreading forest damage in central and northern Europe—damage that now covers more than 19 million hectares. But the precise mechanisms at work are surrounded by uncertainty. Curiously, the destruction unfolded during a period when the use of fossil fuels had more or less leveled off in many countries, including West Germany. The long-term cumulative effects of chemical stress apparently have overwhelmed the trees' levels of tolerance, making them less able to cope with natural stresses such as extreme cold, wind, insects, and drought.

While temperate-zone forests are being pushed beyond a threshold of pollution tolerance, those in the tropics are being pushed below a critical moisture threshold. Conventional wisdom holds that tropical rain forests are typically too wet to burn naturally, but in late 1982 and early 1983 some seven forest fires spread through Indonesia's East Kalimantan province and Malaysia's Sabah province, both on the island of Borneo. They consumed 3.5 million hectares of tropical rain forest, and area almost the size of Taiwan and equal to nearly half the average annual loss of moist tropical forests from all causes.

The forest that ignited in Kalimantan and Sabah had been degraded and destabilized by land clearing for resettlement programs, slash-and-burn farming, and commercial logging. The severe El Nino drought of 1982 and 1983 tipped the balance by reducing soil moisture to a level below that needed to protect the forest from fire. U.S. scientists studying the fires concluded that they "were ecological events of major proportions that have profoundly affected the human, plant, and animal communities of a tropical ecosystem already subjected to numerous pressures."

Far away, in Ivory Coast, some 450,000 hectares of forest were destroyed by fire during the 1983 drought, apparently linked to similar human pressures. And in neighboring Ghana, fires during the same drought destroyed not only an extensive stand of forest, but also 10% of the country's cacao plantations. With pressure building on rain forests throughout the tropics, the moisture level below which they become more vulnerable to fire is likely to be crossed in an ever-widening area.

THE WARMING OF THE EARTH

The world is now uncomfortably close to what may be the most economically costly threshold of all. For at least a century, the annual release of carbon into the atmosphere from human activities—mainly fossil-fuel combustion and deforestation—has exceeded the uptake of carbon by terrestrial vegetation and the oceans. As a result, carbon dioxide has been building up in the atmosphere. Analyses of air trapped in glaciers indicate that the atmospheric carbon dioxide level in 1860 was about 260 parts per million (ppm). Today CO_2 measures 346 ppm, a 30% increase. Since just 1958, when scientists began routinely monitoring CO_2, the concentration has risen 9%.

Climate modelers warn that if the CO_2 concentration approaches double preindustrial levels, a dramatic change in climate will result. By pushing the release of CO_2 into the atmosphere above the rate at which it could be assimilated by natural systems, we have crossed one threshold. But we can still avoid crossing a second threshold: the level of atmospheric CO_2 that will cause an unprecedented and irreversible change in climate.

One of the most feared consequences of the projected global warming is the rise in sea level that will result from melting of glaciers and polar ice caps. A 1°C increase in the temperature of the ocean would raise the sea level an estimated 60 centimeters, or roughly two feet.

Calculating the effect of the warming on the earth's ice sheets is more complicated. Scientists agree that the warming will be more pronounced at the poles. If the earth as a whole warms by 2° to 4°C, as is predicted with a doubling of preindustrial CO_2 levels, polar temperatures are likely to rise 6° to 8°. Current estimates suggest that the rise in ocean levels from such a warming would be on the order of one meter.

Coastal areas are obviously most at risk from rising seas. Many major cities are close to sea level, including Shanghai, London, and New York. Low-lying, densely populated regions of Asia, including parts of Bangladesh and Indonesia and the deltas of the Indus, Mekong, and Yangtze rivers, would be especially threatened.

Faced with increased risks of flooding, governments would have to decide whether to abandon such low-lying regions, evacuating populations to higher elevations, or to build dikes such as the Dutch have done to reclaim the land from the Zuider Zee. The cost of protecting the rice-growing plains and deltas of Asia and the densely populated coastal regions found throughout the world are incalculable. One 2.4-kilometer storm-surge barrier dam and dike system completed by the Dutch in the Scheldt River delta in 1986 to minimize the risk of flooding from severe storms cost several billion dollars. For some poor countries such as Bangladesh, a rising ocean level combined with the agricultural adjustments needed to adapt to climate change could mean using a large share of available investment capital just to maintain the status quo.

SUPPORTING
THE EARTH'S PEOPLES

As the human population continues to expand, the ability of the earth's biological systems to support it adequately is diminishing.

An increasing share of the earth's net primary productivity—the total amount of solar energy fixed biologically through photosynthesis minus the amount of energy respired by plants—is being spent on meeting human demands. Stanford University biologist Peter M. Vitousek and his colleagues estimate that nearly 40% of the potential net primary productivity on land is now used directly or indirectly by human populations—mostly for food production but also for fiber, lumber and fuel—or is lost as a result of human activities. The portion remaining to sustain all other species, and to maintain the integrity of natural systems, gets smaller and smaller as the size and demands of the human population mount. Deprived of needed energy, natural support systems could begin to deteriorate on a large scale.

Identifying environmental thresholds and pinpointing when they will be crossed are not easy tasks. To have predicted the onset of population-induced forest damage, for example, would have required detailed knowledge of how trees respond to various levels of pollution and how natural stresses and pollutants jointly affect trees, as well as a finely tuned monitoring system for tracking forest health. Such extensive data and depth of understanding simply do not yet exist for most natural systems. This inability to recognize thresholds and predict when they will be breached makes efforts to relieve resource imbalances and environmental stresses all the more crucial.

THREATS TO OUR CIVILIZATION

In the modern world, the aura of high technology, sophisticated industrial processes, and a century of unprecedented growth might easily lead us to think that we are immune from the kinds of stresses that could cause a civilization to collapse. Yet the citizens of flourishing societies from the past would probably never have believed that their cultures could deteriorate so rapidly.

Population pressures and environmental stresses are mounting in many parts of the Third World. Per capita grain production in Africa has fallen by roughly one-fifth since 1970, and in Latin America, by 8% in just the last five years. In agrarian societies, declining per capita food production inevitably translates into declining per capita income. Both Africa and Latin America are projected to end this decade with lower income per person than they began it with.

Northern Africa, especially, is experiencing clear symptoms of decline today. Deterioration of its agricultural resources—its soils, forests, and water supplies—compounds stresses stemming from rapid population growth, unsound economic policies, and warfare. Per capita food production is diminishing, malnutrition is spreading, and societal tensions are rising.

Over the last three years, Egypt, Morocco, and Tunisia have each experienced riots or demonstrations connected with increases in food prices. It is difficult to believe that some 2,000 years ago, northern Africa's fertile fields made it the granary of the expanding Roman Empire. Today, vast deserts cover the region, and fully half of its grain supplies are imported.

For the world as a whole, destabilizing stresses could arise from the global economy's pervasive dependence on oil. Hints of that vulnerability emerged with the oil price increases of the 1970s, which in many countries triggered rampant inflation, declining rates of economic growth, and rising unemployment. Whether oil-dependent nations successfully adjust to a reconcentration of oil production in the Middle East, and to the inevitable decline in total production, will strongly influence prospects for economic growth and social stability.

OUR NEW RESPONSIBILITY

As we near the end of the twentieth century, we are entering uncharted territory. Localized changes in natural systems are now being overlaid with continental and global ones, some of which may be irreversible. Everyday human activities, such as driving automobiles, generating electricity, and producing food, may collectively cause changes of geological proportions within a matter of decades.

A human population of 5 billion, expanding at 83 million per year, has combined with the power of industrial technologies to create unprecedented momentum toward human-induced environmental change. We have inadvertently set in motion grand ecological experiments involving the entire earth without yet having the means to systematically monitor the results.

Pollution-induced forest damage and the potential depletion of the earth's ozone layer are relatively recent discoveries. Yet the activities believed to have brought about these threats—fossil-fuel pollutants and the rise of chlorofluorocarbons—have been under way for decades. Taken further by surprise, industrial societies may trap themselves into costly and dubious tasks of planetary maintenance—perhaps seeding clouds in attempts to trigger rainfall where it has diminished with climatic change, or seeking means of protection from increased exposure to ultraviolet radiation, or liming vast areas of land sterilized by acidification.

The existence of thresholds beyond which change occurs rapidly and unpredictably creates an urgent need for early warning systems and mechanisms for averting disastrous effects. Despite impressive progress, the scientific groundwork has yet to be laid for monitoring the pulse of the earth's life-support systems. Meanwhile, the pace of change quickens.

We have crossed many natural thresholds in a short period of time. No one knows how the affected natural systems will respond, much less how changes in natural systems will in turn affect economic and political systems. We can be reasonably certain that deforestation will disrupt hydrologic cycles and that ozone depletion will induce more skin cancer. But beyond these first-order effects, scientists can provide little detail.

Any system pushed out of equilibrium behaves in unpredictable ways. Small external pressures may be sufficient to cause dramatic changes. Stresses may become self-reinforcing, rapidly increasing the system's instability.

Economic systems, with which we are perhaps more familiar, display some of these features. If a heavily indebted developing country reaches a point where it can no longer pay all the interest on its debt, the unpaid interest is added to the principal. The principal grows, further raising the interest. After a point, without debt forgiveness or other outside intervention, the debt grows out of control, and the system moves toward bankruptcy. Mexico is perhaps the most prominent of many developing countries now on this path.

Never have so many systems vital to the earth's habitability been out of equilibrium simultaneously. New environmental problems also span time periods and geographic areas that stretch beyond the authority of existing political and social institutions. No single nation can stabilize the earth's climate, protect the ozone layer, or preserve the planet's mantle of forests and soils. Only a sustained international commitment will suffice.

Matters of the global environment now warrant the kind of high-level attention and concern that the global economy receives. World leaders historically have cooperated to preserve economic stability, even to the point of completely overhauling the international monetary system at the 1944 conference in Bretton Woods. Summit meetings are held periodically to attempt to iron out international economic problems. Policy makers carefully track economic indicators to determine when adjustments—national or international—are required. Similar efforts are needed to delineate the bounds of environmental stability, along with mechanisms for making prompt adjustments when these bounds draw near.

With so many natural systems becoming unstable within such a short period of time, discontinuous, surprising, and rapid changes may become commonplace. Stresses on economies and governments will accumulate. Societies faced with self-generated stresses that are becoming unmanageable have two options: initiate the needed reforms in population, energy, agriculture, and economic policies, or risk deterioration and decline.

POSTSCRIPT

Is the Environment Improving?

Simon argues that the media misleads the public with frightening headlines of environmental problems and famines. In contrast to the media, he looks at scientific data which prove that the environment is improving and resources are becoming more available. He agrees that mankind has environmental and resource problems to work on, but he is confident that they will be taken care of by human effort and inventiveness. He expects necessity to give birth to inventions, because technological developments will reap substantial economic rewards as resources become scarce. Simon's problem-solving thesis is supported by Charles Maurice and Charles W. Smith with ten major historical examples in *The Doomsday Myth, Ten Thousand Years of Economic Crisis* (Hoover Institution Press, 1985).

Lester Brown and Sandra Postel would see Simon as a mythmaker whose optimism requires selective scanning of data on the environment. Furthermore, environmentalists such as Brown and Postel think economists such as Simon fail to understand environmental principles, one of which is that the environment gives off few signals of population overshoot and other environmental dangers until it is too late for species to moderate their growth and come into balance with the environment. The environmentalists argue that many regional and local ecosystems throughout the world are decreasing their natural productivity and major ecocatastrophes loom on the horizon.

Some of the prominent optimists on the issues of the availability of resources and health of the environment include Herman Kahn, *World Economic Development 1979 and Beyond* (Westville Press, 1979); Christopher Freeman and Marie Jahoda, eds., *World Futures: The Great Debate* (Universe Books, 1978); Julian L. Simon, *The Ultimate Resource* (Princeton University, 1981); and Julian L. Simon and Herman Kahn, eds., *The Resourceful Earth: A Response to Global 2000* (Basil Blackwell, 1984). Some of the prominent pessimists include Ferdinand E. Banks, *Scarcity, Energy, and Economic Progress* (Lexington Books, 1977); W. Jackson Davis, *The Seventh Year: Industrial Civilization in Transition* (Norton, 1979); S. R. Eye, *The Real Wealth of Nations* (St. Martin's Press, 1978); *The Global 2000 Report to The President* (Government Printing Office, 1980); Robert Stobaugh and Daniel Yerkin, eds., *Energy Future: Report of the Energy Project at the Harvard Business School* (Random House, 1979); William Catton, *Overshoot* (University of Illinois Press, 1980); and Lester R. Brown et al., *State of the World, 1987* (W. W. Norton, 1987). For a balanced review of both sides of the debate see Barry B. Hughes *World Futures: A Critical Analysis of Alternatives* (Johns Hopkins University Press, 1985).

ISSUE 20

Is America Headed for an Economic Bust?

YES: Richard Lamm, from *Megatraumas: America at the Year 2000* (Houghton Mifflin, 1985)

NO: Marshall Loeb, from "The Economy of 1987—and Beyond," *Vital Speeches of the Day* (April 1, 1987)

ISSUE SUMMARY

YES: Richard Lamm argues that America is heading into an era of economic crisis brought on by reckless spending and inadequate investment.
No: Marshall Loeb predicts that America is entering a prolonged period of economic growth.

In the Fall of 1928, ex-Secretary of State Charles Evans Hughes looked forward to a future of American prosperity, a prosperity that "feeds upon itself," and Treasury Secretary Andrew Mellon assured the American people that "the high tide of prosperity will continue." Their enthusiasm seemed well founded for the stock market had been booming for almost a decade. Irving Fisher, a distinguished economics professor at Yale, summed up the conventional wisdom when he announced that stock prices "have reached what looks like a permanently high plateau." Republican presidential candidate Herbert Hoover was sure that we were "in sight of the day when poverty will be banished from the nation."

A year later, on October 29, 1929, the bottom dropped out of the stock market. On "Black Tuesday," approximately sixteen and a half million shares were traded, and stocks dropped by as much as 80 percent. Within a few years, many businesses faltered and collapsed, and a quarter of the nation's work force was unemployed. People sold apples in the streets, waited in bread lines, built shanties in parks, and wandered through the countryside in desperate search of work. It was the worst depression in the nation's history, and it lasted ten years, until World War II spending finally got the economy moving again.

In 1987 the economy was booming—in fact, had been for five consecutive years. There were concerns about record trade and budget deficits, but profits were up and unemployment had fallen to the lowest level in seven years. Treasury Secretary James Baker noted that a higher percentage of Americans were employed "than at any time in our history." By August of 1987, the Dow Jones Industrial Average had gone up almost 740 points for the year; measured over a five-year period, the value of the Dow had more than tripled. The head of the stock futures department at Shearson Lehman Brothers echoed a view widely held on Wall Street when he said, "I think there's a lot more to come."

On October 19, 1987, the stock market collapsed on a scale never seen before, not even in 1929. Even before noon of what was instantly called "Black Monday," prices had dropped so sharply that the entire year's gain was wiped out. The selling was frantic. Traders were shaking their heads, hardly able to believe that it was happening. By the time of the 4 P.M. closing bell at the New York Stock Exchange, the Dow Industrial Average had plunged 508 points, causing a loss of $500 billion in paper value, a sum equal to the gross national product of France.

What is the significance of this new crash? What were its causes? What will its effects eventually be? The experts are divided, as they usually are about such matters. Most corporate economists, at least, reject the parallels to the stock market crash of 1929; they insist that conditions are greatly different today than they were back then. Others are not so sure; they note that stock market performance is a least one leading indicator of future economic conditions, and the American stock market really took a beating in the fall of 1987. Perhaps only time will tell us whether there are really many parallels to 1929 and the ensuing Great Depression of the 1930s.

Meanwhile, beyond the immediate ups and downs of the stock market, is the larger question of how healthy our economy has been in recent years. Does our economic structure give businesses and consumers the right incentives for growth? Does it give meaningful and remunerative employment to the average American worker? Is it turning out quality products that can successfully compete with foreign-made products? What is our government doing to help or hurt our economy? What should it do? These are the more basic questions, and they are question to which Colorado Governor Richard Lamm and Marshall Loeb, managing editor of *Fortune* magazine, give quite different answers.

YES

Richard D. Lamm

AMERICA AT THE YEAR 2000

PROLOGUE

I believe that America is heading into an era of multiple traumas. For the past fifteen years, our economy has been staggered by a number of external shocks and internal inadequacies. The United States is now a debtor nation. A long-term continued growth of the economic pie, which is so necessary to democracy, is simply not happening. The average American made less money—adjusted for inflation—in 1983 than he did in 1973. Nineteen eighty-four, while posting record economic growth, was a year of recovery built on the quicksand of record deficits. In the early days of my career, political efforts to redistribute some percentage of the national wealth were favored by a growing economic pie. Now that the pie has remained the same size—if not grown smaller—we still try to divide fairly by readjusting the size of the shares.

At the same time, we are not doing enough to restart our economic growth. Have we forgotten such a fundamental truth as the fact that a nation's wealth is its productive capacity—a capacity constituted of a willingness to work hard, to sacrifice, to acquire education and skills, and to invest in tomorrow? That is the part of productive capacity that comes from morale. The other part is the plant, the actual wealth-creating machinery—and both have grown rusty in America.

Our successful rivals among industrial nations have spent on research and development while we have scrimped. They train engineers while we train lawyers. We spend money on doctors and overbuilt hospitals and they spend money on health. The engineers they graduate go to work in the domestic economy to build better exports while 40 percent of our engineers and scientists work at building a defense system.

These countries take an ever-greater share of the world market away from us. They build factories while we build opulent homes. They have pre-empted the leadership in technological innovation in many areas. Their exports grow while our imports grow. They emphasize responsibilities when

Excerpt from *Megatraumas: America at the Year 2000*, by Richard D. Lamm (Boston: Houghton Mifflin Company), pp. 3–4, 14–23. Copyright © 1985 by Richard D. Lamm. Reprinted by permission of Houghton Mifflin Company.

we emphasize rights. They invest in their future as we mortgage ours. They save and add to their national wealth; we spend and dissipate our national wealth.

The United States is a nation in liquidation. . . .

SPEECH BY THE SECRETARY OF THE TREASURY TO THE U.S. CHAMBER OF COMMERCE APRIL 15, 2000

. . . This is the first presidency of the twenty-first century, and it would be nice to think that we could start this century unencumbered by past mistakes. But you must understand that each president inherits the mistakes of his or her predecessors. This isn't a kind of political checkers where we can start a new game when we want to. Every four or eight years a new man or woman steps into the stream of time and plays the pieces that were put into position by previous presidents. We are thus controlled by the dead hands of past politicians and we must live with their mistakes, grapple with their institutions, cope with their inflation, and suffer under the hate and distrust that their foreign policies have engendered.

We've had a succession of presidents who have purchased temporary tranquility at the expense of the future. Every president since the 1960s campaigned for a balanced budget and came into office with the best of intentions. Yet they all failed to balance the federal budget. Ronald Reagan, who complained the most vigorously about the unbalanced budget, accumulated more deficits in five years than his thirty-eight predecessors did in one hundred ninety-two years. Government has been a giant pyramid scheme, a chain letter to the future, and the problem that this administration faces is that the future is *now*. "Political tomorrow" has arrived. This isn't 1980 or 1985 or even 1990; this is the year 2000, and we live with a legacy of staggering political malpractice on the part of both political parties. . . .

Let us first examine the whole question of national wealth. This country has been allowing its wealth to hemorrhage away. When I first assumed public office in 1974, more than twenty-five years ago, this nation had a $9 billion trade surplus. By 1984, it had turned into a $130 billion trade deficit. In 1970, the United States produced 40 percent of the world's gross product. By 1980, it was down to 30 percent and continued to fall after that. In 1970, we were unmistakably first in average per-worker income. By 1980, we were fourth in per-worker income. The United States made the mistake all great empires of history have made. We assumed that it would last forever. We took our prosperity for granted, believing that God was on our side and would protect us from harm. We should have listened to the important words of a wise man who said, "Of the world's known civilizations, the majority have died. Not from enemy activity, but from the decay from within, and the progression has always been the same: from bondage to spiritual faith, from spiritual faith to great courage, from great courage to liberty, from liberty to abundance, from abundance to apathy, from apathy to dependence, and from dependence, once again, into bondage."

It is not enough for a nation to have a handful of heroes. What we need are generations of responsible people. Heroes are important, but they cannot be a substitute for a society of reliable people who steadfastly place the public interest before their own private interest. We reap what we sow, and a nation that has forgotten how to work hard, how to obey the law, how to sacrifice for the national destiny, is not a nation that can be sustained for any great period of time. . . .

In 1985 The United States turned from a creditor nation into a debtor nation. Today we are not only the world's largest debtor nation, we owe more than all the developing nations put together. The world, much of it in poverty, is loaning the United States money to continue its extravagant lifestyle. We thus have two debt crises on our hands: first, the uncollectable funds we have loaned the Third World: second, the very collectable funds we have borrowed from the rest of the world to finance our deficits and sustain our economy. We are the authors of our own economic crisis.

You really must understand how much change I have seen just in my political lifetime. When I graduated from college in 1967, most new cars sold for between $3500 and $5000. My wife and I bought a brand new Volkswagen for $1800. The average single-family home sold for less than $15,000. Gasoline was about thirty cents a gallon and gold was selling for $32 an ounce. Between 1967 and 1984, gasoline prices rose 450 percent. The average home tripled in value and precious metals appreciated 1200 percent. The dollar lost 70 percent of its value between 1967 and 1984. . . .

. . . We Americans are suckers for good news. As Adlai Stevenson said, "Given the choice between disagreeable fact and agreeable fantasy, we will choose agreeable fantasy." The public was fed political pabulum rather than reality, and consequently, this administration has had to take some drastic measures.

I do not like the idea of suspending civil liberties or the imposition of martial law, but the inflation riots of last year left us with no alternative. This administration didn't cause the inflation; we inherited it. America ended up paying for the 1970s oil crisis three times: once when oil went from $3 a barrel to $30; again when inflation caused by OPEC robbed us of our buying power; and the third time when the Arabs deposited their new resources in our banks, and we lent them to countries who couldn't pay us back. It would be funny if it wasn't so tragic. But actions like that caused the hyperinflation with which we now must deal. Martial law is the least onerous of our choices. Hyperinflation is to politics what gasoline is to fire. Hyperinflation preceded Hitler's Germany, Lenin's Russia, and Mussolini's Italy. We are taking away freedom in the name of freedom.

Arnold Toynbee also warned of the fragility of freedom. He observed:

Man is a social animal; mankind cannot survive in anarchy; and if democracy fails to provide stability, it will assuredly be replaced by some socially stabilizing regime, however uncongenial this alternative regime may be. A community that has purchased freedom at the cost of losing stability will find itself constrained to re-purchase stability at the price of sacrificing its freedom. This happened in the Graeco-Roman world; it could happen in our world too if we were to continue to fail to make democratic institutions work. Freedom is expendable; stability is indispensable.

It is this administration's contention that that is exactly what has happened. An early French philosopher said that "freedom is the luxury of self-discipline," but we did not turn out to be a disciplined people, we did not have disciplined politicians, and we did not have a disciplined political system. We became accustomed to instant gratification, and the glue that held us together as Americans simply became unstuck.

At the same time that our national economy was stagnant, the debts against that national economy increased geometrically. Neither political party had the backbone to stabilize the national spending. The Democrats refused to acknowledge that our domestic programs were out of control and growing by unsustainable rates (for instance, Medicare and Medicaid rose all during the 1970s and early 1980s at 17 or 18 percent a year) and the Republicans refused to recognize that military spending was out of control. The military paid $600 for goods available in local hardware stores for $7. Neither party practiced what it preached or preached what it practiced. And this administration is now left with a national austerity program that we think is our only alternative. Medicare accumulated a deficit of more than $300 billion between 1983 and 1995. And we've had to rescue the Social Security system again. Again, we didn't listen to the warnings. The intermediate assumptions of the Social Security Administration on the actuarial soundness of the Social Security, for instance, in 1983, were that there would be only 5.5 percent unemployment by 1995 and a low rate of inflation, that the United States was going to have a rather dramatic increase in its birthrate, and that there would be no substantial increase in life expectancy in the United States. In an almost perverse manner, every one of those assumptions has proven false. Social Security has taken an unacceptably large portion of the worker's paycheck and has certainly accounted for the intergenerational antago-

nism that has been so plaguing this country for the last fifteen years.

Military pensions and federal civil service pensions were equally unsustainable. They were gifts from generous politicians who purchased present popularity for themselves without regard for the consequences. In 1980, for instance, the $27 billion paid to three million federal military and civil service retirees was almost twice the $15 billion paid to the nine million retirees in the private sector. The federal government in 1982 spent more on the retirement of its employees than it did on all its programs for the needy. In that year, the civil service retirement system alone cost $31.4 billion, while the combined total for food stamps, housing assistance, and welfare was $26.9 billion. We attacked the poor, but we didn't have the courage to attack the everyday "you-and-me" subsidies that were really running up the national debt.

Our health care system was also clearly out of control. Again, we myopically failed to see that medical science was rushing us toward a day when we would be faced with the fact that our hospitals were filled with ill people whose physical existence could be prolonged almost indefinitely, but whose quality of life had become intolerable. The cost of this technological torture in the name of health care undercut our economy. We now have a great medical system sitting atop a shattered economy.

Looking back on these mistakes with the wisdom of hindsight, you can see how politicians were able to defer their problems, leaving them to the next generation of politicians. They were essentially faced with three alternatives in dealing with the economy: (1) they could commit political suicide by eliminating sacred spending programs; (2) they could commit political suicide by doubling taxes; or (3) they could start the printing presses and destroy the future by ignoring the problem. As Charlie Brown in "Peanuts" said, "There is no problem so big you can't run away from it." That's what politicians did all through the 1980s and 1990s.

It is understandable, though not excusable, that they might choose to do so. In 1984, for instance, to pay off one year's worth of government debts (the 1984 deficit), each man, woman, and child in the United States would have had to come with $800 in additional taxes. In other words, to really have pay-as-you-go government, taxes would have had to almost double to offset just 1984's budget deficit, with the tax bill being an extra $3200 for a family of four. By 1989, annual interest on the national debt was $750 per person. Caught between the inability to say no to social programs and the inability to say yes to new taxes for them, the politicians debased our money, ran up massive federal deficits, and ignored the consequences. The blind led the bland.

A society ultimately becomes what it invests in. Capital is the stored flexibility that we have available to meet the future. A nation can print money, but it can't print capital. Capital is real wealth. How we spend it is more than just an important issue. In may cases, it is *the* important issue. A society that does not maintain its investment, or that invests in the present at the expense of the future, or invests in superfluous or nonessential items rather than productive capacity soon finds that it doesn't have a future. The future isn't something that we inherit. It's something that we create by our choices. Maybe we didn't see that earlier, but this administration has been mugged by reality.

Our predecessors made multiple mistakes. Again with the wisdom of hindsight, let me try to list some of them:

1. We assumed continued prosperity. We took for granted a rising level of income and shunned the reinvestment and hard work that our international competitors did not shrink from. They prospered while we declined. Freedom, democracy, and abundance are not ironclad guarantees. In fact, they are the historical exceptions, not the rule. Progress is a challenge, not a promise.

2. We didn't control our systems. We didn't reform our health care systems, our pension systems, or any of our federal programs until it was too late. We paid Social Security to rich retirees, farm subsidies to rich corporate farmers, veterans' benefits to wealthy vets, medicare to retired doctors, civil service and military pensions to triple dippers, and unemployment to the deliberately idle. We dissipated our store of national wealth so painfully built up over two hundred years.

3. Our elections became bidding contests, rather than debates over truth. They were occasions for conveying promises rather than challenges and political pabulum rather than political reality. A number of people tried to warn us, but we ignored them. It was like giving blind men flashlights.

4. We didn't pay our own way. We borrowed from the future to finance a way of life that clearly couldn't continue. We thought we had a divine destiny, but instead we had only a deadly decadence.

5. We didn't secure our resource base. We didn't adequately value our own topsoil, for example; it was disappearing even in the 1960s, 1970s, and 1980s at an alarming rate. And we didn't recognize that our strategic fossil fuel and minerals

came from two of the most potentially anarchic areas in the world, the Arabian Peninsula and South Africa. We are now strategically isolated.

6. We let our education system deteriorate. In 1983, a report called "A Nation at Risk" (issued by the National Commission on Excellence in Education) stated simply that the United States in the previous fifteen years had committed acts of unilateral educational disarmament in letting its education system deteriorate. We left our children defenseless.

7. Politicians of both parties acted as if they had a duty to lie. Their constituents rewarded them for protecting them from reality. Truth may be in scarce supply, but it always seems to exceed demand.

This administration is not going to be that way. We are trying to rally people around reality, to force our society to make the hard choices that were never made in the '70s, the '80s, or the '90s.

To survive, we must control our excesses, make all our institutions more responsive and efficient, and examine all our governmental goals to make sure they are realistic and compassionate. We must bring back the virtues that built this country: imagination, sacrifice, restraint, thrift, self-discipline. Government is through making promises that we can't keep; we must now learn to manage scarcity. . . .

NO

Marshall Loeb

THE ECONOMY OF 1987—AND BEYOND: SOCIAL, POLITICAL AND ECONOMIC CHANGES

. . . In this era of rapid and wrenching change, let me sketch *seven* of the sweeping social, political and economic changes that I think will substantially affect our country and its economy, our personal lives and our livelihoods in 1987 and indeed through the 1990s.

Point Number One. The American nation, and much of the rest of the world, is going through a *conservative revolution* of remarkable depth and breadth. This revolution extends far beyond the economy and into society and politics. Furthermore, the revolution is only in its *infancy.* It will continue and in some ways it will accelerate.

The cause is clear: For the first time in history, after centuries, after millenia of living as peasants or subsistence farmers, millions of people in many countries of the world are beginning to possess something in the way of material *assets.* They are struggling into the broadening middle class. They have too recently seen these assets eaten away by the twin scourges of high taxation and runaway inflation, and so they are apprehensively fighting above all else to *conserve* those assets. As a consequence, they are changing their politics, their attitudes and their lifestyles. They are shifting to support conservative policies and they are electing conservative governments. . . .

A conservative revolution is also sweeping over and sweeping up our young people. They grew up in a rare time of *declining* expectations, an era— several years ago—of oppressive inflation and scary unemployment. Consequently, they value a job, and they put a premium on careers. The new young—particularly people aged from their late teens to their early thirties— show all signs of returning to *conservative* values.

If you visit the universities of our country, you'll see that our young people are the most career-minded, business-oriented generation in memory. In fact, the most sought after major course of study on campus in America is business. Most important, every freshman class is more conservative, realis-

From "The Economy of 1987—and Beyond," by Marshall Loeb, *Vital Speeches of the Day,* April 1, 1987. Reprinted by permission.

tic, moderate—pick your word—than the previous one. The students are more conservative, realistic, moderate than their instructors and professors. In just the last several years, we have turned the whole campus equation on its head.

Point Number Two. We are entering a technology- and service-oriented era.

The countries, the regions, the companies that master the new technologies or that develop the information services and the financial services that productively enhance the new technologies, those will be the countries, the regions, the companies that will prosper economically, will dominate politically, will inherit the future. But, the regions where business people try to hang on to and artificially protect and prop up the old, those will be the regions that will continue to be in trouble. . . .

The *problem* is that the United States is rapidly—and perhaps dangerously—becoming *two countries*. It is becoming two countries in terms of its regions, its races and its economy.

Socially, we are also becoming two countries. One America consists of the educated, the skilled people. They get jobs in the highly demanding businesses of the new economy; they put their money in all those high growth investments that we are constantly telling them about in *Fortune*, and their lives grow better. But the uneducated, the unskilled fall further and further behind. The good life, the American dream becomes ever more elusive for them.

Surely, one of the American nation's greatest challenges in the next ten years will be to find means for the American underclass to lift themselves out of their economic and emotional slough. Even my fellow social liberals have to admit: Most of our government programs and

institutions have *failed.* Our public housing has created public slums. Our public welfare has created despair, dependence and hopelessness among millions of our fellow Americans.

So, I believe that *private* enterprise—working with government tax incentives, credits and guarantees, but within the private economy—will have to take on more and more of the job of razing and then rebuilding the slums, of creating the factories and offices, and even, in some cases, of providing the basic schooling, as American business today is increasingly providing basic schooling to its employees. Surely all that will be a continuing challenge and opportunity for every American. We cannot allow ourselves to be comfortable so long as so many of our fellow citizens remain so helplessly far behind.

Point Number Three. In foreign affairs, the United States just may have the opportunity for a rather revolutionary change in its relations with the Soviet Union.

It would be foolish to predict any quick change, yet the conditions are tantalizingly in place for some movement. The Soviets, paralyzed for many years by illness, death and revolving succession among its geriatric leadership, has at long last turned to a younger generation of chiefs. They are desperately trying to make their cosseted economic system more efficient. At least there is the hope that they ultimately will turn out to be more pragmatic, more worldly than their xenophobic predecessors, that they will be willing to open up their economy for more trade with us, that they will be willing to slow the devastatingly expensive arms race in order to spend more for the modern technology that they can buy from us. The man with the toughest management problem in the world today is Mikhael Gorbachev, because he wants to wrench an incredibly backward Soviet economy into the modern era without losing too much central control.

Our American foreign policy should be to help induce the Soviets to free up their political and their economic system, and to switch more of their limited capital resources out of arms and adventurism and into buying what we have to sell.

Point Number Four. In the United States, we are in for a period of rather prolonged, sustained economic expansion.

True enough, I have never seen such a spotty, fractionated economy. Some communities and some businesses are thriving; others are taking it on the chin. In sum, it is hard to talk about the total economy without first recognizing that there are—and will continue to be— sharp differences among its various communities.

But taking it as a whole, the United States economy has been enjoying a remarkably prolonged, sustained expansion, and we expect it to continue through this year and well into next year. . . .

Productivity will rise as all those new entrants to the labor force—notably the baby boomers and women—gain experience in their jobs. Unemployment among the *unskilled* will persist, particularly as the economy becomes more complex and sophisticated. But simultaneously, the big job problem of the late 1980s and the 1990s will be *shortages* of skilled workers. Birth rates declined sharply in the U.S. after 1964, and so we know that far fewer workers will be entering the labor force in the immediate future than in the immediate past.

Longer term, our *Fortune* forecast is that between now and the end of the century—that is, over the next 13 years— industrial production will rise at an average 3 percent annual rate. To repeat: that is not a boom, but it qualifies as a rather large bang compared with average annual increases of 1.8 percent over the past seven years.

All of what I've said is not to suggest that the economy, and our nation, do not have problems. They do—*huge* problems.

Foremost among them, of course, are the four Big D's: the twelve-digit federal budget deficit, the twelve-digit U.S. trade deficit, the thirteen-digit third-world debt and the thirteen-digit U.S. federal debt.

But I have hopes that we will manage to surmount all four without disaster. We expect that the trade deficit will decline by about $50 billion this year because exports will grow much faster than imports. As for the third world debt, many big U.S. and European banks are already gradually writing off their third world loans, so they may just declare victory and walk away.

Regarding the federal deficit and the federal debt, we will have the rare opportunity to save ourselves in the 1990s thanks to a lucky break of demographics. A very small generation of babies were born in the U.S. between 1930 (just after the Depression began) and 1946 (when the boys marched home from World War II). Consequently, beginning about 1990 and continuing through about the year 2010, we will have a remarkably small generation of new retirees entering the social security system and claiming benefits. Simultaneously, the post-World War II baby boomers will be reaching their peak earning years, and pouring huge sums into the Social Security coffers. The Social Security System may well be running a surplus of $200 billion a year late in the 1990s and a surplus of $1 trillion for the whole decade. The question, of course, is whether Congress will persist in being Congress and will spend all that windfall, or will use it to close the deficit and narrow the debt.

Point Number Five. Investment markets in the U.S. should do well—over the intermediate term and the long term.

The market has shot up so rapidly that I can absolutely guarantee you that it will *fall*—fall quite possibly by 10 percent, 20 percent or perhaps more. The trouble is I cannot tell you when. As the economists say, "Give them a figure or a date, but never both." I do not know—and I do not know anybody who knows—whether the stock market will be higher a week from today or a month from today than it is today. And I do not believe that it matters very much, because almost all of us should be evaluating the stock market from a *long-term* point of view. But I believe strongly that the market will be higher a year from now, and *significantly* higher five years from now, than it is today.

There are several reasons to expect that, even if stocks fall temporarily in the near future, we are in the midst of a *long* bull market: Speculation in the market is certainly not excessive; recession in the economy is nowhere in sight; inflation and interest rates show no sign of roaring up in the near future; and despite the recent surge, the Dow Jones Industrial Average is substantially *under*valued.

In terms of real purchasing power, stocks are 9 percent *lower* than they were in early 1966. That is, had you invested $10,000 in the stocks of the Standard and Poor's 500 Index back then, your money by now would have grown—but in 1966 dollars it would have a purchasing power of just $9,000 or so. Not only are stocks fairly cheap by some historical methods, but they are also worth relatively more because tax reform, by lowering income tax rates, allows you to pocket and keep more of your dividends than you could in years past. Dividends also look relatively more attractive since interest rates have come down and you can get only 5½ percent or so on your money market fund. . . .

Point Number Six. There will be a dramatic expansion of the quality market. Americans everywhere are becoming more quality-conscious. They are not necessarily picking the fanciest designer label or paying the highest possible price, but they are showing a new sophisticated awareness that high quality is more efficient and reliable, and therefore more economical in the long run, that spending for high quality goods and services is a sound investment.

A remarkable change is occurring in American marketing. As you go across the country and you study markets—whether they are markets for magazines or cars or clothes or food—you see that the goods that are selling well are those that deliver real value for money, high quality, reliability, durability. And the goods that are selling poorly are those that do not have lasting value—the faddish, the flashy, the easily discarded goods.

Our standards of value will change but, at least for the broad mass of the American people, our standards of living will rise. And business men and women—as well as entrepreneurs, journalists and others—who produce and deliver quality goods and quality services will surely prosper. . . .

And now my final point, point number seven. Let me observe that we are entering an era when the countries that possess the rare combination of human and material resources will prosper and inherit the future.

If my colleagues at *Fortune* are right about our current problems—and they are many—as well as our future potentials—and they, too, are many—there will be five—just five ingredients for the economic, the political, the social success of a nation in the next ten years. Societies, peoples, countries will do well if they have a number of the following five.

First, a rich, a modern, a highly productive agricultural base, giving a country the capacity not only to feed its own people but also to export—for economic gain, occasionally for political leverage, certainly for humanitarian purposes.

Second, an abundant base of energy-bearing raw materials—not only oil and natural gas but also coal, hydro-electric power, geopressured methane, uranium, and all the rest.

Third, a vital, a strong base of other non-energy raw materials—iron ore, copper, lead, phosphate, zinc, and the like.

Fourth, an advanced, an automated, a highly developed technology and industry, notably including information and financial services industries.

Fifth, and most important, an educated, a motivated, a well-informed, a skilled, a sophisticated population.

I've gone down the list of all the member nations of the United Nations—159 at latest count. It's fascinating, it's revealing if you try to apply these five criteria. You very quickly see that the Soviet Union, for all of its vaunted military might, and I do not demean that for a moment—it's very real and will be a threat to us for the rest of our life-times—but the Soviets, if you are generous to them, qualify under perhaps two of the five headings. They suffer from grave problems because of the totally inefficient, bankrupt Soviet agriculture, because of the erratic nature of Soviet industry, because of the questionable skills and education of so much of the Soviet population.

China has a brilliant future, but a distant one. It suffers from severe problems and shortages—and will continue to do so for the rest of this century and probably well into the 21st century.

Germany and Japan are fairly well off, but only fairly so, because they lack the food and the fuel to supply their own populations, let alone to export.

The Netherlands, Norway and Britain have significant economic and social problems at the moment. But, given their advanced industries, their skilled, educated populations, and their vast energy resources, they face potentially very bright futures—*if* they choose the proper policies now.

But, ladies and gentlemen, there are three, and only three, nations on the face of the earth that qualify by all five measures of rich agriculture, abundant energy and non-energy resources, advanced industrial technology, and skilled, educated populations. And those three are Canada, Australia and, of course, the United States.

What our nation *lacks* is also apparent. It is the will, the methods, the procedures and often the institutions to exploit those resources; it is the leaders with skill and vision to rally the people; it is the resolve to surmount individual interests for the benefit of all.

But these are purely psychological and institutional constraints, and thus they can be surmounted. That is where we come in. Surely we—you and I, partic-

ularly you in this great capital of technological prowess and business intelligence—we *can* make a difference.

Ladies and gentlemen, the United
States has *no* major physical or material
limitations. That is quite a superlative
statement, but is indisputably correct.
So, despite all of our immediate and very
visible problems, if we Americans follow
sensible policies of government dereg-
ulation, of investment stimulation, of
energy conservation and energy development, then the economic, the political
and the social future of the United States
in the rest of the revolutionary 1980s and
the 1990s is absolutely *dazzling*.

POSTSCRIPT

Is America Headed for an Economic Bust?

In some cases, Lamm and Loeb are looking at the same facts but analyzing them quite differently. The aging of the American population is one such case. Lamm worries about what will happen when the "baby boomer"—the big bulge of Americans born between 1945 and 1965—reach retirement age and start collecting Social Security. But Loeb notes that the baby boom generation is now entering its most productive years. That should give the economy a near-term boost, perhaps giving it enough momentum to push it through the time when the boomers start retiring and collecting their money. At least that is what Loeb hopes. Whether his hope is more justified than Lamm's fear is for you to decide right now. The final indisputable decision will come in the future.

Adversity is just around the corner, argues Ravi Batra in *The Great Depression of 1990* (Simon and Schuster, 1987). The essays published in Martin Bronfenbrenner's *Is the Business Cycle Obsolete?* (Wylie-Interscience, 1969) are more optimistic. Their common agreement, the editor notes, is that "another catastrophe of the 1929–1933 type is, if not impossible, conceivable only by an extraordinary combination of erroneous policies." In a pessimistic vein is William Ophuls' *Ecology and the Politics of Scarcity* (W. H. Freeman, 1977) and Robert Heilbronner's *An Inquiry into the Human Prospect* (W. H. Freeman, 1977). Barry H. Hughes seeks a balanced assessment in his review of some of the predictions of "futurists." See his *World Futures: A Critical Analysis of Alternatives* (Johns Hopkins, 1985).

Whether it is possible to predict the future of our society remains in dispute. History is full of surprises, and many confident predictions have turned out to be wildly mistaken. Futurists, however, continue to speculate about the direction of history, and some have produced thoughtful works, such as those mentioned above. Anyone interested in futurism might wish to look through issues of *The Futurist* magazine, a publication of the World Futurist Society. The Society also holds annual conferences and publishes anthologies of its best papers.

CONTRIBUTORS
TO THIS VOLUME

EDITORS

KURT FINSTERBUSCH received his bachelor's degree in history from Princeton University in 1957, and a bachelor of Divinity degree from Grace Theological Seminary in 1960. His Ph.D. in Sociology, from Columbia University, was conferred in 1969. He is the author or several books, including *Understanding Social Impacts* (Sage Publications, 1980), and *Social Research for Policy Decisions* (Wadsworth Publishing, 1980), with Annabelle Bender Motz. He is currently teaching at the University of Maryland, College Park, and is the academic editor for the Dushkin Publishing Group's *Annual Editions: Sociology.*

GEORGE McKENNA received his bachelor's degree from the University of Chicago in 1959, his M.A. from the University of Massachusetts in 1962, and his Ph.D. from Fordham University in 1967. He has been teaching political science at City College of New York since 1963. Among his publications are *American Populism* (Putnam, 1974) and *American Politics: Ideals and Realities* (McGraw-Hill, 1976). He has written articles in the fields of American government and political theory and has edited other volumes in the *Taking Sides* series.

STAFF

Marguerite L. Egan   Program Manager
Brenda S. Filley   Production Manager
Whit Vye   Designer
Libra Ann Cusack   Typesetting Coordinator
Lynn Shannon   Graphics Coordinator
Diane Barker   Editorial Assistant
Richard Tietjen   Editorial Systems Analyst

AUTHORS

EDWARD C. BANFIELD is professor of urban studies at Harvard University and author of a number of articles and books on urban problems, including the *Un-Heavenly City Revisited* (Little, Brown, 1974).

BETTY WINSTON BAYE is a reporter for the *Courier Journal* in Louisville, Kentucky, and the author of *The Africans* (Banbury Books, 1983).

DAVID BAZELON has been chief judge of the United States Court of Appeals for the District of Columbia circuit since 1962.

ROBERT N. BELLAH is a sociologist and educator who is currently Ford Professor of Sociology and Comparative Studies at the Unversity of California, Berkeley.

LESTER R. BROWN is president of the Worldwatch Institute, a research organization with an interdisciplinary approach to global, environmental problem-solving.

C. R. CREEKMORE is a free-lance writer who lives in Amherst, Massachusetts, and frequently writes on topics of sociological and psychological interest.

BARBARA DECKARD is an author and observer of the women's movement. She has written *The Women's Movement: Political, Socioeconomic*

and Psychological Issues, Second Edition (Harper and Row, 1979).

G. WILLIAM DOMHOFF is professor of psychology and sociology at the University of California, Santa Cruz.

HENRY FAIRLIE, a Londoner who has lived in the United States for many years, is a keen observer of British and American politics. His comments are frequently found in articles and books such as *The Life of Politics* and *The Spoiled Child of the Western World: The Miscarriage of the American Idea in Our Time.*

JOHN KENNETH GALBRAITH is an internationally renowned economisct who, before his retirement in 1975, was Paul M. Warburg Professor of Economics at Harvard University.

GEORGE GILDER is a widely published social commentator.

ROBERT GORDIS is Rappaport Professor of the Bible at the Jewish Theological Seminary in New York City. He is also the editor of *Judaism* magazine.

ALVIN GOULDNER is professor of sociology at Washington University in St. Louis and has published a number of classic articles in the field, including "Patterns of Bureaucracy," "The Coming Crisis in

Western Sociology," and "Enter Plato."

JEANNINE GRAMICK, a School Sister of Notre Dame, is a co-founder of New Ways Ministry, a Catholic group working with gays and lesbians within the Christian community. She recently completed a sociological study of lesbian women.

ANDREW GREELEY, a Catholic priest and professor of sociology at the University of Arizona, is also program director at the National Opinion Research Center in Chicago.

IRVING LOUIS HOROWITZ is the Hannah Arendt Distinguished Professor of Sociology and Political Science at Rutgers University and editor-in-chief of *Society* magazine. Among his publications are *The Rise and Fall of Project Camelot: The Relationship Between Social Science and Practical Politics* (MIT Press) and *The Use and Abuse of Social Science* (Transaction Books).

GARY IMHOFF is a free-lance writer in Washington, D.C., who specializes in public policy issues. He is the co-author of *The Immigration Time Bomb: The Fragmenting of America* (Dutton, 1986).

CHRISTOPHER JENCKS is professor of sociology and urban affairs at Northwestern University. His books include *Who Gets Ahead?* and *Inequality*.

CHARLES KRAUTHAMMER is a psychiatrist and associate editor of the *New Republic*.

RICHARD D. LAMM was the governor of Colorado from 1975 to 1986 and writes frequently on issues relating to health care, agriculture, and future prospects for America.

MARSHALL LOEB is managing editor of *Fortune* magazine.

GLENN C. LOURY is professor of political economy at Harvard University's John F. Kennedy School of Government.

THOMAS A. W. MILLER is a senior analyst and the publication director at Roper, the polling organization, in New York City. He is also the editor of *The Public Pulse*, Roper's newsletter on American attitudes, lifestyles, and behavior.

STEVEN MUMFORD is an expert in the area of population growth. He has authored *Population Growth Control: The Next Move is America's* (Philosophical Library, 1977). He recieved a Ph.D. in population studies from the University of Texas.

CHARLES MURRAY is a senior research fellow at the Manhattan Institute.

SANDRA POSTEL is a senior researcher at the Worldwatch Institute, a research organization with an interdisciplinary approach to global, environmental problem-solving.

WILLIAM RYAN is professor of psychology at Boston College and a consultant in the fields of mental health, community planning, and social problems. Besides *Blaming the Victim*, his publications include *Distress in the City* (UPB, 1969).

JONATHAN SCHELL is a staff writer for the *New Yorker* magazine and has written several books, including *The Military Half*, and *Time of Illusion* (Knopf, 1976).

PHYLLIS SCHLAFLY is the national chairwoman of *Stop ERA* and the president of Eagle Forum. Her publications include *A Choice, Not an Echo* (Pere Marquette, 1964), *The Betrayers* (Pere Marquette, 1968), and *The Power of the Positive Woman* (Jove Publications, 1977).

HERMAN SCHWARTZ teaches law at the American University and is the director of the Wm. O. Douglas Inquiry into the State of Individual Freedom.

JULIAN L. SIMON is a fellow at the Heritage Foundation and teaches economics at the University of Maryland.

WILLIAM SIMON is a former treasury secretary who writes on topics of current social and economic interest.

DONALD SINGLETARY is a free-lance writer and public-relations consultant in New York City.

SHIRLEY WILKINS is the president of Roper, the polling organization, and she currently directs the Virginia Slims American Women Opinon Poll, a series conducted annually by Roper since 1970.

CHARLES V. WILLIE, professor of education and urban studies at Harvard Graduate School of Education, is a former president of the Eastern Sociological Society. He has authored several books on minority relations including *Black/Brown/White Relations* (Transaction Books, 1977).

JAMES Q. WILSON is professor of government at Harvard University and the author of *The Amateur Democrat* (University of Chicago Press, 1966), *Negro Politics* (Free Press, 1960), and *Varieties of Police Behavior* (Harvard University Press, 1968).

WILLIAM JULIUS WILSON, professor of sociology at the University of Chicago, is the author of *Power, Racism and Privilege* (Free Press, 1976) and the co-editor of *Through Different Eyes* (Oxford University Press, 1977).

INDEX

Capitalism and the Welfare State (Gilbert), 235
capital punishment, 258, 263
carbon dioxide: 338; and greenhouse effect, 341, 342
careers: commitments of women to, 92–105; vs. marriage and motherhood as priority, 74–91
Carter, Jimmy, 190, 192, 210, 214
Catholic Church, *see* Roman Catholic Church
Chicago Sun-Times, 194
child mortality, decrease in, 333
child-rearing studies, on lower class, 32
children: education of poor, 27, 28; mortality rates for, 333; *see also,* child-rearing studies
China: birthrate in, 324; economic future of, 358; and homosexuality, 242, 250; population control in, 319–321
Chinatown, 287
chlorofluorocarbons, and ozone, 338, 343
choice: of career and family by women, 95–105; as freedom, 52–53
Christian Democrats, 208
Christianity: 200; and homosexuality, 240, 241, 243, 245
Churchill, Winston: 209; on nuclear deterrence, 305, 307
cities: global growth of, 70; negative view of life in, 56–63, 70, 71; positive view of life in, 56, 57, 64–71
civil liberties, and big government, 206
civic responsibility, vs. individualism, 36–48
Civil War, 182
class: vs. status, 34; *see also,* lower class; middle class; ruling class; upper class; working class
classical liberalism, and role of government, 200, 201
coal, 334
coalitions, as proof of nonexistence of power elite in America, 198
college loans, and social welfare, 227
"color-blindness," doctrine of, 165, 179
Communist Manifesto, 7
community, vs. individualism, 5, 6, 36–55
community action programs, effectiveness of, to aid the poor, 25–26
commuters, irrational life-style of, 59–61
companionate marriage, as middle-class American ideal, 86
compensatory education, for poor children, 29
Congress: and power elite, 190; and welfare, 214, 229
consensus, economic and social, and effect on government policy, 208–212
conservatives, and welfare, 226
Constitution: and nationalism, 285; and power elite in America, 182

consumer, rights of, in supermarket vs. village shop, 50–53
consumerism: 46; in defense of, 36, 37
consumer pollution, 333
conventional arms, and nuclear disarmament, 303, 304
corporate liberalism, 7
corporations, and power elite in America, 184, 185, 187–192
Costa Rica, birthrate in, 324
country life, *see* rural life
Creekmore, C. R., positive view of, on urban life, 56, 57, 64–71
crime: 5; effect of family on, 270–271; homosexuality as, 242; incapacitation as solution, to, 258–272; prevention, 258, 273–281
crimes of passion, 274
crowding, in cities, 61, 65
Cuba, birthrate in, 324
"cultural deprivation," and education of poor children, 27, 28
culture of poverty thesis: 20–26, 35; criticism of, 20, 21, 27–35

Daley, Mayor, 194
da Vinci, Leonardo, as homosexual, 249, 250
day care, 100
death penalty, 258, 263
debt crisis, of United States, 350
Deckard, Barbara, on traditional role of women as demeaning, 74, 75, 83–91
Declaration of Independence, 182
Deferred Need Gratification, of middle class vs. lower class, 32
de Gaulle, Charles, 209
Democracy for the Few (Parenti), 199
Democracy in America (de Tocqueville), 39
demographic transition, and relationship of fertility to economic development, 324
deserving poor: 203; *see also,* lower class; poor; poverty; underclass
deterrence: as crime prevention, 260–281; nuclear, 294–315
de Tocqueville, Alexis, 36, 37, 38, 39, 164
developed countries vs. less developed countries, and relationship of population growth to economic growth, 325
developing countries: and population growth, 319, 315; *see also,* less developed countries; Third World
deviance, debate over homosexuality as example of, 239–257
disabled people, and welfare, 214
disarmament, nuclear, 303
discrimination: affirmative action as reverse, 164–179; and homosexuality, 242–243; sex, 97, 103

division of labor, within nuclear family, 74–90
doctrine of nuclear deterrence: 295, 299; and first strike capability, 300, 301, 302
Domhoff, G. William, and debate over existence of power elite in America, 182–193, 199
Doomsday Myth, Ten Thousand Years of Economic Crisis (Maurice and Smith), 345
draft evasion, as example of relationship of certainty of punishment and deterrence, 262, 263
Drucker, Peter, 186
drugs, and Rockefeller drug laws, 263, 264, 265, 276
Dye, Thomas R., 188

earnings capacity, of men vs. women, 103–104
Earnings Capacity Utilization Rates, 133
ecological systems, effect of overpopulation on earth's, 316, 317
economic crisis, as coming, 346–359
economic development: effect of, on environment, 330; and fertility, 324
economic expansion, 355, 356
economic freedom, and big government, 212
economic growth: and crashes of 1929 compared with 1987; and debate over crisis of, in America, 346–359; and health of United States, 353–359; negative effects of, 340; relationship of, with population growth, 324–328, 339–340
economic inequality, ethics of American, 122–147
economic liberty: individualism as necessary to, 36, 37, 49–55; relationship of, with political liberty, 205–206
economics, laissez-faire, 201
Economics and the Public Purpose (Galbraith), 213
economies of scale, and population growth, 325, 326
ecosystem, and controversy over pollution of, 330, 331
education: and academic performance of blacks vs. whites, 168; compensatory, for poor, 29–30; and immigrants, 291; lower class value of, 31; place of political values in, 12, 15; of poor blacks, 159–161; of poor as "culturally deprived," 27, 28
educator, place of political values of, in school, 12, 15
Edward II, as a homosexual, 249
egalitarianism, 204, 205
Ehrlich, Paul, and population, 316, 317, 330
eighteenth century, government in, 200
Eisenhower, Dwight D., 209
elite rule: conspiracy of, in control of foreign and fiscal policy, 6–7; debate over

existence of, in America, 182–199; *see also,* power elite
elitism, *see* power elite
elitist-conspiracy model, 6–7
Ellwood, David, 231
energy: and oil, 333, 334; scarcity of, and new source of, 334, 335; solar, 342
entitlements, *see* welfare
environment, controversy over condition of, 332–344
Environmental Protection Agency (EPA), 333
Ephesians 5, feminist protests against reading of, 80
Equal Rights Amendment (ERA), 109
Essay on Population (Malthus), 323
estate-multiplier method, 187
ethics: and income inequality in America, 122–147; of individualism at expense of community, 36–48; as concern of sociology, 3
ethnocentrism, and nationalism, 285
Europe, individualism in, compared to America, 53–54
excessive government, debate over existence of, 200–213
ex-convicts, and supported-work project, 267, 268
exercise, and urban life, 62
external sovereignty, 285

Fairlie, Henry: on individualism as necessary to freedom and pursuit of happiness, 36, 37, 49–55; negative views of, on urban life, 56–63, 70, 71
Fair Play vs. Fair Shares view of income distribution, 136–146
Fair Shares vs. Fair Play view of income distribution, 136–146
Fallaci, Oriana, 79
fallout, 299
family: effect of, on criminality, 270, 271; poverty and breakdown of, 133–135, 215; traditional role of women in nuclear, 74–82; stereotype of nuclear, as myth, 83–90; and welfare, 215; women who combine career and, 92–105
family capitalism, and power elite in America, 186, 187, 188
family ownership, of stock in corporation and control, 186, 187, 188
famine deaths, 335
Famine 1975 (Paddock), 331
Fate of the Earth, The (Schell), 305
federal deficit, 356
Feminine Mystique, The (Friedan), 92, 109
feminist movement, *see* women's liberation movement
fertility, and population growth, 324

fireball, and nuclear explosion, 297
first strike: and doctrine of deterrence, 300,
301, 302; and nuclear arms freeze, 308
Fisher, Irving, 346
Five Thousand American Families (Morgan),
143
flagellation, 246
flexible response, policy of, as limited nuclear
war, 311
food production, world, 318, 335, 339, 343
food shortages, 318, 319, 331
food stamps, 223, 227, 229
Ford, Gerald, 209
forest damage, global, due to pollution, 340,
341, 343, 344
fossil-fuel, burning of, and buildup of carbon
dioxide in atmosphere, 341, 342
fraud, and welfare, 214
freedom: economic, and big government,
212; impact of individualism on, 36–55; *see
also,* personal freedom
free market, 207
freeze campaign, nuclear, 307–310
Freud, Sigmund, and homosexuality, 242
Friedan, Betty, 92, 109
Friedman, Milton, 211, 213
"friendly visitor" system, of early social
services, 24
fund raisers, and influence of power elite on
government, 189
future, of sociology, 10
Future Shock (Toffler), 108

Galbraith, John Kenneth, and debate on
government intervention, 200, 201, 208–213
gay liberation, 238, 243, 246, 257
gay pride, 246
gay rights, 238
gemeinschaft, 57
gender differences, *see* sex differences
General Motors, 194
Genesis, Chapter 19 of, and homosexuality,
240
genetics, and homosexuality, 239, 244, 245
gentrification, 58, 70
Gerasimov, Gennadi, 282
Germany, and government intervention, 202
gesellschaft, 57
Giant in the Earth, A (Katz), 317
Gilder, George: 35, 226; on career
commitments of women vs. men, 92, 93,
102–105; justification of income inequalities
in America by, 122–135, 147
Global 2000 Report to the President, The:
317; on population growth, 329
global warming, 341, 342
GNP: and government intervention, 206; and
poverty, 227

God, and theological explanation for
homosexuality, 253, 254
Goldberg, Itzhak, 262
Gordis, Robert, on homosexuality as an
abnormal behavior, 238–247, 257
Gordon, Diana, 276, 278
Gouldner, Alvin, 2
government: activism, 201; and economic
and social consensus, 208–212;
controversy over existence of excessive,
200–213; view of, by liberals, 200, 201; and
debate over power elite in, 184–199; debate
over welfare programs of, 214–215
government intervention: John Kenneth
Galbraith on, as not excessive, 208–212;
William Simon on, as excessive, 202–207
Gramick, Jeannine, on homosexuality as a
natural and normal behavior, 238, 239,
248–256
Great Depression, 201, 347
Great Society, and welfare, 217
Greek government, 200
Greeks: and homosexuality, 241, 250; effect
of increased population on, 327
Greeley, Andrew M., and debate over
existence of power elite in America, 182,
183, 194–199
greenhouse gases, 338
green revolution, 319
gross world product, 339
guilt, of working mothers, 92, 93
gun control, and power elite in America, 195

hamartia, 244
Hamilton, Alexander, 213
Handlin, Oscar, 287
Harrington, Michael, 35
Hayek, Friedrich, 210
Haymarket Riot, 287
health: of Americans as improved, 333; of
city-dwellers, 64; *see also,* mental health
health care: of poor, 28–30; in United States,
351
Heath, Edward, 209
het, 244
Hewlett, Sylvia Ann, 93
Higham, John, 287
*High Frontier: A Strategy for National
Survival* (Graham), 313
"high frontier" strategy, and nuclear
deterrence, 313
Hiroshima, 298
history: and homosexuality, 249, 250; and
racial oppression in America, 151, 152
Hobbes, Thomas, on man's quest for power,
47
homophilia, 257
homophobia, and AIDS, 239

homosexuality: as abnormal behavior, 238–247, 257; and AIDS, 239; as defined by different disciplines, 249–254; historical evidence of public opposition to, 241; as normal and natural behavior, 248–256

Hoover, Herbert, 190, 346

Horowitz, Irving Louis, in favor of value-free sociology, 2–10, 17

housing, for the poor, 28

human mind, as natural resource, 336, 337

human rights: and homosexuality, 238; and standard of living, 20

hunger-induced social disorganization, 319

hyperinflation, 350, 354

illegal immigration: and population control in United States, 321; effect of, on United States, 282, 283

Imhoff, Gary, on danger of uncontrolled immigration to United States, 282–289, 292

immigrants: and influence of, on economic development, 336, 337; examples of financially successful, in America, 127–130

immigration: benefits of, 290–292; dangers of uncontrolled, to United States, 282–289; myths about open-, 290–292; in United States and population control, 321

Immigration and Naturalization Service, 289

incapacitation, controversy over, as solution to crime problem, 258–281

incarceration, see incapacitation

incest, 240

income: effects of improving lower class, 24; increase in per capita world, 336; effect of, on population, 324; see also, income gap; income inequality

income gap: between whites and blacks, 158; see also, income inequality

income inequality: as immoral, 122, 123, 136–147; justification of, 122–135, 147

India, birthrate in, 324

individualism: excessive, vs. good of community, 5, 6, 36–48, 55; and freedom in pursuit of happiness, 36, 37, 49–55; effect of government intervention on, 202

Indochina War, 194

industrial pollution, 333

infant mortality, decrease in, 333

inflation: 227; and government intervention, 208; runaway, 350, 354

in-kind payments, see welfare

inner-city schools, 27, 28

instinct: homosexuality and bisexuality as, 251, 252; maternal, 76, 77, 79, 90; and procreation, 323

internal sovereignty, 285

intravenous drug use, and AIDS, 239

Jacksonian Democrats, 182

Japan: economic future of, 358; and homosexuality, 250

Jefferson, Thomas, 200

Jencks, Christopher: 44; on welfare as necessary to meet needs of poor people, 214, 215, 226–235

Job Corps, 267

job creation, and crime prevention, 266, 267, 268, 279

job opportunities, for black Americans, 154–157

job safety, 208

Johnson, Lyndon, 192

Judaism, and attitude toward homosexuality, 241

Kahn, Herman, 317

Katz, Robert, 317

Kelley, Nick, as example of a successful entrepreneur, 127–130

Kennedy, John F., 192

Kennedy-Hatfield amendment, 309

kerosene, 334

Kiwai of New Guinea, and homosexuality, 251

koheleth, 243

Krauthammer, Charles, on necessity of nuclear arms race, 294, 295, 305–312, 313

labor force: women in, and career commitment, 92–105; young people in, and effect on economy, 325

Labour Party, 208

Laffer, Arthur, 211

Laffer Curve, 211

laissez-faire government, 200, 201

Lamm, Richard, and debate over economic bust in America, 346–353

Lampman, Robert, 187

Lasch, Christopher, 75

laws, and population control, 320

law of diminishing returns, 324

laws of nature, and homosexuality, 252, 253

Lazarus, Emma, 293

LDCs, see less developed countries

Lee, Richard Henry, 182

lesbianism, 242

less developed countries: vs. developed countries, and relationship of population growth to economic growth, 325; and income trends in, 336; and pollution, 333; see also, developing countries; Third World

Lesser Life: The Myth of Women's Liberation in America, A (Hewlett), 93

Leviathan (Hobbes), 47

Lewis, Oscar, 23
Lewis, Hylan, child-rearing studies of, 32
liberals: view of role of government by, 200,
201, 208; and welfare, 226
libertarians, and government intervention,
201
life expectancy, increase in, 332
life-styles: and homosexuality, 245; of lower
class, 22–26, 33; rural, as ideal, 59; *see
also,* personal life-style
limited nuclear war, 305, 310, 311
Limits to Growth, The (Malthus), 324
Locke, John, as champion of individualism,
36
Locker, Michael, 188
Loeb, Marshall, and debate over economic
crisis in America, 346, 347, 353–359
Lonely Crowd, The (Riesman), 199
Losing Ground (Murray), 35, 215, 216, 227,
229, 233, 329
Lot, 240
Louis XIV, 239
Loury, Glenn C., on affirmative action as
reverse discrimination, 164–172
Lovejoy, Thomas, 335
lower class: culture of, as cause of poverty,
20–26, 35; as victims of poverty, 20, 21,
27–35; *see also,* lower income families;
poor; poverty
lower class value stretch, 32
low income families: and welfare, 214–235;
see also, lower class; poor; poverty

Maimonides, 243
malnourished people, number of, 329
Malthus, Thomas, 323, 324
mandatory sentencing, as crime deterrence,
275
Manpower Demonstration Research
Corporation (MDRC), 267, 268
macroeconomic management, and
government intervention into
unemployment and inflation, 208
marriage(s): expectations vs. realities of,
84–89; effect of, on male work effort,
133–135; sex differences in happiness with,
87–88; shared responsibility in, 98–99; and
traditional role of women as fulfilling,
74–82, 91
marriage contracts, criticism of, 81
Marxism, vs. populism, and elitism in
America, 183
Massachusetts, and Bartley-Fox gun law,
263, 265
"mass society": 36, 37; as fiction, 49–50
masturbation, 253
maternal instinct, as innate, 76, 77, 79, 90

Mazzoli, Romano, 283, 290
McKinley, William, 192
Means, Gardner, 186
means tested benefits, and welfare, 221
Medicaid, 220, 223, 227
medical insurance: 208; *see also,* Medicaid;
Medicare
Medicare, and immigrants, 291
Meir, Golda, on women's liberation
movement, 78, 79
Mellon, Andrew, 346
men: marital happiness of, 88; poverty and
breakdown of family role of, 133–135;
traditional role of, in nuclear family, 76–78,
80–81; views of modern women by,
108–115; women's views of, 108, 109,
116–118
mental health: of city-dwellers, 64–65; of
housewives and mothers, 81, 87–90
men vs. women, *see* sex differences
meritocracy, 136–146
metropolitan areas: *see* cities; urban life
Michelangelo, 250
Middle Ages, government in, 200
middle class: married women, and
expectations vs. realities, 84–86; values of,
compared to lower class, 31–32
military, U.S., and global security in relation
to overpopulation, 321
military pension, 351
Miller, Thomas A. W., on career commitments
of women, 92–101
Mintz, Beth, 192
Miranda rule, 276
mixed signals, in today's changing sex roles,
108–119
Mobilization for Youth, 26
modern liberalism, and New Deal, 201
Molly Maguires, 287
moneyites, 182
motherhood: as fulfilling and rewarding
career, 74–82, 91; and maternal instinct,
76, 77, 79, 90; and overmothering, 85–86;
see also, mothers
mothers: welfare, 231; working, 92–105; *see
also,* motherhood
Mumford, Steven, on overpopulation as
threat to our lives and security, 316–322,
329
murder, capital punishment as deterrent to,
263
Murdock, George, on nuclear family as
universal, 89
Murray, Charles: 35; criticism of position of,
on welfare dependency, 229–231; on
welfare dependency of poor, 214–225, 227
Mutually Assured Destruction (MAD), 295,
300, 305
mutual verifiable freeze: 309; *see also,*
nuclear freeze

National Gay Task Force, 238
nationalism, and immigration, 285, 286, 287
National Research Council, 261
National Rifle Association, 195
national security: and need for consensus,
  12; and illegal immigration, 282–289; and
  population, 318
national sovereignty: and doctrine of nuclear
  deterrence, 302; and immigration, 284–287
National Welfare Rights Organization, 26
nation-state, and nationalism, 285
nativism, 286, 288
national resource(s): and global
  interdependence, 318; and decline in oil
  use, 333, 334; people as, 326–328
"Negro family," connotations of, 28
Neighborhood Youth Corps, 267
Nelson, Brian R., 285
New American Poverty, The (Harrington), 235
New Deal: 7, 192; and modern liberalism,
  201
New York, and scenario of a nuclear bomb
  explosion in, 296–304
New York Stock Exchange, 186
New York Times, 191
1984 (Orwell), 320
Nixon, Richard M., 190, 192, 214
no-first-use policy, and nuclear deterrence,
  311, 312
noise, effects of, in cities, 65
nuclear arms race: 355; and consequences
  of nuclear war, 294–304; as a necessity to
  global security, 294, 295, 305–313
nuclear deterrence: doctrine, 295, 299;
  mutually assured destruction as, 295, 300,
  305; and pros and cons of nuclear arms
  race, 294–312
nuclear family: functions of, 74–75;
  stereotype of, as myth, 83–90; traditional
  sex roles within, 74–82; see also, family
nuclear freeze: 307, 308, 309; criticism of,
  310
nuclear war: consequences of, 294–304;
  prevention of, 294, 305–312; role of
  sociology in prevention of, 12
nuclear warning shots, 305
nuclear winter, 294

oil embargo, 331
old age pensions, 208
OPEC, 331
open immigration: 286; myths about,
  290–292
oral intercourse, 253
Organization of Petroleum Exporting
  Countries, see OPEC
organized crime, 274
Other America, The (Harrington), 35, 235

ozone, 338

Paine, Thomas, 200
Panel on Research on Deterrent and
  Incapacitative Effects, 260, 261
"peak experiences," 47
pension(s): 208; funds, 186; military, 227, 351
people's capitalism, 186
People's party, and anti-elitism, 183
personal freedom: 320; effect of government
  intervention on, 205; see also, freedom;
  individualism
personal life-style: effect of overpopulation
  on, 320; see also, life-styles
physical health, of city-dwellers, 64
physiocrats, 200
pigeons, and homosexuality, 253
Plato: and homosexuality, 249; on man's
  relationship to community, 38
plea bargain, 263
pluralism: as argument against existence of
  power elite in America, 183, 194–199; effect
  of, on social reform, 196, 197
Plutarch, and homosexuality, 249
policy-making process, and influence of
  power elite on, in government, 191, 192
politicalization of sociology: arguments
  favoring, 2, 3, 11–16; arguments opposing,
  2–10
Pollutant Standard Index, 333
pollution: air, and forest damage, 340, 341;
  debate over environmental improvement
  concerning, 330, 331; water and air, 333
Pol Pot, 319
poor: blacks, 148–163; and crime, 266, 267,
  279, 280; improvement of conditions of,
  after 1965, 227; and welfare controversy,
  214–235; see also, lower income families;
  lower class; poverty
Population Bomb, The (Ehrlich), 316, 330
population density, see crowding
population growth: American leadership in
  control of, 319, 320; animal ecology
  experiments as models of human, 323;
  benefits of, 323–328, 337; in cities of world,
  70; control of, 319–322; dangers of current
  rate of, 316–322; relationship of, with
  economic growth, 323–328, 339, 340;
  effect of, on environment, 331, 342, 343;
  pros and cons of, 316–329; and technology,
  327, 328; and Zero Population Growth
  (ZPG), 316, 317
populism, vs. Marxism, and elitism in
  America, 183
porpoises, and homosexuality, 252
positive woman, role of, 75–82, 91
Postel, Sandra L., on poor condition of
  environment, 330, 331, 338–344

settlement house, 25
seventeenth century, government in, 200
sex differences: in earnings capacity;
103–104; physiological and psychological,
76–78, 82; in attitudes toward shared-
responsibility marriages, 98; in attitudes
toward work, 99, 104–105
sex discrimination, of working women, 97,
103
sex roles: changing female, 94–101, 108–118;
negative view of traditional female, 74, 75,
83–90; positive view of traditional female,
74–82
sexual communes, 242
*Sexual Practices: The Story of Human
Sexuality* (Gregersen), 257
shaman, 251
"Shulmans' marriage agreement," 81
Silent Spring (Carson), 330
Simon, Julian L.: on environmental
improvements for human life, 330–337; on
limitation of immigration into United States,
282, 283, 290–293; on population growth
as beneficial, 316, 317, 323–329
Simon, William, and debate on government
intervention, 200–207, 213
Simpson, Alan, 283, 290
Simpson-Mazzoli Immigration Reform and
Control Act, 283, 284, 290
sin, concept of, and homosexuality, 244
Singapore, and birthrate in, 324
single mothers, and welfare, 228, 229
Singletary, Donald, view of, on modern
woman's confused sex role, 108–115
Sixties: poverty in, and welfare, 216, 217;
welfare of Seventies compared to, 218–221
slash-and-burn farming, 341
slums, 28
Smith, Adam, 124, 200
Smith, James D., 187
Social Darwinism, 226
Social Democrats, 208
social disorganization, hunger-induced, 319
social ecology, need to revive, 44–45
social mobility: as myth, 141–142; and power
elite in America, 184
social reforms, as evidence of nonexistence
of power elite in America, 196, 197
social relationships, urban vs. rural, 67, 71
Social Security: 220, 227, 228, 351; and
immigrants, 290
social services: early efforts of, to aid lower
class, 24, 25; and functions of nuclear
family, 74, 75; *see also,* welfare
social welfare, *see* welfare
social workers, 215
society, relationship of individual to, 5, 6,
36–55
sociology: as a science, 2–10; ethical
responsibility of, 2, 3, 11–16

Sodom, 240
sodomy, 246
solar energy, 342
South Korea, birthrate in, 324
Soviet Union: 8; homosexuality as a crime in,
242; and nuclear war with United States,
294, 305; population growth control in, 320
Sowell, Thomas, 226
special-interest process, and influence of
power elite in government, 190, 191, 195
species extinction: 331; decrease in, 335,
336
Sprague, Peter, as example of financially
successful entrepreneur in America,
130–132
Stages of Economic Growth, The (Rostow),
330
standards of living, for minimum and
intermediate budget, 139–140
Star Wars, 313
Statue of Liberty, 293
status: vs. class, 34; changing, of women in
society, 96
stereotypes, of "Negro family," 28
stock ownership: and debate over existence
of power elite in America, 186, 187; family,
and control of company, 187, 188
Strategic Defense Initiative, *see* Star Wars
Strategy of Conflict (Schelling), 301
street crime, prevention of, by attacking root
causes, 273–279
stress, of urban life vs. rural life, 65–67
subsidized housing, and welfare, 223
suburbs, life in, 58, 59, 60
sulfur dioxide, and air pollution, 333
supermarket vs. village shop, as example of
individualism as beneficial, 50–53
"supported work" program, 267, 268
support services, urban vs. rural, 67
Supreme Court, on affirmative action, 165,
175, 176, 177, 178

Taft, William H., 189, 190, 192
Taiwan, birthrate in, 324
Talmud, and homosexuality, 241
taxes, and immigrants, 291
tax incentives, and children, 320
technology, and population growth, 327, 328
terrorism, 288
teshubbah, 244
Thatcher, Margaret, 210
theology: and homosexuality, 240, 241, 253,
254; and population control, 322
Third World: cities in, 70; and debt crisis in
America, 350; immigration from, to United
States, 282, 283; and standard of living,
339; *see also,* developing countries; less
developed countries

374

Til Eulenspiegel Society, 246
Toennies, Ferdinand, on urban vs. rural relationships, 57
Toffler, Alvin, 108
Tong wars, 287
Torah, and homosexuality, 240
Tory Party, 208
Toynbee, Arnold, 350
trade deficit, 349, 356
traffic, problems of, in city, 60
tropical forests, 335, 336, 341
two-party system, and power elite, 189

underclass, 355
undeserving poor, 203, 209, 228
unemployment: 356; and big government, 212; relationship of, with crime, 265–268; and government intervention, 208; and immigration, 291
unemployment compensation, 232
unemployment insurance, 208, 222, 223, 225
unilateral disarmament, 307
unrepresentative elite, debate over existence of, in America, 182–199
unwed mothers, and welfare, 231
upper class, and debate over existence of power elite in America, 182–199
Urban Danger (Merry), 268
urban life: negative view of, 56–63, 70, 71; positive view of, 56, 57, 64–71
Useem, Michael, 188

value-free sociology: arguments against, 2, 3, 11–16; arguments favoring, 2–10
values: of American individualism and freedom, 36–55; of lower class, 22–26, 31–32; sex differences in, 76–78; work with intrinsic, 44–45, 48
veto groups, and power elite in America, 195, 199
victim-blaming ideology, of poverty, 20, 21, 27–35
Vietnam War, as evidence for nonexistence of power elite in America, 195, 196, 199
village shop vs. supermarket, as example of individualism as beneficial, 50–53
Virginia Slims American Women's Opinion Poll, 77, 94–99

wage gap, between men and women, 104–105
Wallace, George, 258
Wall Street Journal, 191

War on Poverty, 216
Washington, George, 192
Washington Post, 191
Watergate, and evaluating existence of power elite in America, 199
water pollution, improvements in, 333
Wealth and Poverty (Gilder), 35
"wealth is theft" concept, and big government, 203
Wealth of Nations, The (Smith), 124
Weathermen, 288
Weber, Max: 2, 3, criticism of views of, 11, 12
welfare: 143, 355; and effect of big government on economic freedom, 207; and childbirth, 320; dependency, 214, 216–225; effects of elimination of, 223, 224; and government intervention, 209, 213; and immigrants, 283, 290; as necessary, 214, 215, 226–235; as social control, 6; and supported work program, 267; *see also,* social services
Welfare (Anderson), 235
Welfare Industry, The (Hobbs), 235
welfare queens, 214, 235
whale oil, 334
white collar crime, 263, 274, 276
white racism, and crime, 258, 279
Who Governs? (Dahl), 199
wife-swapping, 242
Wilde, Oscar, 242
Wilkins, Shirley, on career commitments of women, 92–101
Willie, Charles V., on racial oppression in America, as increasing, 148, 149, 158–163
Wilson, James Q., on incapacitation as solution to crime problem, 258, 259–272, 275, 276, 280, 281
Wilson, William Julius, on racial oppression in America as declining, 148–157, 163
Wilson, Woodrow, 192
winds, and nuclear explosion, 296
Wolpin, Kenneth I., 263
women: career commitments by, 92–105; male view of modern, 108–115; negative view of role of, in traditional families, 74, 75, 83–90; positive view of role of, in traditional families, 74–82; view of men by modern, 108, 109, 116–118; and welfare, 214
women's liberation movement: 109; criticism of, 77, 78, 79
women vs. men, *see* sex differences
work: intrinsic value of, 44–45, 48; negative view of, in city, 60–61; welfare as disincentive to, 214, 215
workers compensation, 223
working class: dissatisfaction of, with capitalism, 7–8; married women, and expectations vs. realities of, 86–87
Workingmen's Party, 287